ALIEN WORLDS

Religion and Politics

Michael Barkun, *Series Editor*

OTHER TITLES IN RELIGION AND POLITICS

Augusto "César" Sandino: Messiah of Light and Truth
Marco Aurelio Navarro-Génie

*The Church Universal and Triumphant: Elizabeth Clare
Prophet's Apocalyptic Movement*
Bradley C. Whitsel

Contemporary Muslim Apocalyptic Literature
David Cook

*From Slogans to Mantras: Social Protest
and Religious Conversion in the Late Vietnam Era*
Stephen A. Kent

Hearing the Voices of Jonestown
Mary McCormick Maaga

*Learning Lessons from Waco: When Parties Bring
Their Gods to the Negotiation Table*
Jayne Seminare Docherty

Millennialism, Persecution, and Violence: Historical Cases
Catherine Wessinger, ed.

*Perfectionist Politics: Abolitionism
and the Religious Tensions of American Democracy*
Douglas M. Strong

*Radical Religion in America: Millenarian Movements
from the Far Right to the Children of Noah*
Jeffrey Kaplan

*William Dudley Pelley: A Life in Right-Wing
Extremism and the Occult*
Scott Beekman

ALIEN

Social and Religious Dimensions of Extraterrestrial Contact

WORLDS

EDITED BY

DIANA G. TUMMINIA

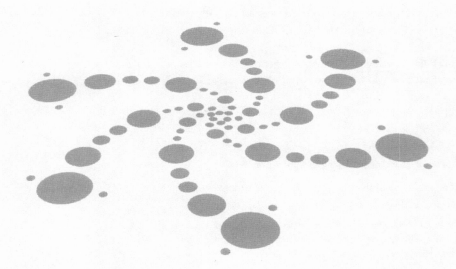

SYU   SYRACUSE UNIVERSITY PRESS

Copyright © 2007 by Syracuse University Press
Syracuse, New York 13244-5290

First Edition 2007

11   12   13   14   15   16   7   6   5   4   3   2

The paper used in this publication meets the minimum requirements
of American National Standard for Information Sciences—Permanence
of Paper for Printed Library Materials, ANSI Z39.48–1984.∞™

For a listing of other books published by Syracuse University Press,
visit the SUP Web site at http://www.SyracuseUniversityPress.syr.edu.

ISBN-13: 978–0–8156–0858–5
ISBN-10: 0–8156–0858–6

Library of Congress Cataloging-in-Publication Data

Alien worlds : social and religious dimensions of extraterrestrial
contact / edited by Diana G. Tumminia.—1st ed.
p. cm.—(Religion and politics)
Includes bibliographical references and index.
ISBN-13: 978–0–8156–0858–5 (pbk. : alk. paper)
ISBN-10: 0–8156–0858–6 (pbk. : alk. paper)
1. Human-alien encounters—Social aspects. 2. Human-alien
encounters—Religious aspects. 3. Alien abduction. I. Tumminia, Diana G.
BF2050.A37 2007
001.942—dc22   2006102594

Manufactured in the United States of America

Dedicated to

Professor Walter R. Allen of UCLA,

scholar, teacher, mentor,

an inspiration to work with,

a principled sociologist

committed to social justice

and real education

Contents

PART FOUR

Ufological "Science" and Therapy

Illustrations

Tables

Acknowledgments

This project began with the work and efforts of the noted scholar James R. Lewis, professor of religion at the University of Wisconsin, Stevens Point, who has spent decades researching the many facets of the sociology of religion. He is particularly noted for his groundbreaking books on the spiritual aspects of UFO phenomena, as well as for volumes on new religious movements. He also edited several reference works in the field, some of which have won awards, one of the most recent being *UFOs and Popular Culture.* Lewis contacted and developed a relationship with leading scholars around the world on the subject of contacteeism, alien abductions, and other UFO cultural phenomena. He compiled the original manuscript for *Alien Worlds* in the hopes of shedding more light on this area of human spirituality and cosmic mystery. Because of family concerns, he turned the manuscript over to me to edit. Without his efforts, the book would never have come to fruition.

The open dialogue on the controversial subjects of UFOs and extraterrestrial phenomena has sparked debates in numerous disciplines and in alternative arenas of information sharing. In that spirit, this volume presents a dialectical range of discourse from sociology to ufology, which I hope will lead to a new synthesis on the part of the reader. Everyone involved in this volume values the work of the anonymous reviewers and the help of sociologist Richard P. Nadeau, who made suggestions and helped proofread the manuscript. I want to also acknowledge Salvador Jimenez Murguia, who sent me information on Pana-Wave Laboratory, a Japanese contactee religion.

Some chapters appeared first elsewhere. Mikael Rothstein's "Hagiography and Text in the Aetherius Society" first appeared in *New Religions in a Postmodern World,* edited by Rothstein and Reender Kranenborg and published by Aarhus University Press in 2003 and is reprinted here with permission. "Presumed Immanent" by Bryan Sentes and Susan Palmer is reprinted by permission from the journal *Nova Religio* (vol. 4, no. 1) published in October 2000 by UC Press. My chapter "In the Dreamtime of the Saucer People" is reprinted in an abridged form with permission from the *Journal of Contemporary Ethnography* of Sage Publications. It originally appeared in volume 31, no. 6:675–705 in December 2002. Some of that chapter also appeared in a different form in *When Prophecy Never Fails* (Tumminia 2005).

I want to express my appreciation to the Unarius Academy of Science for its cooperation in allowing the ethnographic research that made my study possible. I also recognize the members of the One World Family Commune and Allen Michael for their assistance and feedback in the study of the Universal Industrial Church of the New World Comforter.

Author Pierre Lagrange wishes to thank veteran UFO researcher Henri Chaloupek and science reporter Robert Clarke for providing him with copies of the magazine *Ouranos*. His chapter owes much to the comments of Robert E. Bartholomew and James R. Lewis. Lagrange also thanks Bruno Latour for years of theoretical discussions on the subject of knowledge construction and UFOs.

Because a picture is worth a thousand words, I thank the various organizations that donated photos or illustrations: the Unarius Academy of Science, the Aetherius Society, International Raëlian Movement, CUFOs, Ascension Mastery International, and the Universal Church of the New World Comforter.

Two authors wish to publicly acknowledge my efforts. Pierre Lagrange is particularly appreciative of the time I spent assisting him in editing his chapter for English. On a similar note, Christopher D. Bader thanks me for "invaluable help and advice editing and shaping" his chapter. It has been my distinct pleasure to work on such a project. From several corners of the academic universe, I have put together what I hope will be an educational foray into the extraordinary social worlds of UFOs, abductees, and contactees.

Sacramento, California   Diana G. Tumminia
October 2006

Contributors

Pia Andersson studied archaeology and religious studies at Stockholm University. She has written extensively on archaeology, archaeoastronomy, and fringe archaeology.

Christopher D. Bader is an assistant professor of sociology at Baylor University. He has conducted participant observations of several novel religious movements, including the ritual abuse subculture, UFO abductees, and Bigfoot hunters. His articles have appeared in the *Journal for the Scientific Study of Religion, Teaching Sociology,* and *Western Criminology Review.*

Jerome Clark is a well-known independent writer and researcher. He authored the definitive *UFO Encyclopedia* and *Extraordinary Encounters: An Encyclopedia of Extraterrestrials and Otherworldly Beings* among other works.

Anne Cross is a sociologist who teaches at the School of Law Enforcement and Criminal Justice at Metropolitan State University in Saint Paul, Minnesota. Some of her scholarly work focuses on the ufological subculture and the social construction of science.

Christopher Helland is currently researching religious accommodation and innovation in relation to the scientific and technological developments of the late twentieth century. His research also focuses upon the relationship between new religious movements and science, UFO religions being a primary example of that amalgamation.

Anna E. Kubiak is a Polish cultural anthropologist researching religion, in particular New Age religion. Her project, New Age Culture in Poland, has produced several articles, including "New Age Made in Poland" and "New Age or How to Commune." She published the books *Delicje i lewa reka Kryszny* and *Jednak New Age.*

Pierre Lagrange is a former researcher at the Centre de Sociologie de l'Innovation of the Ecole des Mines of Paris, where he taught the sociology of science and parascience. He has published articles on the construction of paranormal phenomena and on the science-parascience controversy. He is also the author of a book on the Roswell controversy.

Susan Palmer is an adjunct professor at Concordia University and a tenured professor at Dawson College, both in Montreal, Quebec. In addition to more than sixty articles, she has written and edited several books on new religious movements. Her latest book, *Aliens Adored,* examines the International Raëlian Movement.

Jennifer E. Porter is assistant professor of religion and modern culture at Memorial University of Newfoundland. She is the author of several articles on the religious and ritual dimensions of Star Trek fandom and is the coeditor of *Star Trek and Sacred Ground: Explorations of Star Trek, Religion, and American Culture.* Her research interests include religion and popular culture, contemporary alternative spirituality, and implicit religion. She is currently researching the impact of the *Star Wars* series on the spiritual lives of fans.

Georg M. Rønnevig received his doctoral degree in the history of religions from the University of Oslo in 1999 with a dissertation on alien abductions. Among his publications are articles on UFOs and New Age religion. He holds a position as a senior executive officer at the Norwegian Immigration Appeals Board. He lives in Oslo, and is the author of the book *Romvesener,* published in Norway.

Mikael Rothstein is assistant professor in the Department of History of Religions at the University of Copenhagen. He specializes in the study of new religions. He is editor-in-chief of *Chaos,* a Danish-Norwegian journal on the history of religions. He edited the anthology *New Age Religion and Globalization.*

Benson Saler is professor emeritus of anthropology at Brandeis University. His major ethnographic fieldwork has been with the Maya-Quiché in Guatemala and Wayú (Guajiro) in northern Colombia and Venezuela. His publications include *UFO Crash at Roswell: The Genesis of a Modern Myth* with Charles A. Ziegler and Charles B. Moore.

Scott Scribner studied astronomy and cultural anthropology at Harvard University's Mount Hermon Liberal Studies Program; physics and sociology at Rensselaer Polytechnic Institute (where he joined NASA's Mars Survey Vehicle Development Group); philosophy and cognition at the University of New Hampshire; and the relationship between psychology and theology at Fuller Theological Seminary. His recent doctoral research examines descriptions of fear in alien abduction narratives.

Bryan Sentes is a member of the English Department at Dawson College and a teacher of creative writing at Concordia University in Montreal, Canada.

James F. Strange is a distinguished professor of religious studies and director of graduate studies at the University of South Florida. He specializes in biblical and social archeology. Two of his many publications are *Archaeology, the Rabbis, and Early Christianity* and *Excavations in the Ancient Synagogue of Gush Halav.* He served as director of excavations at Sepphoris, Israel.

Diana G. Tumminia teaches sociology at California State University at Sacramento. She wrote *When Prophecy Never Fails* about the Unarius Academy of Science, as well as numerous articles about new religions, mythology, and millenarian groups. She studied social psychology at UCLA, where she was mentored by Ralph H. Turner and Walter R. Allen.

Jacques Vallee was born in France, educated as an astrophysicist, and received his doctorate in computer science in the United States. With his mentor, J. Allen Hynek, he studied UFOs, becoming the model for the scientist in Steven Spielberg's *Close Encounters of the Third Kind.* Considered one of the leading experts in the field, he has written numerous books on the phenomenon.

Introduction

Diana G. Tumminia

Welcome to an exploration of the sociological and psychological worlds of extraterrestrial contact and other related phenomena. Space aliens seem to have become part our emergent reality, but where did they come from? Did they travel millions of miles to materialize from the starry haze of the universe, or did they sprout organically from the deepest recesses of our imaginations? Since prehistory, humans have shaped apparitions into their own images as they conveyed their otherworldly visions to one another. Now in the twenty-first century, our species continues to reinvent mythological visitors with supernatural powers, some of whom are the subject of this book. In the past few decades, serious academics and skeptical observers have only begun to make sense out of the cultural relationships people have been establishing with alleged aliens from outer space. Although many intellectuals still shun the subject, judging it the epitome of irrationality, we now see that various disciplines from anthropology to psychiatry have researchers analyzing the human response to UFO-related phenomena. Scholars of religion, as well as folklorists, turn their eyes to the expanding collection of tales told about celestial interlopers who are said to be our allies, long-lost cosmic cousins, and occasional enemies.

In terms of a cultural icon, the extraterrestrial presence pervades countless niches of our societal discourse and representational art, making old themes new, as folklorist Thomas E. Bullard (2000a) might say. Today our populace swims in a sea of extraterrestrial imagery (Dean 1998). Got aliens? Many people believe Area 51 does have aliens and alien technology. In fact, Nevada officially named the much-visited ninety-eight-mile stretch of road (State Route 375), which borders the top-secret military base, the Extraterrestrial Highway. If you stop in Rachel, Nevada, on the edge of base, you can acquire an Area 51 T-shirt, and you can spend a night at the Little A'Le'Inn motel. Do not forget Mount Shasta in northern California, where clouds sometimes resemble spaceships and where certain locals regularly communicate with interstellar beings. The reputation of Roswell, New Mexico, proudly beckons tourists who purchase green-alien refrigerator magnets and fluorescent UFO bumper stickers as souvenirs of their pilgrimages. The curious also chase sightings at UFO hot spots in such places as Marfa, Texas, or Sedona, Arizona. Others find that aliens visit them in their own bedrooms. Moreover, some say that God is an alien.

Extraterrestrials (or ETs for short) seem to have become part of everyday life. At the supermarket checkout line, we can buy candy encased in a plastic flying-saucer toy, whilst we read the latest fringe tabloid headlines about aliens impregnating innocent women. Hollywood cranks out a few movies about aliens each year, and television supplies us with more on a daily basis as we visually encounter dozens of comical cosmic intruders and scores of menacing tricksters from outer space. Media mainlines ETs into the storehouse of our common experience, so much so that we can easily fit them into our casual conversations. For instance, the average American knows more about *Star Wars* than any real war ever fought. I would wager that Americans are more likely to know the names of fictional alien characters than of any important government official. Nowadays, many people can freely debate the virtues and shortcomings of the various generations of the *Star Trek* series, but they may have trouble articulating the complexities of civic issues that directly affect their lives. Extraterrestrials have a strong cultural presence, but what are we to make of it all? To paraphrase the ideas of political scientist Jodi Dean (1998), aliens have invaded the world as we know it.

Whether real or imagined, extraterrestrial contact and the interrelated subject of UFO phenomena provide a wealth of symbolic material for the student, scholar, or skeptic. Relatively newer publications fill in some previous gaps in research. Pioneering volumes created by religion scholar James R. Lewis, *The Gods Have Landed: New Religions from Other Worlds* (1995), *UFOs and Popular Culture: An Encyclopedia of Contemporary Myth* (2000), and the *Encyclopedic Sourcebook of UFO Religions* (2003a), speak to the diverse cultural activity resulting from the diffusion of ideas about extraterrestrials. Using a postmodernist approach, Jodi Dean's *Aliens in America* (1998) addressed the bewildering cacophony of alien discourses that have flowered during the Information Age. Independent scholar Brenda Denzler (2001) investigated the ufological subcultures by charting the confusing labyrinth of mythology and skepticism from her first-hand inquiry into its many facets. Professor of political science Michael Barkun (2003) shed light on the shadowy world of alien conspiracy theories by mapping its themes, which run the gamut from audacious warnings of reptilian invaders to hidden strains of anti-Semitism. For further reading on the mystical aspects of alien contact, consult *UFO Religions* (2003) edited by Christopher Partridge, as well as his newer book *New Religions: A Guide* (2004). While primarily socioanalytical in orientation, these books contain varied points of view that are of interest to those curious about new religions and mythologies.

The Spectrum of Activity

Reports of aliens and the interrelated subject of UFOs encompass a wide spectrum of cultural activity from rumor to legend. Since ancient times legendary accounts of angels, demons, flying people, and chariots have been reported by various cultures in their mythologies (Jacobs 1975; Miller 1985; Williams 1991). Inexplicable airborne phenomena have appeared and inspired a wide range of public reactions in every historic age (Flammonde 1976; Bartholomew and Howard 1998; Lewis 2000). In the United States, the 1896–97 sightings of mystery airships prompted a few vague theories of extraterrestrials and bogus reports of cow abduction. Decades later, World War II–era pilots described flying fireballs and disk-shaped objects, eventually named foo-fighters. After the war, some people spotted so-called ghost rockets throughout Europe, particularly in Sweden (Spencer 1991; Lewis 2000). The euphemism "flying saucer" only gained public acceptance after a single event (Jacobs 1975; Spencer 1991; Lewis 2000).[1]

On June 24, 1947, experienced pilot Kenneth Arnold spotted bright flashes of light and what he described as nine crescent-shaped craft soaring at more than one thousand miles per hour. According to Spencer (1991, 24), Arnold quipped that they moved "like a saucer would if you skipped it across water." A reporter from UPI sent in a story about flying saucers, and the rest is history. In a matter of weeks, the term became part of our language. Undeniably, the culture of the Western world morphed a bit after the 1947 rumors of flying saucers impacted popular imagina-

---

1. According to Spencer (1991), the term "saucer" was a description first used in 1878 when a Texan reported a dark saucer flying over his farm. However, the public did not say "flying saucer" until after the Arnold sighting in 1947. It also took some time before the public used the acronym UFO. According Michael David Hall and Wendy Ann Connors (2000), Captain Edward J. Ruppelt, the project chief of the early Air Force investigations, influenced the adoption of the expression UFO. George Adamski saw a mysterious flying object in 1946 but did not describe it as a UFO or flying saucer (Lewis 2003b) because the terms had not been adopted yet. Nonetheless, the idea of aliens predates the notion of flying saucers.

tion. Unidentifiable flying objects occasionally made news throughout history, but 1947 marked a turning point.

The mysterious discs captured the public imagination in response to wide-spread publicity in newspapers and national magazines (Jacobs 1975). No news of this kind had hit the front pages since the mysterious airship stories of 1896–97. An AP wire service bulletin (Berlitz and Moore 1980, 24) dated July 7, 1947, read, "Flying Saucers Seen in Most States Now." Then a highly controversial story came on the heels of the Arnold sighting. On July 8, 1947, the headline of Roswell, New Mexico's *Daily Record* read, "RAAF Captures Flying Saucer on Ranch in Roswell Region. No Details of the Flying Discs Revealed." The belated official Air Force explanation for the Roswell incident asserted that a weather balloon had crashed, not a flying saucer. By eight weeks after the initial Arnold sighting, 90 percent of Americans had heard about flying saucers, according to the Gallup Poll (Jacobs 1975). Some scientific investigation did ensue, but the phenomenon quickly became entangled with a diffusion of religious expression, media-driven myth, and paranormal claims. Because science ideally should be free of cultural impositions, this diffusion presented the greatest of dilemmas for research.

The images of flying discs sparked a societal inkblot test that is still in the process of being interpreted (Thompson 1991); part of that cultural take on UFOs associated them with extraterrestrial beings. Later reports of actual alien encounters and abductions added more complexity to this mystery of alien contact. The last half-century gave birth to several levels of societal reaction to extraterrestrial rumors, one of which was the establishment of an ethos of belief that settled into certain pockets of the society. Those subcultural niches (Denzler 2001) contain many complementary and competing ideologies, from legitimate science to legitimate religion and everything in between. Aspects that concentrate on empirical data-gathering and analysis are referred to as ufology (or UFOlogy), although the term unfortunately also connotes highly speculative investigation because of the inundation of far-fetched theories into this field despite more serious scientific efforts. By the beginning of the twenty-first century, any real science of UFOs had become clouded in the public eye because of the exponential expansion of supernatural ideas about alien phenomenon and the cessation of public funding for research.

The contemporary legacy of UFOs affects places in Western culture that are now poised to expand through the globalization of the Information Age. Ufological subcultures intersect with other types of narrative production based on a spectrum of UFO imagery, science fiction, and extraterrestrial lore in a cultural feedback loop of human interpretation. These segments of society include the following:

- Freelance skeptics and unaffiliated enthusiasts;
- Investigation organizations that hold conferences and form social networks of information exchange (e.g., MUFON);
- Established and emergent mythology (occult legends, space-oriented cosmologies, ancient astronauts, alien conspiracies, and alien abduction narratives);
- Literary and media-based myth-making in pulp magazines (e.g., *Fate Magazine*), in books (*Chariots of the Gods?*, etc.), on the radio (e.g., the *Art Bell Show*), on the Internet (e.g., uforia.com), and in films and television (*Star Wars* and *The X-Files*, among others);
- Believers in extraterrestrial paranormalism (healing, channeling, ESP, New Age fads);
- Pseudo-psychotherapeutic social networks (abduction psychologists, alien abduction support groups and workshops, past-life regression therapies, and UFO retreats, like the Sattva Sanctuary in Mount Adams, Oregon);
- Psychic and mystic contacteeism (contact with extraterrestrials, e.g., George Adamski);
- Recognizable religious groups (e.g., the Aetherius Society); and
- Sci-fi fandoms, like the self-styled Trekkies, who display quasi-religious behaviors based on myths of extraterrestrial contact.

This patchwork of cultural activity is only loosely sewn together, and it has many overlapping divisions that span both fact and fiction. Many writers call the core of these multiple lines of development the UFO Movement; however, there has been no real social movement in the strict sociological sense of the word, which implies long-term, focused social organization (Turner and Killian 1987). True social movements reach a level of continuity, integration, organization, and stability not found in the collectivities referred to here. Public interest in these areas rises and falls without a consolidated or consistent institutional thrust. Rather, history tells us these numerous expressions spread out in loosely related waves of subcultural activity, something sociologists of collective behavior call a *quasi-movement*.

David L. Miller (1985, 2000) attempted to clarify the amazing assortment of activities by categorizing three types of UFO organizations: the UFO investigation group, the contactee group, and the UFO cult. According to Miller (1985), *UFO investigation groups* are secular civilian organizations, such as APRO, NICAP, CUFOS, and MUFON, which have some connections to credentialed scientists. Generally, UFO organizations take an enthusiastically agnostic stance toward the UFO controversy; at the same time, they encourage the scientific study of UFOs via sophisticated technology. The oldest organization, Aerial Phenomena Research Organization (APRO), began with the work of the civilian pioneers Coral and James Lorenzen in 1952. Now greatly scaled down, the National Investigations Committee on Aerial Phenomena (NICAP) has carried on historic examinations of UFOs since the fifties, when it was headed for many years by Marine Corps Major Donald E. Keyhoe, a major critic of the Air Force's UFO investigations. Presently, NICAP maintains an extensive informational Web site.

Formerly directed by astronomer Dr. J. Allen Hynek (1910–1986), the Center for UFO Studies (CUFOS) works with invited scientists and maintains a computerized data bank. In addition to its own collection, CUFOS preserves NICAP's old research files and continues its research as the J. Allen Hynek Center for UFO Studies. CUFOS looks after the largest collection of UFO reports in the world, and it publishes the *International UFO Reporter* and the *Journal of UFO Studies*. It conducts and assists selected research projects. Currently, CUFOS takes reports on UFO sightings. The Mutual UFO Network (MUFON), established in 1969, ranks as the most recognizable contemporary organization within the investigation group category. Sponsoring annual conferences and publishing journals, MUFON and its chapters in many countries around the world from the United States to Malaysia carry on the mission of investigating UFOs. BUFORA (British UFO Research Association) plays a similar role in England.

Comparatively speaking, UFO investigation groups ideally retain some semblance of skepticism toward contacteeism and paranormal explanations, although individual members may independently embrace the phenomena. In contrast to investigation groups, *contactee groups* claim that one or more of their members have had an actual encounter with aliens. Contactees should not be confused with abductees (people believed to have been kidnapped by extraterrestrials), who constitute a related but separate phenomenon. Miller (1985, 137) explained, "Contactees frequently claim to have been given messages from, or given missions to perform, by the occupants of UFOs." When investigation groups mingle with contactees or abductees, an interaction that is now common, their operations become suspect in the eyes of established scientific circles and public opinion (Jacobs 1975). For example, critics charge that organizations like MUFON are so peppered with uncritical true believers that the groups have become less objective.

Overall, contactee groups seem to be on the increase. Here are just a few examples among many. The Adamski Foundation, which was established around the work of the world's most renowned UFO mystic, George Adamski (1891–1965), is a comparatively old American contactee group that paved the way for similar organizations that are still emerging. The much younger Society for the Greater Community Way of Knowledge in Boulder, Colorado, was set up as a nonprofit educational organization in 1992. It promotes the messages of Marshall Vian Summers (2001) who states that extraterrestrials serve as allies to humanity.

Small formal organizations, such as the Amalgamated Flying Saucer Clubs of America (AFSCA) and the National Investigations Committee on UFOs (NICUFO), fall into this category of contactee groups (Miller 1985). In its heyday, AFSCA published newsletters and advocated that contactee cases be taken seriously. Their general advocacy ran along the lines of convincing the public that aliens offered the wisdom that would solve planetary woes. Founded in 1959, AFSCA based much of its philosophy on the 1951 movie *The Day the Earth Stood Still* and on information derived from visits with aliens hailing from Alpha Centauri. In 1972, AFSCA ran space-age candidates Gabriel Green for president and Daniel Fry for vice-president. UFO lecturer Frank E. Stranges started NICUFO in 1967, giving it a board of directors composed mostly of contactees (Miller 2000). Although the organization waned, Stranges kept up his career as a speaker on the ufological circuit. His publications are still well-known and sought after. Stranges wrote *Outwitting Tomorrow,* attributing authorship to Commander Valiant Thor, a Venusian who possessed a secret underground base in Nevada for a time. Operating as platform societies, these quasi-spiritual organizations like NICUFO have scheduled speaking engagements around the country attracting numerous followers; however, they have remained ineffectual at influencing national public opinion on the validity of contacteeism.

Miller's typology defines *UFO cults* as groups that believe God sends UFOs to save humankind. He designated the Universal Industrial Church of the New World Comforter, Mark-Age, and the Universariun Foundation as examples of UFO cults. The still-active Universal Industrial Church of the New World Comforter has its own cable-access television show (see chapter 3). The group called Mark-Age, started by Charles Boyd Gentzel (Mark) and Pauline Sharp (Nada-Yolanda), teaches that UFOs have always guided Earth's development. Mark-Agers anticipated the return of Christ (Sananda) in the year 2000, when God was to set up a worldwide spiritual government. When it was visibly active, the Universariun Foundation created by Zelrun and Daisy Karsleigh maintained clairvoyant contact with Sri Souda, Lord Michael, and Koot Hoomi, as well as space people poised to save the faithful.

There are semantic problems with Miller's UFO cult terminology. Although Miller (2000) calls Heaven's Gate and Unarius contactee groups, they are more accurately identified as *contactee religions* or as UFO cults (the term he uses). For sociologists of religion, the definition of a cult implies a relatively new, independent spiritual group headed by a charismatic leader (Robbins 1988). Because the term "cult" now connotes an invalid and dangerous religion rather than a new religion, some academics have stopped using it, replacing it with the expression "new religious movement" (NRM). Furthermore, Miller used the term "UFO" the way most Americans and some scholars do, as interchangeable with the words "flying saucer." The UFO acronym stands for *unidentified flying object*, not an extraterrestrial spacecraft, a conceptual nuance with interpretive consequences that are lost on most people. Groups Miller classified as UFO cults were categorized by J. Gordon Melton as flying-saucer groups in the *Encyclopedia of American Religions* (1989). Whether we refer to these organizations as UFO cults, flying-saucer groups, UFO religions, or contactee religions appears to be a matter of semantic style. I would argue for the use of the term contactee religion because it better describes the channeling practice these groups use. By focusing on the word contactee, we can see how much this spiritual practice has in common with other forms of communication with the supernatural.

It is difficult to find the line of demarcation between contactee groups and contactee religions because it is essentially the dividing line between quasi-religion and full religion. Some activities clearly border on religion but do not cross the line. Like many categories in this field, boundaries blur in the flurry of cultural production. Is there a dividing line between quasi-religion and religion? There are probably no clear divisions, although sociologists look for some markers (Glock and Bellah 1976; Stark and Bainbridge 1985; Robbins 1988). We generally first look to see whether adherents consider what they are doing a religion. It is more complicated in the case of the contactee religions that consider themselves scientific organizations, although any glimpse at their cosmologies will show a strong religious deviation from science. Sociologists look for rituals oriented toward the sacred and the supernatural, as well as designations between the sacred and the profane, in order to define a group as religious. One common ritual is the act of listening to the contactee channel messages. Members convert the content of these messages into sacred teachings. As a determining factor, religions place more importance on proper ritual performance and correct belief.

Another indicator that identifies a religion is the amount of deference paid to keynoting individuals, especially founders. Do the roles such keynoters play contain strong supernatural meanings? Are certain people believed to be empowered by supernatural forces? If that is true, the interactions are within the definition of religion. While some contactee activities contain abundant mythical and religious symbolism, believers do not always ascribe the deepest magical or sacred meanings to it, which shifts everything into the gray area called quasi-religion. How success-fully organized are followers in terms of their spiritual focus? Are they a free-floating audience (Stark and Bainbridge 1985), or do they have an established community of believers more common to religion? Sociologists take note of the type of zeal that adherents express in the practice of their beliefs, as well as their goals for social change. Within some contactee organizations, many hold fast to their group's millenarian message, and they believe their organization will trans-form the planet Earth. Strongly organized millenarianism falls into the category of religion.

Contactee Religions and Their Origins

With the exception of a handful of groundbreaking researchers, contactee religions were not generally taken seriously as objects of scholarly study until the Heaven's Gate suicides of 1997. That this should have been the case is in a certain sense puz-zling, considering that these religions can reveal so much about the psychological nature of belief itself. The Heaven's Gate suicides shocked enough people that ques-tions arose about the nature of such groups. Were they all cults with crazy leaders? Had the public anything to fear? For those who looked past the cult stereotype, there were more refined and measured cultural questions to be asked (Lewis 2000; Balch 1995; Balch and Taylor 2003).

There are about twenty-five traceable groups around the world, with dozens that may not visible to social scientists. For a list of various contactee religions, see ap-pendix A. An objective observer of contactee religions would acknowledge the psy-chological sources of these new expressions, as well as the trends in social thought that primed them with magical ideology. Thoughtful observers ask why people form religions around UFOs or extraterrestrials, and they find the imagery significant. UFOs contain abundantly evocative symbols steeped in ambiguity, a condition Paris Flammonde (1976, 62) calls the "sky of the beholder." Thus, early UFOs rumors pos-sessed enough raw materials and enough vagueness to provide incipient mystics, some already occupied in metaphysics, with platforms for building improvisational religions (Tumminia 2003; Tumminia and Kirkpatrick 2003). Our inclination to en-vision deities as floating through the clouds gives us an opportunity to perceive un-usual flying beings in spiritual terms. Flying itself represents the greatest of freedoms, freedom from the bonds of gravity and physical limitations. Flying sym-bolizes the powers of supernatural beings evoking wonder and possibility.

Where did these ideas come from? Academics sought the origins of extraterrestrial spirituality, which definitely predate the 1947 Arnold incident (Lewis 2000, 2003a; Partridge 2003), and they found that Western culture contained many long-standing animistic assumptions about extraterrestrials (Melton 1995). People have believed in extraterrestrials for centuries, according to David Stupple (1984), who noted that American colonists presumed that beings inhabited other planets. The nineteenth-century astronomer Percival Lowell reasoned that lines on the surface of Mars indicated channels dug by Martians. Science-fiction writer H. G. Wells published *War of the Worlds* in 1898, which also demonstrates some of the long lineage of extraterrestrial imagery. Aliens progressively gained more sophistication in every decade of the twentieth century as science-fiction writers captivated popular culture with their stories.

Commenting on the spiritual lineage, Robert S. Ellwood (1983) traced the antecedent religious beliefs in extraterrestrials back to the nineteenth-century syncretism of Swedenborgianism, Theosophy, Spiritualism, and native shamanism. Containing early contactee themes (Ellwood 1983; Melton 1995; Partridge 2003), Emmanuel Swedenborg's ideas about divine communication with moon-men and other planetary spirits eventually merged into Spiritualist mediumship and Theosophy, as did traditional Hindu beliefs in reincarnation and karma. Theosophy's Madame Blavatsky maintained contact with ascended masters and lords of mystical realms who lived on the planet Venus and other worlds, setting the stage for subsequent groups. In turn, the metaphysical milieu influenced by Theosophy and Spiritualism gave rise to fanciful mythologies of lost civilizations of Atlantis and Lemuria that challenged traditional explanations of human origins. Several scholars (Stupple 1984; Lewis 1995; Partridge 2003) have pointed out that certain contactee religions have a theosophically based worldview. In the twentieth century, belief in reincarnation diffused into Western spirituality (Glock and Bellah 1976) to reappear in some contemporary contactee religions, such as Unarius and Ashtar Command, among others. As a matter of course, the notion of alien karma emerged in many of the contactee cosmologies known today.

Pre-1947 contactees talked to otherworldly beings on other planets (Melton 1995). In a once-popular book, Thomas Blot describes his conversation with a Martian in his home in 1891. In a work published in 1930, Willard M. Magoon recounts how he was taken by an invisible force to Mars, where he beheld the beautiful landscape and was introduced to Martian technology. In accounts published in 1935, Guy Ballard explains how he stumbled upon a mystical being on the slopes of Mount Shasta. Ballard later journeyed to meet twelve Venusian Masters at Royal Teton Mountain, where they showed him scenes of their homeland and visions of their advanced technology. Ballard's Venusians echoed theosophical forms. Here we do see a dichotomy because Ballard sustained a religious following, while Blot and Magoon did not.

George Adamski launched the contemporary contactee era on November 20, 1952, when he purportedly came face to face with Orthon of Venus in the California desert (Peebles 1994). Achieving national fame by garnering media attention and selling books, he secured his place as the father of modern contacteeism, despite psychic Mark Probert's making earlier contacts (See chapter 2). Many contactees of this period claimed that they had taken rides in flying saucers. Orfeo Angelucci, Howard Menger, and Truman Bethurum also gained fame, but their audiences did not develop into full-fledged religions. The older groups, like Unarius and Mark-Age, incorporated the narratives of early contactees. Unarius, for example, received channeled messages from Adamski and others whom they regarded as ascended masters living on other planets; those communiqués stand alongside messages from Space Brothers on Mars, Venus, and other celestial worlds (Tumminia 2005).

The product of many influences, a contactee religion is an organized following that forms around a contactee mystic. These religions exhibit strong mythological components, usually derived from the visionary pronouncements of the leader and in some cases from the trusted followers. Most employ channeling as a practice and ritual for establishing and maintaining belief. Nearly all now espouse an amalgamated millenarian worldview with resynthesized themes from these influences: science (Lewis 2003b), pseudo-science (Wallis 1979), ufology (Flammonde 1976; Jacobs 1983; Denzler 2001), paranormalism (Goode 2000), metaphysics (Kerr and Crow 1983), Spiritualism (Melton 1995; Lewis 2003b), Theosophy (Ellwood 1983; Partridge 2003), media (Barkun 2003; Tumminia 2005), and more recently New Age thought (Heelas 1996).

Science is an important theme and symbol to many contactee religions. Most contactee religions fuse images from science fiction with spiritual mysticism, frequently repackaging ancient spiritual practices into a futuristic cosmology. Science in the populist imagination denotes the miraculous power to solve problems with new technologies and to heal the sick. The very word, science, carries a legitimacy that older religions have lost (Lewis 2003b). Many contactee religions claim legitimacy because they profess to be scientific, although their versions of science match no established academic standards (Dolby 1979; Giere 1979; Wallis 1979; Goode 2000). While older contactee sects relied on the possibility of manipulating some elements of Newton's mechanical universe via their philosophies, contemporary mystics now have the holographic universes of cutting-edge science to legitimate their cosmic spirituality (Talbot 1991). Nothing in the realm of time and space is the way we perceive it to be, says modern-day science through the avenues of quantum physics, superstring theory, and M-theory (Lidsey, Wands, and Copeland 2000). Certain physicists now theorize the existence of eleven dimensions and multiple universes that may operate outside the known laws of physics. Some even speak of scientific scenarios for time travel. Today's inventive contactee spiritualities use these types of iconoclastic paradigms about time and space to validate their ideas.

As Lewis (2003b) observes, it is from our encounters with science and technology that we absorb modern notions of power and legitimacy. There is, however, a distinct difference between popular notions of science and science proper. The average person's exposure to science comes from experiences with technology. Thus, science appears to solve practical problems, such as inventing electricity and providing gadgets that run on unseen energy. Quite the reverse of traditional religions, many newer spiritualities preach improvement of this earthly life, rather than solely the acquisition of a transcendental afterlife. This is what religion scholar Christopher Partridge (2003, 22) calls a "physicalist" influence. The metaphysical tradition that encompasses contacteeism promises to transform and to improve the lives of ordinary individuals. On this point, contactee religions intersect with New Age groups, which also champion a better life here and now. In the case of contactee religions, many proclaim that extraterrestrials reveal advanced scientific laws through chosen leaders and that aliens will provide new technologies (and healing techniques) to solve social problems. Some groups await a millennial arrival of spaceships with technological cargo that will improve life on our planet (Tumminia and Kirkpatrick 1995; Trompf 2003).

Spiritualism remains part of the metaphysical milieu that influenced the channeling methods practiced by many contactee religions (Swatos 1990; Lewis 2003b). Most contactee religions draw upon the mediumship technique of channeling the voices and thoughts of extraterrestrials (Porter 1996), sometimes calling it a scientific type of communication. They employ telepathic contact and psychic communication with space beings from other planets, dimensions, or spaceships. Revealed messages and prophecies supposedly communicated from other planetary beings commonly make up the teachings of these religions.[2] In nonindustrial cultures,

---

2. Many are aware that L. Ron Hubbard, the originator of Scientology, was a science-fiction writer. While Scientology's origin myth (Tumminia and Kirkpatrick 2003) refers to an ancient intergalactic war and spaceships, no element of psychic contact or interplanetary revelation is used in rituals. Ordinarily, Scientology is not classified as a UFO religion or contactee religion, but it is considered a new religious movement (NRM).

leaders of such groups would be called shamans or religious mystics because they speak with spirits and receive their visions. Commonly, contactee leaders (e.g., the Normans, George King, Sister Thedra, and Chino Yuko) have a history of study in metaphysical groups, like Spiritualism, Theosophy, or yogic mysticism, which influenced their cosmological inventions. This suggests an opportunistic transition from preexisting groups and ideologies into contactee religions, especially for those groups that espouse channeling and mediumship.

Social Science and the Anomalous

Space aliens and UFOs have reputations for being elusive, and the academic literature on those who believe in them is as scattered as the sightings. A social-psychological survey of the field encompasses many competing explanations about the true nature of experience. Religion scholar John A. Saliba (1992 [reprinted in Lewis 1995]; 2003) attempted at least two summaries that show the vast range of the debate from mass hysteria to Jungian psychology and from cult activity to psychiatric illness.

In a summary of the literature, Saliba reviewed over a hundred social science works on UFO phenomena, flying saucers, abductees, and contactees. He lamented the cynicism linked to the subject as a whole:

> One of the main difficulties encountered in the study of UFO reports is that they are not open to the same process of investigation that has become the normal procedure in the modern scientific world. First of all, UFO phenomena cannot be analyzed directly, immediately, and thoroughly by the scientific community. Second, UFO phenomena cannot be easily categorized—they do not fall into one of the established areas of academic study and there are no universally acknowledged specialists who can be entrusted with the task of verification. Third, the scientific world may not be able to deal with reports that combine both empirical data with the religious and psychic overtones that permeate many UFO reports and accounts of contacts with, and visitations from, alien beings. Four, there is a mysterious quality about UFOs which leaves the door wide open for all kinds of interpretations, both plausible and far-fetched. It is, thus, understandable, if unfortunate, that many natural scientists have been unreceptive to the need for studying the flying saucer phenomenon with an open mind. (1992, 63–64)

Recognizing the interpretive problems inherent with the topic, Saliba went on to cite the main orientations adopted by scholars toward contactee groups and religions. These orientations see the social-psychological aspects of UFO phenomena in three ways: (1) as stemming from projections of psychological need, (2) as rooted in the psychiatric problems of individuals, (3) or as entirely within the realm of myth and religion. Most researchers mentioned in Saliba's summary viewed the phenomena as illusory or as matters that should be relegated to the dubious fields of psychic experience and pseudoscience. My criticism extends to those researchers who emphasize a psychogenic, rather than sociogenic, etiology in contactee and abductee activity.

The very idea of alien contact has long been coupled with the stigmatized notion of hysteria and folly. Hadley Cantril, Hazel Gaudet, and Herta Herzon (1940) reported on the panic precipitated by the radio broadcast of *War of the Worlds* in 1938, when some listeners actually believed Martians were invading Earth! That response was not an isolated one. When a UFO wave engulfed France in 1954, one man shot at his neighbor because he thought he was a Martian. Shortly afterward, a local beet picker was also mistaken for a Martian.[3] This notion of hysteria may be valid in some instances, especially when a population suffers fear precipitated by rumors of threat or attack, but certainly it is not applicable in all cases and does not speak to the widespread cultural diffusion going on today. Most cultural research now shows a spectrum of extraterrestrial-related belief that is settling into the fabric of Western culture and that belies any single explanation.

Social-psychological studies from the 1950s and 1960s labeled UFO believers as irrational or deviant, and questions about the sanity of UFO seekers seemed perfunctory (Buckner 1966, 1968). Perhaps the most widely known work on a contactee group remains *When Prophecy Fails* (Festinger, Riecken, and Schachter 1956), which attempted to explain why people would believe in something that had been proven false. In essence, it sought to explain why people clung to irrational beliefs. Leon Festinger, Henry W. Riecken, and Stanley Schachter described their covert observations of a millenarian group and its leader, who prophesied an immense flood that was to be coupled with the rescue of the faithful by means of flying saucers.

3. This information comes from cover stories of the French newspaper *Radar,* from the Oct. 31, 1954, and Nov. 7, 1954, issues respectively. Suffice it to say, the earliest social-psychological studies of reactions to mysterious flying objects linked the phenomenon to mass hysteria (Miller 2000), and to the belief that UFOs were spacecraft piloted by aliens. Older references to flying-saucer hysteria as connected to anxiety or enthusiastic contagion are found in the work of Neil J. Smelser (1962, 90) and Orrin E. Klapp (1972, 132–33) on collective behavior. In the United States, UFO sightings sharply peaked in 1952 with the so-called Summer of the Saucers, and social psychologists linked the phenomenon to mass hysteria caused by Cold War jitters (Klapp 1972; Hall and Conners 2000).

When no flood or saucers ever appeared, the closest followers continued to believe in their leader and the messages she conveyed. Festinger and his colleagues asked why people would hold such deep convictions despite evidence to the contrary. As an answer, the researchers emphasized the role of social cohesion and member commitment in the maintenance of belief.[4] More important, they linked belief to group influence and involvement.

In another wing of social science, mainstream psychological assessments of contactees and of abductees have not been couched in the neutral language of cultural relativism; behavioral medicine, like the larger society, has come to lump contactees and abductees together as one indistinguishable bundle of odd pathology. Contactees and abductees who have come to the attention of the mental health profession run the risk of being involuntarily labeled mentally ill and being diagnosed with dissociative disorders (Krippner and Powers 1997; Holden and French 2002). The stigma of such anomalous experience appears to be fixed, despite the popular culture's growing fascination with the subject. Conventional psychiatry and psychology focus more closely on indicators of mental health (e.g., personality traits, sadomasochistic tendencies, depressive symptoms, etc.), understanding coupled with treatment (Goldberg 2000), and the physiology of sleep states when assessing contactees and abductees. Psychologists Mahzarin R. Banaji and John F. Kihlstrom (1996) call for a more naturalistic approach to the study of abductees that would incorporate environmental factors and social contingencies in order to demystify the phenomenon. If this were actually done, we might find that there are a multiplicity of ways in which aliens have entered our culture and psyches.

In one attempt to restate the case for contactees and against the psychopathological label, Robert E. Bartholomew, Keith Basterfield, and George S. Howard (1991) asked clinicians to consider the alternative diagnosis of the fantasy-prone personality, a classification invented by Sheryl C. Wilson and T. X. Barber. According to Wilson and Barber's criteria, a person with a fantasy-prone personality spends more than half of a working day in fantasy and has vivid sensory experiences in everyday life (such as seeing, smelling, and feeling the words heard in conversations or on television). Thus, what had previously been labeled grossly abnormal could be seen within a gentler classification, more akin to an overactive imagination or a compulsive, albeit harmless, need for fantasy. Researchers Nicholas P. Spanos et al. (1993) found no psychopathology or lack of intelligence after testing a sample of contactees and UFO observers. However, their study did show that UFO experi-

---

4. For a lengthy analysis of *When Prophecy Fails*, see *When Prophecy Never Fails* (Tumminia 2005).

ences were more probable in people who subscribed to esoteric beliefs and who were more oriented toward fantasy. Although Lewis (2000) reports that subsequent researchers found no empirical data to support the fantasy-prone personality hypothesis, psychological testing for such individual traits is still going on. Leading skeptical experts, such as Richard J. McNally et al. (2004) and Susan A. Clancy (2005), tested abductee subjects on psychometric indexes of fantasy, dissociation, and magical ideation, finding significant correlations.

Psychopathological and fantasy-prone approaches place the origin of contactee activity within the individual in contradistinction to a social origin, a perspective to which many scholars of religion and sociology would object. It is difficult not to hypothesize a link between fantasy, magical thinking, and alien contact. The genre swells with fanciful stories embellished by the most dubious of details that are supported by the most ambiguous evidence. However, to their detriment, psychopathological and fantasy-prone approaches do not differentiate between isolated contactees/abductees (who are not part of a group) and group-oriented contactees/abductees. These perspectives fail to account for the small, but viable, contactee subculture and quasi-movement activity that function as areas of socialization.

Alien Abduction?

Currently, alien abduction narratives (AANs) coexist with contactee accounts and derive legitimacy from some strains of ufology. Students of UFO-related phenomena know that various people claim to have been abducted by aliens and that these claims meet with great skepticism (Brookesmith 1998; McNally et al. 2004; Clancy 2005).[5] For many years, folklorists like Bullard (1989) have asserted the mythmaking potential of the phenomena. Bullard focused upon the ways alien abduction narra-

---

5. The following are reputedly some of the symptoms of alien abduction as professed by many abduction researchers and therapists: missing time (time that cannot be accounted for), feeling paralyzed in bed, unexplained scars or indentations in the skin (evidence of skin scoops and implants), strange dreams, feeling chosen, feeling you have a mission to perform, psychic awareness, false pregnancy, genital soreness, sexual problems, awakening in odd position or strange place, seeing UFOs or mysterious lights, strong fears, life problems, self-esteem problems, feeling watched, reactions to ET images, nose bleeds, ringing in ears, sleep problems, hearing a voice or voices in head, channeling messages, and an inability to remember an abduction. For a further introduction to abduction scenarios, see the International Center for Abduction Research Web site at http://www.ufoabduction.com/straighttalk.htm. This site is connected with the work of David M. Jacobs. Other organizations include FEARS (Founda-

tives resemble the older folk tales of flying ships and kidnappings by otherworldly creatures, such as fairies or other supernatural beings. For millennia, people have heard stories about others being spirited away to some other extraordinary realm of existence. Today's abductees and some ufologists assert that the culprits have been aliens all along. Subcultures of abduction belief classify various types of alien abduction and distinct types of extraterrestrials. See appendix B to learn about some of the many types of supposed aliens. For further study, read *The Field Guide to Extraterrestrials* (Huyghe 1996), *Faces of the Visitors* (Randle and Estes 1997), and *Spaceships of the Visitors* (Randle and Estes 2000). These subcultures of abduction belief exhibit highly animistic themes describing folkloric images of impish aliens, as well as angelic contacts. People who experience this phenomenon assert its reality. As one Web site claims, "real" aliens are different from the ones found on television.

Certain believers rely on a growing substratum of abduction entrepreneurs found easily on the Internet and through word of mouth. Although mainstream psychiatry dismisses these abduction claims as a type of dissociative mental disorder (Krippner and Powers 1997) or false memory, alternative therapies and support groups for abductees have mushroomed (Bader 2003). Social scientists are now concerned with *recovered memories* of alien abduction (Loftus and Ketcham 1994; Clark and Loftus 1996; Newman and Baumeister 1998; Holden and French 2002; Clancy 2005), especially when associated with specific therapies, like hypnosis. Clancy et al. (2002) found a higher level of false recall on word tests among subjects reporting recovered memories of alien abduction. Academics remain skeptical about the validity of hypnosis as a vehicle for recalling alien abduction. The Alvin Lawson experiments first conducted in 1977 showed that unaffected test subjects produced stories about abductions and drawings of aliens under hypnosis, leading the researcher to conclude the stories were spurious (Kerr and Crow 1983, 228). Such evidence prompts many social scientists to hypothesize that these types of memories are false memories, produced in the context of a subculture of belief in alien abduction narratives.

Because of the stigma of being labeled abnormal or psychopathological by psychiatrists, a segment of abduction believers have formed alternative support groups. Some seek out unconventional practitioners who claim to be able to undo the trauma caused by alien abduction. This type of extra-institutional activity points to

---

tion for Abduction Research and Support) and MAAR (Malevolent Alien Abduction Research). See also the chapters on abduction in this book, particularly chapters 6, 8, and 17, which mention other organizations.

the function of abductee groups as folk-healing enterprises. Some practitioners have their own clinics or nonprofit educational institutions, and many give talks at UFO or New Age meetings where they find clients. The Internet and certain ufological networks assist seekers in finding groups and therapists. As one example, Marilyn and Doug Ruben (2003) sell their e-book, *Healing the Hurt of Alien Abduction,* online where they also advertised their services as abduction therapists. This subject is explored in chapters 6 and 17.

Certain authors tie some aspects of the alien abduction to a physiological state called sleep paralysis (Cheyne 2003; Perina 2003). Devon Hinton, David Hufford, and Laurence Kirmayer define it this way:

> In sleep paralysis, the person, during sleep onset or awakening, finds themselves [*sic*] completely awake but unable to move their limbs or speak. Often, the person sees a form, which may shadow-like or indistinct, move toward him or her; frequently, the experience is also associated with an oppressive feeling of chest tightness, weight on the chest or the body, or sensation of shortness of breath. The paralysis is understood as a disturbance of the normal regulation of sleep in which the muscular paralysis characteristic of REM sleep occurs during a state of waking arousal. (2005, 6)

Hufford (2005) points out that this universally reported sleep experience takes place independent of cultural learning and that some features consistent with sleep paralysis are conducive to spiritual interpretation (e.g., apparitions, out of the body experiences, feelings of flying). McNally and Clancy (2005) also propose that the alien abduction experience may originate from bouts of sleep paralysis. The subject of sleep paralysis is discussed more extensively in chapter 6.

Modern Media and Alien Myths

Looking at our mass psychology for the moment, we must admit that alien imagery has embedded itself in our technological iconography. Academics (Kuhn 1990; Jenkins 1992; Porter and McLaren 1999; Lewis 2000) note the interplay of media and mythic morality. In the world's oldest religions, people passed on their sacred stories to later generations on stone, on animal skins, or on parchment, creating collective memories of the sacred. Even in the recent past, the metaphysical precursors to contacteeism preserved their otherworldly messages in books. In the more secular twenty-first century, electronic media (Web sites, e-mail, movies, and television)

supplement traditional efforts to pass on spiritual narratives. Nowhere are extraterrestrials more visible than within the media of the present era.

Alien imagery imprints our mass consciousness through the vehicles of films
and television. Some of us have observed the death and resurrection of Jesus Christ
on film, but we have also witnessed the death and resurrection of Mr. Spock. As
postmodern audiences, we partake of an overabundance of space-oriented origin
myths and a plethora of metaphorical battles between good and evil involving
countless animistic space beings. Through a process of osmosis, popular culture has
absorbed alien and UFO imagery as a staple of allegorical storytelling. Has some of
the burden of teaching metaphysical philosophy shifted from mainstream religion
to the thinly veiled morality tales from media-driven science fiction? How much attention do we pay to the spiritual messages created for us by film and television? In
Star Wars, the Jedi knights practiced an ancient religion that sounded a bit like Tao-
ism tempered by Manichaean misgivings. Does this sort of mysticism have purely
an entertainment value or do some people cling to its philosophy? Hmm. What
would Master Yoda say about all this?

One cultural response to our postmodern world of aliens has been the development of fan activity. The word fan is derived the Latin words for temple, *fanum,* and
religious fanaticism, *fanaticus.* We have only to examine the sincerity of the most
dedicated fans of science-fiction media to see the parallels with religious phenomena; they consume and even act out the mythology of space travel and alien contact.
Fandom does occupy that gray area referred to earlier as *quasi-religion,* the more
secular reflection of formal religious expression. Michael Jindra (1994) referred to
Star Trek fan activity as a disguised religion with deep mythological elements. The
basic plots of *Star Trek* involve a heroic magical voyage to seek out and to explore
new life on alien worlds, using outer space and alien contact as a background for
moral tales and humanistic philosophy. Jindra likened fan conventions to pilgrimages replete with costumed rituals, and the popularity of *Star Trek* to a type of civil
religion. The anthology *Star Trek and Sacred Ground* (Porter and McLaren 1999)
points out the multilayered themes pulsing through the many years of storylines.
Science fiction, like religion, often engages in sharp social criticism. While implicitly
critiquing the sociocultural conditions of the past century on a number of issues
such as the status of women, race relations, and human folly, the *Star Trek* series un-
apologetically intertwined science with mysticism. The scripts meshed the value of
intuition with importance of rationality as Starfleet humanized the cosmos with its
ethical superiority. The more recent generations of *Star Trek* utilize images from the
latest theories of quantum physics alongside its perennial depictions of complicated

group dynamics, warfare, and occasional sexual attraction. Notwithstanding its sci-fi predecessors, *Star Trek* dramatically went where no one had gone before, sparking a multitude of imitations and taking the popular imagination with it. For a study of Klingon fandom, see chapter 12.

Media in its many forms cultivates permutations of themes that then become our psychic tattoos. Barkun (2003) contends that media provides a haven for the propagation of stigmatized knowledge, like alien conspiracy theories, and preserves them for mass-cultural consumption in television and film (e.g., *The X-Files*). Dean (1998) argues that extraterrestrials have invaded the popular culture's iconography and that they supply a reference point within the new millennium's implosion of meaning, brought about the overly complex political and technocratic conditions characteristic of postmodern overload. Aliens are everywhere, she asserts, even where they ought not to show up by any measure of reason.

Chapters in the Book

For a wide variety of reasons, alien narratives are here to stay. The thoughtful reflections of the contributors to the present volume offer insights into why that is the case, and they analyze many types of related phenomena from a continuum of different theoretical perspectives. Clearly, the effort to foster a deeper understanding of such topics will do more to advance the study of how humans create reality than will the popular tendency to simply dismiss these activities as trivial and ridiculous.

This book concentrates on a survey of the societal discourse that ranges from obvious science fiction to the social construction of scientific facts around aliens and UFOs. No attempt is made to present a comprehensive chronicle of alien contact or ufology, since these fields undergo constant revision in response to new claims about prehistory and history (e.g., aliens created Adam and Eve or UFOs visited Pharoah Thutmose II and the prophet Ezekiel, etc.). Although this anthology touches upon many verifiable events as background information, it is by no means an exhaustive history. Such themes are best addressed by experts from those specific areas, and as several chronicles already exist (Jacobs 1975; Flammonde 1976; Thompson 1991; Williams 1991; Peebles 1994; Bartholomew and Howard 1998; Lewis 2000; Denzler 2001), any effort here would be superfluous. This collection mostly ponders religious themes and other open questions within social science. It aims to supplement the knowledge of the cultural response to alleged alien contact, using both descriptive and theoretical approaches.

The present compilation brings together some of the newer scholarship in this expanding field of study. The majority of contributors are senior scholars who have been researching and reflecting in this area for years. In the following chapters, the reader can explore aspects of extraterrestrial contact, the riddle of alien abduction, contactee spirituality, aliens from the media, and various strains of ufology.

The first chapter, by Mikael Rothstein, discusses the hagiography (sacred biography) of George King, the founder of the Aetherius Society. The Aetherius Society began in 1954 as one of the earliest religions established upon the belief in spiritual contact with alien beings, or Cosmic Masters. "Hagiography and Text in the Aetherius Society" reveals the ways the group constructs the story of George King's life, pointing out its spiritual markers.

Students of social psychology may be familiar with *When Prophecy Fails.* Festinger, Riecken, and Schachter (1956) dubbed the leader of the group they observed Mrs. Keech, but her real name was Dorothy Martin (1900–1992). The book showed how people do not have to see to believe and that failed prophecy does not necessarily deter believers. Jerome Clark brings us up to date on the story of Mrs. Keech in our second chapter. She was also known as Sister Thedra. What ever happened to her? "The Odyssey of Sister Thedra" traces her rise and passage into history. Sister Thedra still has followers based at Mount Shasta and around the world, who carry on her work. Some of her many admirers post Web sites to honor her memory and teachings.

In the chapter that follows, I describe the history and beliefs of the Universal Industrial Church of the New World Comforter. Little academic research exists about the group that has lived a communal hippie lifestyle since the sixties. In contrast to the Raëlians, it is the smallest contactee religion. We learn about the story of contactee Allen Michael and his visions for a new society based on extraterrestrial intelligence (ETI) in "Galactic Messenger!"

The contemporary UFO religion that can claim the largest worldwide membership is the International Raëlian Movement, or the Raëlian Religion, as it is known in Canada. The Raëlians, who trace their origins to space travelers called the Elohim, grabbed headlines around the world when they announced the alleged successful cloning of a human being. Their leader, Raël (Claude Vorilhon), appeared on the popular television show *Dr. Phil* in 2003, although he abruptly ended his interview when Dr. Phil McGraw failed to show the deference he required. Who are the Raëlians and why does their leader demand so much reverence?

Some postmodernists argue that metanarratives of the nineteenth and twentieth centuries, like the teachings of the great religions and scientific rationalism, have crumbled in favor of emergent cut-and-paste philosophies of the postmodern age that weave media iconography into a collage of novel perspectives. Bryan Sentes and Susan Palmer discuss the Raëlians' curious philosophy and news-making activities. They examine in "Presumed Immanent" the extensive Raëlian history, tying its symbolism to the postmodern condition and explaining how UFO mysticism resolves the perceptual conflict between science and religion.

Many of the authors in this book analyze the writings and beliefs of contactee religions from the perspective of the sociology of knowledge. With "In the Dreamtime of the Saucer People," I present an ethnomethodological analysis of the Unarius Academy of Science. This chapter describes what life is like living within the Unarian reality. Although other chapters link close encounters and abduction narratives to various sleep states, that is not my thesis. Rather I contend that any person, whether a reputable scientist or contactee, produces evidence to support his or her belief system. Dreams are one *valid* way of explaining reality for Unarians.

In "Toward an Explanation of the Abduction Epidemic," Georg M. Rønnevig writes about some supposed, albeit renowned, cases of alien abduction and the possible connection of the abduction syndrome to sleep states. Rønnevig makes the case that alternative therapies, such as hypnotherapy and abductee support groups, create rituals of belonging and meaning for those who believe they have been abducted.

In "Secondary Beliefs and the Alien Abduction Phenomenon" Benson Saler proposes a multicausal approach to the social scientific understanding of alien abduction narratives. What can account for the range of reactions to alien abduction narratives among believers, skeptics, and debunkers? This chapter speaks to those who already have a background in the AAN debate.

Scott R. Scribner draws a parallel between religious tales, in particular biblical passages, and alien abduction stories. How is that we may accept the biblical account of visions, but not those of contactees? His chapter "Alien Abduction Narratives and Religious Contexts" articulates a current investigation of the nature of alien abduction narratives as a specialized subset of UFO-related culture. Scribner notes that these narratives seem to be losing their thematic connections to spacecraft. He proposes there is a similarity between some many religious references and alien abduction narratives.

In "Close Encounters of the French Kind," Pierre Lagrange expounds upon the sociology of knowledge as he details the case of the French history of ufology. In the tradition of Bruno Latour, who gave us groundbreaking analysis in the sociology of science, Lagrange attempts a sociological analysis of the narratives of paranormal "science" of flying saucers. Aptly, he calls this subject a "sociological untouchable" because of its association with the irrational. Lagrange deconstructs the ideological history of the UFO debate in France by describing the divisions in the types of proof and evidence characteristic of ufologists, contactees, and reputable scientists. What constitutes logic and reason for each camp interested in the phenomena?

In "Consciousness, Culture, and UFOs," the noted author Jacques Vallee examines the complexity of belief in UFOs as he puts into historical and cultural context the difficulties of doing objective scientific research on the subject. He asks what kind of real research can be done in the climate of "social-trance formation." Have the symbolic explorations of the cultural inventions surrounding the topic forever sidetracked science from finding out what is really going on? Vallee comments on the present state of affairs with understanding and insight.

In "Aliens from the Cosmos," Anna E. Kubiak, a Polish scholar of New Age religions, comments on some elements of UFO myth. She assigns the scattered nature of the retellings of the myth through media, pseudoscience, and abduction narratives to the fragmentation of the postmodern consciousness.

A widely sold pop culture poster reads, "All I Need to Know, I Learned from Watching *Star Trek*." Jennifer E. Porter enlightens us about a special segment of *Star Trek* fans in her chapter, "All I Ever Want to Be, I Learned from Playing Klingon." What do people derive from dressing up and going to *Star Trek* conventions? What happens when fans become the characters they so love from television and the movies? Her chapter allows us to learn something about Klingon culture and mythology, as well as *Star Trek* fans themselves. Of the 331 extraterrestrial species in the *Star Trek* universe, Klingons possess the greatest popularity (*Star Trek* Web site 2004).

While many of the other authors in this book take a social constructionist stance or a doubtful posture toward extraterrestrial visitation, James F. Strange asks what-if questions of our readers. He addresses the disputed science of UFO archeology in "Observations from Archaeology and Religious Studies on First Contact and ETI Evidence." Taking an advocate's stance, Strange makes the case for this enterprise arguing that it is often misunderstood and faces prejudice from the scientific establishment and the public at large. What would happen if scientists found an actual UFO artifact? What would happen if we actually made contact?

Sociologist Anne Cross shares her ethnographic work on the subculture of ufology in "A Confederacy of Fact and Faith." She notes how segments of the ufological subculture "scienticize" religion by meshing discordant paradigms into explanations of ancients astronauts and extraterrestrial presence. She observed meetings and conventions within the milieu, including a lecture by Erich von Däniken, renowned for his books touting the archeological evidence of alien visitations. Her descriptive study informs us on the elements of this subcultural activity and the logic employed in the construction of its reality.

Along the same lines of debate, Pia Andersson investigates the UFO archeology arguments in "Ancient Alien Brothers, Ancient Terrestrial Remains: Archaeology or Religion?" by pointing out the ways believers fuse science and religion. What is the reasoning behind the blending of ancient myths and archaeological sites with the newer narratives about alien visitation? Andersson surveys the field, explaining the various connections made by ufologists and ancient astronaut enthusiasts.

Christopher Helland gives us more information about the Raëlians and their quest to introduce cloning as a viable option for human beings. How do Raëlians use science to legitimate their belief system? As Helland shows, Raëlians view their push for human cloning not as a scientific experiment with ethical problems, but rather as a continuation of the spiritual intervention of the Elohim. In 2003, researchers euthanized Dolly, the world's first cloned sheep, because she developed lung disease, arthritis, and signs of premature aging. This event raises further ethical questions about the cloning of human beings at this point in history, a caution ignored by the current Raëlian vision. While mainstream scientists fret over cloning experiments with animals, Raëlians claim success in cloning humans. By examining their philosophy, Helland explains the ways the group links scientific notions about cloning to their extensive worldview in "The Raëlian Creation Myth and the Art of Cloning."

In the final chapter, sociologist Christopher D. Bader reports his research on a sample of the abductee support group members. "Abductee Support Groups: Who Are the Members?" outlines his demographic and qualitative findings. These groups employ a maverick form of psychology that walks the line between folk religion and therapy.

Readers can use this book as one tool in study of the cultural response to presumed aliens for outer space. As beneficiary of the change of attitude within the academic community, the reader is encouraged to explore the topic using the many references now available in reputable books and journals. I also recommend checking out the Internet for more worlds of information. Most contactee religions now have their own Web sites, as do the various ufologists and their critics. Any average Internet surfer can access various levels of documentation about UFOs, extraterrestrials, abductions, or disputed claims of contact that would probably take a lifetime to read. In closing, good luck with your research, and may all your contacts be of the friendly kind.

PART ONE

Contactee Religions

Hagiography and Text in the Aetherius Society

Aspects of the Social Construction of a Religious Leader

Mikael Rothstein

In hagiographies, followers produce sacred biographies of their religious leaders that cloud facts with spiritual discourse. Very often, there is no easy access to plain historical facts, whereas legends, myths, and theological elaborations on a leader's life and work are found in abundance. Similarly, externally obtained data remain relatively rare. Brief biographies, as those found in J. Gordon Melton's *Biographical Dictionary of American Cult and Sect Leaders,* give valuable scholarly information, but very often it is difficult to measure the validity of biographical details provided about religious leaders by their own supporters.[1]

This lack of objective factual information is very much the case with religious leaders or innovators of the past, such as Muhammad, Siddhartha Gautama Buddha, or Jesus, to mention a few, but it certainly is also a common feature regarding religious leaders of the present. Most new or alternative religions will describe and explain all matters concerning their leaders that are of interest to the believers. Those selective explanations support their beliefs about the extraordinary nature of their leaders (Wallis 1986; Palmer 2004; Tumminia 2005). Information of other kinds, however, is often much harder to retrieve. A prominent example of this mechanism is Scientology's passionate preoccupation with L. Ron Hubbard, his life, and his work. The Church of Scientology's literature transformed the person of

---

1. This book (Melton 1986) only deals with religious leaders who died before January 1, 1983.

Hubbard into a superior being of ultimate good and ultimate competence. Although not declared divine, Hubbard is adored and emulated by the believers of the Church's inner circle. Yet when it comes to the verifiable and sometimes unflattering details of Hubbard's life, Scientology remains silent. Similar examples include the lives of Maharishi Mahesh Yogi of Transcendental Meditation, Madame Blavatsky of the Theosophical Society, and Sun Myung Moon of the Unification Church.[2]

Although the actual historical and social conditions behind any religious leader are of general relevance to the study of religion, these facts are not always the most important ones to followers. If scholarly interest focuses attention on the historical and social preconditions for a religious group to emerge, it will be natural to consider the history and personal background of its leader. However, at other times, attention will focus on the religious interpretation or the making of the religious leader, and then the need for precise historical facts will be of less importance. For instance, the historical facts surrounding Muhammad are of less interest than the legendary *hadith* traditions, if the intention is to understand the image of Muhammad as the ideal prophet for Islam. Likewise, the actual place and time of Jesus' birth are of no significance if we are interested in the mythological foundation of Christian Christmas celebrations or the understanding of the infant Jesus in Christian lore or iconography. Similarly, the actual objective analysis of L. Ron Hubbard's life is of little interest to the average Scientologist because the foundation for all Scientology's standards is the mythological rendition of Hubbard (Wallis 1977).

The images of religious leaders are generally social constructions, and the narratives about them will very often form actual hagiographic traditions. Thus, studying the image of the religious leader or founder is not usually a survey of accurate historical facts. Rather, it may well be an investigation into comprehensive mythological texts and narratives. However, very few historians of religion have taken up the challenge of analyzing the hagiographies (sacred biographies) of contemporary religious leaders by means of religious texts.[3] An indication is found in *The Encyclopedia of Religion* in which the entry "Biography" (explained to mean "sacred biography") written by William R. LaFleur only refers to classical religions, and among those primarily to Christian traditions. There is no mention of the literally thou-

2. There are, of course, exceptions. The life of Bhaktivedanta Swami Prabhupada, guru and founder of ISKCON, for instance, has been described with many details and in all aspects in several books written by his disciples.

3. See Dorthe Refslund Christensen (1997a, 1997b, 1997c, 2005) and Rothstein (1992, 1993) on the hagiographic tradition surrounding L. Ron Hubbard.

sands of hagiographic legends outside the realm of traditional Christianity, Islam, Buddhism, and Confucianism. This chapter aims at a hermeneutical investigation into religious texts in order to understand the sacred biography of one relatively unknown modern religious leader, approaching the subject from the field of the history of religions.

George King in the Texts of the Aetherius Society

No significant attempts were made by scholars to research the official image of George King (1919–1997), the founder of the Aetherius Society, until his death.[4] Available information indicates that all external descriptions of King and his life refer to internal sources of documentation. Consequently, in the biographical note on King by sociologist of religion Eileen Barker (1991), she based her information on books issued by the Aetherius Society.[5] What she then emphasized was the religious conceptualization of King, who was not an ordinary man in the eyes of his followers, showing how such academic biographies in turn also rely on the perception of the adherents.

The common description of King, whether internal or external, will therefore involve the same mixture of myth and historical facts that constitutes any sacred biography. Religion historian William R. LaFleur writes:

> Whereas mythology will usually tell only of random deeds of deities in a largely episodic and nonconsecutive manner, the subjects of a sacred biography will tend to be treated as persons whose life stories need to be told as discrete and continuous lives. The subject of a sacred biography will tend to be treated as someone whose

---

4. George King died in July 1997 just as I completed an early draft of this chapter. Hence, I deliberated on all my conclusions before the death of King, and I have followed them up to see if they still applied to Aetherius.

5. Eileen Barker's (1991, 216) biographical sketch of King reads: "Founder and President of the Aetherius Society, 'An International Spiritual Brotherhood.' He is known as the Metropolitan Archbishop, His Eminence Sir George King, OSP, PhD, ThD, DD. Sir George was born in Shropshire; his father was a schoolteacher, his mother a practicing spiritual healer. He became a London taxi driver and a conscientious objector during the World War II; he served as a section leader in the Fire Service. He practiced yoga and studied a number of Eastern and New Age philosophies. In 1954, he claims to have received the command 'Prepare yourself! You are to become the voice of the Interplanetary Parliament.' Sir George has since channeled numerous messages, especially from a Cosmic Master from Venus, known as Aetherius, and Master Jesus."

life story can be told from birth to death and, to that degree at least, as it would be treated in a secular biography. The difference from the latter, however, lies in the degree to which such a subject will be represented as carrying out a divinely planned "call" or visions authenticating such a mission, and having either infallible knowledge or supernatural powers. (LaFleur 1993, 220)

Every aspect of this characterization suits the example of George King nicely. Moreover, in order to capture the tradition that developed around King, the perspective of the believers becomes unavoidable. From a hagiographic standpoint, it is of no direct interest that before his career as a religious leader, King earned his money as a taxi driver. However, it is of great importance to understand that his former position as an anonymous taxi driver signifies something crucial to his followers: their religious leader started out as nothing more than an ordinary man who was destined for greatness. Hence, this frequently reported detail of King's professional life before his religious awakening appears spiritually meaningful. Nonetheless, "ordinary man" is not really a fitting description for King because his followers paint him as an extraordinary personage. In fact, the books and pamphlets of the Aetherius Society repeatedly state that King was "a Western Master of Yoga," or "a Western Yoga Adept" at the time extraterrestrial beings of superior intelligence approached him in 1954. Moreover, the texts say that King passed through various developmental phases in his spiritual evolution, leaving behind many elementary stages of consciousness in the process.[6] The image we receive is that of a common man who reached splendid heights through diverse forms of spiritual knowledge and practice. The Aetherius Society depicts King as a self-realized man who attained what we all potentially could aspire to, although it is only spiritually accomplished by a select few. Members of the Aetherius Society occasionally suggest that King was, in fact, a Cosmic Master himself, but this idea has never been officially confirmed.[7]

Various texts issued by the Aetherius Society introduce King by more or less the

6. Usually this claim is not stated explicitly, but the principle is often emphasized, for instance in King and Avery ([1975]1982, 15) where it says: "[the law of karma] will place each individual exactly where he belongs to be; exactly what he has earned will be given him."

7. When members of Aetherius were asked about the status of George King, a common answer was the following: "A lot of people think that he is an adept, but it has never been verified by his Eminence himself" (Bang 1996, 48). When King received the title of Master, this meant spiritual leader rather than Cosmic Master. Elsewhere, concerning Claude Vorilhon (Raël), the leader of the International Raëlian Movement, I have pointed to the fact that religious leaders often will avoid discussing their spiritual status (Rothstein 1993, 143). They will often leave it up to their followers to decide. This

1.1. George King founded the Aetherius Society in 1954. In the group, he is referred to as His Eminence, Dr. George King. Courtesy of the Aetherius Society.

same standard phrases. The hagiographic emphasis is always placed on his unique personal qualities and the immense importance of his spiritual task, while little is mentioned of his life before receiving the religious call. The following quote encapsulates the society's presentation of its spiritual leader:

His Eminence Sir George King. Primary Terrestrial Mental Channel. His Eminence Sir George King was born on January 23rd, 1919, in Wellington, Shropshire, England. His father was a schoolmaster and his mother a noted clairvoyant and Healer. From a very early age, he showed a profound interest in Religion—at that time, orthodox Christianity. The World War II years were spent in the London Fire Brigade, battling the effects of the Nazi Luftwaffe incendiary and high-explosive raids on London and surrounding areas. During this time he learned personally and deeply of man's inhumanity to man—as well as much about man's capacity for self-sacrifice and bravery.

His interest had turned by this time to the more profound Truths of advanced metaphysics and he became a student of Yoga, practicing ever more difficult and challenging Yoga exercises for up to ten hours daily. His own psychic abilities became very pronounced, including his ability to project into the Higher Realms to pursue his intense search for the highest Truth, with the assistance of advanced in-

is the case with Raël, Maharishi Mahesh Yogi of TM, Sun Myung Moon of the Unification Church, and Jesus.

telligences there. By 1954, he was deeply engrossed in Spiritual Healing and had already received advanced Initiations on the Higher Planes.

It was in this year that he received the well-known "Command" to prepare himself to become the voice of Interplanetary Parliament and was soon shown, through a series of highly specialized exercises, how to bring about that elevated state of consciousness absolutely necessary to establish a mental rapport with the Beings Who inhabit the other Planets. He mastered the science of Raja, Gnani, and Kundalini Yoga until he could consciously attain the state of Samadhi. It was then the Cosmic Masters of the Solar System began using him as Primary Terrestrial Mental Channel. . . .

To Members of The Aetherius Society throughout the world His Eminence Sir George King is acknowledged Primary Terrestrial Mental Channel for Interplanetary Parliament and recognized as their Spiritual Master in these latter days before the dawning of a New Age upon Earth! (Abrahamson 1994, 14–15)[8]

The Age of Aetherius describes King's numerous achievements in detail in several additional texts, consistently referring to the many prizes, awards, titles, and acknowledgments King received. An addendum to the 1982 version is a good example of hagiographic construction (King and Avery [1975] 1982). The actual information is not questioned here. Rather, the reader should focus analytically on the way it is presented.[9] A partial list of King's achievements reads:

Long-deserved recognition of the outstanding abilities and achievements of Doctor George King began to arrive in 1977, when the academic degree of Doctor of Philosophy was conferred upon him. Soon to follow were other degrees: Doctor of Sacred Humanities, Doctor of Literature with an appointment as Professor in Human Relations at North-West London University, a well-established and highly-reputed one in England, also issued to the Author [King], on the recommendation of several outstanding European scholars who had reviewed his works, a Citation

8. The reader should note that hagiographic texts often capitalize words that otherwise would not be capitalized in order to emphasize their spiritual importance. This is true of the texts quoted in this chapter.

9. The book gives a line of references to other Aetherius Society publications or texts of a similar kind.

mentioning the author's publications, *You Too Can Heal, The Day the Gods Came,* and *The Nine Freedoms,* as well as his research thesis entitled "The Behavior of Humanity and the Psychological Approach to Humanity."

From the Academy of Science in Rome came the Gold Medal of Merit in Science and the Medal of Honor with Collare Grand Croce d'Onore al Merito con Bandia d'Italia Marce Tuillo Cicerone, together with the Diploma Solenne in Science conferring the title, "Immortal of Rome." The nobility and royalty of the world also began to take note of his humanitarian achievements and he was soon invested in Knighthood in many Orders of Chivalry in Europe. (King and Avery [1975] 1982, 77–78)

Further in the text, Aetherius describes how George King was crowned by His Royal and Imperial Highness Prince Henri III Paleologue (apparently King's cousin), who bestowed upon him additional orders and titles. Following that, another account reports on King's own successful efforts to establish new orders of chivalry, including his enthronement as Prince Grand Master of his own order, the Mystical Order of Saint Peter, on June 20, 1982. Characteristically, the text emphasizes King's authority as Archbishop and Metropolitan Archbishop of the Aetherius Church. Additionally, Aetherius listed several other distinctions, including his appointment as "Honorary Consul-at-Large, Minister of State, and Special Adviser to the President of the Republic of Free Poland (in Exile)]," where, accordingly, he was also honored with "its highest awards including Virtuti Militari and the Grand Cordon of the Order of Polonia Restituta."

According to *The Age of Aetherius,* the International Evangelism Crusades voted George King Minister of the Year for 1981, and he received the Prize of Peace and Justice with the rank of Knight of Humanity in 1981 from UNICEF and the UCCI (Union of Capital Cities of Latin [Ibero] America). A comment in the text reads: "this Prize being only somewhat less prestigious than the famed Nobel Prize" (King and Avery [1975] 1982, 77–78). The text ends with the following:

Honors and awards too numerous to list here have been received from all over the Western world where the humanitarian works, Spiritual abilities and insight of this outstanding Master of Yoga have begun to win the recognition which they have so long deserved. Others are sure to follow and will be added to the addenda of future editions of this book. (King and Avery [1975] 1982, 79)

Aetherius touts the auspicious astrological alignment of the planets on the day of King's birth, as evidence of his great importance.[10] On his seventy-eighth birthday (January 23, 1997), Aetherius awarded George King more accolades when they invited all of humankind to partake in a cosmic tribute to King. The invitation stated that he had already received many "temporal and divine" recognitions, but on that day they promised a special heavenly tribute would be bestowed.

In addition to cosmic awards and honors, Aetherius portrays King as a unique religious leader in other ways. In one text, for instance, King describes how he met Master Jesus face to face at the top of the mountain known as Holdstone Down on July 23, 1958, in Devon, England. The text that describes the photo of this auspicious site where the meeting took place reads: "The small pile of boulders in the foreground marks where Master Jesus stood on this historic occasion. . . . Thousands of pilgrims have followed our Master to this spot" (Abrahamson 1994, 22).

In other texts, the elevated masters themselves acclaim that King is special. One text, *The Twelve Blessings,* contains a note saying, "Jesus blessed this book." The note states that in a spacecraft, George King's mother, Mary, meets with Jesus at his request after being mentally instructed to bring the book. "This must not be touched by any . . . save our Mental Channel," the voice tells her. After a wonderful journey, the spaceship enters a "Mother Craft" where Jesus approaches Mary King. "Give me the Book," he says, and takes it in his hands. Then Master Jesus exclaims:

> Oh Supreme Master of all Creation
> Higher than Highest
> Mightier than the Mightiest
> Greater than all Greatness
> We bring to Thee this offering in Love and Humility
> From our beloved brother of Earth—George,
> The one Whom Thou didst choose to be a Leader
> Among men of Earth, in this their New Age.
> (Aetherius Society 1974, 11)

In this text, George King emerges as "a beloved brother" to Master Jesus and a leader among men, chosen by the Supreme Master of all Creation, apparently the

---

10. The source document is the Aetherius home page (http://www.aetherius.org) accessed from the Internet on December 28, 1996. For more discussion of the Aetherius Society's beliefs, see Rothstein (2003) and Saliba's chapter in Lewis (2003a).

same entity others call God. The authority speaking here is none other than Jesus, the single most authoritative figure in Western religion, but the narrative does not question the fact that the words came from King himself. The narrative is constructed so that this vital information is provided through the memory of Mary King, who went to the far end of the solar system with the Cosmic Masters. Hence, it is somebody else who tells of King's unique qualities, not himself—a fact that obviously strengthens his credibility. This characteristic theme appears throughout many texts, making it seem that the universe sings praises to George King.

After praising George King, Jesus places the book in a box, and Mary King hears beautiful music filling the room. Deeply moved, she weeps aloud. After a few moments of "cosmic music," Jesus turns to say:

> Blessed is he, who reading this Book doth understand.
> But exalted is he, even among Angels,
> Who reading this Book, doth take it to his heart
> And follow its precepts.
> Tell my Son, that this Book is now and forever—Holy.
>
> (Aetherius Society 1974, 12)

The last sentence is obviously of greatest interest to us because Jesus is talking directly to Mary King, and there is no doubt that "my Son" means George. As the text gives no indication of actual family bonds, the meaning is probably symbolic.[11] However, what we have is the explicit mention of a close relationship between Jesus and George King, and none other than George's mother serves as the mediator. Although the theological context is different, the word "Son" points to Christian conceptualizations, and King echoes the figure of Jesus Christ in Christianity. In Christianity, Jesus is the Son of God, and in this text, King becomes symbolically the Son of Jesus. The important point is that the text thereby positions King as some

---

11. Another UFO prophet, Frenchman Claude Vorilhon, known to his followers as Raël, claims that his mother, whose name also is Mary (Marie), was once abducted into a spacecraft and inseminated with sperm from the leader of the Planet of the Eternals, Jahwe (Yahweh). Later on, Claude was born as the child of an earthly mother and a celestial father, who had never had sex in the terrestrial way. When mature, during a visit to his extraterrestrial father's home, he was informed of this event, and he was introduced to his half-brother, Jesus, whom he heartily embraced. In the International Raëlian Movement, this origin myth serves to give Vorilhon his image and authority, just as the somewhat softer Aetherius' version supports George King's charisma. For a full account of the Raël story, see Rothstein (1993).

kind of savior, as a chosen one—similar to the status of Jesus in Christian beliefs as the model. The hagiographic tale of King's meeting with Jesus on a mountain is another example of the same type. The narrative structure reflects that of Moses on Mount Sinai and the myth of the transfiguration of Christ on a mountain as well. Thus, King encounters the divine in the same manner as prominent figures from biblical myths. In this perspective, King inherits the biblical tradition of the prophets, and through the notion of Cosmic Masters of a superior spiritual standing, is being embedded in an easily recognizable Theosophical tradition.[12]

In all, the text affirms King and his teachings as unique and of utmost value. Further, the book contains minute descriptions of how King reacts during "overshadowing" from the Cosmic Masters, thus forming a legitimation for his charismatic status in the group. Finally, we may observe that the language of the Master Jesus is similar in style to traditional biblical language, not because Venusians read the King James version of the Bible, but because that kind of language signals religious authority to many. Thus, there is an easily recognizable idiomatic tradition in the Aetherius Society, and in that sense, the texts of the Aetherius Society are quite traditional. Apparently, Cosmic Masters tend to prefer older forms of English whenever they approach humankind with spiritual messages.

Further Examinations of the Texts

A brief examination of texts such as the one cited above reveals several characteristic themes that support the charismatic image of George King. First, his closest associates in the organization (although King may personally be the general author or editor of the books in which the quotes are found) describe him as extraordinary. Hence, his followers recognize and promote King as divinely chosen. Self-promotion also occurs, namely in connection with discussions of the religious preconditions, goals, and the ritual practices of the Aetherius Society. Sometimes he channels acclaims from the Cosmic Masters, but this kind of recognition is more powerfully expressed through others. As previously mentioned, his own mother carries messages from Master Jesus about his divinity. Second, the Aetherius Society's texts praise King through lists of acknowledgments, but most titles and

---

12. George King's teaching legitimizes itself through various references to Christianity. *The Twelve Blessings* (Aetherius Society 1974) is, for instance, seen as an extension of Jesus' Sermon on the Mount, which now, according to the believers, "includes a Cosmic concept."

awards refer to ethereal institutions beyond the verification of persons outside the group. Third, the Aetherius Society's texts portray King not only as a superior spiritual leader and as adept at various mystical techniques but also as an outstanding intellectual and humanitarian. As is typical of sacred biographies, King's birth and childhood indicate his future greatness.[13] Fourth, while Aetherius does not perceive King as the only bona fide contactee, he certainly is presented as the most salient and competent one, a fact corroborated by astrology and the planetary alignments of his birth. Fifth, Aetherius acknowledges that King fully deserves all the abundance of accolades bestowed on him.

At this point, we may refer to the Aetherius Society's Web site, which, of course, also contains hagiographic presentations of George King. For instance, it states that King had abandoned "all business interests and materialistic ambitions" and that he had acted "upon instructions from Cosmic Authority." The Web site emphasizes several other titles and marks of honor, including "the International Prize of Peace and Justice from H. H. Prince Pensavalle, President of the International Union of Christian Chivalry" in 1981. Additionally, it stresses that in 1991, King was "presented Letters Patent of Armorial Bearings also known as a Grant of Arms, by Bluemantle Pursuivant, a Herald of Her Majesty's College of Arms in England." [14]

It appears that the presentation of George King, which has been much the same throughout the entire history of the Aetherius Society, serves insiders more than outsiders. The hagiographic texts are not inducements to join the society. Rather, the texts provide stimulating information to those already engaged in the society's endeavors. Indeed, the quotes cited above are from books meant for people already familiar with King's teachings. The texts do not present convincing arguments of any kind for impartial outsiders because they do not refer to specific earthly facts and physically verifiable events. In Aetherius, King's virtues are a given reality. If the reader is reasonably well acquainted with the beliefs of the Aetherius Society, the description of King becomes meaningful, but a reader not well-versed in the doctrine might find it overstated or even ridiculous. Therefore, these texts are statements of faith written by leaders of the movement to the average member. The texts communicate the message of King's unique status and the general meaning of the Aetherius Society's work, and repetition of these statements serves to internalize them as

13. For comparisons to the legends of L. Ron Hubbard, see Refslund Christensen (1997).

14. The source is the Aetherius home page (http://www.aetherius.org) accessed on December 28, 1996.

foundational knowledge in the minds of the believers. Thus, the hagiographic materials add to the group's internal solidarity rather than providing seeds for missionary work.

According to Eileen Barker, the leader's divine qualities are of direct relevance only to believers, while outsiders will find them hard to accept, to say the least (Barker 1993, 194). I take this hagiographic relevancy to be a common feature in all small religious groups that form a cultic milieu around their leader (but in fact, it is also a well-known mechanism in larger social contexts; e.g., the person of Jesus is of no immediate relevance to nonbelievers in Christian environments). In the Aetherius Society, the outsiders' lack of deference for, and understanding of, George King is (at least among certain members) turned into something positive. During my talks with members of the society in London in 1993, two women told me that skepticism from nonbelievers was perfectly understandable, and that no one should be expected to understand George King "just like that." However, learning about him would, as they saw it, lead to a natural awe for his person.

As I understood these women, their special (we might say esoteric) knowledge of King was a strong force in their religious commitment. They had access to details and resources unknown to the general public, and thus, the ignorance of others was no personal burden to them. My interview research was limited to these two respondents, but if this interpretation is correct, it appears that the hagiography of King as an expression of insiders' narratives serves an important purpose. It helps the believers to identify themselves in contrast to those who have not been initiated into the sacred knowledge. Hence, internal social stability may be gained through a somewhat restricted communication to potential converts. The partly esoteric nature of the society's inner movement involves the true understanding of King, and, therefore, limited knowledge of the religious leader among outsiders is of internal value.

Actually, external communications are carried out in very different ways from internal communications. During 1996, the Aetherius Society conducted a lecture tour throughout the United Kingdom (eighteen major cities), but the message did not have George King as the central figure; rather, "public information" on UFOs and the destiny of our planet was the focus. Richard Lawrence, spokesperson for the Aetherius Society in London, said, "What we want is to get the message out to as many people as we can. . . . It's a matter of getting the message out to people and letting them decide" (King and Lawrence 1996).[15] While King's qualities are success-

15. Charles Abrahamson was interviewed by Mel Richards in the magazine *Encounters* in 1996. See page 64. A small book by King and Lawrence (1996) was issued in that occasion.

fully defined within the internal religious community, they are not emphasized to outsiders because the society downplays King's role when dialoguing with nonbelievers. However, that does not diminish King's importance; rather, it is a matter of missionary strategy. Therefore, among fellow believers, the society will tirelessly promote George King, while during the conversion process new members will gradually learn to appreciate King's extraordinary qualities. However, the Aetherius Society does not seem to be too interested in gathering a larger membership. Lawrence said, "We will always say to people, don't join us unless you really know what we are" (King and Lawrence 1996). The importance of George King is unquestionable among believers, but the Aetherius Society concedes that not everyone may feel the same.

In a message on the Aetherius Society's Web site, which is probably visited mainly by those already acquainted with the group, a paragraph explains that King's influence can be seen everywhere, although not everyone is able to realize it. This again speaks to his extraordinary spiritual status. A four-page presentation of King ends with the following:

> Indeed is the legacy created and built by Sir George a massive and almost unbelievable one. He is truly an inspiration to all on Earth, most especially to those interested in working to bring in The New Age on Earth. For Sir George has shown us the Way for these modern days. . . . By living amongst the many, contacting the Spark of God within and then returning to teach, heal and uplift mankind in all ways possible. (Aetherius Society 1996)

This brief text, just as those cited earlier, is addressed to inner members. Texts addressing the general public hold quite another perspective, for the overall soteriological importance of King is neglected in favor of a much more restrained rhetoric. In a flyer advertising a series of lectures delivered by Aetherius Society leaders in London during a "Festival for Mind, Body and Spirit," King is presented in the following way, "It [Aetherius Society] was founded in August 1956 by Western Master of Yoga, His Eminence Sir George King, who has produced many books and cassettes on a wide variety of metaphysical and occult subjects."[16]

16. The information is from a leaflet for the Festival for Mind, Body, and Spirit at the Royal Horticultural Halls in London on May 20–29, 1995.

To outsiders, the books and cassettes mentioned may seem bizarre, naïve or all too complicated, but to the initiates, everything becomes clear because King, who channeled the basic parts of the society's literature, stays in permanent tune with beings of spiritual superiority. In short, a precondition to appreciating the Aetherius Society's publications is the knowledge of George King as a unique religious authority.

Construction of Charisma in Hagiography

Having discussed the depiction of George King by the Aetherius Society, we may be able to establish some kind of external categorization. One possibility is to analyze King's case along the lines of Max Weber's classical conceptualization of religious prophets (Wallis 1974). Weber distinguishes between two types of prophets, the emissary type and the exemplary. The emissary type of prophet is a religious preacher who believes he or she has received a message of general or specific import, and it is his or her task to communicate it to others (Weber 1963, 46ff). In contrast, the exemplary type of prophet bases authority on his or her own experience, which serves as an example to others. Most leaders of contemporary new religious movements are of the exemplary type, but some are emissaries from divine beings. George King appears to be a mixture.

The Aetherius Society understands and describes King in three distinct functions: (1) he is the especially chosen Primary Terrestrial Mental Channel who receives and communicates concise and decisive information from the Spiritual Masters; (2) he is the self-made expert of all sorts of metaphysical techniques and thus glorious, as seen from his achievements; and (3) he is a great human being in the ordinary sense of the word, a great humanitarian, a self-sacrificing and trustworthy man. In other words, King unites the two standard types of religious leadership suggested by Weber. He communicates messages from powers beyond and personally serves in all possible ways as a guiding light to his followers. The Aetherius Society's texts always point to the fact that King's spiritual development preceded the "command" from a higher calling. Thus, we get the impression that the Cosmic Masters chose him because of his self-made (although karmically determined) character. On the other hand, his authority is very much based on the position given him by the Masters. In this way, the two dimensions of his religious authority meld together, forming a unity of expression and embodiment.

Pursuing Weber's ideas further, recent scholars have used the concept of charisma to understand some leaders of new religions. Sociologist of religion Roy

Wallis (1993) explored one case in which the leader's charisma was not just inherent but was constructed by his followers. Moses David (aka David Berg) led the Family (formerly known as the Children of God) until his death in 1994. Of his charisma, Wallis writes:

> [Charisma] emerges out of a particular structure of social relationships in which an exchange takes place of mutual attribution of status and worth. The putative charismatic leader emboldened by this flattering recognition of the status and identity to which he aspires, then seeks to realize in his behavior the powers and status with which he has been credited: to live up to the image with which he has been endowed. In the process others are elevated with him as intimates or lieutenants. Their significance derives from him. Having been raised up, and recognized as special by him, they add to the recognition of the leader, endowing him with still further significance as author of the movement and their own fortunate condition, leading him to take ever more seriously the conception of himself as someone out-of-the-ordinary. (Wallis 1993, 172)[17]

As Wallis and others (Weber 1963; Tumminia 2005) suggest, followers construct the charisma of leaders through various means. Hagiography is one of the methods that preserves the charismatic construction for posterity. The primary books of the Aetherius Society were issued entirely by King and his "intimates and lieutenants." They were either written by close associates who also may have served as editors of King's texts or in cooperation with King himself. As a matter of fact, only two or three names reappear often in written materials. As far as I can judge, by the time of his death, King was never approached by any but those chosen few. Prior to his death, it was often mentioned that King was ill, and that his hard work had affected him.[18] That, of course, made the contributions of these assistants even more necessary, and their positions even stronger. These individuals have, according to King, "dedicated all their essential energy to the cause of World Peace and Enlightenment." He adds, "These few, under my personal direction, are responsible for a staggering work load which benefits all life on Earth in a very direct manner" (King and Avery [1975] 1982, 50–51). In return, they propagated King as a religious ideal when he was among them, and they continue to do so after his death.

17. Wallis is quoting himself from "The Social Construction of Charisma" (Wallis 1986).

18. King himself explains how the process of channeling the messages from the Space Masters was of great danger to his health in King and Avery ([1975] 1982, 52–53).

In this way, the texts of the Aetherius Society reflect the general social mechanism described by Wallis. King's closest associates managed his image; in sociological terms, they socially constructed his image. In addition, ordinary members who valued this charismatic narrative about their leader bolstered this construction by the continued recognition of King's special character. In the aftermath of King's death, the practice continues. The written materials published today by the Aetherius Society are, in fact, the tangible result of a complex hagiographic process that adherents experience in their devotion to King. At the same time, the literature of the organization is a resource in that ongoing maintenance of King's legendary status.

A concrete example of how texts serve as hagiographic resources is the internal interpretation and description of King's 1959 appearance on British television (BBC, May 21, 1959). According to online Aetherius texts, King demonstrated "a Yogic Samadhic trance so that a Cosmic Master from another Planet could actually speak to Britain!" The event is called "unique and historic," and it is said that it was "re-broadcast again and again through ensuing years" owing to its popularity. The fact that King appeared on national television in 1959 is still (over forty years later) looked upon as a great accomplishment; so great that it is still recorded in the most recently written updates of the society. However, Jerome Clark, a commentator on the UFO debate, points to several other instances in which King aroused everything but pleasure in the media. In the fifties, a London newspaper speculated that the Aetherius Society might be a Communist front, and during a radio interview in New York, King was called a charlatan (Clark 1998).

Such controversies disappear into oblivion in hagiographic texts. Negative images that contradict King's charisma are not recounted, but images of success are constantly invoked. Positive, successful tales of the past nourish hagiography and help create foundational myths (Abrahamson 1994). What members hear today is directly derived from these and other quasi-mythological times. As is typical of hagiographic construction, the Aetherius Society bestows religious meaning upon otherwise minor mundane events, creating a sacred narrative that glorifies its leader. Thus, by conceptualizing the historical past in mythological terms, this religious group is doing exactly what many other religions have done, not least Christianity.

Hagiographies preserve a leader's charisma, and the social construction of hagiographic texts is one way that followers serve their leaders. Barker points to the fact that recognition of the religious leader's charisma must be a learned behavior. Charisma describes a certain type of relationship between the devoted believer and the leader. Barker calls this socialization process *charismatization*. She writes:

The argument is that charismatic authority can result, at least in part, from social processes that take place within the group which is headed by the person who is accorded the authority. . . . It is not until they are in the movement that the followers learn to recognize the charisma of their leader and thereby come to accept that he should have a virtually unlimited say in how they live. (1993, 184)

Few had the opportunity to establish a personal relationship with King, for many members had never even met him. That is not unusual because countless members of New Religious Movements never meet their spiritual masters in person. They may be part of a large audience while the spiritual teacher is present, and a personal audience can be rare indeed. Nevertheless, through hagiography each succeeding generation will read accounts of their teacher's charisma. Those motivated to continue to be committed to the group will recognize their teacher's extraordinary qualities.

Referring back to theories on the subject, we may safely conclude that the charisma of George King is embedded in Aetherius's texts. Needless to say, his "intimates and lieutenants" acted as key people in that hagiographic process. Even before his death, the religious authority of George King stood on a social construction based upon the mythological rendering of his life, rather than on George King the person. King's death has not prompted a decline in his legendary status. New followers now meet him as that social construction, a symbol of meaning alive in the group's literature.[19] The "routinization" of King's charisma takes the form of "textualization" from which current leaders of Aetherius derive their authority. The hagiographic depictions of King provide all that is necessary for devotees to feel comfortable that the charismatic mantle of his authority has been passed on to the succeeding generation of leaders.

A prominent and relatively recent example is the book on "Operation Starlight," which relates the story of how King and a few close followers charged mountains with spiritual healing energy from the Cosmic Master's spaceships.[20] In

---

19. See Weber (1975, 89–104). [Editor's note: The classic sociologist Max Weber theorized the followers of a leader created charismatic authority by their recognition of the leader's gift of grace or extraordinary nature. The *routinization of charisma* means that the mantle of authority is passed to the next generation of leaders after a charismatic leader dies or steps aside. Typically, the next generation does not possess the charisma of the original leader. Thus, authority becomes routine, instead of exciting, according to Weber (Tumminia 2005).]

20. See Abrahamson (1994). The front cover of this particular book gives a beautiful example of the iconographic promotion of George King as the Master of the Society. Standing in full mountain-

this way, through the language of the texts, the minds of current members integrate the heroic history of King and the spiritual importance of his creation, the Aetherius Society. At an earlier stage, King presided as a living founder at the center of the movement, but in the years leading up to his death, his physical contact with members declined. Nonetheless, after his death, he remains ever present in the institutionalized memory of Aetherius. When King was old and sick, he still served as the Primary Terrestrial Mental Channel to the Cosmic Masters, and his physical absence from the organization's daily routine was of little consequence. Now, after his death, legends about his persona are developing, and, owing to an ongoing process of charismatization, he remains just as vital a symbol as he ever was.[21]

George King and Other Contactees

At this point, we may ask whether the concept of UFOs as cosmic messengers, which is at the heart of George King's teachings, has anything to do with King's emergence as a religious leader. One may ask why the concept of UFOs was integrated at all into King's religious thinking? Why did extraterrestrials aboard UFOs approach King? Why not Cosmic Masters of a more familiar or traditional sort?

When we take the time and place into consideration, these questions answer themselves. A major capital of the English-speaking Western world during 1954, London provided a perfect frame for King's experience. In this specific case, King's initial contact with Master Aetherius of Venus took place at a time when the most famous contactee of all, George Adamski, had just come forward. The year before King's contact with the Cosmic Masters in 1954, Desmond Leslie and his coauthor Adamski issued the best-selling *Flying Saucers Have Landed* (1953), which was simultaneously published in London by Werner Laurie and in New York by the

---

climbing outfit on the top of a rock, a beam of light is entering him from above. On the black-and-white photo the light forms a corona around his head and shoulders. The light, of course, is interpreted as healing spiritual energy beamed from the spacecraft high above Earth. A note in the book explains that the picture is no fraud, and that similar beams of light were seen around George King during the entire climb. Otherwise, King is only shown in old photographs—sometimes as a mountaineer, sometimes in full bishop's gown, but usually as a thoughtful and serious man in plain clothing.

21. In this chapter, I have restricted the issue to religious texts. However, George King, although physically absent, is now also experienced by members through tape recordings and photos.

1.2. In the Aetherius Society, Operation Starlight consisted of charging certain mountains with spiritual energy. This Aetherius expedition climbed Castle Rock in Colorado in 1960. Courtesy of the Aetherius Society.

British Book Center.[22] Adamski's book was the subject of much popular discussion, and anyone with an interest in the paranormal would have noted it.

The similarities between King's experiences and those of Adamski are remarkable. Both encountered spiritual masters from Venus; these entities are described in much the same way, and the messages given are of the same principal type. The masters chose their contactees for a specific mission with one primary objective: to

22. Further bibliographic details may be found in volume 2 of Eberhart (1986, 831), and see also Clark (1998).

teach humans how to live in love and peace. Further, as is well known, Adamski had been occupied with various kinds of spiritual and occult endeavors prior to his first encounter with Orthon from Venus.[23] According to information from the Aetherius Society, King likewise received diverse forms of spiritual training and erudition when approached by the superior intelligence from beyond. Finally, of course, both men claimed to have been taken aboard flying saucers and given unimaginable tours of other worlds.[24]

Considering the large number of subsequent contactees who may have unintentionally assimilated Adamski's philosophy (among others, George Van Tassel, who contacted Ashtar Command; Pauline Sharp, who was known as Nada-Yolanda of Mark-Age; Tuella of Guardian Action; and Ruth and Ernest Norman of the Unarius Academy of Science), it is hard to ignore the possibility that the Leslie and Adamski text influenced King as well.[25] The official position of the Aetherius Society holds that others may also have had contacts similar to those of King, and that other groups work along the same lines. However, no organization deserves the same status in the cosmic field of saving humanity as that of the Aetherius Society.

Thus, while King's followers do not rule out the possibility that the Cosmic Masters may have sought contact with others before and after meeting with King, they clearly state that since 1954 no one in the world has had the same intense and decisive contact as King did. Reverend Charles Abrahamson of the Aetherius Society in London commented:

> We are not saying that he is the only contactee at all, but we do think he has a unique role. We don't think there is anyone else who for over 42 years has consistently been in contact on a weekly basis without a break. I don't think there is anyone in the world to even claim that, or who has built up an organization, which has done as many things as we have. (King and Lawrence 1996).

23. See Abrahamson (1994, 14) and King ([1963] 1974, 7).

24. For further comments on the heritage of Adamski/Theosophy in contactee groups, see chapter 5 in Flaherty (1990). I have only come across one reference to Adamski in Aetherius materials. Under the heading "A Miraculous Healing. A Personal Discovery" on the home page of the Aetherius Society (http://www.aetherius.org), a woman tells of how she miraculously overcame severe illness by mentally contacting healers on Venus. Her inspiration was Adamski's book, which is explicitly mentioned. I take this to be an indication of good will toward Adamski and organizations that revere him.

25. The Aetherius Society has argued for its special distinction in the field of contactee groups in all sorts of ways, for instance through a numerological and astrological analysis of the organization. Hence, divination forms an important part in the construction of the Aetherius Society's image.

In addition to the early contactees, a well-known religious tradition, namely Theosophy, influenced King, and in a sense, it could be said that King borrows some of its charismatic authority along with its beliefs. In 2004, the church's Web page bore a link to another page about Theosophy, which was provided to help beginners understand Aetherius. The society never mentions the theosophical influence outright, but the model seems obvious. In fact, in the wake of this metaphysical legacy, many contactee mystics formed special alliances with celestial adepts, as Theosophists did. The researcher David Stupple (1984) observed a direct theological link between the mahatmas of Theosophy and the Space Brothers of contactees like King. However, King made his own path through a consistent UFO-related theology and through special affiliations to specific Masters, such as Master Jesus, Mars Sector 6, and, of course, Master Aetherius.

The Aetherius Society venerates George King because of his much-touted personal accomplishments, but also because he has placed himself in a tradition in which religious leaders are automatically elevated in status. This is simply because no theosophically inspired leader or religious innovator can function without personal contact with the superior beings of the cosmic realms. Thus, by definition, persons in tune with the Cosmic Masters are special. The sacred biography surrounding him is a natural effect of this particular religious engagement with the exalted Masters. The fact that the Cosmic Masters work through massive spaceships and other sorts of alien technology is a matter of keeping up with the times.[26] As far as the literature of the Aetherius Society is concerned, all of these mechanisms are reflected in every book and pamphlet, and above all, the channeled knowledge is related to the information received by Madame Blavatsky and her successors.[27] Hence, George King does not stand alone, but in the presence of cosmic dignitaries who speak only to the most worthy.

Hagiography Legitimates a Leader

Hagiographic texts with exalted characterizations of George King legitimize his teachings, as well as the existence of the Aetherius Society as an organization. Such texts preserve his socially constructed charisma for future generations. By invoking King as the most important human being ever and as the prime source for the salva-

26. Most, if not all, aspects of this development are dealt with in Flaherty 1990.

27. Future research, therefore, should address the question of Theosophical hagiography in general to find similarities and differences in the various narrations about various Theosophical leaders.

tion of humanity, believers place themselves within the same sphere of celestial authority attributed to their leader. Through the narratives that describe the life and achievements of King, the members perceive that they are sharing in benefits of the life and work of their founder.

At the same time, King may be interpreted as a devotional object, for he is revered as the ideal human being, and it seems fair to view him, along with the extraterrestrial Masters, as the objects of devotion for the whole group. Although Aetherius does not explicitly suggest formal worship of King, it seems as if the hagiography legitimates the wider theological, philosophical, and ritual authenticity of the group. If not for George King, then, none would know of the extraterrestrials' plan for Earth, and no one would have the chance to ascend to higher levels. In the context of believers bridging to a higher spiritual level, King occupies the position of humanity's savior in times of dire need. Thus, in this example, the tales of this religious leader serve the same function as the hagiographies of other religious groups; the idealization of the life of the leader as sacred and charismatic underpins the legitimation of religious doctrines, rituals, and dogmas.

The Odyssey
of Sister Thedra

Jerome Clark

The terms—flying saucers, unidentified flying objects, and contactees—existed in no one's vocabulary in 1946, although sightings of unusual aerial phenomena had been reported for at least the previous century and a half (Bullard 1982; Lore and Deneault 1968; Bartholomew and Howard 1998). Historically, Charles Hoy Fort's *Book of the Damned*, a work on what would be later called UFOs, first linked such oddities to visitors from space in 1919. Fort even speculated, perhaps facetiously, that certain individuals were in contact with the pilots of the mysterious objects.[1] If that was so, no one ever owned up to it until the evening of October 9, 1946, when the Kareeta—a long, bullet-shaped structure with large wings that looked as if they belonged to a giant bat—flew over San Diego. Those who saw it said it was dark except for two red lights along the side. Visible for an hour and a half and moving at speeds varying from slow to very fast, it periodically swept a searchlight along the ground.

Not till the following summer, after private pilot Kenneth Arnold's widely publicized 1947 encounter with nine shiny discs over Mount Rainier, Washington, would things like these get to be called flying saucers (Arnold 1950; Maccabee 1995a, 1995b, 1995c). Even in 1946, however, San Diegans did not have to be told that this object was something definitely out of the ordinary. Just how out of the ordinary, however, was left to local medium Mark Probert to say. Probert had been channeling messages from a variety of discarnate beings who discoursed at stultifying length on cosmic philosophical issues for the recently formed, San Diego–based

---

1. "I think that sometimes, in favorable circumstances, emissaries have come to this earth," wrote Charles Hoy Fort (1995, 247) in a book originally published in 1919.

Borderland Sciences Research Associates (BSRA), directed by occult theorist N. Meade Layne (Layne 1949).

As it happened, Probert was among the many San Diegans who had their eyes raised skyward in anticipation of a meteor shower but were surprised to observe the passage of the mysterious structure. While it was still in view, Probert phoned Layne, who urged his associate to attempt telepathic communication with the craft's presumed occupants. The attempt succeeded, Probert would assert, telling a newspaper reporter:

> The strange machine is called the Kareeta. . . . It is attracted at this time because the earth is emitting a column of light which makes it easier of approach. The machine is powered by people possessing a very advanced knowledge of anti-gravity forces. It has 10,000 parts, a small but very powerful motor operating by electricity, and moving the wings, and an outer structure of light balsam wood, coated with an alloy. The people are nonaggressive and have been trying to contact the earth for many years. They have very light bodies. They fear to land, but would be willing to meet a committee of scientists at an isolated spot, or on a mountain top.[2]

Although his name is not now as recognizable as some others, Mark Probert distinguished himself as the first of what soon would be called "contactees" (Clark 1998). Not at first a term of endearment, in time it became merely descriptive, a way of characterizing the worldwide host of human beings who would profess to believe themselves to be recipients of messages from friendly extraterrestrials looking out for our best interests. The scattered contactee subculture coalesced into an identifiable movement in January 1952, when aircraft mechanic George W. Van Tassel initiated a series of public gatherings in the high desert country of Southern California. Van Tassel channeled elaborate messages from starship ("ventla") commanders (Van Tassel 1952), soon introducing the first metaphysical superstar of the flying-saucer age, Ashtar, "commandant quadra sector, patrol section Schare, all projections, all waves"—an extraterrestrial and interdimensional being who even today communes with a small army of mediums and automatic writers.[3]

On November 20, 1952, George Adamski entered occult history through his claimed meeting with Orthon, a golden-haired Venusian, near Desert Center, California (Leslie and Adamski 1953; Welch 1952; Zinsstag 1990; Zinsstag and Good

---

2. Quoted in Harold T. Wilkins (1954, 45).

3. See Tuella (1989). Tuella is a pseudonym of the late Thelma B. Terrell.

1983). In no time at all, others were alleging physical encounters with benevolently intentioned "Space Brothers" here to rescue the human race from imminent nuclear war. As if to up the ante, contactees soon recounted rides in flying saucers into outer space or to neighboring planets.[4]

One figure who quickly rose to prominence, occult and maverick anthropologist George Hunt Williamson, first heard from extraterrestrials in mid-1952, when a Martian named Nah-9 psychically warned him and his associates that evil space people were conspiring with evil earthlings to wreak havoc (Williamson and Bailey 1954). As the messages grew ever more ominous, a frightened Williamson wrote a friend in Guatemala that "time is very, very short! . . . Disaster will come before Dec. 1st, this year! So only a few weeks remain!" He went on, "We have been told that a man will contact us soon, when all is in readiness! And there will be a landing in this vicinity by special ship direct from Mars within two or three weeks from now! . . . The landing will be near here" (Aharon 1957).[5] Nonetheless, Williamson was able to pull himself together enough to be in Desert Center on November 20, when he served as one of the six "witnesses"—albeit at some considerable distance—to the epochal rendezvous of Adamski with Orthon.

Truman Bethurum also joined the swelling contactee ranks with his own tale of friendly space people. He met them one night in July 1952, he said, while employed as a heavy-equipment operator in the Nevada desert. Eight little men with "Latin" features interrupted his nap as he caught a few winks between shifts. They guided him to a nearby flying saucer and its captain, "a gorgeous woman, shorter than any of the men, neatly attired, and also having a Latin appearance: coal black hair and olive complexion. She appeared to be about 42 years old" (Bethurum 1954). Bethurum subsequently learned that she was actually hundreds of years old. Her name, she told him, was Aura Rhanes. She and the crew of the "scow" (spaceship) hailed from the planet Clarion, a world never visible to us because it is always on the other side of the moon (Bethurum 1954). As Bethurum would learn in subsequent contacts, Clarion is an idyllic world devoid of conflict or disease. Clarionites had come here out of concern that human beings might blow up their planet in a nuclear war (Beckley 1970).

On April 4, 1954, the first major contactee gathering, the Interplanetary Spacecraft Convention, brought several thousand space communicants, true believers,

---

4. See, for example, George Adamski's *Inside the Space Ships* (1955), Howard Menger's *From Outer Space to You* (1959), and Buck Nelson's *My Trip to Mars, the Moon, and Venus* (1956).

5. Aharon's pseudonym is Yonah Fortner.

and curiosity-seekers to Van Tassel's residence at Giant Rock (literally a giant rock), between Lucerne Valley and Twenty-Nine Palms, California (Anonymous 1954, 13; Sanders 1954). The Giant Rock meetings, which were held every year until 1977, provided a forum in which contactees could exchange information and ideas. In the process, they borrowed names and concepts from one another, even as the meaning and context changed from telling to telling. Although contactees agreed on a general cosmology, no two of them described a precisely similar one (Gray Barker 1976; Bishop and Thomas 1999; Max B. Miller 1963; Ruppelt 1994). Believers either ignored these discrepancies or dismissed them as meaningless, much to the exasperation of skeptics. One of them, ufologist Isabel L. Davis, wrote:

> Where was Clarion . . . during the night of August 23–24, 1954? On that night, Adamski claims, he was shown both sides of the Moon by Ramu of Saturn, through an instrument on the Venusian carrier ship. . . . As the ship goes around from the familiar toward the unfamiliar side, ahead of it in the sky should have been Captain Aura Rhanes' Clarion. But neither Ramu nor Adamski mention[s] it. Adamski certainly knew about Clarion—for Bethurum had visited Palomar Gardens [Adamski's residence] during the summer of 1953, and Adamski had then accepted Bethurum's story. But with a whole planet missing from where it should be, Adamski is neither surprised nor curious. (Davis 1957)

Dorothy Martin

Despite its increasing vitality, the contactee movement of the early 1950s attracted little attention from the larger world, except for occasional newspaper articles. For the most part, only those who were interested in UFOs were aware of the small but growing army of believers in Space Brothers. Press coverage was scant except for scattered articles in local newspapers, most of them in Southern California where the movement was most active. All of that would change, however, with a strange episode that began in a Chicago suburb in 1954.

Like most who would become contactees, Dorothy Martin had long been drawn to unorthodox ideas. She was introduced to occultism while living in New York City in the late 1930s, when she attended a lecture on Theosophy. She began reading a variety of esoteric works and became active in Dianetics, later called Scientology. She turned to the works of Guy Warren Ballard, who as Godfré Ray King created the I AM movement, arguably the first religious group to make extraterrestrial contacts a central tenet.[6] (Among other claims Ballard reported meeting twelve Venusians—"Lords of the Flame." Ballard essentially created the image of the golden-haired, angelic Venusian that Adamski would bring into the saucer age.) Martin also read *Oahspe,* a massive text channeled by John Ballou Newbrough and first published in 1882. *Oahspe* depicts a complex, richly populated spiritual cosmos whose inhabitants included guardian angels known as "ashars" who sail the universe in ethereal (other-dimensional) ships.[7]

One day in 1952 or early 1953, Mrs. Martin awoke in her home in Oak Park, Illinois, with "a kind of tingling or numbness in my arm, and my whole arm felt warm right up to the shoulder. . . . Without knowing why, I picked up a pencil and a pad that were lying on the table near my bed," and she started writing a message from her deceased father. The message was a trivial one. It consisted of instructions to his still-living widow on planting flowers, instructions that her mother rejected. Yet it was the beginning of an odyssey that eventually would catapult Martin into the headlines and shape the rest of her life.[8]

Meantime, the couple who would play a large role in the drama to come was also being swept up by events. For Charles and Lillian Laughead (pronounced law-head) it started in Egypt, where the couple served as Protestant missionaries from 1946 to 1949. During that time, Mrs. Laughead fell victim to recurring nightmares and irrational fears, which she could not will to stop nor could her husband, a physician, treat successfully. Looking for a cure, they turned to esoteric literature and read many of the same books Martin was scrutinizing. When they returned to the United States, Dr. Laughead took a staff position at the Michigan State College Hospital in East Lansing. By then, the couple had become full-fledged occult enthusiasts, and almost inevitably they soon incorporated flying saucers into their newly found faith.

6. For more information, see J. Gordon Melton (1995) and David W. Stupple (1994).

7. See John B. Newbrough's *Oahspe* (1882) and Martin Gardner (1996). The full text of *Oahspe* is available at different Web sites, and it can be found by searching the Internet.

8. Unless otherwise indicated, the account of the 1954 events draws on the reconstruction in Leon Festinger, Henry W. Riecken, and Stanley Schachter's *When Prophecy Fails* (1956). I have, however, removed the pseudonyms the authors gave the principals and restored their real names; thus, "Marian Keech" is now Dorothy Martin, "Thomas Armstrong" is Charles A. Laughead, and so on. The authors' "Lake City," often assumed to be the real name of a Twin Cities suburb, is in fact Oak Park, Illinois, where Martin lived during the episode in question. Page numbers are given in parentheses where available.

On a trip to Southern California to see the Rose Bowl Game in early January 1953, Dr. Laughead met Adamski, whose recent meeting with Orthon was electrifying occultists and saucer buffs. Adamski told him that the Venusian had left tracks in the desert sand. Each contained within it a distinct set of mysterious symbols.[9] Laughead took home a drawing of the prints, which he showed to his wife. Intrigued, Mrs. Laughead devoted the next five months to an effort to decipher the symbols. She decided that the left track, in her interpretation, represented the sinking of the lost continents of Mu and Atlantis. The right predicted their reemergence from the ocean floor following geological cataclysms that would soon befall the Earth.

Not long after his visit with Adamski, another source of inspiration for Dr. Laughead came in the form of an automatic-writing message delivered by a ministerial student. The message, according to Laughead, "was from the Elder Brother who later identified himself as being Jesus the Christ and also Sananda. In this message, I was told to keep telling the truth about the saucers. The Venusians, he said, would contact me, and I would work with them."

For her part, Martin was seeking to improve her automatic-writing skills. After her late father proved boring and immature as an otherworldly contact—trapped, she deduced, in the imbecilic region of the spirit world—she found her way to an entity who called himself the Elder Brother, and then to other beings she would call the Guardians. One, who introduced himself in April 1954 as Sananda, now a resident of the utopian planet Clarion, was no less than Jesus in his earlier, earthly incarnation.

Although Martin got the name of the planet Clarion from Bethurum, her Clarion existed not on the other side of the moon but in an etheric realm. A companion planet, Cerus (sometimes confusingly referred to also as a "constellation"), housed other space beings who kept Martin's arm and hand in furious motion as they acted on their promise to teach her cosmic wisdom. The Elder Brother said she would not be doing this alone: "We will teach them that seek and are ready to follow in the light. . . . Be patient and learn, for we are there preparing the work for you as a connoiter. That is an earthly liaison duty before I come. That will be soon. . . . They that have told you that they do not believe shall see us when the time is right" (37).

Soon a woman from a nearby town began typing up these messages and distributing them. Martin joined a local occult discussion group and started talking about

---

9. The symbols fascinated early contactee followers and generated a small but intense literature. See, for example, Williamson (1957, 95–151) and Strickland (1962).

her experiences. She also passed them on to another group in Chicago, where she spoke with John Otto, a nationally known UFO enthusiast and lecturer. Thus, the story of her space communications gradually came to be known in the larger community of New Agers.

The Laugheads met Otto in March 1954, when the latter attended a George Adamski lecture sponsored by the contactee-oriented Detroit Flying Saucer Club. Credulous and excitable by nature, Otto took space communications of all kinds very seriously.[10] At some point, either in Detroit or in subsequent correspondence with the couple, he told the Laugheads about Dorothy Martin's messages and expressed the conviction that they represented something important. Intrigued, the Laugheads wrote Martin and recounted their own occult explorations.

Somewhere around this time, Martin received a message urging her to go to East Lansing to seek "a child . . . to whom I am trying to get through with light." She took it to mean the Laugheads because she had never heard of anyone else from that city. She quickly replied to the letter, and soon the three would form a tight association, based in part on Mrs. Laughead's conviction that she was the "child." For some time, she said, she had sensed overtures from the Guardians.

The Laugheads and Dorothy Martin met for the first time in late June, when the couple drove down from Michigan to visit Martin's home. (Martin was married to a gentle man who did not believe in space messages, but who did not discourage her activities. He had little if anything to do with the events to come.) By this time, Martin was receiving as many as ten messages in a day, and they were taking an increasingly foreboding tone, warning of imminent disasters and cataclysms. However, the messages assured that those who would "listen and believe" would enter a New Age of knowledge and happiness.

Gray Barker of Clarksburg, West Virginia, listened, but he did not believe Martin's accounts. Barker was drawn to the UFO field in September 1952 through newspaper reports of a landing and encounter with a monstrous creature near the tiny town of Flatwoods in his native state. After interviewing the witnesses, he wrote an article on the incident for a popular paranormal digest (Barker 1953). Soon he

---

10. Otto's gullibility later led him to involvement with contactee/lifelong grifter Reinhold O. Schmidt, who from November 1957 into 1961 claimed extensive interactions with German-speaking saucer crews from Saturn. Schmidt used information allegedly acquired during spaceship excursions to peddle bogus treasure schemes to naïve investors. On October 26, 1961, an Oakland, California, court sentenced him to prison on charges of grand theft. See Jerome Clark (1998, 822–23).

was an active presence in ufology, and in September 1953 he started his own small-circulation bulletin, *The Saucerian,* which covered both seemingly credible sightings and saucerdom's most outlandish aspects.

Martin, a native West Virginian, wrote Barker in early 1954 to subscribe to the publication. In a follow-up letter in April, she wrote, "I have apparently been contacting the visitors, but the messages are beyond my comprehension. . . . They told me once before they would land in Flatwoods. This time the contact was stronger and more positive." She enclosed a message addressed to Barker from a spaceman named Garcia Sai:

> I am in contact with the pilot of an active space craft in the vicinity of Flatwoods. We have made contact there and expect to land in May or June.
>
> At that time you will be contacted. The contact will be one of the space people. You will look for a scar on the left cheek the color of the hair.
>
> The last time there was so much confusion they [presumably the witnesses to what the press called the "Flatwoods monster"] failed to see what did happen. This time it will be planned so there will be a contact on earth to receive us. (Barker 1953)

Barker pressed for more details, more out of idle curiosity than any conviction that Martin's messages signified anything but self-delusion. A few weeks later Barker did meet a young man with a scar on his face, but he knew him to be a local man whose injury had come about in a car accident.

Though privately skeptical—"amused" probably best characterizes his attitude—Barker continued to play along with Martin. He solicited further messages. After another space communicant, one Sara, assured him that contact was imminent, he concocted a story about meeting a strange man near the post office and seeing him vanish into thin air. Sara quickly assured Martin that "the young man who contacted Gray Barker was our contact and had a message for him." Later, reflecting on these matters after Dorothy Martin had fallen victim to worldwide headlines and international ridicule, Barker would observe that from his point of view, "Mrs. Martin had contacted some rather inept extraterrestrials—or . . . the information was coming from quite a remarkable subconscious" (Barker 1955).

Meanwhile, the messages kept pouring into Oak Park. Though of course they purported to be from extraterrestrial interdimensional Guardians, their true source was traceable to the occult literature to which Martin had exposed herself. For example, in a July 8 communication, the Guardians described themselves as "beings of the UN [mind of the High Self] . . . who can and do create by the UN the casement or vehicle they chose to use in the seen." Earlier, Barker noted, N. Meade Layne had written, "The aeroforms [flying saucers] are thought-constructs, mind constructs. As such, they are, in effect, the vehicle of the actual entity who creates them" (Barker 1953). Significantly, Martin subscribed to *Round Robin,* the bulletin of Layne's Borderland Sciences Research Associates.

The messages from Sananda and other Guardians more and more took on a prophetic tone. Spaceships would land and make contact with earthlings in May or June. Selected people would be flown to other planets, along with space people who had been on secret Earth assignment. The messages also alluded darkly to imminent nuclear holocaust: "The people of Earth are rushing, rushing toward the suicide of themselves. . . . To this we are answering with signs and wonders in the sky." The space people would see to it that those responsible were brought to swift justice.

On several occasions, Martin was instructed to go to different locations in the Chicago metropolitan area either to see spacecraft or to receive direct messages from extraterrestrials in physical form. Nothing came of these ventures, except—in Martin's judgment—on one occasion. A saucer was to land at a nearby military base at noon on August 1. "It will be as if the world was coming to an end at the field when the landing occurs," the Guardians declared. They added, "The operators will not believe their senses when they see the craft of outer space in the midst of the field." They assured Martin that she should trust this message: "It is a very accurate cast that we give."

So at the appointed hour Martin, the Laugheads (who were visiting for the weekend), and nine other believers parked near the gate and awaited the arrival. No spaceship appeared, but Martin took comfort from the sudden appearance of a stranger who showed up unexpectedly along the highway. She thought he had "eyes that looked through my soul. . . . I knew something was going on that I didn't understand." He declined her offer of a sandwich and a glass of fruit juice, then wandered off saying nothing more. The next day, through automatic writing, Martin learned, "It was I, Sananda, who appeared on the roadside in the guise of the sice." "Sice," in extraterrestrialese, is "one who comes in disguise." It would not be the last time Martin would inflate a mundane incident into a signal from the cosmos. Nor would it be the last of the unfulfilled prophecies.

The most important of these came through on August 2, the same day that Sananda pronounced himself the man on the road. He also delivered these chilling words:

2.1. This portrait of Sananda, the Cosmic Christ, depicts the supernatural being with whom Sister Thedra spoke. Courtesy of Ascension Mastery International.

The Earthling will awaken to the great casting [conditions to be fulfilled] of the lake seething and the great destruction of the tall buildings of the local city—the case that the lake bed is sinking to the degree that it will be as a great scoop of wind from the bottom of the lake throughout the countryside. You shall tell the world that this is to be, for such it is given. To you the date only is secret, for the panic of men knows no bounds. (55)

In subsequent messages that month, Sananda warned of enormous geological upheaval. North America would soon break in two:

In the area of the Mississippi, in the region of Canada, Great Lakes and the Mississippi, to the Gulf of Mexico, into the Central America will be as changed. The great tilting of the land of the U.S. to the East will throw up mountains along the Central States, along the Great New Sea, along North and South—to the South. The new mountain range shall be called The Argone Range, which will signify the ones who have been there are gone—the old has gone past now—the new is. This will be as a monument to the old races; to the new will be the Altar of the Rockies and the Alleghenies. (56)

Not only North America would feel the impact of the upheaval. The Egyptian desert would be transformed into a green valley. Much of Europe, from Britain to Russia, would sink under the sea, and Mu (also known as Lemuria, a mythical Pacific lost continent invented in nineteenth-century occult writing) would rise. Stunned and awed, Martin and the Laugheads reported these revelations to the larger world in a seven-page mimeographed document, "Open Letter to American Editors and Publishers," sent out on August 30. A handwritten addendum appended at the last minute cited December 20 as the "date of evacuation"—in other words, the final day on which human beings living in the affected areas could save themselves.

A second mailing two weeks later concerned the "terrific wave" that would rise from Lake Michigan at dawn on December 21 and overwhelm Chicago before spreading east and west:

> Glad are the actors who have awaited the coming of the Guardians. Amid the cries of anguish the question is heard: "Why didn't someone tell us that we might have moved to safety?" But in the days of the warnings they were told of the safe places—the eastern slopes of the Rockies, the Catskills, and the Allegheny Mountains—but they said, "It can't happen here!" (58–59)

The first press story to report the curious beliefs of Martin and her disciples appeared in a Chicago newspaper on September 23. The reporter missed another flying saucer–related apocalyptic prophecy, which had been published six days earlier in a small Oklahoma paper. Gladys White Eagle, a Cheyenne woman, claimed to have seen a UFO land with a roaring sound on the north bank of the Canadian River a month or so earlier. A tall, thin man with a long beard stepped outside. Speaking in "twisted words" and with an unpleasant cackle, he declared that a great earthquake and atomic bombs would destroy the United States on October 13. He asked her to return to the same spot on September 17. "I'm not going back because I'm scared," White Eagle told the newspaper.[11]

Although Martin saw no one emerge from a spacecraft, it was a spaceman, she believed, who came to her door in the wake of the press coverage of her prophecies. One man, who did all the talking, identified himself as an earthling, but went on to disclose that his companion was from another world. The man directed Martin to desist from further publicity and to await orders. It did not occur to Martin that these callers might be practical jokers. Her sole concern was whether they represented good extraterrestrials or bad ones trying to shut down the Earth-Clarion link.

Among those who were congregating in Martin's home by this time, besides the

11. These and comparable occult views of flying saucers are expressed in N. Meade Layne (1950).

predictable coterie of New Age seekers, the curious, and the gullible, were five psychologists, sociologists, and graduate students under the direction of the Laboratory for Research in Social Relations of the University of Minnesota. Learning of the ongoing saga from the newspaper story, three university professors—Leon Festinger, Henry W. Riecken, and Stanley Schachter—saw the chance to research firsthand a prophetic movement at work. They were especially interested in what would happen to its participants when the anticipated events did not occur—thus the title of the classic book they would write about the episode: *When Prophecy Fails.*

Although Martin, Laughead, and the others waxed hot and cold on publicity and proselytization, it would have been impossible to conceal what was going on. For one thing, there were followers not just in the Chicago area but also in East Lansing and Detroit. In the former Laughead led a church-related Quest group. He also had ties to the Detroit saucer community, dominated by contactees and mystics, including medium Rose Phillips, whose spirit guide—a discarnate physician—had his own cosmic sources *(Clinton Daily News* 1954a, 1954b).[12] In fact, some of Martin's Michigan followers would go to Phillips to seek confirmation or disconfirmation of the December 21 prophecy. To the confusion or irritation of the inquirers, Phillips managed to provide both, agreeing that the described cataclysm would occur but offering conflicting testimony on the date.

In any case, as December 21 grew closer, the Laugheads spent more and more time away from their East Lansing home. Participants debated whether to quit their jobs and otherwise cut off earthly ties, and all awaited anxiously for further signs. As tensions mounted, one member began channeling her own communications from "the Creator." For a time the often discordant testimony coming through the two women created a rift within the group, but soon Martin's strong personality—one manifestation of which was the greater relative clarity of Sananda's messages—won out.

All the while, however, the larger outside world was closing in. Besides pressure from disbelieving family members and friends, the believers experienced a particular jolt when Laughead lost his job because of his beliefs. On November 22, the university asked him to resign his position (effective December 1) with the college health service, though word of the firing would be withheld for another three weeks. On December 17, Michigan State College president John A. Hannah told the Associated Press that students had complained about Laughead's "propagandizing"

---

12. An interesting, albeit idiosyncratic, account of Detroit's saucer scene can be found in contactee Laura Mundo's *Flying Saucer Up-Day!* (published in the mid-1970s).

them "on a particular set of beliefs of questionable validity" that would "affect ad-versely the quality of their college work." Before this public announcement, only school officials, the Laugheads, and—when Laughead confided to them a week later—the members of the Martin group knew about this stunning turn of events.

With time running out, the Laugheads moved into the Martin residence and prepared for the coming landing. Each member received a "passport" consisting of a sheet of blank paper inside a stamped envelope. This, along with the "password" ("I left my hat at home"), ensured each believer a seat on the flying saucer. On Decem-ber 16, Laughead slipped away to address a local saucer club. "Some sound tapes were run off," he told an Associated Press reporter there. "Nobody understood them, but it was obvious that an organized attempt at communication with the earth had been captured on the tapes," said Laughead (*Buffalo Courier-Express* 1954).

The next day the relative privacy that had shielded the group from ridicule ended when a Chicago paper exposed Martin's strange beliefs and reported Laugh-ead's loss of employment. Other papers across the country, and soon afterwards the world, picked up the story, and over the next few days Martin and Laughead did their best to convince journalists, who were playing the episode for laughs, that they were not crazy. Laughead did most of the talking, trying to come across as a reason-able man who simply followed the evidence—unlike the reporters, who he thought were confused and unknowledgeable.

The publicity left the relentlessly gullible group open to the most obvious pranks, including phone calls from self-identified space people. The most absurd of these came from "Captain Video"—the hero of a popular television series for chil-dren—who on the day of the newspaper article's appearance informed Martin of a spaceship landing to occur at four o'clock that afternoon in her own backyard. In-credibly, Martin directed the group to prepare for the pickup. Only Mrs. Laughead suspected a joke, but Martin would have none of it.

Soon everyone was busy ripping the metal out of his or her clothes—the space people had warned that metal could not safely be worn aboard a saucer—and scan-ning the sky. At four, the believers walked out the door, some in mid-conversation with reporters and curiosity-seekers, in full expectation that within moments they would be whisked into space. After an hour and a half of no saucer, however, they trooped back inside and watched Captain Video—the real one—on television. Mar-tin suspected that the space people would send a coded message through the show, but even with her considerable imaginative powers she discerned none.

Late that evening Martin received a psychic message that a spaceship was on its way; anyone who was not ready when it arrived would be left behind. For more than three hours, until about 3:20 in the morning, the small band shivered outside in the frigid air. Finally, a message arrived from the space people praising the believers' patience and commitment and releasing them from the vigil. Not everybody was able to sustain the faith, and the ranks dwindled as one by one those who could not contain their growing doubts slipped away. The others let themselves be persuaded that the space people were merely testing them to prove that they were worthy of rescue from the coming cataclysm.

On the morning of December 20, less than twenty-four hours before the tidal wave would wipe Chicago off the face of the planet and forever reshape Earth's geography, Martin got these words from the Guardians:

> At the hour of midnight you shall be put into parked cars and taken to a place where ye shall be put aboard a porch [flying saucer] and ye shall be purposed by the time you are there. At that time you shall have the fortunate ones forget the few who have not come—and at no time are they to be called for, they are but enacting a scene and not a person who should be there will fail to be there and at the time you are to say "What is your question? . . ." and at no time are you to ask what is what and not a plan shall go astray and for the time being be glad and be fortunate to be among the favored. And be ye ready for further instructions. (158–59)

Martin and the others spent the day rehearsing the passwords and rituals that would enable them to board the spaceship when it arrived. One message disclosed that the escape from Earth would begin precisely at midnight, when a spaceman would knock at the door. He was to be greeted with these words: "What is your question?" When no spaceman showed up at the designated hour, one member began intermittent channeling from the Creator, who promised a miracle. None happened. For the first time, even the most hardened believers were facing the possibility that maybe nothing was going to happen, at least any time soon. Martin suggested that maybe "it was this little group spreading light here that prevented the flood." Not long afterwards, not surprisingly, a message from Sananda confirmed this interpretation. Laughead took over the phone to call reporters and wire services with the happy news: the Earth had been saved. The result was a fresh round of ridicule-filled news stories. Even worse, group members who had given up jobs and cut ties with skeptical family members faced uncertain immediate futures.

As the day went by and the press and the curious marched in and out of Martin's door, there was growing anxiety that members were missing hidden messages from the space people. At nine that night, Martin took a call from someone identifying himself as a spaceman. Taking him at his word, she engaged him in prolonged conversation. Another prank call sent her off on a brief, embarrassing venture to a boy's door. A teenaged UFO buff who came to the house was assumed to be a spaceman and pressed for orders.

Martin also claimed that earthquakes, which had occurred in Italy and California, validated her prophecy. By then, she was grasping at anything. The next day, when Sananda directed her to turn on her tape recorder at 8 P.M. so that a flying saucer could beam down a song sung by an extraterrestrial "boys' glee club," all that came of it was a blank tape. As if things were not already farcical enough, a message on the twenty-third ordered everyone to stand in front of the Martin home at 6 P.M. and to sing Christmas carols. At that moment—what else?—a flying saucer would land, and spacemen would talk with the carolers in person. The message further directed the group to publicize the new prophecy and to encourage anyone who wanted to be there. Interviewed later that evening about this additional failed prophecy, Laughead could only offer this feeble explanation: "There may have been spacemen there in disguise." On Christmas Day, one of the sociologist-observers called on Martin. Taking him to be a spaceman, she asked him what orders he had for her.

The Aftermath

Of the group, only Martin and the Laugheads, bottomlessly faithful, managed to sustain belief in the extraterrestrials who promised so much and delivered nothing beyond ever shakier rationalizations for each successive unfulfilled prophecy. Laughead survived a psychiatric hearing initiated by his sister, who was trying to take custody of his three daughters, but that did not deter him. As late as May, the Laugheads acted on instructions channeled through Detroit medium Rose Phillips. They waited with Phillips at a hotel garage ramp in East Lansing for a new saucer landing.

For Martin, things were even worse. To her Oak Park neighbors, the caroling episode, which had precipitated a near riot and brought police to the scene to quell an unruly crowd, was the final irritation. Community pressure forced the police to draw up a warrant against Martin and Laughead, charging them with disturbing the peace and contributing to the delinquency of minors. Though clearly reluctant to act on the warrant, the police warned the Martins to shut down the meetings. They also intimated that if there were any further problems, Mrs. Martin would face psychiatric examination and possible institutionalization.

Early in January 1955, Dorothy Martin slipped out of town. Under an alias, she flew to Arizona. (Or, as one sympathetic account has it, "Sananda told her to burn her bridges behind her. Just minutes before a sanity warrant was to be served, committing her for 'observation,' Sananda sent ones who whisked her away to a place of safety, never to return to her home again.")[13] In her new residence, she found herself much closer to the hub of contactee activity. Both Truman Bethurum and George Hunt Williamson lived in Arizona. The Laugheads, living by then in Southern California, dropped in from time to time.

Through Williamson's channelings, the Laugheads and Martin, who by then at Sananda's urging thought of herself as "Sister Thedra," learned of the Brotherhood of the Seven Rays. According to an extraterrestrial named Aramu-Muru:

> The Brotherhood of the Seven Rays traces its origin back many thousands of years ago to the post-Lemurian period. It really goes back further than that, but it knew its monastery in post-Lemurian times at Lake Titicaca, Peru. It worked then and it continues to work now with other Brotherhoods throughout the world. It is in close association with Master Koot Hoomi Lah Singh at Shigatse, Tibet, and with the master teacher of the great White Brotherhood at Mt. Shasta, California. There are several others located throughout the world in fellowship with the Brotherhood of the Seven Rays. (Norkin 1957, 115–16)

In another session, on February 19, 1956, the planetary spirit of Venus, Sanat Kumara, who ordinarily communicated with Martin but this time spoke through Williamson (aka "Brother Philip"), assured Martin that her apocalyptic prophecy would prove true after all:

> Very soon, beloved of my being, the winds shall howl, sooner than we realize. It is already upon us, for I have witnessed it in the plane which is just above that of physical expression upon the earth, and that means that if it descends one more plane, it shall find reality. And that which you knew must come on a December not many months ago shall find its reality, for it is in the plane ready to descend into form and motion upon the earth. (Norkin 1957, 90)

Guided by such prophecies, Martin, Williamson, and others moved to Lake Titicaca to establish the Priory of All Saints in the remote northern Peruvian town Moyobamba, while the Laugheads kept the North American faithful abreast of de-

13. The information is from a now-defunct Web page with no date entitled, "Sister Thedra," http://sfsu.edu/~rsmith/thedra.htm.

velopments from Hemet, California. From Peru, a bulletin reported day-to-day activities, and a transcript of channeled or automatically written messages, often with
apocalyptic overtones, accompanied each report. Soon, these messages said that
cataclysmic changes would bring flying saucers down from the skies, and then
Lemuria and Atlantis would rise up from the ocean depths.

By the summer of 1957, however, nearly all of the spiritual pilgrims were back in
the United States. Williamson went off elsewhere in Peru, and only Dorothy Martin,
whom Sananda directed to stay behind, remained in Moyobamba. Living under
primitive conditions and suffering from poverty and ill health, Martin barely survived. She felt that her colleagues had betrayed her. She spent a portion of her mea-
ger income on postage for mailings to North America, but no one seemed to listen or
care. Even so, the messages continued to come at a furious pace. They included dramatic visionary encounters with various space people, angels, and religious figures.[14]

Although expecting to spend the rest of her life in the Andes, Martin was surprised to receive instructions to return to the United States in 1961. She moved to
Southern California and was there for nearly a year before heading to the northern
tip of the state and Mount Shasta, long an attraction to America's mystically
minded.[15] Occult legend held that a colony of Lemurians lived inside or under the
mountain. The Lemurians maintained contacts with extraterrestrials who regularly
arrived in UFOs. Sananda and Sanat Kumara directed Martin to establish the Association of Sananda and Sanat Kumara. Finding peace and stability at last, she took
up residence in the Shasta area and worked with a small but devoted group of followers who carefully recorded and circulated the messages she received daily.

By 1988, the space people dictated yet another move, to Sedona, Arizona, the
New Age center of North America. It was here on June 13, 1992, that Sister Thedra's
long, strange trip ended. Just before her death, Sananda told her of his plans for her
in the next world. As her body failed, her hand guided a pen one last time to write
the final message from her beloved cosmic friend: "It is now come the time that ye
come out of the place wherein ye are. . . . Let it be, for many shall greet thee with
glad shouts." [16]

14. One message, which bears no date, was recorded by Sister Thedra and distributed by the Association of Sananda and Sanat Kumara.

15. See, for example, Frank (1998).

16. This message, which also bears no date, was recorded by Sister Thedra and distributed by the
Association of Sananda and Sanat Kumara.

Galactic Messenger!

Overview of the Universal Industrial
Church of the New World Comforter

Diana G. Tumminia

In the realm of academic writing, the Universal Industrial Church of the New World Comforter (UICNWC) remains seldom noted beyond a few references. In the interest of furthering research into the subject of contactee religions, this chapter fills in some of the gaps in knowledge about this little-known group. Mentioned in *The Encyclopedia of American Religions* (Melton 1989) and in David Miller's glimpse at so-called UFO cults (1985, 2000), the low-profile church remains underscrutinized perhaps because it has created no imminent prophecies, suicide pacts, or headline-grabbing scandals. Philip Lamy (1999) briefly identifies it as one of the many millennial groups that await an impending cosmic transformation. During 2004–6, UICNWC had ten members, making them the world's smallest contactee religion. In comparison with other groups (listed in appendix A), UICNWC shows some commonalities, as well as clear differences, in social structure and beliefs.

UICNWC resembles many other contactee religions in that its millennial message purportedly originates from outer space or otherworldly celestial planets. Like every other contactee religion, it relies on clairvoyant communication with extraterrestrial divinities who provide superior guidance on matters cosmic and eternal. The 1950s marked a pivotal time in the contactee career of UICNWC's leader, Allen Michael; this period is concurrent with the early contacteeism of Sister Thedra of the Association of Sananda and Sanat Kumara, Ernest Norman of Unarius, and George King of Aetherius. For UICNWC members, their founder holds the reverential status of being divinely gifted by his special calling from the powerful spiritual realms above planet Earth, a fact that parallels almost all other such groups whose visionary worldviews are derived from the creative pronouncements of charismatic leaders. Similar to the Raëlian Movement in one respect, UICNWC's teachings utilize idiosyncratic interpretations of biblical references that speak to an alien genesis and salvation.

What may make UICNWC truly unique is its touch of Marxism and its flowering in the hippie subculture of the psychedelic sixties with its free-love philosophy. On the surface, this may resound of the Raëlian omnisensual philosophy; however, UICNWC's free love emphasizes only heterosexuality. In contrast to some other contactee religions, UICNWC's millenarian prophecy of impending transformation by extraterrestrial forces lacks an exact manifestation date, and, thus, it differs from the unfulfilled prophecies of Chen Tao, Unarius, Sister Thedra's group, or Ashtar Command, which all tried to pinpoint the exact date of the advent of their space beings. UICNWC stands apart from other contactee religions with its overt political and economic messages and with the creation of its own political party, albeit small in comparison to other political entities. This stance may sound a bit reminiscent of Amalgamated Flying Saucer Clubs of America (AFSCA) space-age candidates Gabriel Green and Daniel Fry, who were part of the world of early UFO conventions that Michael Allen attended. Presently, most other contactee religions place their efforts outside all forms of political expression.

The public may know UICNWC by another name, the One World Family Commune. As the church's core, the commune bases itself on the teachings of Allen Michael, formerly Allen Ward Noonan, who as of this writing is still alive and living in the commune in Santa Rosa, California. Through a field visit, interviews and e-mail correspondence with four different members, in addition to a study of its literature and videos, I learned some of the history and practices of the One World Family Commune. The commune introduced me to Allen Michael, who at the time was recuperating from an illness. At present, the ten-person commune is virtually the whole membership of the church, although they do have outside supporters around the country. Despite their small size, the group maintains a Web site (Galactic 2004) and a public-access television show, *Galactic Messenger*. The commune operates on donations for services (educational talks) and goods (food, books, tapes, artwork), as well as on other types of charitable contributions. Older members rely on social security for income.

The One World Family Commune views itself as an educational institution, rather than a stereotypic church, because its goal is to teach about extraterrestrial scientific principles that they profess can rid the world of economic and social problems.

Galactic Contact

Before Allen Michael became the Galactic Messenger, he led a simple life (Michael 1982). Born in Britt, Iowa, in 1916, he grew up with an enterprising spirit. He ran track in high school, and he became interested in art. Although he won a scholarship to college, he dropped out to work as a sign painter. During World War II, he served as a noncombatant making camouflage for the military. After the war, he married a woman named Marian, with whom he had a son. Michael worked for peace through a local Presbyterian Church.

Extraterrestrials contacted Allen Michael in April 1947 when he resided in Long Beach, California. It states in a handout, entitled "My Encounter with Galactic Space Beings," that during his childhood Michael received visits from angels while he played. Since then, he has felt extraordinarily blessed because he experienced God in a very personal way. When he was thirty-one years old and working as a sign painter, he received a spiritual contact with ETI (Extraterrestrial Intelligence). Describing this, Michael says,

> A shaft of ultraviolet light entwined with gold threads enveloped me and I, the entity in this body, was taken up into a great room inside a space ship. . . . I was connected with the Galactic Logos, the Great Galactic Being manifesting as this whole Galaxy. A beautiful, yet powerful voice like thunder and lightning spoke to me. The voice was audible to me, coming out of a brilliant beam of silver and golden light and it was projected on out to either side and above and below me. . . . The powerful words that came booming out to me were as follows: "My Son, will you be the savior of the world?" (Michael 1982, 445)

Michael recalls that he traveled psychically out of his body into another level of existence to a mother ship of the Galactic Command Space Complex. Later in 1947, he channeled information called "The New Covenant Bill of Rights," which is a foundation of the group's thinking (Michael 1982). It represents the guidelines for living, as well ETI's vision for a renewed world, and reads as follows:

The New Covenant World Bill of Rights
Let each of us share all the world—the Kingdom of God, and call one place of our choosing our own, and be free to come and go in the world and stay at any dwelling place accommodating travelers.

3.1. Allen Michael, ca. 2001. Allen Michael heads the Universal Industrial Church of the New World Comforter. The group produces a public-access cable television show called *The Galactic Messenger.* A skilled graphic artist and woodworker, Allen Michael paints and makes backdrops for his television show. Courtesy of Starmast Productions.

Let each of us give to the extent of our abilities to the One World Company, and in return all things shall be added unto us.

Let each of us be judged only by our conscience in God, and let no people judge their fellow beings, but rather take judgement [*sic*] of their own thought and action.

Let no person or group hold any authority over another, except that people be willingly led by wisdom and true personality.

Let the government be of the people, where the people are self-governed; by the people, where the people enjoy perfect freedom; for the people, where the people give themselves abundant living.

Let the government seat be only the storehouse and inventory of the people's products.

Let all things be done unto edification, for God is not the author of confusion. (Michael 2001, 16]

Michael's marriage to his first wife broke up shortly after his cosmic initiation in 1947. He continued to reside in Long Beach, taking time to travel to all the early

UFO conventions at Giant Rock, California, and various other locations, where he encountered George Van Tassel, George Adamski, Gabriel Green, and other prominent speakers who professed the coming of the flying saucers.[1] This subculture, rather than alternative religion, was an important influence.

In July 1954, after hearing a voice telling him to follow a cloud, he drove to Giant Rock, where he hoped to meet up with otherworldly beings. He camped out overnight awaiting instructions as clouds formed where spaceships hovered. Allen Michael describes his first physical contact with Space Beings:

> After the sun went down and the sky was pitch dark with stars shining brightly, I saw flashes of light move across the sky. About 9:30 P.M., I got on my mattress in the station wagon and fell asleep. In a dream, I was in the flying saucer with those I had been with before. . . . At about 10 A.M. the round spaceship materialized about 6 feet off the ground 75 feet away. . . . An opening in the ship and a platform shot out. Three beings floated out on it. From left to right, as I faced them, were Favelron, Celeste and Jameston. I was aware I had been on voyages with them before. (Michael n.d., 2)

The extraterrestrials threw him kisses as they sped off in a flash of light. Because he was still in his earth body, he could not go up to them. This close encounter was "really" a holographic projection from the "Mothership." The differences in dimensional energies made it impossible for the extraterrestrials to meet physically with their chosen one, Allen Michael.

After encountering the extraterrestrials, Michael (1982) started a proto–New Age business and communal experiment in Long Beach. He operated an art studio and a coffeehouse called the House of Meditation until 1967. By accounts, that phase provided a successful artistic outlet for the community. Michael remembers that the popular singer Jackson Browne got his start there with coffeehouse performances. However, his early commune attracted some problematic individuals who hastened its demise (Michael 1982). Michael says he followed the voice of the God force in his head as he started to write down all the channeled messages coming through him from the "God-Mind." In 1967, telepathic guidance led him to San Francisco to set up a natural food restaurant and the One World Family Commune. About 1969, Allen married again to a commune member, Dian (although they later

---

1. Various biographical information came from an e-mail (Dec. 5, 2005) from member Joseph Antaree, who asked Allen Michael some specific questions for me.

divorced, they both remain in the commune today). When the group moved to Berkeley, he experienced another significant epiphany while walking to a coffeehouse. According the Allen Michael, he was taken out of his body to a mother spaceship. Twelve other souls were taken with him to the planet Altamira, where they were given assignments as Cosmic Masters. The extraterrestrials assigned Allen to the Archangel Michael, hence his name change. Since beginning his cosmic mission, Michael has led his followers through several decades and into the twenty-first century, propagating the faith with a small collection of books, pamphlets, and a public-access television show.

Beliefs

Like others within the subculture, the group grafts disparate themes together, a process Michael Barkun (2003) calls improvisational millennialism and postmodernists label *bricolage*. The key beliefs of the One World Family Commune focus upon reincarnation, a concept called Uni-Communism, the Hegelian dialectic (Thesis, Anti-Thesis, and Synthesis), and extraterrestrial assistance that will bring about the salvation of planet Earth. The One Worlders are millenarian utopians who advocate total disarmament, elimination of economic exploitation, and the promotion of leisure and creativity through lifestyle changes. They practice a natural food philosophy ("eliminating meat and processed non-food") and extol the virtues of communal sharing. They recognize that certain prophets and teachers have channeled higher knowledge from the God Mind, like Edgar Cayce, Mary Baker Eddy, and Nikola Tesla, to name a few who have tried to bring God consciousness to others.

The group reveres extraterrestrials called the Galactic Elohim of Galactica, an advanced spiritual civilization in perfect attunement with twelfth-density consciousness of the Universal Mind. Allen Michael writes, "Altamedia and Altamira are the first two of the twenty-four Galactic Worlds in close orbit around the Great Central Sun, and [they] include the headquarters of the Galactic Elohim assigned to set up this planet as a special healing station" (2001, 87). The Galactic name for Earth is Placentia, the planet of plenty and rebirth. The creation project here on Earth began six million years ago, after the "Solar Catastrophe" caused by Baal, an oppositional entity. The Galactic creators cloned plant life and animals from God Mind Imagination, a part of the higher spiritual intelligence of the Supreme Being. In some of the later Galactic Elohim projects, these creators provided the technology to build the pyramids and to carve the statues on Easter Island (Michael 1982).

A member explained the process of pyramid building in an e-mail letter: "The main thing about UFOs is that we believe they built the pyramids first with computerized spacecraft that lasered the stone into triangles and then levitated them up and took them to the building site and teleported them into position and later on heat set the whole triangle with rooms underneath, etc., so the blocks would bond." [2]

Galactica is poised to bring about a transformation of planet Earth. Some time in the future, the Galactic Elohim will engage in a great "demonstration in the skies" and appear on radio and television to announce the New Age of spiritual energy (Michael 2001, 61). The New Jerusalem Mothership will orbit Earth, sending out many shuttles to pick up people and take them on board the Autonomous New World Government headquarters, with all flights being scheduled through the Internet. According to a handout, the Galactic Space Command is preparing the Internet for the World Computer Government, which will schedule the production and distribution of all goods and services. As the One World Family Commune views the Galactic Mothership as existing in a higher plane of transcendental energy, its vision for the future does not require verification through any ordinary physical means. Nevertheless, the social changes that Extraterrestrial Intelligence makes at that future time will be obvious to everyone.

The millennial vision for a better world predicts that a free supply of nonpolluting energy will be drawn from outer space. [3] This abundant energy of the universe will supply free of charge all things needed, ushering a transformational age that ends all social and economic inequality. Cars will be obsolete as people travel in "crash-proof" spaceships (Michael 2001, 319). This space energy already powers the New Jerusalem (the Galactic Mothership that oversees Earth), and it has been available for many years. Members point out that both Nikola Tesla and Wilhelm Reich spoke of this energy source. When society runs on that kind of energy, it will abandon its dependence on fossil fuels, which is arguably one source of war and exploitation.

One Worlders envision their Space Beings as divine, as opposed to other extraterrestrials, particularly the Greys, whose presence has been reported by various witnesses around the world. Technically in UICNWC teachings, the Greys are not extraterrestrials at all, but humans who went underground, where they mutated

---

2. This quote is from my e-mail correspondence with commune member Michael Bobier in February 2004. The capitalization of words in the chapter conforms to the style in church literature.

3. The theme of free energy from outer space is also a theme of the prophecy of the Unarius Academy of Science. Unarius also cites this wisdom as coming from Nikola Tesla. See Tumminia (2005). Another contactee religion that reveres Tesla is Pana-Wave Laboratory (see appendix A).

into another species. As Michael (2001) first told their story at an early flying-saucer convention in the sixties, the Galactic Elohim gave Greys spaceships and taught them how to use their psychic powers. The proverbial Greys fly ships, reside underground in extinct volcanoes, and intercept aircraft that are "bent on murder." Greys telepathically communicate with the military to get them "to stop fighting." Michael remarked that the Bible mentioned Grey activity in Revelation 9:2–4, which makes a symbolic reference to smoke rising and locusts emerging from the smoke. According to Michael, Greys have the "power of scorpions to sting those who do not have the mark of God on their foreheads (CIA and the armies they control)" (2001, 207). Greys serve a purpose, but because of their karma from past lives, they are not spiritually advanced. Michael channeled this information about Greys:

> Now let it be known that Galactica has delivered spaceships to the Grey Aliens, who inhabit mutations from the earth strain of bodies. Grey aliens are souls in mutated devolution bodies who, because of their negative conditioning by the Luciferic energies, have been unable to incarnate in normal earth strain bodies. (Michael 2001, 206)

As a spiritual practice, the group listens to the channeled messages of Allen Michael, who speaks from the God Mind, Universal Christ Consciousness, and the Universal Mind of ETI. These channeled messages comprise the content of books and television shows. Allen Michael encourages others to be channels themselves, in other words to tune into the Universal Mind and let "It" speak to and through them. He has sometimes asked close followers to channel on particular topics. The group believes songs, poems, and artwork are similarly inspired by higher intelligence.

Allen Michael defines his role as that of the Galactic Messenger (a Space Being representing Galactic Space Command) and that of the New World Comforter (explaining Spirit God's Master Plan to people of Earth). After Michael's first encounter with Space Beings, he read the Bible to clarify his mission. The Bible verses John 14:16–18 explained that his purpose was one of being a spiritual comforter, like the Holy Spirit:

> And I will pray the Father, and he shall give you another Comforter, that he may abide with you forever;
>   Even the Spirit of truth; whom the world cannot receive, because it seeth him not, neither knoweth him: but ye know him; for he dwelleth with you, and shall be in you.

I will not leave you comfortless; I will come to you.

Most published materials quote biblical verses as explanations of the inspired teachings. The writings capitalize the first letters in Space Being when referring to Michael, giving the reader the idea that he and the Galactic Elohim are exalted souls of a high spiritual consciousness and energy. Likewise, members capitalize key words in written texts to signify their spiritual importance.

The church's worldview professes that good and evil forces compete for the souls of people, planets, and societies. One member explained this cosmology to me:

> We have come to recognize that the struggle between good and evil is a result of The Solar Catastrophe, and only as we (all the people on the planet) find The Synthesis, which comes to reconcile The Thesis (good) and The Antithesis (evil) and return to a state of harmony and oneness with Creation Universe will transcend that struggle. One element of The Antithesis is The Dragon (World Usury Bank), Revelation 12.[4]

In the New Age that ETI initiates, souls will return to the "normal Universe," and people will express their loving and sharing natures. In the meantime, however, One Worlders refer to Earth as part of a "ruined solar system," a present state of affairs initiated by the cosmic fall caused by Baal-Lucifer, who initiated the "Solar Catastrophe." The cosmology (Michael 2001) refers to an oppositional force (Anti-Thesis) which manifests in various forms, identified by terms like these: Anti-Christ, Babylon (a system of satanic power), Anti-Matter (satanic power in the electromagnetic field), the Beast (military-industrial complex), Gog (forces of the evil Anti-Christ, like the Nazis, militarists, or KKK), and 666 (electronic bar codes on products, ATM cards, etc.). Most of these references, of course, come from the biblical Book of Revelation. Conversely, they see the conduits for good (Thesis) as follows: ETI Space Beings, Galactic Elohim who appear in spaceships, God Mind, Omni God, Spirit God, and Christ Consciousness, to name a few. Both forces serve as synthesizing energies viewed within the Hegelian dialectic of intergalactic change. The resolution between these forces will come in apocalyptic Armageddon (or *Karma-geddon* as One Worlders might say).

4. This quote is from my e-mail correspondence with an anonymous commune member in February 2004.

Referring to the manifestations of the negative force, Michael assigns many of the world's problems to "Zionist" conspiracies that extend to the International Monetary Fund, the Federal Reserve System, the CIA, the Secret World Government, and general destructive tendencies toward "Babylonian usury" (capitalistic economic exploitation based on lending money at high interest rates) (1994, 2001). Because Allen Michael uses the term *Zionist* throughout his texts, the members of the One World Family Commune wanted to it to be known that he was not being anti-Semitic. According to UICNWC, the use of the term Zionist in Michael's writings *does not* refer to Judaism or being Jewish. One member explained it to me this way, "My comment is that Zionism is not equivalent to Judaism, but rather refers to those who control the world through money and believe they are building God's Kingdom on Earth, people like President Bush, who is not Jewish." Another member, who was also concerned that the word Zionist would be misunderstood by outsiders, wrote me saying his children are half Jewish; he and others in the commune underscore the fact that they subscribe to a philosophy of unity and love for all people without exception. One Worlders say that the term Zionist has an idiosyncratic meaning within the group, which unfortunately is misconstrued by outsiders.[5]

Michael's themes express a familiarity with certain UFO conspiracy theories, a body of marginal knowledge studied by political scientist Michael Barkun (2003). For example, *The Everlasting Gospel* (Michael 2001, 299) acknowledges John Coleman for his book, *Conspirators Hierarchy: The Story of the Committee of 300,* that in part refers to a contrived drug war against mind-expanding substances. The book explicates the purported network of connections between an international elite, economic commissions, and secret societies (Barkun 2003), which parallels but does not literally resemble Michael's references to satanic conspiracies.

On the war in Iraq, One Worlders take an antiwar stance, and they believe that large triangular spaceships levitate young people on board so that they will learn to be conscientious objectors. When these people become sufficiently enlightened,

5. This appears to be a poor choice of wording; Michael says that "Zionism" represents money and ownership, as opposed to communism, which refers to the elimination of capital and ownership (2001, 274). One Worlders say this is just a matter of distinctive semantics because Zionism means any type of monetary exploitation and does not refer to any single group. Many of the terms Michael uses, like the hollow/inner-earth theory, Zionist, return of the Antichrist, or the New World Order, figure prominently in some segments of the UFO conspiracy literature that is Anti-Semitic (Barkun 2003). However, if one studies UICNWC's literature and illustrations of their philosophy, it emphasizes interracial unity and love. Michael also condemns the Nazis for their genocide of Jews.

they will teach others to follow the commandment "Thou shalt not kill." Bush is viewed as a tool of the Lucifer Group, the Dragon of Revelation 13:4, whose militaristic ways will lead to a karmic cleansing and a prophesied civil war in the United States. On this matter, Allen Michael has foretold that Bush and all economic elites will be exposed for their satanic natures as the spiritual consequences of the Iraqi War manifest.

Michael's books frequently comment on world affairs, like the NAFTA treaty and the dealings of the World Trade Organization (WTO), as manifestations of the negative force. His philosophy rails against capitalism. He advocates that people bring about a worldwide work stoppage to change the world economic system. The group also seeks to abolish the penal system and replace it with a health-care system that "loves and lifts all people" regardless of their circumstances. The group seeks to end all wars and to provide a true education connected with service, creativity, and extraterrestrial guidance. GROM is one acronym they use for "Get Rid of Money." Until all things are free and shared, the group suggests the printing of free transitional money, but only until the world's economic base changes completely through Galactic initiation. When the "New World" brings about a total-sharing economy, money will be obsolete.

The One Worlders espouse a belief in reincarnation and karma, two factors that produce lessons for souls on this planet of healing (Earth). Karma equates to the great cosmic law of cause and effect, while reincarnation allows souls to take on successive lifetimes in order to make up for past misdeeds. During their transmigrations, souls inhabit bodies of different genders, races, and social classes. One can be born a white king, but reincarnate as a black slave girl. For that matter, one could be born a black queen, and then become a white slave boy. As in the case of many New Agers, they see any social relationship in this life as based upon the karma of past lives. In this vein, planet Earth is a school where souls reincarnate until they learn their spiritual lessons and their true higher calling. Characteristically, they explain history and economics as *karmic arrangements*. This type of explanation is commonly found in New Age groups and other contactee religions with theosophical influences derived from metaphysical subculture. Because souls live many lifetimes in many bodies, their external bodily identifications have more to do with their karmic history than with any earthly struggle for social change.

Economics and race relations reflect the veiled actions of spiritual machinations. In referring to the former economic and racial exploitation of blacks in South Africa under apartheid, Allen Michael writes, "Our etheric body or soul carries into our next life the instinctive emotional programming of our former lifetimes" (1994,

3.2. "Workers of the World Unite." The Universal Industrial Church of the New World Comforter envisions a new world of harmony among all races of people and elimination of exploitation. Their New Age will increase love and eliminate war. This illustration appears in their first volume of *The Everlasting Gospel* (1982). Courtesy of Starmast Productions.

16). For example, blacks under apartheid were formerly oppressors in past lives; through the karmic wheel of justice, they received what they meted out in previous existences. In other writings, Michael deems African Americans as important role models for nonviolent civil disobedience, but in any case, sociopolitical relationships and race relations translate into karmic arrangements with long spiritual histories. Within this rather New Age interpretation of the karmic dimensions of human relations (race, social class, gender, and oppression), the group advocates equality for all.

One World Family Commune

From its inception, the One World Family Commune based itself on the utmost principles of fellowship and equality. Rejecting the worst aspects of individualistic and materialistic culture of twentieth-century America, members came forward to create a utopian living situation that could be a model for the future society. Many members saw mainstream religion as flawed by greed and hypocrisy. They sought official recognition as a church in the 1970s, but they could not relate to the more negative connotation of a church that has to do with an antiquated notion of piety or the corrupt acquisition of personal wealth. On a one-page handout, entitled "ONE WORLD FAMILY COMMUNE: The Idea Whose Time Has Come," commune members explain their affiliation: "We are not a church in the established sense of the word, but a church in the true meaning—a congregation of people who have come together to live according to our highest ideals for the betterment of humanity and, in doing this, we become channels of the higher truths."

The One World Family Commune lives by the ideals of utopian communism, its version being Uni-Communism, which espouses total sharing, nonmonogamous love arrangements, natural foods, and vegetarianism. In its philosophy, Uni-Communism equates with Christ Communalism. Michael (1994) justifies the communalist approach with biblical verses (Acts 4:32–35) and with channeled messages from the God Mind via Galactica. According to these verses and cosmic communiqués, followers of Christ are to hold all things in common and distribute them according to each person's need. In this context, the members of the commune view their philosophy as a lifestyle of loving service. Uni-Communism also relates to the ideas of Karl Marx, who advocated the abolition of private property and economic changes that honored workers. From his perspective, Michael synthesizes Marx and Christ through the guidance he imparts as the Galactic Messenger.

The entire church including the commune has seen significant attrition from its early years in the Haight-Ashbury district of San Francisco. According to member statements, Allen Michael moved to Haight-Ashbury in the spring of 1967 before the Summer of Love began. He opened up a vegetarian health food restaurant called the Here and Now, where he attracted followers who came and went.

In 1968, the FBI "busted" Allen Michael after an agent posing as a teacher asked him for marijuana. Michael sold him a "lid," or about an eighth of an ounce, which led to his arrest and that of one other commune member. Michael spent six months in Vacaville prison, but it became a spiritual experience for him, as there he channeled what would become *The Everlasting Gospel* material.

In 1969, the restaurant moved to Mill Valley Redwood Shopping Center in Marin County, where the restaurant's name changed to The Mustard Seed. However, shopping center management asked the group to leave because there were "too many hippies eating outside." Hippies, of course, were welcomed by Allen Michael, who held the view that ETI beamed New Age vibrations to the hippie generation. In recalling those bygone days, a member said that certain people in the group took LSD and experimented with drugs during that period. Michael (2001) indicates that the government waged an unjust war on drugs and psychedelics because it failed to see their value in opening the doors of perception. At that period, the Flower Power culture incited rebellion and alternative-lifestyle thinking, so the group appeared to be in tune with the psychedelic utopianism of the times. Most followers by 1970 were in their twenties or thirties when they moved to Berkeley to run a cafeteria-style restaurant on the corner of Haste and Telegraph Avenues. Once each week, Allen Michael channeled messages at an evening assemblage of flower children and bohemian seekers. During this period in 1973–74, they incorporated into a church.

In 1973, Michael published the first in his series of *The Everlasting Gospel* books, entitled *To the Youth of the World,* with the help of the newly formed Starmast Productions, the media arm of the church. The popular *Cosmic Cookery,* written by Kathryn Hannaford, came out in 1974.

Of that period one member said, "We lived out the Berkeley days and the Vietnam War did end [1975], and our books came out and some of us went out as missionaries of sorts to spread the word of Jesus, sharing all things common as the sensible civil way to live."[6]

In 1975, the One World Family Commune moved to Stockton, California, where they rented a mansion and some other housing for the forty people left over from Berkeley. By 1978, there were only twenty adults left. Of this period one member wrote, "We were all vegetarian and strict for the most part. We had natural selection classes whereby we practiced Tantra Yoga [sexual energy yoga] in a shared group. The sharing was difficult for some and easy for others."[7] During the Stockton era (1975–87), they published three additional volumes of the *Everlasting Gospel*

6. This quote is from my e-mail correspondence with Michael Bobier, who signed his e-mails with the salutation, LSD (Love Is Service Done), in February 2004.

7. This quote is from my e-mail correspondence with Michael Bobier in February 2004.

series: *ETI Space Beings Intercept Earthlings, UFO ETI World Master Plan,* and *God Ultimate Unlimited Mind-Speaks.*

Inspired by extraterrestrial intelligence, Allen Michael had consistently sought to educate the public about his world economic plan. In 1980, while in Stockton, the One Worlders helped him with his presidential campaign when he ran as the candidate for his own Utopian Synthesis Party. Michael based his platform on the idea of printing free money, which in his opinion would end unemployment, taxation, inflation, and recessions. He campaigned for a worldwide work stoppage and the canceling of all debts, and for the principle that all goods be freely distributed without care for payment. Furthermore, he advocated the 30/30 Plan, in which people rotate responsibilities by working thirty days and by having leisure for thirty days (Michael 2001). All these ideas still constitute the solutions to world problems promoted by the group as the principles of positive spiritual revolution.

In 1991, the group moved to Santa Rosa, where they now educate about natural foods, produce their television show, and send out books and tapes. In the 1990s they published the *Little Book* volumes (Michael 1994), which are additional channeled messages in the *Everlasting Gospel* series. The legacy of the sixties still shows in the church philosophy of "make love, not war." Reminiscent of that era are Michael's references to an unjust war on psychedelics and drugs (2001, 239). Even now, the commune practices a free love sensibility in the sense that no one pairs off. Members do not marry or form monogamous unions.

Some passages in Allen Michael's writings condemn the sexual practices in Sodom and Gomorrah, which prompted me to ask about any restrictions on sexual orientation. A member who wrote me said that sex was a "mystery" that they were still exploring. Another member indicated that sex had an obvious function in procreation, and beyond this, they acknowledged that sex was a normal part of a normal life. In this regard, the group also honors celibacy and bisexuality as choices, but tends to lean more toward a nonmonogamous, heterosexual tantric yoga practice. One female member wrote, "We recognize the sexual union as being a natural health-giving communion between males and females in the exchange of higher energy and hormones."[8]

One World Family Commune's Web site indicates that the members view themselves as space beings, assistants in a cosmic plan for the redemption of souls so that they may return to the "Normal Universe." A commune member described what that meant in e-mail correspondence:

---

8. This comment is from my e-mail correspondence with member Del Ranier in 2004.

We consider ourselves space beings in as much as we believe we have an etheric eternal double in space (in the New Jerusalem Mothership), and that double comes to us in spurts to be one with us, if we let it. The key is to let it, and when it comes as a channel or channelings, it isn't weird or strange, but common sense at best. We believe we are volunteers from the space command who let higher beings or higher concepts enter into us as consciousness.[9]

The One World Family Commune objects to classification as a UFO cult, stating that they have nothing in common with mind-control organizations like Jim Jones' People's Temple, Rajneesh, or Heaven's Gate. In contrast, they characterize themselves as "autonomous beings" preparing themselves (and others by example) for the Autonomous Self-Government that will be the basis of what they call the "New World." The commune does not view Allen Michael as a guru. To members, he leads by inspiration.

They raise this issue because reporters rushed to interview them after the Heaven's Gate suicides, asking if they were going to kill themselves. They know that outsiders may wrongly equate their leader with the dangerous cult gurus of other groups that made headline news for their misdeeds. Contrary to the stereotypes others placed upon them, they see their lives in the context of spiritual service. One member wrote, "We all espouse to love and to be of service to all people as one people, and to each other as we take turns cooking and shopping and doing chores, and serving one another without thought of remuneration."[10]

The Future

In late 2004, the commune contemplated a move to a larger house and grounds because they hoped to have more room to expand and to provide a bigger workshop for Allen Michael's art projects. For now, the world's smallest millenarian contactee religion will probably remain small because of the reluctance of potential members to commit to its communal lifestyle. The present average age of adult commune members is 64.5 years. Most of the children of members have left and will not be serving as replacement members. Their nonproselytizing approach coupled with their principled communal lifestyle hampers any exponential growth in followers for the moment. Even though they are not reluctant to take on new members, one

---

9. This quote is from my e-mail correspondence with Michael Bobier in February 2004.

10. This quote is from my e-mail correspondence with Michael Bobier in February 2004.

person indicated that they are not a group that someone could easily join. In his words, it was not impossible, but it was highly unlikely that the average person would be able to adapt to the dedicated communal way they live. However, they do believe that they are in spiritual contact with others who will come forward at the appropriate time. An "elect" of 144,000 will recognize the truth of the *Everlasting Gospel,* and they will join them when circumstances allow for an awakening.

The passing of a charismatic leader saddens followers, but the death of a leader inevitably happens in every group. Like other members of spiritual groups, they believe that their leader will never die in the sense that the soul ("Being") never dies. He will also live on through his messages of "higher truths" for the "end times." Because they have admittedly made no provisions for a transition of leadership when Allen Michael dies, they will probably continue the organization in their power-sharing style of communal consensus.[11] The One World Family Commune already takes care of the functional aspects of the church anyway, so the transition should go smoothly. This strategy may serve them for a time, although just as inevitably any group needs new members. Members are aware of their small numbers, but they are making no special efforts to bring in new people. Given their place in the history of contactee religions, it will be interesting to see how long they will continue to transmit their vision on behalf of the Galactic Space Command and how they will go about making future transitions.

11. Editor's note: Allen Michael died at 93 on March 25, 2010.

Presumed Immanent

The Raëlians, UFO Religions,
and the Postmodern Condition

Bryan Sentes *and* Susan Palmer

In 1974, Claude Vorilhon, a French race-car driver, pop singer, and journalist who later took the name Raël, published his first book, which describes his meeting with extraterrestrials and their revelations concerning humankind and the cosmos. Today, Raëlianism is the largest flying-saucer religion in the world, claiming a membership of 60,000 in ninety countries (Raëlian Church 2004). It is millenarian and evangelistic in its goals, yet world-affirming in its orientation toward society. Raëlians do not fit the anticult movement's stereotype of a cult, nor do they correspond neatly to Roy Wallis's (1984) tripartite typology of "world rejecting/affirming/accommodating" new religious movements (NRMs). Thus, Raëlians present an enigma: they are fundamentalists but also modernists. Their actions are based on the belief in the literal and infallible truth embodied in their sacred texts, which contain Raël's accounts of his meetings and communications with his extraterrestrials, the Elohim or "those who come from the sky." Essentially, these communications transform premodern scripture into a postmodern discourse. These texts bear at least a prima facie consistency with Robert S. Ellwood's suggestion that the appeal of "UFO cults" might reside in their offering "classic religious eschatologies revamped to meet the fears and dramas of the modern world" (1973, 334).

In this study, we will explore the Raëlian eschatology within the context of the "fears and dramas of the modern world" and the historical horizon within which the modern world and Raëlianism both find their context. Briefly, Raëlianism replaces the supernatural with the extraterrestrial and technological in order to demystify and demythologize primarily the Abrahamic religions, simultaneously (if unconsciously) mythologizing and ideologizing science and technology. The

Raëlian hermeneutic and attendant worldviews ground their unique—if somewhat extreme—solutions to some of the most troubling topics of the late twentieth century, such as ecology, sexuality, globalization, and genetics.

UFOs, the Death of God, and the Postmodern Condition

Despite its explicit protestation that its members are not ufologists (Raëlian Church 2004), the Raëlian Movement would not exist if it were not for the historical advent of the UFO phenomenon. In his *Flying Saucers: A Modern Myth of Things Seen in the Skies,* Carl Jung proposes that flying saucers are "manifestations of psychic changes which always appear at the end of one Platonic month and at the beginning of another. Apparently they are changes in the constellation of psychic dominants, or the archetypes, or 'gods' as they used to be called, which bring about . . . long-lasting transformations of the collective psyche" (1978, 5).

The historical developments accompanying or marking Jung's "changes in the constellation of psychic dominants" are the advent of a global culture and its simultaneous division into two mortally adversarial camps armed with the newly discovered and harnessed energies at the nucleus of the atom. Regarding this transformation, Jung insightfully points out that "the whole collective psychological problem that has been opened up by the Saucer epidemic stands in compensatory antithesis to our scientific picture of the world" (1978, 135). Where Jung, perhaps, would see this compensation relative only to the historical developments following World War II and the beginning of the Cold War, we propose a bolder and more far-reaching thesis. The appearance of UFOs on our historical horizon as objects inspiring religious behavior "stands in compensatory antithesis" to the scientific worldview as such and its practical, social, and spiritual effects since the Scientific and Industrial Revolutions, and that this standing "in compensatory antithesis" is ambivalent, being simultaneously an affirmation, critique, and transcendence of science and technology and the mortal threats they are seen as presenting (e.g., the environmental crisis and the danger of nuclear war). New religions arising within the context of the contemporary developed world whose sources of revelation are extraterrestrial spontaneously take their space-age deities to be merely natural or immanent rather than supernatural or transcendent, precisely because they exist within the horizon of our postmodern condition (i.e., within the horizon of the death of God).

Both the death of God and postmodernity are admittedly ambivalent notions. The idea of the death of God as a traditionally defined metanarrative is one of the most important manifestations of the postmodern condition. Philosophically, the postmodern condition has been articulated as an "incredulity toward metanarratives" (overarching, universal explanations, e.g., the Christian eschatological version of human history)[1] or the death of the Cartesian subject as the epistemological and metaphysical foundation of the modern, scientific worldview (Gadamer 1981).[2] The death of God more generally signifies the replacement of a theological interpretation of the world by a natural scientific interpretation. The death of God is, then, the withdrawal or dispersion or disappearance of the metaphysical, the supernatural, or the supersensuous world upon which hitherto the sensuous, natural, physical world relied for its substance, meaning, and value (Heidegger 1977). Contemporary science and technology do not need to include God, the Absolute, or Being in their theories, measurements, calculations, or planning; the discourse of science and technology that dominates our practical affairs holds the ideas of God, the Absolute, and Being as being of no account. The social effects of this change in dominant worldviews are well-known. Existing religions have been increasingly required to justify themselves against the theoretical and practical worlds articulated and con-

1. James A. Aho's analysis (1997) of the postmodern condition is both more sociologically oriented and pointed than Jean-François Lyotard's now-classic presentation (1987), though certainly consistent with the latter's basic thesis. Likewise, Martin Heidegger's characterization of the metanarrative as place-holder for God is both relatively early and germane: "Into the position of the vanished authority of God and of the teaching office of the Church steps the authority of conscience, obtrudes the authority of reason. Against these the social instinct rises up. The flight from the world into the suprasensory is replaced by historical progress. The otherworldly goal of everlasting bliss is transformed into the earthly happiness of the greatest number. The careful maintenance of the cult of religion is relaxed through enthusiasm for the creating of a culture or the spreading of civilization. Creativity, previously the unique property of the biblical god, becomes the distinctive mark of human activity. Human creativity finally passes over into business enterprise" (1977, 64).

2. The philosopher Hans-Georg Gadamer succinctly articulates this version: "Self-understanding can no longer be integrally related to a complete self-transparency in the sense of a full self-presence of ourselves to ourselves. Self-understanding is always on-the-way; it is on a path whose completion is a clear impossibility. If there is an entire dimension of unilluminated unconscious; if all our actions, wishes, drives, decisions, and models of conduct (and so the totality of our human social existence) are based on the obscure and veiled dimension of the connotations of our animality, if all our conscious representations can be masks, pretexts, under which our vital energy or our social interests pursue their own goals in an unconscious way; if all the insights we have, as obvious and self-evident as they may be, are threatened by such doubt; then self-understanding cannot designate patent self-transparency of our human existence. We have to repudiate the illusion of completely illuminating the darkness of our motivations and tendencies" (1981, 103–4).

structed during the Scientific and Industrial Revolutions, and they have often fought a losing battle in their efforts to do so, as the nature of the reality described by science has changed with each new discovery. Today secular consciousness understands Earth to be but one planet orbiting one of billions of stars, it and its sun billions of years old, this planet the home of *Homo sapiens,* only one of millions of species, each of which but a momentary genetic variation proper to the momentary environment within which it lives.

NRMs Within the Horizon of the Death of God

Some new religious movements arising within the context of the disappearance of the supersensuous world tend to articulate themselves, often with a popular fluency, in the discourses of the natural sciences and seek to justify their beliefs by means of para- or pseudoscientific investigation or argument. For example, in 1915 Sir Oliver Lodge dedicated *The Survival of Man* (a work on life after death) to "the founders of the Society for Psychical Research, the truest and most patient workers in an unpopular region of science."[3] The society's research attempted to reinvent, transform, or translate beliefs about the unseen or invisible world into the discourse (and truth conditions) of the natural sciences.

As J. Gordon Melton (1995) observes, since 1750, many of those who claim contact with otherworldly beings articulate themselves relative to the scientific discourse of the day. Something new has appeared in the past five hundred years to which religions old and new have felt required to react either by attacking or by conversing. Simply put, the present takes as a given the scientific worldview; so, new religious intuitions that seek to articulate themselves often take for granted the truth of that worldview and seek to harmonize it with their religious sentiments. Thus NRMs whose theology is centered around otherworldly beings paradoxically attempt to articulate a religious worldview within a purely immanent horizon wherein the gods no longer hail from a region outside of space and time (i.e., outside nature) but rather from some distant planet, star, or other universe (i.e., another spatiotemporal-temporal dimension).

Although these gods are no longer supernatural in the traditional sense of the word, they possess technology a premodern mind could interpret only as miraculous. However, since these beings must exist within the laws of nature that the natu-

---

3. This quotation occurs on an unnumbered page of Lodge (1915). The book, *The Survival of Man*, was first published in 1909.

ral sciences articulate and that technology exploits, their technical prowess appears paranormal, yet-to-be-understood by science. The technology of the flying saucer is miraculous in the sense that it transcends not the laws of nature but only our present ("primitive") understanding of these laws. John A. Saliba's solid and comprehensive study (1995) confirms this collapsing of the miraculous into the supertechnological, especially in the case of Christian interpretations of UFO phenomena. These two ideas—that in time our science will come to understand paranormal phenomena (and thereby acquire new technologies of paranormal power) and that the ufonauts are technologically and spiritually more advanced or superior to us—orbit an affirmation of science and technology that takes them to be natural to all forms of intelligent life, on and off the earth, thereby ideologizing the developed world's dominant cultural practice.

Furthermore, these two absolutely contingent (and perhaps profoundly short-lived) cultural accidents (i.e., science and technology) are understood not only as natural but as progressing or evolving. Alongside or bound up with this assumption of science as a naturally evolving universal tendency of life is the belief that the way out of the profound problems industrialization has presented is technological ingenuity itself. Indeed, the argument often offered for funding a search for extraterrestrial intelligence (well-known by its acronym, SETI) is that any race advanced enough for interstellar communication will have undergone the crises we ourselves presently face and, therefore, may share their solutions to our most pressing ecological problems. Thus, an optimism is part and parcel of the mere appearance of flying saucers as extraterrestrial spaceships (whether "nuts-and-bolts" or of a "higher etheric vibratory plane") and of the revelations and admonitions of their pilots.

Within the context of the developed world, whose development is taken as the product of a natural tendency of intelligence, the flying saucer appears as both a critique of the present (as existing at and thereby showing the limits of a particular viewpoint) and the transcendence of it (expressing the present's ultimate and assured goal). Those NRMs for which the UFO is such a vehicle of enlightenment occur not only within the postmodern horizon of the death of God, but, more narrowly, within that of the UFO phenomenon as such. More specifically, their membership affirms what is called the extraterrestrial hypothesis (ETH) in some ufological circles, which proposes that "real" UFOs (i.e., those that are not misidentifications or hallucinations) are spaceships manufactured and piloted by intelligent, extraterrestrial creatures. Some proponents are "contactees" who claim to have had communication, whether face-to-face or telepathic, with the ufonauts and to have received from them religious messages or missions. Around some of these contactees, new religions have formed, such as George King's Aetherius Society (Wallis 1974), Ernest and Ruth Norman's Unarius (Tumminia 1998, 2005), Human Individual Metamorphosis (later known as Heaven's Gate) led by Marshall Herff Applewhite and Bonnie Lu Nettles (Balch 1995), and many others (Lewis 2000, 2003a; Partridge 2003). The Raëlians (Palmer 2004) are the most prominent of all these groups. It must be noted that some contactee religions and groups do dispense with the iconic saucer, corporeal extraterrestrials, and any claims of scientific legitimacy, but they still depart from the older metanarratives of God and science by communicating with holographic and interdimensional aliens.

The International Raëlian Movement: Introduction and History

Although a passing familiarity with the discourses of UFO religions suggests they all address the same family of concerns, each has evolved its own answers and solutions. Those of Raël are strikingly original. They offer, on the one hand, a critical view of society, politics, morals, and the environment, while, on the other hand, outlining an optimistic vision of the transcendence of these quandaries. Raël's creative theology corresponds closely to the characteristics noted by Jung in his study of the psychological significance of the flying saucer, characteristics that Jung felt accounted for our deep fascination with this phenomenon. Raël addresses the profound trepidation evoked by the threat of a global nuclear holocaust by criticizing our aggressive abuse of the fruits of science and technology and by encouraging our corresponding aspirations to become equal to our creators, who are "25,000 years ahead of us."

The "truth" communicated to Raël by his extraterrestrial teachers is essentially an interpretation of the Bible analogous to that of proponents of the ancient-astronaut hypothesis. Saliba sums up the ancient-astronaut biblical hermeneutic as follows:

> God becomes an astronaut, a superior being who lives in a more advanced civilization in some other faraway galaxy. Divine revelations are nothing but teachings from space creatures and miracles are awesome interventions by intelligences who are technologically superior to the human race. The supernatural, in this view, is reduced to the super-technological. God is a superior humanoid creature living on another planet. He has made himself immortal through technology and has created the human race. (1995, 34)

This view (always marked by reading Ezekiel's vision as a UFO sighting report) has found popular expression for some decades now. The year 1968 is a watershed for the widespread paperback publication of this genre of ufological literature: Erich von Däniken's first two books, published in German; in England, W. Raymond Drake's theosophically inclined *Gods and Spacemen in the Ancient East;* in America, Otto Binder's *Unsolved Mysteries of the Past;* and, most significantly, Jean Sendy's quasi-cabalistic *La lune: Clé de la Bible.* This last book, along with Sendy's two others, all published in French before 1970, essay an ancient-astronaut reading of Genesis and the Bible at points identical to Raël's. Similar views are expressed in Jacques Bergier's *Extraterrestrial Visitations from Prehistoric Times to the Present* and Serge Hutin's *Alien Races and Fantastic Civilizations,* both published in French in 1970. That views strikingly similar to Raël's precede the publication of his own does not necessarily entail any plagiarism on his part, but their presence and popularity certainly aids in understanding the appeal of Raël's overtly religious articulation of these views.

Raël's First Encounter and the Founding of MADECH

The story of the Raëlianism starts on December 13, 1973, in the Clermont-Ferrand region of France. In his first book, *The Book Which Tells the Truth,* published in French in 1974, Vorilhon tells how he witnessed a flying saucer land and then met its small, greenish, humanoid occupant, who identified himself as one of the Elohim of Genesis (Vorilhon 1986b).[4] Vorilhon boarded the flying saucer, where the extraterrestrial explained over the course of six days the "true" meaning of the Bible, the essence of which interpretation constitutes the majority of what is called the "Message."

Broadly, the Message is that all life on Earth is neither the end-product of divine creation nor that of continuing evolution, but the creation of extraterrestrial biotechnologists who made all life "from scratch" by means of their complete knowledge of DNA and their ability to synthesize and manipulate it. *Homo sapiens* is "created in their own image." The Elohim's revelation is, essentially, a reading of the Bible as the story of an extraterrestrial biotechnological research project, whose

---

4. Raël's first book in translation is the first half of Claude Vorilhon's *The Message Given to Me by Extra-Terrestrials: They Took Me to Their Planet* (1986b). *The Book Which Tells the Truth* is also part of *The True Face of God.*

drama bears a curious resemblance to present-day research and debate. The reason the Elohim created life on Earth is that the population of their own planet feared the consequences of experiments in biotechnology and the creation of artificial life forms. The Elohim scientists were required to remove their research to a distant planet for safety's sake (Vorilhon 1986b, 14). Their creation of creatures in their own image, as well as their revealing to their creations their true artificial nature (and thereby the newly made human beings' power to create new life, in turn, by technological means), were both surreptitious and illegal acts, whose consequences were the expulsion from Eden and the Flood, for example, the termination of the experiment and the sterilization of laboratory Earth.

In this reading of Genesis, Yahweh becomes the leader of the scientists who created all life on Earth; the Serpent, those Elohim who gave to humankind the knowledge of good and evil, that is, the awareness of their being artificial life forms; and Satan, the leader of the faction on the Elohim's home planet critical of the scientists' research and its results (Vorilhon 1986b, 20–30). That this scenario bears on present anxieties concerning biotechnology needs little explanation. In fact, the Raëlian Movement pointed to the world-famous cloning of Dolly as confirmation of the Elohim's revelations, that is, that humanity is attaining a level of technology already reached by the Elohim in Earth's distant past.

The Message given to Vorilhon by his extraterrestrial teacher comprises not only this ancient-astronaut interpretation of the Bible, but also a set of "New Commandments." With this prescriptive portion of the Message, Vorilhon received his new, charismatic name, Raël, meaning Light, Light of God, Ambassador of the Elohim, and messenger (Vorilhon 1986b, 105–6). Raël is told to promote world government by "the most intelligent," a system called geniocracy (109). This one-world government also includes the institution of a single, worldwide currency and an international, artificial language (113). In addition to the global unification of currencies, the Elohim's prescribed economic reforms also include an economic system they call "Humanitarianism," based primarily upon the abolition of inheritance (111). The condition for this one-world economy and government is the elimination of military conscription (114).

Raël is then given the mission to spread the message of humankind's true origins and destiny and to build an embassy "on neutral territory" where the Elohim will land and meet the representatives of all nations if a sufficient number of human beings come to believe in them and humanity abandons its warlike ways (Vorilhon 1986b, 115–17). In this case, the Elohim will share their advanced scientific knowledge with humanity, ushering in a "Golden Age" of peace and prosperity. The practical implementation of the Message began with the founding of MADECH (Mouvement pour Accueil des Elohim Createurs de l'Humanité) in 1974 and the publication of Raël's first book. MADECH became the Raëlian Movement International between 1975 and 1995. In 1995, it sought recognition as an official church and became known as the Raëlian Religion in Canada. It now calls itself the International Raëlian Movement or Raëlian Revolution.

Raël's Second Encounter

Raël's second alleged close encounter, on October 7, 1975, is recounted in his next book, published in French the same year, *Les extra-terrestres m'ont emmené sur leur planète (Extraterrestrials Took Me to Their Planet).* As the title attests, this book recounts a twenty-four-hour visit to a paradisal planet "relatively close to the Earth," where Raël is further enlightened as to the nature of humankind and its creators (Vorilhon 1986b). His Elohim teacher now identifies himself as Yahweh, "president of the council of eternals." Raël is introduced to Jesus, Moses, Elijah, Buddha, and Muhammed, now immortal by means of serial cloning. Not only does a 700-member Elohim council of eternals inhabit the planet, but so also do 8,400 "people from Earth . . . who, during their lives, reached a sufficient level of open-mindedness on the infinite, or who enabled humanity to progress from its primitive level by their discoveries, their writings, their way of organizing society, their exemplary acts of fraternity, of love or of unselfishness" (197).

Raël is shown the machine that instantaneously manufactures the clones whereby the Elohim and deserving human beings maintain their immortality. A temporary clone of Raël himself is produced from a cell sample taken from between his eyes. Not only are the deserving rewarded with immortality by means of cloning, but "[a]ll those on Earth who preached violence, wickedness, aggressiveness, and obscurantism . . . will be re-created to undergo the punishment which they deserve after being judged by those whom they made suffer or by their ancestors or descendants" (Vorilhon 1986b, 205). This technology, together with extensive automatization, accomplishes "all the dirty work [and] all the work that is uninteresting [i.e.,] all the maintenance work" by means of "biological robots" (198). Not only do these robots perform all the onerous and tiresome labor, but they also provide erotic pleasure, as six female robots, one of each human race, demonstrate during Raël's first and only night on the Elohim's planet (206–8).

Later, back on Earth, Raël is telepathically given supplementary commandments and sixteen "Keys" that highlight and expand the original message. Humanitarianism and geniocracy are reaffirmed and explained in greater detail. "The transmission of the cellular plan" is introduced, whereby a Raëlian's genetic code is transmitted to the Elohim and a square centimeter of bone tissue from between the eyes is secured to facilitate being cloned on the planet of eternals after death. A system of tithing is advocated, to help Raël, "the Guide of Guides . . . devote himself full time to his mission" (Vorilhon 1986b, 215). A relatively detailed code of behavior is presented, covering diet (e.g., prohibiting stimulants and recreational drugs), sexual behavior, child rearing and education, and meditative practices.

Schism, Consolidation, and the New Raëlians

In 1975, the Raëlian Movement International emerged out of a schism within MADECH. The membership of the new movement was divided into two levels: the more committed "Guides" who composed the "Structure" and the more loosely affiliated "Raëlians" who received the group's bulletin, titled "Apocalypse." This restructuring and concomitant articulation of social and ethical values combined to create a relatively stable structure of organization and beliefs, which continues to this day. Following this consolidation, Raël was to devote an entire volume to his teachers' political philosophy (Vorilhon 1977), as well as to the practice of "sensual meditation," by which the practitioner aims at attaining telepathic communication with the Elohim, activates his or her psychic potential, and grows new neural pathways (Vorilhon 1986c).

In 1979, Raël published *Accueillir les extra-terrestres*, later translated and published in English as *Let's Welcome Our Fathers from Space: They Created Humanity in Their Laboratories* (Vorilhon 1986a), wherein his charismatic claims are intensified. It is revealed to him that the Eloha Yahweh is his father and Jesus his half-brother; he is the "last of forty prophets" being born in "the Age of Apocalypse" (the era following the detonation of the first atomic bomb, the discovery of DNA, and the revelation of humankind's true nature through Raël by the Elohim). Despite these intensifications, this latter book is essentially a reformulation and repetition of earlier material. Although there have been some additions to the Message since the mid-1980s, none are so radical as to alter substantially the basic character of the religion. Indeed, the development of and the debate around biotechnology, and the popularization of the idea of "terraforming" serve—admittedly, to a limited extent—to harmonize the religion's concerns with more mainstream society.

Today, the Message continues to be evangelized, according to annual instructions Raël receives telepathically from the Eloha Yahweh, his father. These instruc-

4.1. The founder of the International Raëlian Movement, Raël, was born Claude Vorilhon in France. Courtesy of the International Raëlian Movement.

tions name a particular nation which is to be the special focus of the movement for that coming year. The Movement's own version of its history is organized according to year and country in this way. Furthermore, in 1985 the Movement instituted Planetary Week, to be held commencing each April 5, focused around a different theme each year. Each national branch of the religion is encouraged to hold a conference to publicize the Message. To court the press, often an outrageous or controversial act is performed. Actions considered outrageous by more mainstream society are not restricted to the branches' conferences. As the *Toronto Star* reported on November 11, 1992, the Raëlians distributed 10,000 condoms to Roman

Catholic high school students in Montreal, Canada, putatively to protest the Montreal Catholic School Commission's decision against installing condom dispensers in its high schools.

Consistent with the goal of one world government and planetary political unity is the Movement's advocacy of racial integration—not through intermarriage and procreation, but through interracial sexual relationships. In photographs, Raël is sometimes depicted as surrounded by a racially mixed circle of bikini-clad young women, reminiscent of promotional photographs for a Miss World Beauty Pageant (Palmer 1995). To attract more interest in their cause, the religion also opened UFO Land in 1997 near Valcourt, Quebec, a theme park presenting the Message by means of multimedia displays. In another provocative move, the religion organized a bilingual "conference-debate" entitled "Yes to Human Cloning" in Montreal on June 18, 1999.[5]

Beliefs, Values, and Politics

Beliefs

From its inception, Raëlianism rigorously excised all residue of the transcendent in its rereading of the Bible according to its own version of the ancient-astronaut hypothesis. Cosmologically, any supernatural realm where a First Cause, for life or the cosmos, might reside is excluded by positing an infinite regression of causes in answer to the question, "Why is there something rather than nothing?" The cosmos extends infinitely into the past and future (Vorilhon 1986a, 52). Likewise, the material (i.e., atomic) order extends into the infinitely small and large. The atom is depicted as a microcosmic solar system; the solar system, a macrocosmic atom, and so on. As Raël explains it:

> Once we have attained sufficient open-mindedness we can understand that in space the Earth is but a particle of the atom of the atoms of the hand of a gigantic being, who himself contemplates a starlit sky which composes the hand, the stomach or the foot of a being even more gigantic, who finds himself under a sky, etc., etc. and this ad infinitum. The same process applies for the infinitely small. On the atom of the atoms of our hands, there exist intelligent beings for whom these par-

5. Source is the Web site: http://www.netside.net/~valiant/PRO61499.html.

ticles are planets and stars, and these beings are composed of atoms of which the particles are the stars and the planets on which there are intelligent beings, etc., etc . . . also to Infinity. (1986a, 52)

It is no exaggeration, then, to characterize the Raëlian cosmology as being one of absolute immanence. That this immanence is, furthermore, exclusively material is reinforced not only by the identical atomistic structures of the micro- and macro-cosmos ("as above, so below" in Raëlian terms), but by the derision terms like "im-material" or "impalpable" receive, especially when predicated of more orthodox depictions of God. Already, in his first book, Raël's Elohim teacher speaks in a man-ner that echoes the more popular understanding of the death of God: "In scientifi-cally developed countries . . . [n]o one can believe any longer in a 'heavenly God' with a white beard, perched upon a cloud, omniscient and omnipotent, which is what the Church wants us to believe in. Neither can they believe in delightful little guardian angels, nor in a devil with horns and hooves" (Vorilhon 1986b, 90).

In its views concerning the origins of humanity, the Raëlian Movement is no less consistent in its insistent monistic materialism. Where almost all other propo-nents of the ancient-astronaut biblical hermeneutic interpret *Homo sapiens* to be a hybrid of "those who come from the heavens" (in Genesis, "Sons of God") and protohuman females ("Daughters of Men," Genesis 6:2), Raël is more radical: his Elohim reveal that humankind is literally made in their image by means of biotech-nology. Indeed, the Elohim are responsible for all life on Earth. Furthermore, Raël explains in a section of his *Let's Welcome Our Fathers from Space: They Created Hu-manity in Their Laboratories* entitled "Questions Which Are Most Often Asked" that the Elohim in turn are themselves the creation of another, superior race, who in turn are themselves created in the same manner (Vorilhon 1986a, 53). This regress of artifice, Raël is told, is infinite: there is no original life whose source is evolution or some supernatural Creator.

Evolution is refuted by the Elohim on the grounds that chance mutation cou-pled to natural selection is incapable of developing higher organisms. As Raël writes:

As Einstein said, there cannot be a watch without a watch-maker. All those people who believe that we come from the monkey through a slow evolutionary process, believe that the beautiful watch which we are, has built itself, by accident. It is a bit like saying that if we put all the components of a watch together in a bag and shook it around for a while, we would eventually get a perfect working watch. (Vorilhon 1986a, 88)

Raëlianism's thoroughgoing atomistic materialism erases not only the distinction between God and Nature but between soul and body; just as there is only material nature, so there is only a physical body. Nonetheless, the traditional promise of immortality for true believers is maintained, as remarked above: immortality by means of cloning. The initiatory rite of the Raëlian Movement is the "transmission of the cellular plan," whereby a new member's genetic code is telepathically transmitted to the Elohim by a Guide, insuring the practicing member's re-creation after death on the planet of eternals, as well as formalizing that member's recognition of the Elohim as his or her creator.

Furthermore, the new member is encouraged to sign a contract permitting a mortician, upon the member's demise, to excise one square centimeter of the "frontal bone" (near the pineal gland or "third eye"), which is then sent to a bank in Geneva, Switzerland, to be stored, awaiting collection by the Elohim. According to Raël:

> The cellular plan, or genetic code, of each individual, is registered in an enormous computer which records all our actions during our life, from the time of our conception, from the meeting of the ovule and the spermatozoon, the moment when a new genetic code is registered, hence, a new individual. The individual will be followed through his lifetime, and at the end of his life, the computer will know if he has the right to eternal life on the planet where the Elohim accept in their midst, only the most worthy of men and women. (Vorilhon 1986a, 29–30)

This characterization of human beings as "nothing more than self-programming, self-reproducing biological computors [sic]" (Vorilhon 1986a, 74) grounds the Raëlian promise of immortality for the deserving. In the Raëlian view, the person is identical to his or her genetic code. During his first encounter, Raël's Elohim teacher explained the means by which an individual gains immortality technologically:

> When we are in full possession of our abilities and our brain is at its maximum efficiency and knowledge, we surgically remove a tiny part of the body which is conserved. When we die, from a minute particle of our body which had already been

preserved, we fully re-create the body, as it was at that time. I say as it was at that time, meaning with all its scientific knowledge, and of course, its personality. (Vorilhon 1986b, 124)

This version of the serial re-creation of the individual is later modified (Vorilhon 1986a, 31): an actual, physical particle is not necessary, as "the enormous computer which records all our actions" also records our genetic codes, whereby those deserving are "re-created young, with a body in full possession of its force and its resources." Where the Raëlian belief concerning immortality by means of cloning may well appear questionable to those familiar with the arguments of identity theory and functionalism in the philosophy of mind, there is no denying that a version of science and technology is being used here to articulate a new religious intuition in terms immediately familiar to a populace for whom news about biotechnology has become commonplace.

Values

Given the centrality of the technology of cloning to the Raëlian worldview, it comes as no surprise that they give their whole-hearted support to developments in biotechnology. The Raëlian Movement has come out explicitly in favor of genetically altered foods, vegetable and animal, on the grounds that since all living matter is originally artificial, the more genetically artificial an organism, the more "natural" it is (Raëlian Church 2004). The Raëlian support for the development of cloning technology, on the other hand, has been more than merely rhetorical. In a press conference held March 11, 1997, in the Las Vegas Flamingo Hilton, Raël announced he had created Valiant Venture Limited with a group of investors, offering "Clonaid" for parents wishing to clone, rather than procreate, a child—at a cost of $200,000. The venture also offers "Insuraclone" that for $50,000 will store a client's child's cells so the child may be cloned in the event of an untimely death. This company was founded in the Bahamas, where cloning is not illegal (Raëlian Church 2004).

Furthermore, on January 13, 1998, the group announced its support, moral and financial, for the research of Chicago-based scientist Dr. Richard Seed, who then claimed that he would clone a baby by mid-1999. Though no Raëlian himself, Dr. Seed's own words, as reported in an article in the *Ottawa Citizen* on January 11, 1998, express sentiments not dissimilar to Raël's: "Cloning and the reprogramming of DNA is the first serious step in becoming one with God."

That such activities have generated controversy is no surprise. The Bahamian government froze the assets of Valiant Venture. Dr. Brigitte Boisselier was fired from her position as director of a research project for a chemical company in Lyons, France, reportedly for speaking publicly in favor of cloning and for admitting to being a Raëlian on television. Dr. Boisselier has said, "Why do people always think about the bad things scientific advances can bring? Why not assume that people are good and will use this knowledge in a responsible way?"[6] Her optimism is matched by a kind of "happy positivism": she has remarked that what can be done, will be done, and that it is better to do it openly and legally so as to prevent exploitation. Such *amor fati* relative to technology is characteristically Raëlian. At the end of 2002, Dr. Boisselier announced the birth of the first cloned human, although Clonaid produced no tangible proof that the child was actually cloned.

The Raëlian enthusiasm for cloning is only one aspect of its general approval of all reproductive technology. The Raëlian affirmation of reproductive technologies finds its context in relation to the religion's approach to individual sexual behavior. Since "life was made to be enjoyed," heterosexual sex is to be emancipated by artificial means from procreation (Vorilhon 1986a, 61). The use of contraception, including abortion, is prescribed as a means to accomplish this emancipation, as well as a means to solve problems of overpopulation (Vorilhon 1986b, 121). All manner of polymorphous consensual sexual activity, hetero-, bi-, or homosexual, is likewise affirmed. Indeed, Clonaid explicitly offers its services to homosexual couples wanting children. Succinctly, as Raël himself phrases it in *Let's Welcome Our Fathers from Space:* "Each individual has the right to do with their body as he or she sees fit" (Vorilhon 1986a, 86).

The extreme value placed on sexuality is best exemplified by the practice of directed hedonistic sensuousness ("sensual meditation"), which is perceived as means to altered states of consciousness, mystical states of oneness with the universe, and telepathic communication with the Elohim. Sexual activity in particular and sensuality in general are said to produce brain cells and to improve neural links (Vorilhon 1986a, 61–70). As Raël writes in the "Keys," "The moment you approach closest to perfect harmony with infinity is when this takes place in your room of sensual meditation with someone you love, by physically uniting with him, and placing yourselves in harmony with infinity during your union" (Vorilhon 1986b, 263).

---

6. This quote is from a personal communication from Dr. Brigitte Boisselier.

Politics

Where the Raëlian approach to sexuality and reproduction would exploit and in-tensify the possibilities presented by recent biomedical developments and social changes, likewise the religion's social and political values affirm contemporary trends, namely global industrial and technological development. The Eloha Yahweh not only advocates universal automation of the means of production, but also goes as far as to criticize organized labor's resistance to it (Vorilhon 1986b, 190). As re-marked above, the social system that would manifest humankind's moral maturity is that of a one-world, geniocratic government, having one global currency and one global language, a vision consistent, in part, with recent world economic trends, for example the formation of the European Economic Union and its adoption of the Euro. Already in Raël's second book the Eloha Yahweh says, "Once the European military is unified, so can the European economy be by creating a single European currency" (Vorilhon 1986b, 184).

However, where recent history has proven amenable to the Raëlian valorization of development, it has been less so in regard to geniocracy. Despite writing a book-length manifesto and the subsequent founding of a short-lived political party, Raël writes in *Let's Welcome Our Fathers from Space:*

> political ideology does not weigh very much when compared to the Messages of the Elohim. . . . The priority of priorities is the building of the Embassy asked for by our Creators so that we can welcome them in the company of the ancient Messen-gers, Moses, Jesus, Buddha and Mohammed. This is my only reason for being on this Earth. This must become the only reason for living of all those people who wish to help me. (Vorilhon 1986a, 51)

The belief that the relative intelligence of a citizen is unproblematically deter-minable through "scientific" testing again highlights the religion's faith in the ab-solute truth available via the scientific method. Perhaps not unsurprisingly, the Raëlian Movement's political ideology has not escaped criticism, particularly in Eu-rope. Because of its overtly elitist dimensions, geniocracy was denounced as "fascist" by the Guyard Report (1996) on sects in France. In its own defense, the Raëlian Movement explicitly argues that it is neither a cult nor a sect (Raëlian Church 2004). Furthermore, in more recent articulations of its politics, Raëlianism has emphasized tolerance and human rights. That all religions ultimately spring from pretechnological humanity's misinterpretations of supertechnological phenomena is offered as grounds for religious, cultural, and racial pluralism (Raëlian Church 2004). Indeed, the Raëlian Movement has gone as far as to post the "United Nations Universal Declaration of Human Rights" on its Web site, stating that the Declaration

> is the text written by Man which applies the best to the Message transmitted by the Elohim. This charter which is already contained in the Message, invites the individual to adopt a panoramic, non-sectarian, and non-fanatic vision of our world. It brings him/her to naturally respect and better yet, to love eachother's [sic] differences. (Raëlian Church 2004)

The utopia to be brought about by the technological developments and social values the Raëlians so affirm is portrayed most concretely in Raël's description of his visit to the Elohim's planet of the eternals. The lifestyle on the Elohim's planet and in the Golden Age promised by technology is characterized as one of material ease provided, imaginably, by sufficient means of production, supplied by automated mechanical means and a workforce of "biological robots," artificial human beings identical to ourselves in every way except their intellect, which is designed solely for a single practical purpose. Automation and mechanization are explicitly advocated by the Eloha Yahweh; he explains to Raël that:

> [y]ou could very soon live in a genuine terrestrial paradise if only the technology which you have was actually put into service for the well-being of people instead of serving violence, the army, or the personal profit of a few. Science and technology can totally liberate humanity not only from the anxiety of hunger in the world, but also from the obligation to work to live. Thanks to automation, machines can quite easily look after the daily chores. Already, in some of your most modern factories, only one person is needed now to simply oversee a computer which commands and carries out all the operations for the building of a car for which not so long ago several hundred people were needed. In the future, even that one person will be unnecessary. (Vorilhon 1986b, 190)

According to the teachings of the group, the "biological robots" who constitute the labor force of this "terrestrial paradise" are:

> created in the same way we [the Elohim] created people on Earth, in a one hundred percent scientific way, but they are voluntarily limited and absolutely submissive to

us. They are also incapable of acting without any order, and are very specialized. They don't have any aspirations of their own, and have no pleasure, except the ones that their specialization requires. They grow old and die like us but the machine which makes them can make far more than we really need. Besides, they are incapable of suffering, of feelings and cannot reproduce themselves. Their life span is similar to ours, that is to say, with the help of a small surgical intervention, about seven hundred years. When one of them must be destroyed because of old age, the machine which created them produces one or several others depending on our needs. They come out of the machine ready for functioning and with their normal height for they have neither growth nor childhood. They know how to do only one thing, to obey people and Elohim and are incapable of the slightest violence. (Vorilhon 1986b, 198)

One is reminded of the eugenic social engineering in Huxley's *Brave New World,* where artificially inseminated ova are altered in utero to the minimal physical and mental demands of their future careers. This life of ease, security, and pleasure (by means of plentiful and readily available sex "robots") can be enjoyed endlessly, by means of immortality through cloning.

Despite—or perhaps because of—the intense value Raëlians place on science and technology, their belief that all life is synthetic inspires an admiration and respect for living organisms. The variety of plant and animal life on Earth is attributed to the artistic faculties of the Elohim biotechnologists. The beauty and variety of nature is held forth not only for appreciation, but also as further evidence against evolution:

You yourself could have realized that an accidental evolution would have little chance of producing such a large variety of forms of life, of colors of birds and their amorous demonstrations, of the shape of the horns of certain antelope. . . . The evolution of the forms of life on Earth is the evolution of the techniques of creation and the sophistication of the brilliant work realized by the creators which led eventually to the creation of people similar to them. (Vorilhon 1986b, 103–4)

In fact, the Raëlian Genesis states that teams of scientists held competitions over whose creations were most beautiful. Each race is said to have been the creation of one particular team, each in one location on Earth's protocontinent, Gondwanaland. Accordingly, the Raëlians have cultivated an appreciation for the beauty of nature; the awe they express over nature's wonders, in their videos and other media, is, however, not that of the Romantic before the Sublime, but that of an appreciator of an artist's abilities. As Raël writes: "Respect nature for as long as you are not capable of re-creating it, and for as long as you are not capable of becoming a creator yourself. By respecting nature, you respect those who created it, our parents, the Elohim" (Vorilhon 1986b, 244).

Interestingly, this conception of organic life as an artificial creation grounds an empathy for all organisms, vegetable and animal, while not leading to the extremes of biocentricism. As Raël indicates:

> Never make animals suffer. You may kill them to feed on their flesh but without making them suffer. For although death is nothing, suffering is an abomination and you must avoid animals suffering as you must prevent human beings from suffering. . . . Plants, too, are alive and suffer in the same way as you do. So do not cause plants to suffer. They are alive just as you are. (Vorilhon 1986a, 244)

This approach to nature and the advocacy of the use of reproductive technology are the religion's primary points of engagement with ecological concerns.

Conclusion

The thoroughgoing centrality of "science" is the feature of the Raëlian worldview that most marks it as the kind of NRM characterized in this study. The Raëlian "demythologization" of the Bible is simultaneously a mythologization or mystification of science. Indeed, Raël echoes Sir Oliver Lodge: "Science should be your religion for the Elohim your creators created you scientifically" (Vorilhon 1986b, 255). Not only should science replace religion, but being scientific is claimed to be the very essence of being human; as the Eloha Yahweh says during Raël's first encounter: "Humanity's objective is scientific progress" (Vorilhon 1986b, 27). Not only is scientific progress the objective of humanity but of all intelligent, humanoid races. Although the Elohim cannot travel in time or foresee the future, they explain that just as the life cycle of a biological organism can be studied, known, and predicted, the same is true for the technological and moral development of any society of intelligent beings (Vorilhon 1986a, 118).

Within this Raëlian view, technological societies experience either a harmony or a disharmony of technological and moral development. In the latter case, the society self-destructs, as our own threatens to do. However, should the society mature morally, its use of technology results in a Golden Age where the problems development and industrialization engender, such as pollution, overpopulation, hunger, and the energy crisis, are themselves solved by "the wise use of science." This reification of science and technology (hardly restricted to the Raëlian Movement) grounds the sense of the claim that the Elohim are "25,000 years ahead" of humanity's present scientific and technological development. Science and technology are repeatedly characterized as a natural pursuit of intelligent beings. In this way, a social and cultural phenomenon is portrayed as if it were natural, necessary, uniform, and universal, and thus, the phenomenon is ideologized.

Despite being primarily a transformation of the Bible, Raëlianism appears more immediately relevant to our most urgent concerns. While religions originating before the Scientific and Industrial Revolutions have sought ways to accommodate to a changing environment and to answer new concerns, the Raëlian Movement might be said to be inspired precisely by the selfsame issues that characterize the present moment in world history. The Raëlian view then affirms existing, traditional theological structures (e.g., the narrative of Genesis), while performing a kind of Hegelian *Aufhebung* (sublation) identical in its logic to that performed on the notion of technology itself by the class of NRMs here studied.

In summary, the advent of the Scientific and Industrial Revolutions usher in today's dominant discourse and practices within which religions orthodox and otherwise must define themselves. The present stands within the horizon of the death of God, understood as the domination of the assumption of the immanence of the world and the consequent disappearance of the metaphysical, the supernatural, and the supersensuous (at least overtly) or their fall into the merely paranormal. The paranormal or paraphysical is that realm of nature yet to be understood (and so ultimately controlled) by science. This assumption that science will continue along the path of discovery, knowledge, and power naturalizes or ideologizes science and technology. When our science and technology poison the biosphere, split the atom to release potentially species-suicidal energies and manipulate the genetic code of living organisms, humanity has taken upon itself powers and potentialities hitherto exclusively the domain of superhuman deities. That science and technology, whose worldview determines how things are, bring us to an unprecedented impasse demands that they must in some way be transcended (i.e., survived). The flying saucer appears within this horizon as a symbol of just such transcendence, promising that precisely the causes of our quandary will be our means of salvation.

In the Dreamtime of the Saucer People

Sense-Making and Interpretive
Boundaries in a Contactee Group

Diana G. Tumminia

Ethnographers expect to encounter new meaning systems, especially when they analyze groups with highly spiritualized understandings of the world. However, few worldviews evoke such deep incredulity as psychic contact with extraterrestrials and the claim that this contact is a legitimate scientific enterprise. The research on contactees (those who telepathically communicate with space aliens) mixed with the studies of religiously oriented flying-saucer groups decades ago (Festinger, Riecken, and Schachter 1956; Buckner 1968; Wallis 1974; Stupple and Dashti 1977). However, most older studies concentrate on the marginality of these belief systems (Wallis 1979; Bartholomew, Basterfield, and Howard 1991; Spanos et al. 1993; Newman and Baumeister 1998), while fewer concentrate on the social-psychological processes of belief itself (Festinger, Riecken, and Schachter 1956; Tumminia 2005).

This ethnographic study discusses the interpretive world of the contactee group Unarius Academy of Science. According to their distinctive logic, all events can be observed and explained through what Unarians call "the Science." The Science teaches that everything consists of energy attuned to harmonic frequencies, and that energy frequencies connect individuals to "memories" of past lives, other dimensions of existence, and prophetic visions. Sometimes called "fourth-dimensional physics" or "interdimensional physics," the Unarian Science explains the ways invisible dimensions guide members into uncovering the "truth" about their existence. The philosophy asks its students to channel messages from the infinite intelligence of Space Brothers and to heal themselves through the practice of past-life therapy. Some of the wisdom of their Science communicates through dreams.

Unarian accounts of the power of their Science sometimes resemble interpretations more akin to that of the Azande chicken oracle (Evans-Pritchard 1937; Mehan and Wood 1975; Pollner 1987) than those of modern science (Giere 1979).[1] To compare Unarius to the Azande does not imply a problem on the part of Unarians. Ethnomethodology views all social actors as *mundane reasoners* (social constructors with typified interpretive procedures), and ethnomethodology makes no distinction between rational and irrational methods of interpretation. Mundane reasoners are average people in the process of interpreting reality. Thus, rocket scientists, the Azande, and Unarians stand as equals in the social construction of reality, although each may have on the surface different styles of fact-finding.

As a referential framework, the Science operates as an incorrigible belief system full of paranormal claims and unfulfilled prophecies (Tumminia 1998). It does not matter that the outside world has a different version of credible science, because Unarians verify the power of the Science through a constant stream of evidence produced in their own way.[2] They gather facts from dreams, recovered memories of past lives, visions, bodily sensations, psychic readings, channelings, and other experiences of Space Brother contact. To Unarians, these common everyday experiences present incontrovertible proof of the authenticity of their brand of scientific logic, and they make up the daily topics of polite conversation within the group. By invok-

1. Pollner (1987) illustrates the idea of mundane reason with the example of the Azande poisoned chicken oracle (Evans-Pritchard 1937; Mehan and Wood 1975). The Azande (also written as Zande) are an African people of the Congo and Sudan who practice divination by giving a poison substance to a chicken. Sometimes the poison kills the chicken, indicating a particular answer to a question. In order to be sure of the answer, the Azande perform the process again in which case the chicken might live. Thus, the Azande face regularly face contradictions, but their cultural beliefs easily explain which answer is correct. Unarians do not kill chickens, but they look for signs of inspired wisdom in everyday objects or events. In this search for wisdom, they sometimes come up against contradictions.

2. The mere mention of science evokes cognitive territoriality. Interpretations of what is true science (Wallis 1979; Gieryn 1983; Giere 1979, 1988) and what is not science define credible academic work. Academic science preserves boundaries tied to notions of logic and empirical observation that exclude reasoning based on magic and faith. According to Thomas F. Gieryn (1983), science demands boundary work to maintain its public image, access to resources, and intellectual territory. Many social scientists would concede that science itself is socially constructed (Mulkay and Gilbert 1982; Gilbert and Mulkay 1984; Latour 1993, 1995). Academics defend their interpretive boundaries in order to function in their own domains. In this book, chapter 9 is about boundary work in the history of French ufology.

ing the reality of the Science, Unarians render their interpretations sensible and reasonable because they are based on their version of empirical observation.

From a phenomenological and ethnomethodological perspective, I examine the
interpretive boundaries between the Unarians and myself as we tried to make sense
out of each other's form of reasoning. I detail some of my encounters with the Unarian lifeworld and the times that their reality seeped into my own, causing me to employ my own explanations of the "truth" of their Science. I also recount the ways that
our divergent interpretations separated our experiences of the same phenomena.

Theories of Reality Interpretation

Clues to our interpretive processes are seen in the ways we talk when making sense
out of a taken-for-granted world we perceive to be intersubjectively shared (Mehan
and Wood 1975; Pollner 1987). Even sense-making activities that create a so-called
unreality (Pollner and McDonald-Wikler 1985) can be observed for procedures of
fact-finding and production of evidence that validate perception. Melvin Pollner
and Lynn McDonald-Wikler examine the case of a severely retarded child whose
parents insisted that their child was competent. In the face of extensive evidence to
the contrary, the parents developed explanatory practices to describe the child's behavior as normal, thus reinforcing the family's view of reality. The parents documented their reality by creating and describing their own facts to dispute the
assessments of others. They rationalized the contrasting views of outsiders by
claiming the child acted retarded in public, but not at home.

Many unconventional beliefs, some calling themselves scientific, draw strict
sense-making boundaries that are sustained even when those beliefs are subject
to disconfirmation. According to Berger (1967), spiritual beliefs retain credibility
through social networks, or plausibility structures, by employing narratives
conducive to upholding those beliefs despite competing information. Referring to
Peter L. Berger and Thomas Luckmann's work (1967), David A. Snow and Richard
Machalek argue that groups support their unusual beliefs utilizing plausibility
structures, or "interaction networks that are simultaneously based on and devoted
to sustaining those very ideas" (1982, 17). Snow and Machalek remind us that most
groups, whether conventional or deviant, rely on plausibility structures that invoke
the natural attitude as a means of self-validation. Even preposterous ideas resist disconfirmation within a group's internal unfalsifiable logic. According to Snow and
Machalek, undeniable disconfirming evidence "goes unnoticed by the believer"
(23).

In contrast, Pollner (1987) explains that mundane reasoners notice contradictory evidence, but they explain it away by pointing out errors others have made in their interpretation of the facts. Mundane reasoners (Tumminia 1998) also produce a host of "facts" from their worldview to counter empirical proof of the falsity of their beliefs. Incorrigible beliefs endure because facts are constantly found to support their credibility and because errors are identified in the ways that other people perceive disconfirming evidence.

Deviant or problematic events (Goffman 1974; Garfinkel 1967; Zaner 1970; Meisenhelder 1979), such as discordant encounters with members, generate brief moments of insight into the taken-for-granted reality of the ethnographer's world. Members of groups may repeatedly challenge an ethnographer's presumptions about reality with words and by involving the researcher in experiences that cannot be readily explained. In the field, the juxtaposition of contradictory worldviews between the ethnographer and the group member delineates their respective interpretive boundaries and is worthy of study in its own right (Mehan and Wood 1975; Wieder 1988; Bloor 1988; Rochford 1992; Pollner 1987). We can see in these borderlands of interpretation some of the presumptions each holds up as real.

In this study, I describe my own boundary recognitions of the questionable ways Unarians documented facts and produced evidence. I also recount the problematic separation I experienced between the ways Unarians framed the meaning of everyday events, especially dreams, and how that separation led me to reflect on our respective methods of reality construction.

Entry into the Field

From the perspective of fieldwork, ethnographers walk the line between the dynamics of inclusion and professional distance. Pollner and Emerson refer to the normal practices fieldworkers use to sustain the boundaries between the "observer and the observed" (1988, 237). Pollner and Emerson recognize that fieldworkers often serve as resources to the groups they study, potentially becoming workers, believers, and close confidants. As the researcher is drawn into activities, the presumption of staying a mere observer begins to fade. Ethnographers can retain their distance by asserting verbal and physical boundaries and by evading inclusion, although they run the risk of alienating their informants. Psychological engulfment remains another risk of immersion in the field. Will the group's reality bleed into the observer's reality? To some extent that is desired in order for the observer to understand the subjectivity presented, but ethnographers must mindfully negotiate such experiential understanding to preserve their epistemological borders.

Before I entered the field, I had anticipated some of challenges Pollner and Emerson (1988) write about; however, I did not know how deeply I would have to deal with these issues. Unarians accounted for anything by referencing its connection to the Science. The assumption of the all-pervasiveness of the Science shaped their sense-making as interpretive territory into which I could not deliberately cross given my role as a fieldworker. Without acknowledging the workings of the Science in every event whether I believed in it or not, I could not interact with them or make sense out of what they said to me. The implicit constant recognition of the action of the Science in everyday life cordoned off the limits of the Unarian lifeworld.

Unarius had a local reputation for being an eccentric group (Parfrey 1995) when R. George Kirkpatrick began the study in 1986 by constructing a questionnaire containing standard demographic and attitudinal inquiries. Unarians initially refused to answer the survey, saying that he was asking the wrong questions. As his assistant, I studied the group from my office by analyzing Unarian books and videos, and by talking to former members who defined Unarius as a "mind-control cult." Unarians eventually took the survey (Kirkpatrick and Tumminia 1989b), but they reported back to us that we were using the wrong methods of scientific investigation. They suggested that we learn the science of past-life therapy by attending their classes. From the beginning, Unarius framed all communications with us in terms of the virtues of their Science and the errors of our own.

From a distance, we knew that the core group of about forty members discussed the minutiae of their lives in the context of spiritual psychotherapy during weekly class sessions. Their therapy consisted of attending classes and receiving past-life readings. They sought the advice of their leader, Uriel the Archangel, and her assistant Antares (Kirkpatrick and Tumminia 1989a). We understood that Unarius functioned as a highly cohesive group for its most committed members. Yet students could come or go if they chose to do so, although the philosophy strongly reminded them that departure meant loss of redemption. In such a small committed group, any fieldworker would have to deal with the requirements for considerable compliance with their mystical worldview. Passing as a member could be problematic given that we did not know what that might actually entail or how far a participant would need to go given the group's reputation. I deemed that posing as member was unsuitable, because the Unarians already knew of our interest. I decided to gain entry as a known researcher in order to provide some official distance from the group

with which I could maintain a skeptical involvement. I clung to this identifiable borderland between us, while Unarians refused to recognize its existence.

In the winter of 1988, Dr. Kirkpatrick sent a letter asking permission for me to
interview Unarians and to attend meetings. When we received no response, we
made a field visit in January to talk with Antares, the coordinator of the center.
Antares welcomed me by giving me a local membership list with phone numbers.
He gave me permission to call anyone and to participate freely, although he took
me aside to caution me not to make the mistake that Dr. Kirkpatrick had made of
classifying Unarius as a religion. He repeatedly made it known to me that Unarius
was a science, not a religion. Because Unarians saw themselves as scientists, they
maintained an interpretive boundary against mysticism. I attended classes and
volunteered when I could. More or less, Unarian members came to view me as
part convert, part Unarian student, and part sociologist. As I visited them repeatedly from 1989 to 2002, I became more empathetic toward their struggle to rid
themselves and the universe of all perceived imperfections. Both of us found ways
to accept each other as long as I cooperated with the framework of Unarian
interpretation.

The key to my acceptance in the field was the patronage of Antares (also known
as Charles Spaegel or Vaughan or Louis Speigel), the director of the Unarius Academy of Science, who passed away in 1999. Under his watchful eye, I became such a
regular fixture that he consequently referred to me as the "resident sociologist."
Antares also treated me as a student of the Science, giving me several boxes of Unarian books and intermittent psychic readings when he thought I needed them. He instructed others to help me collect documents, and he allowed me to browse boxes of
unmarked photos. Antares encouraged me to communicate with their leader, Uriel,
and even to touch her hand during an auspicious event. He allowed me to volunteer
at the center, doing typing, sorting, and mailing, while I also attended classes in
past-life therapy with the other students. My continued relationship with Antares
was based on the singular interpretation that I was ignorant of the Unarian Science
and my past lives with Uriel. I knew as long as I reiterated that I wanted to learn
about the Science and I submitted to its authority, I would be allowed to interact
with the group. Most members ignored my presence, while others welcomed me by
volunteering to be interviewed. Even with Antares' approval, a few students could
barely tolerate me. But to the group's way of thinking, irritation was a clue that I "really" belonged there, because I was "triggering" a memory of a past-life interaction,
and such memories could also surface in dreams.

5.1. Unarius operates out of this building in El Cajon, California. Photograph by Diana Tumminia.

Initially some students befriended me out of their own inclinations, as well as their concern for my spiritual welfare. One student, Nina, gave me a free place to stay after I started to commute from Los Angeles. Antares encouraged me to stick with it, for he assessed my situation as one of divine unknowing. According to him, though I came in the guise of a researcher, I would soon learn that the Space Brothers sent me there to discover my past.

The World According to Unarius

Early in my fieldwork, I often sat at a table with Thomas, who would mind the reading room while he put together a mass mailing. Thomas inevitably opened his conversations with the latest headlines, inasmuch as they held clues to what was "really" happening in the world under the guidance of the Space Brothers. Seventy-year-old Thomas, who held a master's degree in music, served as musical director and official librarian. A student since 1975, Thomas believed he had reincarnated once as a librarian on the continent of Atlantis and then again had served in the fabled Alexandrian Library. In addition to his past lives, he disclosed much of his present life story to me.

His memories of his childhood included a strict, remote father and a significant dream about outer space in which two spiral galaxies rotated in opposite directions. This dream, in his opinion, pointed the way to Unarius. As an adult, he interpreted the dream image as the swirling positive and negative forces of the universe.

Thomas had studied theology at the Swedenborg seminary, which at the time was located across the street from Harvard University. He had enjoyed using the library at Harvard, where he became familiar with the work of Pitirim Sorokin, an early sociologist. In passing, Thomas mentioned Sorokin to show me he knew something about sociology. He added that Sorokin had surely been inspired by the Space Brothers, for he saw history occurring in cycles, the way Unarians did. He, like other Unarians, tried to convince me that enlightened sociology came from channeled messages from outer space.

Thomas's understanding of history and the daily headlines presented a study in contrasts for me. We shared marked interpretive boundaries. Whether they came from the tabloids or from legitimate news sources, headlines documented the work of the Science. At the university, my colleagues met the national news with skepticism, disgust, anger, and derision. Their skepticism usually followed charges of fraud, mismanagement, or international conspiracy. But at Unarius, Thomas embraced the same news as evidence that the promises of the Space Brothers were being fulfilled, or that Uriel was working on a spiritual dimension to bring about world peace and metaphysical change. Unarians saw the handiwork of the Brothers and the promise of the Science in every news story. During the months I occupied the reading room, Thomas credited the Brothers' guidance to Gorbachev's reforms in the former Soviet Union, the protests for democracy in Red China, and the success of the space shuttle program. He explained that some world leaders had come from other planets to shape world events for the better.

Thomas assured me that the recent discovery of nuclear fusion, or cold fusion as it is also known, would save the planet. Cold fusion, according to him, showed the action of the Brothers on the other side. At school, my colleagues expected that the cold fusion story would prove to be a hoax, because they were certain that only dishonest scientists could claim success from such experiments. However, from the Unarian point of view, this news signified the implementation of the Space Brothers' plan to bring free nonpolluting energy to planet Earth.

Thomas also followed "big news" from the tabloid press, where he had learned about the mystery "face" in the Cydonia region of Mars. Thomas told me a Russian space probe had taken photos of a human face, sculpted in surface rock. He said that the "face" bore the message, "Go back. Stay away." Thomas affirmed that this was a message from the Martian underground cities that had battled Earth in an ancient space war.

With a willingness to understand Unarian subjectivity tempered by skepticism, I attended classes on the history of the Martian wars. During these as well as other classes, a few members sometimes fell asleep. This was an accepted practice, because it was believed that students were attuning themselves to the elevated frequencies of the Brothers and that they might awaken with higher knowledge from a dream or a vision.

In the succeeding decade of fieldwork, I adapted to their way of interpreting news by anticipating that every news story would verify the work of the Space Brothers. In 2001, Unarians waited for the realization of their long-held prophecy, the arrival of a spaceship from the planet Muon followed by thirty-three other star-ships of the Interplanetary Confederation. When the events of September 11 tran-spired, I knew the underlying cause of the attack would be explained from their unique perspective. Unarians pointed out that the advent of the "Vehicles of Light" had precipitated the release of negativity, a condition that had been purportedly foretold many years ago. At the year's end, Unarians cited the warlike nature of the Earth world as the reason the spaceships did not land and why they would continue to remain invisible. In one class I attended, the lecturer explained that the Space Brothers would contact students in their dreams with instructions about what role they would play when a physical landing did take place.

To be part of Unarius, one must play the role of a student who reports the work-ing of the Science in dreams, memories, and other experiences. Antares served as my teacher. He pressed me to learn from his life and accumulated knowledge. Holding the second-highest status, next to Uriel the Archangel, Antares claimed he had been reincarnated from Satan, Tyrantus, Kaa (the space traveler), Ta-Nu of Lemuria, Pontius Pilate, Nero, Cardinal Richelieu, and Napoleon. Antares once told me how Uriel realized who he *really* was in a past life. When Uriel awoke from a nap one day, she reported what she had dreamed. She told Antares that he was indeed the Fallen Angel, Satan, who had come to her to redeem himself through the study of Unarius. In an interview, Antares recalled the incident to me, saying that he knew what Uriel said was true, because he felt his solar plexus spin with recognition. In all the subse-quent stories that emerged, Uriel cast Antares as her evil foil. About 1984, Uriel said that he had overcome all this negativity through the study of the Science, hence his name change to Antares.

How Past Lives Make Sense

Unarian sense-making involves finding "scientific" evidence of past lives. Past lives make sense because they account for present appearances, such as illness, emotions, or the content of social interaction. Unarians talk about their past-life revelations

5.2. Antares and Uriel. Uriel (Ruth Norman), the Archangel of the Unarius Academy of Science, gave Antares an award at a celebration in 1989. She led Unarius until her death in 1993, and Antares took over the position until he passed away in 1999. Courtesy of the Unarius Academy of Science.

with sincerity. Narratives remain tenuous for they are subject to group examination and criticism. Without verifications from others, particularly Antares and Uriel, members could not be sure their past-life memories were accurate. Others might counter their stories with contradictory memories or interpretations, but conflicting stories posed no problems for the students, who trusted that the truth would ultimately be revealed. Almost any story, like visions of dancing with snakes on Atlantis or dreams about a past life with Jesus, found recognition as long as the teller did not attack the veracity of the Science or the decisions of their leaders.

As I became a regular fixture at Unarius, people became as curious about my cosmic origins as I was about their social origins. In one of my first encounters with Antares, he told me how the students had lived many lifetimes before inhabiting their bodies here on Earth. In some of those lives, they had studied at "learning centers" on other planets and dimensions. Now they studied here at Unarius, once again absorbing the celestial science. Antares and the students intimated that I had been sent in this same manner, even though I did not consciously know it.

Until I walked into Unarius, I had no past lives. The more time I spent at Unarius, the more past lives would be attributed to me. In a phone conversation, Antares once told me I had been a handmaiden to the goddess Diana, and that I had lived in her temple. One afternoon as I attempted to write in my field notebook, Antares told me I had been a scribe on the planet Orion millions of years ago; then a few days later, he added that I had also been a spy there. The other students verified Antares' analysis, stating the facts as they saw them. They thought I had been a spy too, because I acted like one, always asking questions, collecting documents, and recording events. The facts were clear to them. When I volunteered to help Carol with some computer work, another student, Dave, coldly quipped, "You're letting her into the computer system now! She's a spy." Someone unfamiliar with the ways Unarians speak might have thought I was being labeled an outsider, but the insinuation meant that Dave was remembering an encounter with me in a past life. By being labeled a spy, I had been given an insider status, and to their way of thinking I had been offered an opportunity to clear the wrongs of a previous existence.

Unarians continued to include me in their world and to define me as a student, despite the appearance of my inability to work the Science. When I was asked if the Science had helped me, I said that I was not aware of how it did. When I was asked if I had discovered any of my past lives, I answered, "Antares said that I had a past life on Orion" (or whatever life he had related to me recently). I practiced the ethnographer's art of evading questions (Pollner and Emerson 1988), but I was perceived as ignorant because I did not elaborate on any recovered memories from past lives. Nor did I report the content of my dreams. Those who accepted me as a hanger-on resigned themselves to my ineptness. I volunteered little information about my own thoughts and feelings or any supposed past lives, a sign of an incompetent student of the Science. The perplexing riddle of my lack of advancement was solved when I attended an Interplanetary Confederation Day celebration. The parade leader asked me to carry the banner of the planet Valneza. Later Nina remarked, "Oh, that's why you don't understand the Science. You have a past life in Valneza, the planet of nature worshippers who don't have much development." My incompetence seemed logical and reasonable given this information provided by the Space Brothers.

Dreams and Sightings

In modern presuppositions of our commonly shared world, dreams have lost their validity as real.[3] This is not the case for Unarians. Unarians discuss dreams as part of

---

3. Many peoples embrace the reality of dreams. For example, the biblical story of Joseph tells how he interpreted a pharaoh's dreams as prophetic warnings. The Senoi of Malaysia view dreams as a way

the fact-finding process of the Science. Dreams hold great portent because members believe they travel out of their bodies while they sleep to visit other dimensions. By the same token, they believe that other spiritual dimensions visit them. They say they can receive enlightened messages from their teachers as they sleep, as well as re-solve the problems from past and present lives. Sharing the contents of dreams, both in everyday conversation and in formal testimonials, facilitates the use of this docu-mentary method of obtaining knowledge through the Science. Dream analysis of-fers a tangible way to use the Science. In the Unarian way of seeing things, dreams provide real contact with the Space Brothers.

In their method of uncovering reality, dreams explained illnesses. For instance, dreams of space travel accounted for one member's problem with osteoporosis. The dreams allowed a window into the member's past life in which she spent inordinate time aboard spaceships, depleting the health of her bones. Her past life actions caused her present-day condition. Another student dreamed about experimenting on other members during a past life as an evil scientist. This verified for her the karmic cause of her skin cancer.

Dreams often initiated major mythical revelations in the group. For example, what Unarians call the Great Lemurian Cycle was initiated by the student Crystal's dreams (Unarius Students and Norman 1976). During this cycle, students gave tes-timonials about their past lives on the planet Lemuria, where they were controlled by electronic surveillance, and they lived horrible lives as robot-like zombies. On the basis of their "memories" of this time, they acted in psychodramas that were video-taped "proof" of the power of Unarian Science. Spies infested all of Lemuria. From the perspective of the Science, the reason the Space Brothers had sent me to Unarius was to clear my Lemurian karma as the Unarian students were doing.

Students understood that their spiritual teacher, Uriel, could heal them in their dreams. The dreams contained evidence of her healing powers, as Melanie testified:

> She [Uriel] took me into the bedroom and sat me down. Two students were there with me, Decie and Loretta, and something I have realized, I have a lot of Atlantis karma with these two people. That is why they were there. Uriel said, "Now Melanie, I am going to remove an obsession from you, but I want you to tell me

---

that souls travel via out-of-body experiences and thus gain knowledge. They teach that people can ma-nipulate their dreams to some extent and face fearful dream situations. By doing so, they can overcome evil spirits or negative parts of themselves. They can also tap the dream state for creativity, knowledge, and blessings. Different cultures and groups ascribe different realities to dreams.

what kind of an obsession it is." She kind of waved her hand over me, and I remembered the dream the next day, but that was the end of what I remembered of that dream. So within a very, very short time after that dream, the last sign of my Herpes condition was totally gone. . . . These few dreams were most important to me, because I saw proof of Uriel in these dreams. (Uriel and Unarius Students 1988, 205)

For Unarians, dreams supply real connections with spaceships, especially those belonging to the Space Brothers. Over the years that I talked to students about their dreams, I learned that few students had ever seen a "real" spaceship, except in their dreams or psychic visions. Many students had seen lights in the sky, and they followed news reports of mysterious lights that hovered over distant places. Ernie, who had once been part of the One World Family Commune in the 1970s, remembered big blue balls floating off the cliffs of Big Sur as he drove one afternoon. Another student, Miriam, observed a "craft" as a small ball of white light outside her apartment one night. In addition to psychic and clairvoyant sightings, dreams opened the channels for what they perceived as real contact with the ships.

At one juncture, the academy's classes focused on dreams. During class, a certain student recalled a "healing dream" in which he saw himself sailing to an island to capture King Kong. On the island, he netted and caged two miniature Kongs. As he described it, the sight of the little monsters prompted a deep fear in him. Although he might be able to control the smaller ones, this student feared he would never be able to control the larger beast. He supposed his fear came from the "lower self" to thwart his spiritual progress. He believed he could master his lower nature, as long as he stayed on the positive path of life. His self-revelation brought about the landing of a shimmering spaceship, which invited him within. On board the starship, he found a beautiful woman who led him to a cleansing pool; he dove in to experience remarkable healing. In his dreams, he often saw the "Brothers" in the guise of beautiful women.

Lani worked out her misgivings about Unarius in a dream. She confided in me one day, saying that she had once entertained some doubts about the teachings. She felt that the prophecy of a space fleet landing was hard to believe, even secretly admitting that she really did not believe in the Space Brothers. Lani rescued herself from doubt by surrendering to the power of the Science, conceding that Uriel's knowledge must be much greater than her own. That night she dreamed a large spacecraft landed, which took her and her boyfriend aboard. In the dream Lani asked, "Can anyone see us?" "No," came a reply. "We are in another dimension." Lani asked why they had been taken aboard. The Space Brothers answered, "We know you need proof." Lani explained to me that this was a good example of how a student, who does not put limitations on herself, can open up to higher intelligence and know anything.

Ronald, the printer at the Center, told me a tale of having a vision of a spaceship before class. Quite sleepy, he dozed off only to experience a "memory" of a past life when he rode in a spacecraft above Atlantis. Ronald said that a glowing scientist appeared, beckoning him to follow. They ascended stairs made of light beams. Then this caring scientist instructed him in the principles of "high-energy physics." Ronald warned me, however, "It's a waste of time chasing flying saucers. Let them come to you." This comment referred to the Unarian belief that when a student raised his or her consciousness, the spaceships would ultimately reveal themselves.

Space Brothers Contact Me

Fieldworkers often hear cautions against "going native" or being psychologically engulfed by their subjects (Emerson 1988). In her fieldwork on Spiritualism, Burke Forrest (1986) underwent some unexpected and frightening effects of socialization when she began to see spirits. Intense dream states caused her to leave the field. Joseph Damrell (1977) reported a surprising, nonordinary shift of perception during meditation while studying Vedanta. E. Burke Rochford (1985) wrote that he was converted to Hare Krishna (ISKCON). Tanya Luhrmann (1989) stated that she entered the witches' worldview through a process of interpretive drift, and that as a participant she felt the power of the witches' circle. Ironically, Evans-Pritchard (1937) saw witches travel at night in the form of lights on the horizon. In their statements about the permeability of realities, Hugh Mehan and Houston Wood (1975) noted how the civilized Tobias Schneebaum became a cannibal by joining a tribe in Peruvian jungle. Without ascribing phenomena to the existence of separate metaphysical realities, these examples demonstrate the power of the social to affect subjective perception through participation.

In my lengthy fieldwork, I learned to think like Unarians—and to dream like them. While asleep, their world permeated the cognitive boundaries I had erected against them. During the time I talked extensively with Unarians about their dreams, I experienced my first *vivid dream* about a Space Brother. It is helpful to distinguish vivid dreams from ordinary dreaming. Vivid dreams evoke unforgettable images and feelings. More than just watching pictures in the mind, vivid dreams stimulate deep feelings with emotional responses to color, touch, words, and sounds. The following is an excerpt from my field notes:

I was deeply asleep, so deep into the dream state that I experienced all the following as vividly real and at the time I could not distinguish that I was dreaming. I sensed I was at the San Diego Airport. Everything was dark as I looked out into the night sky to see the stars animatedly twinkle in the deep blackness. On the horizon, I heard a sound that penetrated my body and that made the cells of my body vibrate to its rhythm. In the distance a cluster of stars started to move as if they were a formation of airplanes. As they flew toward me, they formed an image of a woman. Under the pressure of their sound, I staggered back and fell on the ground. Excitement and fear gripped my mind and body as I thought, "The saucers—there are the saucers."

The ships moved closer, but their presence was overwhelming me with their size, luminosity, and vibratory sound. As they landed, I was dwarfed like an insect in a forest of light and sound. A mountainous spaceship opened its doors to reveal its denizen. A red-haired man, looking a bit like the actor Russ Tamblyn of *West Side Story,* emerged in white brocade Nehru suit that sported a gold medallion. He beckoned me aboard. The ramp he extended consisted of sound waves. Excitedly I thought, I *must* see the ship. With each step up the ramp, my cellular structure seemed to transform, which was represented outwardly by different changes in clothing. By the time I made it to the top, I was dressed in a purple and gold sari that periodically sparkled with golden light beams.

There propelled by an inner state of great longing, I threw out my arms to be embraced. The Space Brother enfolded me in his arms. Every cell of my body was awash with waves of loving feeling. In turn, as a monarch might escort a consort on a royal tour, the Space Brother showed me the many chambers in the ship.

In a room with a bronze floor engraved with a map of Earth, the Brother explained to me the karmic destiny of my planet. We rode on hovering metallic plates to different sections of this great map, which as he detailed its significance would act out his words in a holographic display. From this vantage point, I saw civilizations rise only to fall, and radio waves sent from the pyramids of Egypt to the pyramids of Atlantis.

This dream caused me to do sense-making in the light of day, for it was a serious reality disjuncture. If I had been a true Unarian, this dream would have been "scientific" proof of the existence of the Brothers, subjective validation of the power of the Science. Again if I had been a real Unarian, I would have shared my experience during a testimonial in class; thus I could have added credence to the collective reality. I held back because I did not want to contaminate the field setting by having members get involved with my experience instead of their own. Furthermore, I did not want to come under their social control. The less I revealed about myself, the more I felt my own autonomy. That did not mean that the saucer dreams entirely ceased, but with my frequent exits from the field to return to Los Angeles, I could shake off their influence within a few days. I attributed this vivid dream to an unconscious accommodation to the intersubjectivity of the group, although I also entertained other explanations.

Interestingly, my research partner, Dr. Kirkpatrick, also sustained dreams about the spaceships and visits from the Brothers. The most dramatic impact upon him occurred on our way to present a paper on Unarius at the Pacific Sociological Meetings in Reno, Nevada (Kirkpatrick and Tumminia 1989a). We drove from San Diego up Highway 395, making camp along the way at Lake Diaz. During the middle of the night, I heard screams coming from his tent. As I peered out, I saw in the moonlight the occasional bump against the tent fabric; it looked like he was kicking or punching the tent. I reasoned that Dr. Kirkpatrick was having a bad dream, the contents of which I learned the next morning. He said he dreamed that a giant flying saucer the size of the lake landed on the water. Aliens that he could not describe pressed him into joining a plan to introduce a new technology here on the Earth. This technology consisted of inventing a biological equivalent of such objects as cars, houses, and computers, which materialized by accessing the correct genetic code. He fought the aliens off only to escape by waking from his dream.

Here again was a clear interpretive boundary permeated by the alleged Space Brothers. We, like the Unarians, had seen and contacted the spaceships, but we had vastly different interpretations of what the events meant. What for us was evidence of the power of suggestion, fatigue, or with any stretch of the imagination a tap into the collective unconscious, instead would have been for a Unarian unquestionable proof of the truth and the power of their Science. Even after our encounters with the Brothers, their facts remained our fiction.

Reality and Evidence

From a lifeworld perspective, Unarians live within a socially constructed reality guided by Space Brothers who communicate their presence through the experiences of members. Unarians presume that the "scientific" principles of past lives and the actions of their beloved Space Brothers function behind all physical appearances. They, like other social actors, engage in fact-finding pursuits that validate their point of view. Through social interaction, Unarians document their reality by gathering evidence through dreams, psychic readings, and through other types of logical inferences in line with their lifeworld assumptions. Unarians see the evidence of the Science, the great metaphysical law of energy, as it operates throughout all universes and within all human beings. By referencing this invisible world, they account for what is real and for what constitutes a reasonable explanation of any event, including the content of dreams.

Douglas argues that the ability to pass as a member indicates the depth of the researcher's understanding of a group (Douglas 1976; Rochford 1992). A well-socialized participant observer can come to think and to feel some of a group's reality, but probably not without noticing his or her own boundary of interpretation based upon some degree of objectification. My experience of fieldwork in Unarius involved a continual juggling of our respective meaning systems and frequent negotiations of the various reality disjunctures (Pollner 1987) the setting produced. From my orientation, I accounted for Unarian sense-making by pointing to their use of incorrigible propositions (Tumminia 1998). By defining the Unarian experience in that way, I discounted evidence that Unarians would say is proof positive that the Science was working with me. Our discordant worldviews separated our experiences of the same phenomena by placing them within different interpretive boundaries. The guardian of these boundaries is belief; if we do not for an extended length of time suspend disbelief in another's interpretive territory or lifeworld, we cannot make it our own. I would argue that even ethnographers who come to experience group realities deeply would recognize the boundaries of their experiences.

Tempered by academic training, the ethnographer's science processes a personal world of reflexivity with that of the sense-making procedures of the group under observation. The participant observer enters the field with the presumption that the observed social world will remain reasonably separate. As Rochford (1992) and others (Schwartz and Jacobs 1979; Bloor 1988; Pollner and Emerson 1988) observe, fieldworkers anchor themselves in the notion of being objective outsiders, separate from the social settings and the meaning systems they study. As part of this privileged status (Rochford 1992; Pollner 1987), their assumptions about meaning are often taken for granted until members challenge them. Some informants question the reasoning and credentials of fieldworkers in the course of interaction or in solicited encounters of member validation. Within this ironic house of mirrors, the ethnographer imposes meaning on people who are documenting their understanding of how the world works by criticizing the validity of the investigator's interpretation. It is through these discordant exchanges that we understand the limitations of our own perspectives and the subtle ambiguities of the social construction of reality.

PART TWO

Abductees and Contactees

Toward an Explanation of the "Abduction Epidemic"

The Ritualization of Alien Abduction Mythology in Therapeutic Settings

Georg M. Rønnevig

Since the 1960s, ufologists and the media have collected testimonials from people who said that extraterrestrials captured and released them. However, relatively few alien abduction narratives (AANs) reached the public's notice during the 1960s and 1970s compared with the remarkable increase that happened some ten to twenty years later. What caused the dramatic increase in stories about people taken by aliens during the late 1980s and the early 1990s? To point to the fact that stories like these flourished in popular media (movies, books, radio, television, etc.) in the same period does not, in my opinion, provide a sufficient answer. One has to consider several tendencies, trends, and sociocultural events occurring at the same time in our culture in general, as well as within the universe of ufology. With respect to that segment of ufology, one should be aware that, although the structural aspects of the abduction narratives for the most part remained the same from the 1970s to the present, there was a substantial shift in the accounts on how the abductions allegedly took place. The general impression is that alien abductions in the seventies took place out in the countryside, often when people were driving their cars late at night. Increasingly, the stories of aliens abducting people in the 1980s involved new themes, such as the aliens coming inside bedrooms at night and suddenly appearing without witnesses having seen a UFO. The abduction stories took on a darker, more grotesque content, and abduction "investigators," such as Budd Hopkins and others, emphasized the posttraumatic stress that victims faced.

The enigma of alien abduction narratives challenges all researchers in the field. Such narratives arise from multiple causes, and the phenomenon does not easily fit into one single area of analysis. As research progresses, there may well be multiple lines of credible explanations of different alien abduction narratives. Taking my cue from some past research, I contend that many AANs from the 1980s and 1990s could *partially* be explained by looking at the common, nonpathological experience now known as sleep paralysis and its related states. Although these physiological states are not under conscious control, shifts in cultural understanding color interpretations about these experiences, especially when such states can give rise to so many unusual experiences. It is my proposal that the sudden increase in AANs in the late 1980s and early 1990s, as well as the shift from "countryside kidnappings" to "bedroom abductions" during this same period, could *partially* be explained by looking at how sleep paralysis came to be defined as a symptom of abduction by certain key figures involved with the abduction hypothesis. The literary and media attention around this definitional shift contributed to the rise in such reports. Further, I suggest that it is significant for our understanding of the "abduction epidemic" to notice that this shift happened at approximately the same time that our culture saw a dramatic increase in hypnotherapists and victim support groups, as well as other therapeutic means of recovering memories. Many practitioners within these much-criticized forms of therapy and ufological investigation presume that abduction memories are a veiled process with supernatural or superhuman implications and that these memories should be recovered. This influence facilitated the emergence of support groups as ritualized venues for abduction narratives based up the reputed efficacy of this type of treatment and the testimonial evidence of members.

Short History of Alien Abductions

Alien abductions have been a part of the UFO myth since the early 1960s. The legendary story about Betty and Barney Hill and their experiences in 1961 gained much attention when writer John G. Fuller published *The Interrupted Journey* (1966). As the story goes, the Hills saw a UFO while driving home to New Hampshire late at night after a short vacation in Canada. When they finally got home, they realized that their trip had lasted about two hours longer than expected.

In the following weeks, Betty was haunted by nightmares in which she dreamed that she and her husband were forced aboard a spacecraft by small alien creatures and subjected to different medical procedures. The elaborate story about the Hills' abduction did not emerge until about two years later, when they both decided to try hypnotic regression in order to recall what happened that night. Under hypnosis they "remembered" how their car engine stopped as the aliens appeared, how they "floated" into the UFO, were stripped naked, placed on a table, scrutinized, and experimented upon by their abductors. Among other things, Betty "recalled" how the aliens inserted a long needle into her stomach. She was told that this was a pregnancy test. Further, the aliens told her that neither she nor her husband would recall anything of the incident. The Hill case caused internal debates among ufologists in the late 1960s. To some UFO researchers, this and a few other early abduction cases were simply too bizarre to be taken seriously (Jacobs 1999, 18). Abduction reports remained scarce and only twenty-six cases came to light during the period from 1967 to 1972 (Bullard 1987a, 3). Mainstream ufology occupied itself with sighting reports, not abduction stories.

After the public recognition of the Hill case, high profile abduction narratives seemed to increase, keynoting evolving themes of problematic aliens. For example, another famous case, known as the Pascagoula Incident, gained national attention. Entities with claws dragged two fishermen, Calvin Parker and Charlie Hickson, into an oval-shaped object at Pascagoula, Mississippi (Spencer 1991). The supposed incident took place in October 1973, and it corresponded with big waves of UFO activity in 1973 and 1974 (Thompson 1991). Another mysterious story, the Travis Walton case, appeared in 1975, a few weeks after NBC had exposed millions of Americans to the theme of alien abduction by broadcasting a TV movie about Betty and Barney Hill called *The UFO Incident.* By 1980, about two hundred abduction cases were known to ufologists (Newman and Baumeister 1996). Common to most of these stories are how the victims were situated in isolated areas when the UFO suddenly appeared, and how they afterwards, like the Hills, were unable to account for an extended period of time, a phenomenon called *missing time.*

According to Keith Thompson, the "Hill case stands as a primordial precedent, the mythic First—for future alien abductions" (1991, 62). Ufologists continue to return to this presumably authentic account as a prototype for the spectrum of narratives that followed. Abduction researcher Budd Hopkins adopted the Hill case as a reference point in his search for new abductees. However, when Hopkins published his first book, *Missing Time,* in 1981, he claimed to have found cases where persons had been abducted without remembering having seen a UFO. In addition, the narratives published by Hopkins were darker, more frightening, and more of a traumatic character than the previously known cases. Budd Hopkins insisted that abductees were in need of the same therapeutic guidance and help as were the victims of rape or war.

6.1. Betty and Barney Hill. The Betty and Barney Hill abduction in 1961 is one of the most talked-about cases of alien abduction. Courtesy of Mary Evans Picture Library.

At the same time debunker Philip J. Klass criticized Hopkins for publishing a set of symptoms ambiguous enough to plant the idea of UFO abduction as a plausible explanation. It is worth noting that the scope of symptoms allegedly indicating abductions broadened during the 1980s. As already mentioned, most of the abductees in the 1970s reported seeing a UFO and subsequently having a period of time for which they could not account. For ufologists that suggested that abduction had taken place. During the 1980s, however, Budd Hopkins and others started looking for new clues that, according to their extraterrestrial hypothesis, indicated that aliens were abducting people for genetic experiments. They soon picked up information that some people had seen alien-like creatures in their bedrooms at night and that such people could not move during that time. This scenario was all new.

Although this theme would become standard in abduction accounts later, according to Kevin D. Randle, Russ Estes, and William P. Cone (1999), only very few abduction reports from the 1970s told of aliens entering homes to remove the occupants. In the 1980s, ufologists started to see into reports of unexplainable nosebleeds, scars, and body marks the clear indications of alien implants. Veteran ufologist Ann Druffel (1998) demonstrated that a careful study of books written during the 1980s clearly showed a progression of details involving missing fetuses, implants, and alien hybridization that was lacking in earlier accounts. As a measure of the thematic shift, it is worth noting that Betty Hill never reported an alien transplant or a missing fetus, nor did other early abductees. By the 1990s, the field of abduction research had become unbelievably complex, with some people even linking abductions to cattle mutilations (Howe 1989). The continuing elaboration of unconfirmed speculation about the extent of abductions was, according to Thompson, "like a high-dose vitamin shot to the emerging abduction *mythology*" (1991, 172). In the late 1990s and after 2000, the abduction mythology developed even further and split in different directions, including stories of late-stage, adult hybrids almost indistinguishable from humans, prepared to integrate into human society and take control of the earth (Jacobs 1999), stories of benevolent aliens aimed at transforming human consciousness and caring for our planet's ecological future (Mack 1999), and stories of transgenic beings interacting with humans during their routine lives (Hopkins and Rainey 2003). As we shall see later, the bedroom abductions set a new standard that would soon be followed by hundreds of other accounts.

Religious and Mythological Significance

In his essay "Religious Dimensions of the UFO Abductee Experience" (1995), scholar of religion John Whitmore suggests that the very idea of UFO abductions is an intensely religious concept. Whitmore states that the expression of the idea of "the Other" has traditionally fallen under the purview of religion. People at different times, as well as in other cultures, have expressed this idea in terms of some belief in spiritual beings from another order of intelligence, and they have attributed to them superior magical power, such as the ability to pass through walls, to fly, and to communicate telepathically. According to Whitmore, the idea of the Other still takes this form in modern abduction tales. The difference in interpretation is, of course, that while the fanciful beings in other times were conceived of as having magical powers, the aliens of the current abduction lore are said to possess superior technological knowledge and equipment.

As John A. Saliba proposes, this change might be seen as secularization, as well as a remythologization of traditional religious themes. The stories of extraterrestrials visiting our planet secularize religion because they eliminate the supernatural, at least in the words of some authorities on the subject. In the eyes of people like Erich von Däniken, says Saliba, "the miraculous events in the Bible become activities of superhuman beings from other planets, who possess superior technological and psychic powers" (1995, 35) that only appear miraculous because humans have an inferior and underdeveloped culture by comparison. At the same time, the accounts of people kidnapped by aliens, taken from their homes, and subjected to obscure medical procedures remythologize religion, because they introduce an element of mystery and a prenatural force that supposedly is beyond our scientific knowledge (Saliba 1995). It should not come as a surprise that some people view these stories not as religion or folklore, but as indicators of highly advanced technological achievements. In accordance with the rationalistic thinking of the twenty-first century, many people now embed the very understanding of UFOs and aliens in a secularized context.

Although this secular context holds true for a large amount of UFO stories, one should note that since the 1990s there seems to be a tendency to view encounters with aliens in terms of New Age concepts, such as channeling, interplanetary reincarnation, clairvoyance, and spiritual techniques like meditation. This viewpoint seems clear from the standpoint of some ufologists such as John E. Mack (1995, 1999) and Lyssa Royal and Keith Priest (1993). It also makes sense from the perspective of some famous abductees, especially Whitley Strieber (1997, 1998), who views his whole life in terms of what he believes was an initiation into another realm or a higher mode of being. Indeed, some grassroots abduction narratives today do speak of transcendental experiences and altered states of consciousness, not traumatic kidnappings. People like Strieber and others who seem to rely on a more positive New Age interpretation of the abduction phenomenon, speak out against the frightening theories of Budd Hopkins (1987, 1997) and David M. Jacobs (1993, 1999). These two investigators see in the stories of alien encounters nothing but trouble for humankind as they stress the trauma of victims and claim that the aliens are here for their own selfish reasons.

Stressing the relevance of religious significance, John Whitmore concludes his essay on the abductee experience by stating:

> The phenomenon of UFO abduction is a gold mine for scholars of religion. . . . The general patterns of the abduction experience manifest congruencies with numinous encounters, and with archaic shamanistic symbolism. The consequences of the event for the abductee are the same as with other forms of subjective paranormal religious experience. (1995, 81)

What Whitmore fails to recognize is the importance of the social and ritual aspects that often accompany the processes whereby some people come to think of themselves as abductees. Surely, Whitmore is well aware of the fact that many stories of alien abduction emerge during hypnotherapy because he states, "The religious imagery and interpretation brought out by hypnosis could be confabulations of the subject's subconscious and perhaps worked into a UFO narrative in an effort to please the hypnotist" (1995, 68). Despite this recognition, Whitmore seems to place more importance on the part of the individual's subconscious (even on Jung's psychological category "the Shadow") than on sociocognitive processes. This emphasis does not mean that Whitmore's approach is worthless when the task is to analyze the religious content and symbols of the experience, but one should at the same time stress the importance of the social context wherein these symbols become manifest and elaborated into a comprehensive narrative.

As discussed later, becoming an abductee involves a socialization process that deserves study from the viewpoint of a rite of passage. It must be noted that the preferred term for abductee is *experiencer* (Partridge 2003, 30). First, however, we have to look at what often causes a person to seek help from a hypnotherapist whose specialty is "investigation" of the alien abduction phenomenon. In some cases, frightening and inexplicable experiences prompt people to look for abduction therapists. Can we explain any of these experiences outside the abduction assumption?

Sleep Paralysis and Hallucinations

Although there still is some controversy surrounding the issue, it now seems apparent that as much as 50 percent (Randle et al. 1999, 299, 350) of the stories of people kidnapped by aliens could, in part, be explained with reference to related types of phenomena called sleep paralysis, night terror, hypnagogic hallucinations, incubus syndrome, or the Old Hag phenomenon (Druffel 1998; Randle et al. 1999; Randles 1999). The epistemological difficulties of using these terms when focusing upon reported experiences should not be underestimated. First, it should be made clear that these terms do not necessarily refer to the same types of experiences. Second, the rich associations surrounding related concepts, such as nightmares, bedroom visitations, and out-of-body experiences, make them open to misleading ideas about the subject matter. Third, it should also be stated that we are looking at phenomena that have historically lacked proper academic classification and discussion.

Such problems in terminology forced folklorist David Hufford, the author of

The Terror That Comes in the Night: An Experience-Centered Study of Supernatural Assault Traditions, to state in his introduction, "No commonly accepted term exists in modern English for the experience that is the subject of this book" (1982, ix). Hufford's book is not about abductions, but it contains a discussion of a specific kind of experience that people in Newfoundland know as the Old Hag, a mythic tradition about a witchlike being who attacks a sleeper at night (an occurrence referred to as "hagging"). For lack of a better word, Hufford used the term "Old Hag" to denote the experience about which he was writing.[1] The experience of being hagged as found in the Newfoundland tradition is summarized by Hufford as follows:

> (1) Awakening (or an experience immediately preceding sleep); (2) hearing and/or seeing something come into the room and approach the bed; (3) being pressed on the chest or strangled; (4) inability to move or cry out until either being brought out of the state by someone else or breaking through the feeling of paralysis on one's own. This experience is explained as caused by either a supernatural assault, indigestion, or circulatory stagnation, or some kind of combination of these. (1982, 10–11)

More than thirty years after the release of Hufford's book, the commonly accepted term for this experience is "sleep paralysis" and there is a rapidly growing popular and academic interest in the phenomenon. This interest has been reinforced by the discussion of what causes otherwise normal people to report abduction by aliens. Noted psychologists such as Susan Blackmore (1998), Richard J.

---

1. When Hufford attempted to give a precise description of the Old Hag phenomenon, he wrote, "The 'sleep paralysis with hypnagogic hallucinations' comes close, but in current usage the term includes some experiences that are different from the Old Hag and, despite the theoretical importance of this connection, the term is to general and omits many primary and secondary features of the Old Hag" (1982, 246). The term "sleep paralysis" is used differently today. Still, Hufford seems to regard the intrusion of REM activity into waking moments as inadequate to explain sleep paralysis. See Bower (2005) at http://www.sciencenews.org/articles/20050709/bob9.asp. See also Mooney (2005).

Hinton, Hufford, and Kirmayer (2005) stress that sleep paralysis should be distinguished from *nightmares* that can cause a panic attack upon awakening, *nocturnal panic* (waking in terror with no memory of a dream), and *night terrors* (when a person briefly awakens in fear and flails about only to fall asleep again and later awaken with no memory of the incident). In sleep paralysis, one is awake but cannot move. In this state, one can see a shape moving and experiences chest tightness, weight on chest and body, or shortness of breath. They categorized sleep paralysis as a disturbance of the normal sleep pattern when paralysis occurs upon awakening (or sleep onset) instead of in the REM sleep cycle, although others, like Mooney (2005), say it happens during REM sleep.

McNally and Susan A. Clancy (2005), and others (Randles 1999, 150), have argued that sleep paralysis is a key to understanding the abduction phenomenon. Psychophysiologist Kazuhiko Fukuda of the Fukushima University has conducted research on sleep paralysis and brain activity. Fukuda et al. (1987) linked the frightening Japanese sleep experience of *kanashibari* (e.g., seeing a ghost or demon sit on one's chest) to sleep paralysis. The entire March 2005 issue of *Transcultural Psychiatry* is dedicated to sleep paralysis, with contributions from various academic disciplines, including a lead article by Hufford (2005).

Retired professor of psychology Al Cheyne has been researching sleep paralysis for more than a decade (2003). He runs a Web site on the phenomenon and has collected more than 28,000 reports from around the world.[2] Apparently, those in traditional cultures recognize it under other names. For convenience, I will use the term "sleep paralysis" throughout this chapter, but the reader should note that I am referring to the whole complex of related conditions.

What is sleep paralysis? Normal sleep paralysis is a failsafe mechanism that ensures that people do not act out dreams, for example, sleepwalking or flailing around in bed. Sometimes, however, people experience awareness during sleep paralysis, which means that they are in a fully awake state but nonetheless unable to move. The experience may occur during any time of sleep, but very often this condition occurs in hypnagogic and hypnopompic states (Newman and Baumeister 1996; Bowers and Eastwood 1996; Strube 1996; Cheyne, Newby-Clark, and Rueffer 1999). The *hypnagogic* state refers to the drowsiness that precedes actual sleep. The *hypnopompic* state pertains to the partially conscious condition of a sleeper before awakening. It is estimated that approximately a fifth of all people experience sleep paralysis at least once, and to some people this experience is accompanied by terrifying sensations such as buzzing or levitation, and sometimes vivid auditory and visual hallucinations stemming from the REM sleep phase.

According to Randle, Estes, and Cone, the belief that an entity is in the room happens in about 80 percent of the cases of sleep paralysis (1999, 195). As a matter of course, the paralysis soon passes. The unusual tingling sensation in the body disappears, and the person goes back to sleep, or becomes fully awake and can move

2. See Cheyne's Web site at http://watarts.uwaterloo.ca/~acheyne/S_P.html for more information about the physiological aspects of sleep paralysis. His Web site also contains a copy of the Waterloo Unusual Sleep Experiences Scale, used in his research to assess hallucinatory experiences associated with sleep paralysis (e.g., sensed presence; pressure, floating, fear, and auditory, visual, and tactile sensations).

again. Afterward the person is usually convinced that the experience was real and that he or she was awake and not dreaming (Hufford 1982; Newman and Baumeister 1996, 105; Randle, Estes, and Cone 1999, 299–306). Without knowledge that this is a common, nonpathological experience and not a disorder, some people seriously think they are going insane. Others find it hard not to ascribe an otherworldly meaning to the experience. Most abductees insist they were awake when the aliens entered their bedrooms (Fiore 1993; Jacobs 1993, 1999; Hopkins 1987, 1997; Mack 1995, 1999; Strieber 1997). They are probably right considering that sleep paralysis may be described as dreaming with one's eyes wide open.

In the early 1990s, ufologist and abduction researcher David M. Jacobs gave the following description of what characterizes the beginning of a typical nighttime abduction by aliens:

> In the middle of the night she turns over and lies on her back. She is awakened by a light that seems to be glowing in her room. The light moves toward her bed and takes the shape of a small "man" with a bold head and huge black eyes. She is terrified. She wants to run but she cannot move. She wants to scream but she cannot speak. (1993, 50)

The similarities between Jacobs's description and accounts of the Old Hag, or what may happen during sleep paralysis, are obvious. As Randle, Estes, and Cone stated: "In fact, Jacobs in *Secret Life* provides a textbook example of sleep paralysis, apparently without realizing what he has done" (1999, 221). Robert A. Baker made a similar point with respect to Strieber's *Communion* (1987), calling it "a classic, textbook description of a hypnopompic hallucination" (Moffitt 2003, 517). The same could be said about several other books on abduction, including Ann Druffel's *How to Defend Yourself Against Alien Abduction* (1998), which is an interesting manual containing instructions on how to use different resistance techniques in order to break the paralysis and fend off abductions.

An experience of sleep paralysis usually needs a lot of elaboration and reinterpretation before it can be reworked into a comprehensive alien abduction narrative, even if the person visualizes an alien in the form known to his or her cultural background. One of the obvious reasons for reconsideration and retelling lies within the abduction mythology itself. What is clear to everyone who is familiar with abduction narratives is the stress that certain ufologists place on the partial or full amnesia that some people suffer when abducted by aliens. Throughout the abduction litera-

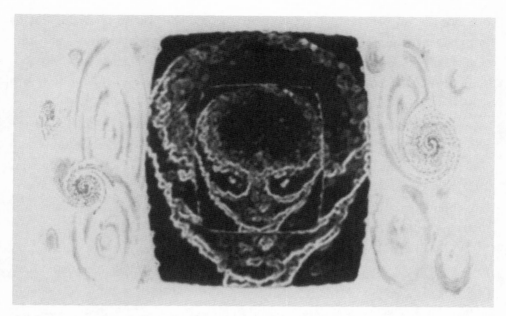

6.2. Some researchers believe the phenomenon of alien abduction is associated with sleep paralysis, dream states, and nightmares. Artwork by Diana Tumminia.

ture the reader is told that it is typical for abductees to remember only fragments of the episodes in which they were abducted. Different ufological theories exist on why people do not remember being abducted. Some theories suggest that abductions are so frightening and traumatic that people repress the memories of them in order to protect their psyches (Fiore 1993), whereas others have suggested that the aliens are responsible for abductee amnesia (Hopkins 1997; Jacobs 1999). Many abduction researchers agree, however, that hypnotic regression can reveal detailed information about these events. Thus, some abduction researchers seem to interpret people's descriptions of sleep paralysis as fragmented or distorted memories of initial and/or final stages of true alien abductions. Later in this chapter, I will return to some of the historical and sociocultural conditions for these assumptions. First, however, I would like to draw attention to another closely related aspect of sleep paralysis.

Sexual Aspects of Alien Abduction and Sleep Paralysis

Sometimes the details of abduction narratives are of an explicit sexual nature. In a famous abduction story from 1957, the young Brazilian farmer Antonio Villas-Boas was working in the fields very late at night. According to Thompson, the hour was one A.M., a time of the night when many people sleep. Reports say his tractor stopped when an alien ship appeared. After being kidnapped and taken aboard a ship, he supposedly had sexual intercourse with a beautiful female alien (1991, 33). Typically in later abduction narratives, however, male abductees tell about how they were unwillingly stimulated to orgasm and forced to ejaculate into cylinders of some sort. Female abductees tell how the aliens performed quasi-gynecological experiments on them, including extractions of ova and artificial fertilizations, and some women report that in subsequent abductions fetuses were removed (Hopkins 1987; Mack 1995; Randle, Estes, and Cone 1999; Randles 1999). According to certain abduction researchers, the aliens are searching for human genetic material in order to revitalize their own race.

Villas-Boas did not ascribe his experience to a dream, but the sexual theme now sounds familiar. The recurring themes of reproduction and alien-human cross-breeding in the abduction mythology have gained increasing significance. In addition, stories have adopted the latest popular jargon about DNA, molecular structure, and cloning. Sometimes abductees tell how they were subjected to extraordinary sexual experiences or how aliens raped them. Sometimes they describe how they were forced to engage in bizarre sexual activities, for example, having intercourse with other abductees aboard a UFO (Jacobs 1999) or having sex with aliens and humans disguised as aliens (Mack 1995).

During an on-camera interview, Leeza, a self-described abductee, was asked about the sexual aspects of her abductions. She said that they were charged with sexual energy and that the aliens often observed her during sexual activities. Randle, Estes, and Cone write:

> Leeza remembered laying on the all too familiar metal table surrounded by the aliens who had just removed a hybrid fetus that they had implanted into her. As she lay there, immobile on the table, one of the five-foot aliens mounted her, looked deep into her eyes, and what she heard him say was, "What you need is a good fuck!" A very earthly and very sexist statement if there was one. The aliens then proceeded to, as she said, "Give me the most profound orgasm of my life!"[3] (1999, 97)

3. Randle, Estes, and Cone continue to state: "While it is quite true that not all abductees suffer from psychological problems, it is also true that many do. Research by several different investigators has suggested that as many as half of the abductees are homosexual, and while homosexuality is not a psychological problem, the influence and opinions of society can certainly create problems for gays. Beyond that, however, as many as 90 percent of the abductees have some kind of sexual dysfunction. Their tales of rape and sexual activity on board the UFO are evidence of these problems. . . . Once

It may seem absurd to suggest that some of these and other sexual details in abduction narratives could be rooted in actual experience. Of course, some things said in therapy may not relate to real experiences at all. However, this account may not be so absurd if one takes into consideration the vast mythology of incubi- and succubi-devils, which have been known from the days of Saint Augustine and throughout the Middle Ages. In old folklore and in different alchemistic and theological speculations, stories exist about incubi-devils that engage in sexual activities with humans. The term incubus is derived from the Latin *incubare,* which means to lie down on. Succubus is derived from the Latin *succubare,* which means to lie under. Both terms refer to demons that were believed to have sexual intercourse with humans (Hufford 1982, 130; Flaherty 1990). A full discussion of the highly interesting incubus traditions cannot be done here, but it should be noted that the topic played a significant role during the European witch hunts. Certainly, the folk cultures of Europe and America had always believed in evil spirits, but the related idea of disincarnate entities grew immensely popular during the sixteenth, seventeenth, and eighteenth centuries with occult groups like the Rosicrucians, Theosophists, and the Spiritualists (Flaherty 1990).

So how does all this relate to alien abductions? It is my suggestion that some of the sexual details in many of today's abduction accounts may be rooted in a kind of sleep-related experience that may occur during dreaming and sleep paralysis. The incubus traditions existed under very different social, cultural, and historical conditions, but they too may be descriptions of certain forms of sleep paralysis. Modern AANs reflect medical and technological images, but it could very well be that some AANs are the same kind of altered states (often defined as religious) that sparked the old incubus traditions.

As previously mentioned, the discussion of the experience now commonly referred to as "sleep paralysis" is a problematic one. Randle, Estes, and Cone, for example, do not distinguish between cases where the experience seems to be of a sexual nature and others where sexual aspects are missing (1999, 299–306). Rather they label them all as sleep paralysis. Hufford claimed to have found only a few explicit sexual details in the Old Hag accounts, and he suggested that these differed from the Old Hag phenomenon in that they lacked the feature of paralysis, and, in

---

again, the scientific and objective evidence leads down a path that does not end with alien creatures. Instead, it leads us to common human problems that are ignored by the researchers" (1999, 100–101). Newman and Baumeister (1996, 1998) think that many abduction narratives stemmed from masochistic fantasies.

several cases, the presence of fear. Hufford thinks that the experiences behind the incubus stories differ from the Old Hag phenomenon. Hufford explains:

> These probably constitute either a distinct subtype of the experience or a different phenomenon altogether. . . . At any rate, it would be a mistake automatically to assume that no more realistic experience lies behind the widespread incubus traditions. To do so would be to invite a repetition of the errors and confusion that have characterized writings about the Old Hag variety of experience. (1982, 131)

This is an important point if the task is to identify the exact nature of a given experience. When discussing alien abductions, it seems plausible to suggest that abduction researchers and therapists have come across a variety of experiences during their work with abductees, and most probably different combinations or clusters of experiences, which they have interpreted and assigned meaning on the basis of the extraterrestrial hypothesis.

Folklorist Robert P. Flaherty writes that the psychiatrist R. B. Raschka defined nightmare as a manifestation of "the Incubus Syndrome, an expression of erotomania in which the individual believes him or herself to be visited by a supernatural lover or, as the case might be, sexual assailant" (1990, 587). This definition of the nightmare explicitly stresses sexual aspects. Hufford, however, noted that the word "nightmare" would be an excellent name for the Old Hag, "if it could be restricted to its older meaning" (1982, 246). While the word "nightmare" as used today simply refers to an unpleasant or bad dream, it originally had direct reference to the experience which is the subject of Hufford's work (53). The word nightmare comes from the Anglo-Saxon *neath* (or *nicht*) and *mara,* and it was used to refer to a being who attacked the sleeper, causing a crushing or oppressing weight on the breast. Although this meaning of the word can still be found, it now seems rather out of date and the traditions that accompanied it have either died or have been changed beyond recognition.[4]

---

4. Ever since Ernest Jones, a psychoanalyst and biographer of Freud, published his book *On the Nightmare* in 1931, there has been much confusion surrounding the academic treatment of nightmares (Hufford 1982). Jones attempted to use psychoanalysis to explore problems in anthropology, history, religious studies, and abnormal psychology. He used the word "nightmare" in a restricted sense, suggesting three cardinal features: agonizing dread; sense of oppression or weight at the chest, which alarmingly interferes with respiration; and conviction of helpless paralysis. According to Hufford, all three of the features Jones selected as definitive are directly related to his use of psychoanalytical theory to interpret the nightmare. As one would expect from a Freudian, Jones (as quoted in

Recent research by McNally and Clancy (2005) may shed new light on the relationship between sleep paralysis and the sexual aspects that sometimes occur. They found that subjects who said they had repressed, recovered, or continuous memories of childhood sexual abuse were more likely to report sleep paralysis than did a control group. Panic attacks, trauma, stress and other factors that disturb sleep, may also indirectly increase the likelihood of experiencing sleep paralysis stress.

An Experience Bereft of Tradition?

Given the obvious similarities between sleep paralysis and what abductees report as the initial and final stages of an abduction, it is not unreasonable to think that this particular experience has played a role in the development of the alien abduction mythology during the late 1980s and early 1990s. However, to understand how this could come about we have to be aware of some important social factors.

According to Hufford, while the occurrence of the experience is high ("15 percent or more of the general population"), the distribution of folk tales, myths, and traditions about the experience vary from culture to culture and "heavily determine the ways the experience is described (or withheld) and interpreted" (1982, 245). This means that while the experience seems to be fairly common, not every culture has developed a mythic tradition that gives the experience a name or an explanation in living, meaningful discourse.

The people of Newfoundland know it by the name of Old Hag, in Mexico it is referred to as *subida del muerto* (the dead getting on top), in Turkish *karabasan* (black buster), and the Eskimos call it *augumangia,* but according to Hufford the great majority of people in the United States are unfamiliar with any tradition that relates to this type of experience (1982, 53). This rather peculiar situation forced

---

Hufford 1982, 126) interpreted the nightmare to be "a form of *Angst* attack, that is essentially due to an intense mental conflict centering [*sic*] around a repressed component of the psycho-sexual instinct, essentially concerned with incest." Jones apparently identified some concepts of the nightmare with some concepts of the incubus, equated their meaning and eventually gave this connection a modern basis in psychoanalytical theory. It is highly problematic to determine if the words nightmare and incubus in earlier times have been understood as significantly different in meaning, even if they may or may not have referred to the single thing, or whether they were used analogously. Jones's emphasis on unconscious meanings tended to blur these distinctions as he thought that people meant the same thing by both terms, whether they knew it or not, and that both the terrifying and the erotic experiences were the same whether or not their content was similar (Hufford 1982, 130).

Hufford to try to answer the question: "How can this experience, which is well known in Newfoundland, be practically unknown in the United States?" (51). Hufford's hypothesis is that the presence of an accessible terminology in Newfoundland indicates a consensus about its applicability, "which in most cases provides assurance that the experience is not somehow monstrous" (52) or unreal. Hufford elaborates:

> One function of the Old Hag tradition in Newfoundland, then, is to provide both a convenient language for talking about this experience, and another is to indicate a consensus that it is acceptable to have undergone it. . . . In the absence of a tradition that would serve both purposes, as is the situation throughout most of the United States, the experience remains largely unshared and unknown except through the occasional use of cautious and potentially misleading analogies. (52)

As will be discussed below, alien abduction mythology in the 1980s and 1990s seem to provide a language for talking about this experience, and abductee support groups and other therapeutic settings specifically aim at making it socially acceptable for a person to share his or her abduction story.

In his book, Hufford took an experience-centered approach, stressing that many people who reported Old Hag attacks had no knowledge of the folklore surrounding these attacks. Thus, the cultural-source hypothesis cannot explain all sides of the phenomenon. In Hufford's view, "the experiential source hypothesis contains elements of experience that are independent of culture" (1982, 15). It is interesting to note that Hufford reported many convincing examples where the experience in question seems to have played an important role, but alien abductions were not listed among these examples. That should not come as a surprise to us, giving the fact that the bedroom variety of alien abductions had not yet become standard in 1982. Hufford noticed, however, that the Old Hag "can be as easily assimilated to UFO beliefs as it can to vampirism, witchcraft, or anxiety neurosis" (234).

Years later, Hufford attended the 1992 Abduction Study Conference held at MIT in Boston. Australian UFO researcher Keith Basterfield notes that Hufford was careful to state that the events his respondents described were not explained by simply labeling them episodes of sleep paralysis (Basterfield 2002). Basterfield quotes Hufford as saying, "They remain anomalous, because there is no current explanation of why the experiential contents of sleep paralysis are so tremendously similar—I have documented a complex, cross-cultural stable perceptual pattern involving more than 30 distinct content features." Hufford further stated that paralysis episodes are global and have been stable since ancient times, whereas UFO abductions are regarded as recent in origin (Basterfield 2002).

1987: The Turning Point

Hufford wrote his book about supernatural assault traditions in 1982, and although stories of alien abductions had been known for three decades, that was still before the so-called abduction epidemic of the late 1980s. Furthermore, the abduction narratives stemming from the pre-1987 period were not only relatively few, but also seemed to suggest other combinations of meaning and experience. With few exceptions, most of the abduction narratives receiving widespread reportage before the Budd Hopkins era took place out in the countryside, typically occurring in isolated places while the person was driving a car. The abductees, it seemed, were targets of opportunity. They were away from civilization, traveling late at night along a deserted portion of road. The UFO would follow them for a period of time before the abduction would take place. Then they would arrive at their destinations aware that they were later than they should have been. According to Randle, Estes, and Cone (1999), this was a pattern that suggested itself over and over again.

Prior to 1987, descriptions of what happened during sleep paralysis and related experiences did not automatically bring the idea of alien abduction to the minds of ufologists or people in general. A lot of people were probably experiencing sleep paralysis anyway, but as Hufford noticed in 1982, there were neither a suitable language for talking about the experience, nor a social arena in which the experience could be shared without fear of ridicule. When both Budd Hopkins and Whitley Strieber had their book successes in 1987 and the media attention around abductions increased as never before, thousands of Americans suddenly recognized a redefined scenario of abduction. Hopkins's *Intruders* made the best-seller list, and Strieber's *Communion* was so popular Hollywood turned it into a movie, starring Christopher Walken. Both books suggest that behind these strange nocturnal experiences there may be hidden memories of alien abductions. Around the country, people reported waking up in the middle of the night, being unable to move, seeing strange lights, and feeling a presence in the room. In 1988, abduction reports became so numerous there were simply not enough investigators to handle the volume of cases on a one-to-one basis. Seemingly, the strange encounters damaged so many people that support groups were being formed to help handle the social and psychological problems they were experiencing (Druffel 1998; Bader 2003).

Within a few years after 1987, during a time in which several talk shows, documentary programs, movies, and popular television series like *The X-Files* touched upon the topic, the implication that sleep paralysis could be a symptom of alien abduction came to be established in the minds of many people. Abduction researchers listed the typical features of sleep paralysis and suggested that these features, such as paralysis and fear, were fragmented memories of alien abductions. This interpretation was made possible because people in general, and, it seems, the abduction researchers too, were largely unfamiliar with the phenomenon of sleep paralysis. Thousands of people who already believed in UFOs were probably more or less ready to accept the abduction interpretation as an explanation for their strange nighttime experiences. If they were to experience sleep paralysis, they might happen to visualize an alien, instead of any number of other cultural icons, like a ghost or the Virgin Mary, adding an image onto a sometimes remembered sleep event. Through informal networks of certain ufologists, abduction researchers, hypnotherapists, and abductees in support groups, some of these people received the emotional, cognitive, and social support necessary to accept the abductee identity and to define themselves as abductees.

Given that the hypothesis that sleep paralysis was being mistaken for alien abduction was not widely known before 1987, one begins to understand the increase in abduction reports. Few knew of the link or how to offer alternative explanations. There are, however, two more important factors that should be given attention in order to get a fuller and a more comprehensible picture of the situation. The first of these is the influence that psychological tradition has had on our culture in general and on the abduction mythology in particular. The second, related to the first, is the twenty-year rise in the number of abduction survivor and abduction support groups, accompanied by an increase in psychotherapists who specialize in abductees.

Ideological Heritage of the Psychological Tradition

The ideological heritage of the psychological tradition and its impact, both on the popular level and on the professional level, is massive. In Western culture, many people assume that traumatic experiences are suppressed into the subconscious. The notions of suppression and repression are widely held by ordinary people and by many psychologists in clinical practice.[5] What was formerly relevant to religion

5. Memory research conducted by cognitive psychologists, however, suggest that traumatic events are not repressed, but often remembered all too well. People who report recovered memories of trau-

or folklore has been "medicalized" by certain contemporary psychiatrists, psychologists, hypnotherapists, and now by segments of the growing UFO subculture.

Not all AANs come from therapeutic intervention. Folklore scholar Thomas E. Bullard investigated the abduction narratives of many known cases. Although there are sometimes corroborating witnesses, he noted that the vast majority of cases occur as events known only by a single abductee (1989, 150); by inference that makes the validity of the event hard to prove. His assessment notes that a segment of abductees say they remember being captured and that they had no significant amnesia, for example, Villas-Boas and the Travis Walton case (see chapter 17). Other abductees experience temporary amnesia, gradually remembering details through dreams or flashbacks, while still others spontaneously recover their memories sometime after the event. Curiously, some have no memories of abduction, but later recall details through therapy. Bullard also contends, "A greater number of abductees tell their full story only under hypnosis, an uncommon way to obtain a narrative but the usual technique for exploring these cases" (150).

The often-postulated notion of abductee amnesia is crucial for understanding how some people are able to interpret an experience of sleep paralysis or so-called missing time as an indicator of alien abduction. Without this particular interpretive factor, the practice could probably not exist in its present form. Given the fact that certain abduction researchers using hypnosis think they can obtain more and more information about alleged abductions by subjecting people to succeeding hypnotherapeutic sessions, the process has been prone to criticism.

As scholar of religion Mikael Rothstein has pointed out, the idea of amnesia as understood within the frames of the abduction mythology makes it possible to suggest that everyone might be a potential abductee (1994, 96). People who believe in UFOs and abductions might, under the right circumstances, start to think that they may have been abducted without actually having any clear memory of it, except perhaps, for puzzling episodes of sleep paralysis. It is possible for people to reach the extraterrestrial hypothesis on their own, based on what they already know about abductions through books, movies, and the Internet. According to Rothstein, however, the process whereby a person reinterprets an episode of sleep paralysis into a

---

matic events, memories that were not remembered before entering therapy, are probably creating false memories (Loftus and Ketcham 1994). McNally et al. state that the "belief that one has been traumatized may generate emotional responses similar to those provoked by recollections of trauma (e.g., combat)" (2004, 493). Nonetheless, many clinicians believe that painful memories can be repressed and later "recovered" with the help of certain psychotherapeutic techniques.

full-blown abduction narrative can involve a hypnotherapist who will encourage the person to "remember" more details of the abduction. Furthermore, the therapist and others with similar convictions will even help to shape and to legitimate the experience in accordance with the alien abduction hypothesis.

Within the short history of modern abduction discourse, the significance of having a UFO encounter has been supplanted by the act of having an emotional response, for instance, to a book about UFOs or alien abductions (Dean 1998, 51). In *Encounters: A Psychologist Reveals Case Studies of Abductions by Extraterrestrials*, Dr. Edith Fiore states:

> Any anxiety reactions experienced while reading this or any other book on UFOs and CEIVs [Close Encounters of the Fourth Kind] is a strong indicator. What is happening is this, as with any reactions of anxiety in relation to this topic, is that you are actually partially reliving the original traumatic experience during which you felt anxiety, maybe even terror. (1993, 257)

Fiore provides the reader with a checklist for indications of a repressed memory of an abduction. Among these, she lists several symptoms: missing time, nightmares or dreams of UFOs, sleep disorders, and waking up with unusual bodily sensations (256).

Surely, it is a long route from experiencing sleep paralysis to the belief that one has been abducted by aliens. But people hold different opinions about what is nonsense, what might be possible, and what might even be the truth. A person who already believes that aliens visit our planet and who finds some plausibility in the stories of alien abductions might be considered a possible candidate for the abductee role. Within the limits of the alien abduction mythology, it is possible that everyone could have been abducted without actually being aware of it, given this mythology's emphasis on how most people do not remember their abductions. Different ufologists have various explanations for why this is so. Some say that the aliens block memories of the events or simply instruct abductees to forget the incident until the day comes when they will be "ready" for it to surface, which in the opinion of some abduction researchers is when the person enters hypnotherapy. Others, however, say that people repress their memories of the abduction because of their traumatic and horrifying nature.

The roots of these explanations run deep into our cultural ways of thinking about the subconscious, trauma, and recovered memory. It is my suggestion that the alien abduction mythology could never have taken on such an extensive role in the media were it not for the fact that many people held quasi-psychological ideas about traumatic experiences, repression, and the possibility of memory recovery through hypnosis. Psychoanalytic thought has had such a profound effect that in some circles it is so common and so ingrained as to be taken for granted, for example, the idea that an adult psychological problem stems from a repressed childhood experience with a parent (Spanos 1996).

Indeed, the very idea of hypnotizing someone who has encountered a UFO requires a specific constellation of notions about memory, trauma, and hypnosis (Dean 1998). John F. Moffitt states, "The best explanation for the postmodernist myth of 'alien abductions' as specifically 'relived' under hypnosis is—according to the title of an excellent monograph treating a now-omnipresent syndrome—*The Myth of Repressed Memory*" (2003, 516). Moffit is, of course, referring to the book by Elizabeth Loftus and Katherine Ketcham (1994) and to the highly controversial topic of false memory syndrome.

The growth of interest in abduction on the part of the therapeutic community in the 1980s and 1990s parallels the rise of work on multiple personality disorder (MPD) and satanic ritual abuse (SRA). While some ufologists were talking about the abduction epidemic in the late 1980s, others, such as the social psychologist Nicholas P. Spanos, aimed their criticism at the enormous increase in reports of MPD. Some investigators even spoke of an MPD epidemic (Spanos 1996). A similar process occurred with the dramatic increase of SRA reports, an alarming occurrence that many researchers thought was caused by specific psychologists imposing their beliefs upon their patients (Pendergrast 1996; Bottoms and Davies 1997; Richardson, Best, and Bromley 1991; Bader 2003). This case against recovered memories strongly suggests that a one-sided focus on experiences such as sleep paralysis does not provide a sufficient explanation for the "abduction epidemic" in the late 1980s. One must keep in mind the rise of influence from the therapeutic community so as not to forget the important social factors that lay therein. This means giving attention to the social dynamics that take place in therapeutic settings.

Rise of Support Groups

A whole psychological industry grew up around the ideas of repressed memories, satanic ritual abuse, and multiple personality disorder, not to mention alien abduction. According to Jodi Dean, there are in the United States alone at least twenty support groups for people who believe they have been abducted by aliens (1998, 52). In addition, there are numerous foundations, Web sites, and UFO organizations that provide information about alien abductions, and each year the numbers grow. Among the best known is the Intruders Foundation, led by ufologist and the leading alien abduction researcher in the 1980s, Budd Hopkins. Another was the Program for Extraordinary Experience Research (PEER), which has now suspended its operations; it was founded by the late John E. Mack, a professor at Harvard Medical School and a psychiatrist who overtook Hopkins's role as an authority on abductions in the 1990s. The John E. Mack Institute now carries on his work.

Several psychologists have been actively treating the alleged trauma of abductions, including Richard Boylan and Edith Fiore. Boylan and Leo Sprinkle established the Academy of Clinical Close Encounter Therapists (ACCET), so that they could develop a program for abductees run by qualified therapists. Sprinkle and Boylan believe that the abductions are real events and not psychological problems.[6] Medical doctors, including Raymond Moody and Richard Neal, have researched the abduction phenomenon. According to Randle, Estes, and Cone (1999, 67), others with advanced degrees involved in abduction research and therapy include Aphrodite Clamar, Barbara Levy, Jeffrey Mishlove, Mary Ellen Trahan, and Roberta Fennig. Dr. Fennig is one of the few fully credentialed psychiatrists treating those who claim they have been abducted. There are also several ufologists practicing hypnotherapy and conducting regular support-group meetings for abductees, which has resulted in a peculiar mix of UFO research and therapy. Several in this field, for instance Richard Boylan, Raymond Fowler, Leo Sprinkle, and Edith Fiore, attest that they have had abduction experiences (Randle, Estes, and Cone 1999, 67).

The point here is that there is no shortage of people with more or less impressive credentials who not only believe that aliens are abducting humans, but are attempting to deal with the supposed psychological trauma of those events and thereby are serving the function of lending their authority, at least in the eyes of the believers, to the alleged phenomenon. People who think that they may have been

---

6. Leo Sprinkle is the past president of the ACCET who has been using hypnosis to recover alleged suppressed or forgotten memories for thirty years or more. The current president of ACCET, Richard Boylan, a onetime licensed psychologist in the state of California, was accused of implanting memories of alien abduction in his patients. In 1995, the Board of Psychology, Department of Consumer Affairs, in the state of California revoked his license after concluding that Boylan's personal beliefs were imposed upon his patients. The documents are available from the state of California and are marked as No. W-14 and OHA No. 9404129 (Randle, Estes, and Cone 1999, 150). ACCET now is headquartered in Boylan's home in Sacramento, California.

abducted and who want to seek out a hypnotherapist or a support group should not have any problems finding one.

"Support groups can be healing," write Randle, Estes, and Cone and further state, "For the last several decades, they have helped countless people deal with loss and pain" (1999, 307–8). While they acknowledge this, they are very critical of what goes on in many of the abductee support groups. They point out the obvious, namely that support groups were originally meant to help people recover from emotional trauma and solve personal problems of a terrestrial kind. People entered a group, talked about their problems, shared their experiences with others, worked through issues, and then moved on. However, according to the authors, many of today's so-called recovery groups in the UFO subculture no longer serve this function. They suggest that the introduction of the idea of "survivor" may have changed the purpose of these support groups. Being a group member used to be part of a healing process, but it now seems to have become a new form of religion (308).

Group members are no longer people with typical psychological problems; instead they are called "abductees," "multiples," and "survivors." Instead of moving toward resolving their own problems, members now learn to incorporate them into their damaged identities as the support group takes on the function of a family and a place of belonging. The most tragic element of many of today's recovery groups, according to Randle, Estes, and Cone, is that recovery is not expected to occur (308). Instead of encouraging members to see themselves as normal humans in pain, several groups attach labels to specific types of pain, like "lifelong abductee." Members of many of today's groups are told that they are different from others, "that they will always be different, and that none but a fellow survivor could possibly understand them" (309).

"In abduction groups," Randle et al. assert, "this feeling of being different is amplified as the abductees are told that they have always been different" (309). Many abductees come to rethink their lives, and thus to reshape their biographies and identities, in terms of what they believe is a lifelong interaction with aliens. The very idea of alien abductions and its corroborating mythology becomes, at least to some abductees, a fruitful ground for exploration and reinterpretation of past events, and hitherto strange, frightening and incomprehensible experiences, like sleep paralysis or missing time, are reinterpreted within the support group's worldview.

According to folklorist Linda Jean Milligan (1988), intimate groups where members confront each other and relate to each other directly provide a context where socializing is characterized by creative consensus building. In this intimate context of social support, the group essentially shares the belief in the realness of UFOs. Because the reality of abduction is not an issue, the telling of memories and sharing experiences tends to produce new or modified aspects of the mythology as the members discuss such topics as why the aliens are abducting people, who the aliens are, where they come from, and what the ultimate goal of their "breeding program" might be. These group processes are also likely to provide a framework in which individual experiences can be given broader meaning (Spanos 1996). For instance, some abductees come to believe they are heroes in a cosmic soteriological project in which alien collections of sperm and eggs are being used to create a new hybrid species suited for a new age. In this socially reinforced point of view, the aliens are attempting to save human genetic material from pollution and an imminent environmental catastrophe (Mack 1995). In the eyes of others, however, the aliens have their own selfish reasons for abducting people, and their ultimate purpose is to use the hybrids to infiltrate legal systems and governments and finally to enslave humanity (Jacobs 1999). The apocalyptic aspects are apparent in both scenarios, but only the first has the soteriological element that gives believers a sense of hope for the future.

In the absence of a tradition, people have difficulty defining expression and often feel uneasy when asked to disclose what they regard as intimate details of personal experience. However, in a therapeutic setting aimed at overcoming the patient's resistance to opening up to the therapist, it becomes possible for the patient to express his or her uneasiness regarding certain experiences. The patient is also most likely to be assured that he or she is not alone, and that many others have had the same kind of experience. In other words, it becomes socially acceptable for the presumed abductee to talk with the therapist, as well as with other abductees in support groups. This acceptance leads us toward another aspect of this rich and complex issue, namely the process whereby people are being initiated into the group.

Becoming an Abductee in Therapy and Support Groups

All abductees do not necessarily undergo hypnosis or join a support group. However, a very vocal segment of abductees do seek the services of UFO researchers, therapists, and groups. When people seek out abduction therapists who do hypnotic regression work, they already carry a more or less well-defined preconception of what they believe has happened to them. They may initially struggle with the validity of the idea of alien abduction (Hopkins 1981; Strieber 1987), but the act of going to a therapist or joining a support group implies some suspension of disbelief. They already have some information about alien abduction through the popular media, books, movies, Web sites, friends, and family members. In other words, when the people first arrive at the therapist's office, they know more or less what to expect when they go under hypnotic regression. What they expect is that they will be able to remember, and even reexperience, the alleged mysterious and frightening incidents of abduction. As already mentioned, this expectation implies that the person also holds certain ideas about how traumatic experiences can be suppressed into the subconscious, or how the aliens are able to block memories. If they submit to certain therapists, they believe (or at least they are told so by their therapists) that their current situations, dominated by stress, anxiety, frightening dreams, and sleeping problems, are symptomatic of one or more previous alien abductions.

When seen as a ritual, the hypnosis session is a situation that helps encourage a subject to use his or her cognitive abilities to remember the experience of abduction. Moreover, the session motivates him or her to enact the role of an abductee. Through reinterpreting one's biography in terms of what is believed about alien intrusions, the subject produces a narrative about a changed life. Hypnosis is a ritual with a long history and has been defined by some as a way to unlock memories from hidden parts of the self. This idea about the qualities of hypnosis is widespread on a popular level but nevertheless contradicts most academic research on the matter. Most psychological research suggests that hypnosis should not be used to recover memories in psychotherapy.[7] Whether or not hypnosis is used, what is recalled frequently contains inaccuracies, distortions, fantasies, and outright fabrications. Moreover, the confidence people place in their recollections is not a good indicator of its accuracy. Memories are easily distorted by leading questions and repeated requests to recall details, as well as other pressures that lie within the hypnotic situation itself (Lynn and Irving 1996; Newman and Baumeister 1996; Spanos 1996; Spiegel 1997; Newman 1997; Lynn et al. 1998).

7. According to Randle, Estes, and Cone, the American Psychiatric Association and the Society for Clinical and Experimental Hypnosis issued a formal statement that hypnosis *should not be used* to enhance recall (1999, 336). Despite the fact that hundreds of studies suggest that hypnosis is a poor tool for that purpose, abduction researchers (e.g., Budd Hopkins, David M. Jacobs, James Harder, and John Carpenter) continue to use the technique of regressive hypnosis to extract memories of alleged alien abduction. In Great Britain, the situation is slightly different. The British UFO Research Association (BUFORA) introduced a complete ban on the use of regression hypnosis in 1988, but this signal to the UFO community went unheeded (Randles 1999, 46).

When the decision is reached to use hypnosis, both the hypnotherapist and the subject are aware of the expectations and the behaviors dictated by the situation (Randle, Estes, and Cone 1999; Sagan 1997). The subject is there to recover memories of abductions. Scholars of religion should perhaps not dwell on the facts that prove how poor our memories are or how unreliable hypnosis is when used as a tool for memory retrieval. What should interest us is that the subject is there to take on a *new identity*. In varying degrees, he or she wants to become known as an abductee. This does not mean that every abductee wants to go on the *Oprah Winfrey Show* (Dean 1996). On the contrary, many abductees are quite reluctant to come forward in the early stages of therapy. Initially, they seek out someone who will lend a sympathetic ear, someone who will listen; they seek social interaction with others who believe they are in the same situation.

Despite what Mack (1995) and other abduction researchers claim, the society of abductees might just be a club that people want to join (Randle, Estes, and Cone 1999). This motivation on part of the subjects should not be overlooked. As has been suggested, the subjects are there to join a specific group, and the very experience of the hypnotic regression itself can be viewed as an initiation rite into a new phase of life. Their new identities will redefine every aspect of their lives and install a cosmic dimension to their current situations. In some cases, the new identity will redefine their belief structure, their choice of friends, and their mental concerns. In other cases, the idea of alien abduction might already be congruent with their worldview. As psychologists Richard McNally et al. (2004) have found, abductees tend to hold a wide range of New Age beliefs and to have a rich fantasy life.

According to anthropologist Michael Kenny, we can gain much insight in the hypnotic situation by choosing a dramaturgical approach to the performative aspects of emotions. As readers familiar with abduction narratives know, abductees often show powerful emotional expression as they "remember" their abductions during hypnosis, and it is not unusual for the subjects to cry, shiver, scream, and by other means give expression for extreme fear. As abduction therapist Mack puts it, "This emotional expression appears altogether authentic to those who are unfamiliar with the abduction phenomenon and witness it for the first time" (Kenny 1998, 275).

After a hypnotic session, which contained several "recalled" details of an abduction, one of Mack's patients, Catherine, said that she thought she

> was making it all up until I started crying. I still don't remember it like a real memory, as in I remember I went to work yesterday. . . . Oh God . . . I'm willing to admit

maybe it's really not all my imagination. My reactions to other things make more sense if this happened. I'm not like a totally irrational person, which is kind of a relief! It doesn't seem like a dream. It seems more real than a dream, but not as real as me talking to you. . . . I don't think I would be sobbing for no apparent reason if there wasn't anything there. (Mack 1995, 153–54)

When seen as a ritual, psychotherapies that encourage or expect emotional catharsis obviously have, according to Kenny, the same suggestive potential as do the possession dramas witnessed by anthropologists in the field. Kenny writes, "The religious imagery is unmistakable, as is the evocation of what is familiar to anthropologists as a rite of passage, whereby—in a ritual punctuated by pain and fear—a person is moved from one stage of life to another" (1998, 277–78). With respect to how emotions performed in a ritual context can be transformational, Kenny is obviously right.

Another patient of John E. Mack, named Joe, explicitly said that his abduction experiences as revealed under hypnosis "were 'like a rite of passage,' a 'step of growth' toward becoming 'more human.' He felt that as a human being he had been part of 'an experiment that went sour,' a kind of aberration of God's creation" (1995, 190). For Joe, as for many other experiencers, the aliens have come in order to save human beings from an imminent catastrophe. The current ecological situation is believed to be a threat to the very existence of humankind. When the aliens collect sperm from males and ova from females to crossbreed them with extraterrestrial DNA and create a new hybrid species, the aliens will preserve, according to Joe, "the human genetic substance, though in some other form" (Mack 1995, 199). As Whitmore noticed, aliens seem to have taken over God's traditional role as a savior and ultimate director of history (1995, 74). The goal of history, according to some abduction narratives, is not the unification of man and God in Christ, but a unification of humans and aliens, a joining of the two species in a new evolutionary form of hybrids, suited for a new time.

Cathartic expression of emotions may be seen as one of several important factors in the creation of a new social status or identity. The therapeutic situation, the very meeting between the abduction researcher and the potential abductee, provides a ritual context, which allows the subject to articulate his or her emotions associated with strange events, such as sleep paralysis, missing time, or nose bleeds. This ritual context further encourages the subject to use his or her fantasies and cognitive abilities to integrate these fragmented "memories" into a fuller, richer, and more comprehensible abduction narrative. The subject goes through a process wherein he or she accepts the confabulation under hypnosis, legitimated by the therapist as real memories of abductions. By attending a support group for abductees where socializing with others strengthens a collective sense of what they believe has happened to them, the subject may start to take on a new identity and may eventually accept a new social status as an abductee, or experiencer.

Seen from a structural and functional point of view, meetings with an abduction therapist who practices hypnosis and social interaction with other abductees in support groups may be looked at as two types of initiation rites that allow subjects to gain new cosmological insight and to be part of a community that holds esoteric wisdom about the ways extraterrestrials relate to humans. The hypnotherapeutic situation itself may be seen as an arena, a scene where different roles are enacted in accordance with more or less well-defined sets of rules for conduct, speech, and behavior. With respect to the phenomenon of sleep paralysis as discussed above, it is worth noting that the therapeutic setting is where one is permitted or, more precisely, expected to give rich descriptions about strange and puzzling experiences that typically occur during the night.

The small communities of abductees that have grown up around abduction researchers and experiencers have become secretive societies of people who believe they are participating, voluntarily or not, in a grand cosmic operation supervised by extraterrestrials. Abductees feel they have experienced something unique, and repeatedly say that anyone who has not experienced what they have will never be able to understand. Instead, they stress how people with any official vested interest in UFOs and aliens are wrongfully subjected to ridicule. In this respect they are on the margins of society at large, and they are most likely aware of it themselves. That might be one of the reasons the support groups, at least for some people, have become a kind of surrogate family, a place for belonging, and a place where uneasy feelings, identity conflicts, and social insecurity may be confronted and worked out in a safe environment. Therapeutic settings, like the hypnotic situation and the meetings between abductees in support groups, may be seen as modern initiation rites in which subjects ritualize the alien abduction mythology in their quest for meaning. Hypnotic sessions and therapy groups for abductees may also, in part, be seen as modern examples of how an old phenomenon like sleep paralysis has manifested itself in yet another social and mythological form.

Abducted?

Throughout this chapter, I have attempted a critical multidimensional approach to the so-called abduction epidemic of the late 1980s and early 1990s. Surely, much more research is needed before all the complicated aspects of this highly interesting phenomenon can be dealt with properly. Nevertheless, some of the specific reasons for the dramatic increase in abduction reports seem clear. During the 1980s, there arose a modified tradition of alien abductions, which served as an interpretative model by which the individuals who were confronted by a perceptual anomaly or were facing extraordinary conditions, could orient their experiences in the light of the culturally available and socially sanctioned concepts of alien abductions. It seems likely that a significant number of these experiences, maybe as many as up to 50 percent, stemmed from conditions akin to sleep paralysis and dreams. Furthermore, it also seems likely that the modified tradition of alien abduction that focused on bedroom intruders not only allowed an extraterrestrial interpretation of ordinary conditions, such as sleep paralysis, but also helped create the abduction epidemic during the late 1980s and early 1990s.

Experience alone is not sufficient for starting a mythology, much less a tradition, unless culture provides a means for giving expression to these experiences. That might just be exactly what happened during the late 1980s when the alien abduction hypothesis became highly available to a large number of citizens who otherwise lacked satisfactory language for dealing with this puzzling phenomenon. In addition, the ideological influence of the psychological tradition and the rise of therapy and support groups in the same period provided the sociocultural conditions necessary for some people to come to terms with an extraterrestrial interpretation of their experiences.

Some alien abduction narratives may be seen as modern examples of how a common experience like sleep paralysis, which in the past would have been called a nightmare or an encounter with an evil spirit, lost the older traditions that defined it. It continued a hidden, "homeless" existence until it manifested itself under the specific sociocultural conditions of the late twentieth century. In this respect the abduction mythology nurtured by therapeutic settings are, in part, social expressions of this very old phenomenon rationalized in accordance with the cultural (specifically psychological and technological) milieu of the current period.

Secondary Beliefs and the Alien Abduction Phenomenon

7

Benson Saler

This chapter reports on some research now in process. My colleague, Charles Ziegler, and I are engaged in a complex project dealing with the nature and multi-faceted significance of belief. Among other things, we are very much interested in the phenomenon of credulity, which we characterize as the acceptance or justification of belief largely or entirely on the testimony of other persons (Saler 2004). Our stipulative definition of credulity does not necessarily connote something pejorative, despite a widespread, popular use of the word to mean an uncritical or unsophisticated readiness to accept belief. Credulity, as we conceive it, is a panhuman phenomenon of immense evolutionary significance. It promotes the accessing and utilization of information stored outside of any given individual, and it facilitates the achievement of cognitive complexity. It is often a cost-effective way of enabling persons within a social group to coordinate their cognitive resources, as well as to benefit from information derived from outsiders. However, there can be costs. Among them are the possible dissemination of misinformation, the narrowing or closing off of avenues of potentially useful investigation and ratiocination, and the diversion of energies that might be gainfully employed elsewhere.

Rather than discuss credulity and related matters mainly in abstract fashion, Ziegler and I attempt to explore them with respect to selected case studies. We are particularly attracted to situations that include expressed differences of opinion within the same society. That is, cases where some members of a given society express what seems to be strong positive conviction, whereas others register skepticism or disbelief. For exploratory, illustrative, and comparative purposes, and

128

confining ourselves to North America, we have chosen these primary case studies: the Salem witchcraft trials of 1692, a rash of trials in the 1980s alleging ritual or "satanic" sexual abuse of young children, and the alien abduction phenomenon. While we depend entirely on published material and studies for our coverage of the first and the second, our exploration of the alien abduction phenomenon is based on interviews and diverse other sources of information. The alien abduction phenomenon is our central case study, and it constitutes our primary substantive focus for the investigation of what we call "secondary beliefs" as they relate to the matter of credulity. This chapter deals only with that case study.

The Modern Abduction Phenomenon

Persons who affirm the reality of alien abductions generally claim that "alien beings" have abducted contemporary residents of our planet. Numbers of people suggest or maintain that earthlings are kidnapped for medical examinations or experiments, and especially for examinations or experiments dealing with procreation. While most of those who make these assertions appear to believe that the aliens are extraterrestrial beings from distant solar systems, some suggest that the abductors either are from "parallel dimensions" or that they are time travelers from the troubled future of our own planet.

The modern abduction phenomenon contains elements that remind several of its interpreters of many other things. These include Celtic and other folklore accounts of fairy abductions, certain events in Greek, Roman, or other myths, Judaic and Christian references to angels, North American Indian captivity narratives, still other captivity stories, and a wide diversity of themes found in science fiction, ufology, and other expressions of contemporary Euro-American popular culture. Indeed, Terry Matheson (1998), professor of literature at the University of Saskatchewan, sees in them and in the analyses made of them by several authors a complex and subtle ambivalence toward technology, along with a related discourse on power. Elsewhere I attempt to relate abduction narratives to certain developments in the postmodern world as sketched by the postmodernists Frederic Jameson and Jean-François Lyotard. I believe that "[c]ommon themes in abduction accounts are the powerlessness of the victims, their vulnerability to exploitation, and the indifference to human dignity and pretensions of autonomy that is a marked aspect of alien hegemony" (Saler, Ziegler, and Moore 1997, 143), albeit more recent accounts of abduction sometimes suggest more positive themes. The alien abduction phenomenon, to be sure, evinces continuity with a long and probably panhuman history of seeing mysterious or remarkable things in the skies, but one can also interpret it as resonating with much else. As a set of Euro-American narratives for our times, it blends in arresting ways power and sexual themes with interests in science, technology, and the occult.

One of the most famous cases of claimed abduction is that of Betty and Barney Hill, who were reportedly abducted from a highway in New Hampshire in September 1961 and who later recalled the full extent of their experiences under hypnosis. From the time of the putative Hill abduction, there have literally been thousands of cases of claimed abductions. No one knows precisely how many, but hundreds have been summarized in a growing literature accessible to the public (e.g., Lorenzen 1963, 1970; Fuller 1966; Lorenzen and Lorenzen 1977; Walton 1978; Fowler 1979, 1982, 1990, 1993; Rogo 1980; Bullard 1987b; Hopkins 1981, 1987; Strieber 1987, 1989; Randles 1988; Bryan 1995; Jacobs 1993, 1999, 2000; Mack 1995; Brookesmith 1998; Randle, Estes, and Cone 1999; Denzler 2001). Still other accounts are stored in the private files and videotape archives of numbers of researchers. Some of the abductees tell their stories under hypnosis, but others furnish reports without being hypnotized.

It is important for scholarly purposes to distinguish between the accounts of people claiming to have been abducted—narratives that are often fragmentary and sometimes inconsistent—and the published or filmed versions of those accounts as fashioned by others. Some commentators have recognized the importance of this distinction. So-called contactees are individuals alleging typically friendly personal contacts with aliens, and abductees are usually removed against their will. Randle, Estes, and Cone remark that the contactee is the focus of his or her tale, whereas in the case of abductions the researcher is "the man in the middle" between the abductee and the general public, because the researcher is the person who "answers questions" (1999, 90).

Terry Matheson makes analogous points in a critical analysis of the writings of several authors dealing with the abduction phenomenon. In his initial examination of the abduction literature, Matheson tells us:

> I made two discoveries regarding these narratives and their crucial role in determining how they were received. By and large, authors of most abduction chronicles favored one interpretive possibility—that the experiences were taking place more or less as the abductees claimed—and relentlessly privileged that possibility even when the evidence pointed in other directions. I also noticed that the original evi-

dence itself—the actual information provided by the abductees—was often less precise and coherent than was the material the public received. In fact, readers of such books were being manipulated to a significant extent, the writers having employed various strategies designed to enhance coherence and lessen the likelihood that alternative conclusions would be reached. (1998, 12)

Matheson goes on to make a point similar to those expressed by Carl Jung (1959), Curtis Peebles (1994), Saler, Ziegler, and Moore (1997), Thomas E. Bullard (2000a, 2000b), and others. As Matheson puts it, "I began to suspect that what was occurring was the creation of a modern, secular myth that we were fortunate enough to be able to observe in the process of being formed and refined" (1998, 13).

Causation and Belief

Proponents of the alien abduction phenomenon sometimes employ a trinomial vocabulary for distinguishing among persons who express opinions about the reality of abductions by aliens. "Believers" are those who accept such abductions as real or as highly probable. "Skeptics" are those who confess to harboring strong doubts. "Debunkers," a subset of skeptics, actively attempt to discredit the idea of alien abductions, sometimes proposing alternative explanations for the claimed experiences.

Proffered explanations alternative to actual abduction by aliens include deliberate lying, screen memories that mask sexual abuse, hypnagogic or hypnopompic states, hysterical contagion, birth traumas, psychopathology, suggestions from hypnotists and others, wish fulfillment, confabulation, fugue states, temporal lobe epilepsy, and special cases of temporal lobe dysfunctions triggered by electromagnetic stimulation stemming from movements of the earth's crust.

Ziegler and I hold that the claims of abductees relate to a diversity of causes—that, indeed, the alien abduction phenomenon is best conceived to be multicausal in origin. Allowance should be made for the very real possibility that different alleged abductees respond to different factors and that no one causal factor can be adduced for all cases. If this be accepted, then not only can efforts to dismiss a possible alternative cause not be taken as significantly strengthening the case for alien abductions, but such efforts are also unlikely to equate to a blanket refutation of the suggested alternative possibility. Various skeptics, for instance, have suggested a phenomenon termed "sleep paralysis" as an alternative explanation for the abduction phenomenon. In doing so, some have been inspired by the folklorist David

Hufford's analysis (1982) of tales about a folkloric being known as "The Old Hag." Hufford argues that a textual approach to understanding Old Hag stories can be enriched by also considering an experiential dimension of such narratives, inasmuch as some people claim to have actually experienced the Hag. Such experiences often involve a sensation of being paralyzed soon before either waking up or going to sleep. Hufford suggests that those experiences may have enriched folkloric repertoires about the Old Hag. While physiological states by themselves, Hufford maintains, cannot account for either Old Hag folklore or for the meanings of experiences that people associate with that folklore, they and the narratives may sometimes be mutually reinforcing. Drawing on their readings of Hufford's nuanced analysis, some students of alien abductions hypothesize that some abductees may "see" aliens in consequence of their physiomental states during the transition from wakefulness to sleep or during the transition from sleep to wakefulness (hypnagogic and hypnopompic states).

The historian David M. Jacobs (1993), however, attempts to discredit that explanation entirely, thus removing a causal possibility alternative to the extraterrestrial agency explanation that he favors. He points out that there are a number of reported abductions that occur in daylight when the reputed abductees are presumably in full wakefulness. If, however, we adopt a multicausal perspective, Jacobs cannot legitimately champion a blanket refutation of the hypnagogic or hypnopompic possibility. Although that possibility cannot account for persons appearing to experience abduction in full wakefulness, hypnagogic and hypnopompic explanations remain as viable alternative explanations for at least some of those persons who reportedly encounter aliens in the bedroom either when going to sleep or when beginning to wake up.

Understandably, most of the literature to date focuses on reputed abductees. Abductees, who are also called "experiencers," relate dramatic tales: arresting stories that stimulate some to suppose that earthlings have been contacted by aliens, while motivating others to offer alternative conjectures as to why their fellow citizens might furnish such narratives. Ziegler and I call the statements affirmed by abductees themselves *primary beliefs.* However edited and packaged they may be on their way to the public arena, they constitute the primary public "data" of the abduction phenomenon.

Yet, while we must take account of and seek to comprehend primary beliefs and those who affirm them, we also have a strong interest in what we call *secondary beliefs* and their proponents. Secondary beliefs are the affirmations of persons who do

7.1. Western culture contains many types of alien abduction narratives. One theme states that aliens transport abductees to their ships by means of teleportation. Artwork by Diana Tumminia.

not claim to have had abduction experiences but who profess to accept and support the reports of those who do claim such experiences.

Secondary believers have not been adequately studied in the academic literature on alien abductions. For scholars of religion they can be as interesting, or perhaps even more interesting, than primary believers. In the histories of religious and secular movements, it is secondary believers, after all, who sometimes turn the claims of experiencers or visionaries into successfully diffused persuasions, and they deserve at least as much attention as the original sources of the narratives that they support and extend.

Considering secondary believers with respect to the alien abduction phenomenon, credulity in the stipulative sense offered earlier is salient. That is because secondary beliefs in the reality of the alien abduction phenomenon rest entirely on the testimonies of persons, whether hypnotized or not. For despite the efforts of dedicated secondary believers, such as Budd Hopkins (1981, 1987), to find unambiguous material evidence for abductions, no such evidence has been produced. Hopkins and others, for example, have explored the possibility that aliens may have "implanted" monitoring or control devices into some abductees. Hopkins showed me two albums of color photographs of skin colorations and other bodily markings that he deemed possible evidence of implants, but I saw nothing unusual in the photographs. Sensational rumors spread by other persons, to the effect that actual implants have been (or are soon to be) surgically recovered, have never, insofar as I am aware, been given credence by the scientific community. Neither claimed implants nor other claims of material evidence have been produced to the satisfaction of interested skeptical observers. Until claims of such evidence are authenticated, I feel obliged to conclude that what people say happened in abductions remains the basis for secondary beliefs.

Some Attractions of Secondary Beliefs

An obvious and immediate question that merits consideration is this: Why do secondary believers appear to believe in alien abductions? Why, indeed, in the face of challenges from skeptics and debunkers within their own society, do they persist in affirming what they affirm? Further, what might be the larger cultural, comparative, and perhaps even evolutionary implications of their affirmations? These are questions that Ziegler and I are addressing in our ongoing research, and it would be premature to attempt to answer all of them here. However, our project is well enough advanced to sketch some answers to the first question posed.

To begin, just as primary believers are best viewed within a multicausal framework, so, too, is it necessary to entertain a variety of hypotheses for attempting to understand what may motivate secondary believers. It must be noted in that regard that not all secondary believers register the same intensity of belief. We have been struck both in our interviewing and in our reading by evidence of diversity in the profession of belief, as well as in the contents being professed. Some secondary believers so hedge their affirmations as to suggest lack of firmness in belief, whereas others give the appearance of strong conviction. In that regard, moreover, second-ary believers mirror in opposition skeptics and debunkers, making for interesting comparisons. Some skeptics, in our experience, are not entirely skeptical, and they sometimes give the appearance of wanting to believe while not being willing to say that they do. Belief in the reality of aliens, after all, can stimulate, as well as be stim-ulated by the imagination. We surmise that it is attractive to some people at least partly (or perhaps largely) on that score.

On the extreme, we have persons who are strongly committed either to affirm-ing or to denying alien abductions and various other claims about UFOs, aliens, and the positions of the government and the military and scientific establishments re-specting UFOs and abductions. Thus, for instance, one of the strongest proponents of the reality of UFOs as alien spacecraft, and one of the strongest claimants that there are government-supported conspiracies to suppress information about UFOs, is Stanton T. Friedman. Mr. Friedman has interviewed numerous witnesses to seemingly unusual events. Certain of his interviews in the late 1970s and there-after, for example, were instrumental in making the so-called "Roswell Incident," the claimed crash of an alien spacecraft near Roswell, New Mexico, in 1947, an impor-tant case in the UFO community's roster of cases (Saler, Ziegler, and Moore 1997). Armed with the Freedom of Information Act, he has tirelessly (and sometimes suc-cessfully) petitioned U.S. government agencies to release hitherto classified docu-ments. Utilizing the purported eyewitness accounts that he and other researchers have collected, along with the documents that he has obtained, Mr. Friedman has devoted many years of his life to lecturing and writing about UFOs and conspiracies (his dedication in that regard is well captured in the Redstar Film documentary *Stanton T. Friedman IS Real*). Mr. Friedman is matched both in zeal and in the allo-cation of much of his lifetime by the dedicated debunker Philip J. Klass. Mr. Klass's numerous publications and many lectures over the years have been directed at re-butting what Mr. Friedman and like-minded others affirm. Karl Pflock, a ufologist who has moved from being a circumspect believer to being a sometimes outspoken debunker in the case of the Roswell Incident, has pointed out to me in a personal communication that Mr. Klass is as much a member of the UFO community as Mr. Friedman. I deem that an astute observation if by "community" we mean a set of persons who evince more that a casual interest in some topic. Much of Mr. Klass's identity is invested in topics of immediate interest to the UFO community.

What motivates such strongly committed persons as Mr. Friedman and Mr. Klass? As of this writing, Ziegler and I have not had the privilege of interviewing ei-ther, so I cannot answer the question that I pose. I do think, however, that it is an interesting one, and I hope that we may later attempt to answer it within a biographical framework.

In our interviews and in our readings, we have also been struck with the frequently expressed opinions of secondary believers respecting the apparent *sincerity* of many abductees or experiencers, a sincerity that secondary believers encounter either on personal contact or through reading accounts or viewing videotapes or films furnished by others. While secondary believers occasionally discount the testimonies of some persons who claim to be experiencers, dismissing them as lies or as suggestive of pathology, they often appear to be favorably impressed by narrations that meet certain standards of reportage. First, those standards include the deliverance of narratives that accord with those furnished by other experiencers. Something of a subculture on alien abductions has crystallized (largely with help from the media—Hollywood and television in particular), and, though still somewhat heterogeneous in details, it includes now a fair degree of consensus about what happens when one is abducted. Second, standards for judging abduction narratives dispose at least some secondary believers to favor stories that are related with shows of emotion that are judged to be convincing.

Emotional expressions adjudged especially convincing are shows of fear or terror. These are deemed appropriate and are accepted as integral elements in the primary narrations. Such expressions on the part of primary believers remind me of a radical form of psychotherapy known as abreaction therapy, which supposedly releases repressed emotions. In that form of treatment, the patient is encouraged to reexperience a trauma and accompanying emotional responses that triggered the disturbance. From the skeptic's point of view, however, abductees would be abreacting nonevents (Holden and French 2002; McNally et al. 2004). If the skeptics are correct, how then are we to explain the seemingly sincere expressions of fear or terror? As displacements? As false memories occasioned by traumatic stress? As playacting? Or as something else?

In any case, the emotional component that primary believers communicate to, or evoke in, secondary believers is a matter that deserves close scholarly attention. Sensitivity to emotive transmissions and triggers would be useful not only with respect to studying the dissemination of narratives of claimed alien abductions, but also for a wider understanding of the spread of what we conventionally term religious narrative.

In a 1973 paper dealing with the nature of belief, the anthropologist Robert Hahn proposed what he called the ethnography of sincerity. Hahn was largely concerned with formal criteria for evaluating propositions. A widened sense of the ethnography of sincerity, a sense that includes attention to the emotions, could well strengthen and extend our scholarly engagements. People, after all, often make efforts to assess the sincerity of messengers as part of their more inclusive efforts to assess the reliability of messages.

Scholars, as we well know, generally seek to situate, analyze, and interpret messages. If they aspire to convincing explanations of why some messages are accepted and others rejected, and by whom, they also need to consider the messengers, their audiences, and the nature of, and constraints on, interactions between them. While we can be guided by general theoretical understandings, those cannot by themselves explain why, within the same society, some people are believers, others are skeptics, and still others are active debunkers. Yet these are matters that need explaining.

Alien Abduction Narratives and Religious Contexts

Scott R. Scribner

This chapter explores, from a psychosocial perspective, some parallels between alien abduction narratives (AANs) and religious phenomena by examining samples of widely published accounts.[1] I acknowledge the potential controversy and resistance that such a proposal may encounter. Some secularists may see little difference among what they generally consider fantastic or irrational accounts. Many religious believers may be offended by any implied equivalency between an orthodox (canonical) narrative and one that is merely "weird" (and also perhaps heretical or demonic). On a personal note, many people have asked me why the study of UFOs or alien abduction could possibly be important in the modern world where "real" social problems need attention (as opposed to imaginary problems). My answer is that the claim that a story is *true,* although it also seems *strange,* raises the possibility of new knowledge that can stimulate both scientific and religious inquiry.

Alien Abduction Narratives (AANs)

For millennia, reports about humans being kidnapped by supernatural beings have appeared in many cultures (Bullard 1989; Sagan 1997). The modern form of alien abduction narrative describes a kidnapping by extraterrestrials who (depending on

1. Some AAN researchers are quite loathe to hear psychosocial interpretations of AANs (Jacobs 1999). One possible explanation for this resistance is that if alien abduction is seen as psychological—subject to explanations using models of cognitive and emotional relevance—it may lose status as potential science or empirical reality.

the point of view) may or may not be classified as supernatural beings. Although reports of abductions by these beings have occurred throughout recorded history, modern researchers agree that attention to abduction reports has dramatically increased since 1966 (Vallee 1965; Thompson 1991), the year that marked the first widespread publicity about the Barney and Betty Hill abduction.

Alien abduction narratives differ from *contactee* narratives in that most contactee narratives are explicitly intended to convey spiritual meaning. Contactees relate how they meet space people, ride in spaceships, receive higher knowledge, and take physical or out-of-body trips to other planets (Lewis 1995; Partridge 2003). For example, the late George King, founder of the Aetherius Society, adapted or developed new theologies based on alleged extraterrestrial contacts, much like religious prophets do following visionary encounters with spirit beings or angels (Wallis 1974). The UFO prophet Raël (1987a) claims to have had mystical meetings with the space-traveling creators of humankind. Uriel the Archangel of Unarius communicated with Space Brothers who reside in fourth-dimensional energy (Tumminia 2005). Contactee messages easily fall into a religious category, especially with their emphasis on revelatory visions.

An AAN can describe a single experience or a group of experiences. Many AANs involve the claim that strange beings took a person out of a bed or an automobile—usually at night—and subjected him or her to quasi-medical examinations and other bizarre treatment. Another reported locale for abduction is an isolated place like a forest or a field. Frequently these accounts include expressions of terror about painful or humiliating procedures. Those who tell such narratives may go public themselves or they may contact AAN researchers. Based on a controversial interpretation of data from a Roper Poll, some UFO abduction researchers claim that two million Americans may have been abducted by aliens (Hopkins, Jacobs, and Westrum 1992).

John Fuller's *Interrupted Journey* brought the abduction story of Betty and Barney Hill to millions of Americans in 1966 when *Look* magazine carried excerpts from the new book. The Hill case is considered paradigmatic for the modern form of the AAN because it contains all the elements just mentioned and because it was the first widely known case (Thompson 1991; Lewis 2000; Denzler 2001). Under hypnosis, Betty Hill drew the so-called Star Map, which located the home world of her abductors and which became evidence to some followers of the veracity of her account. After Barney Hill passed away in 1969, Betty Hill made many public statements and personal appearances, and until her recent death (in 2004) was considered a spokesperson for abductees in general.

Another prominent example of an alien abduction narrative is contained in Raymond Fowler's book *The Andreasson Affair,* published in 1979. Betty Andreasson was a conservative Christian homemaker who lived in southern New England during the 1960s. Betty's alien abduction allegedly occurred on January 25, 1967, although she did not report it until 1974 in response to a *National Enquirer* call for alien abduction stories. Later she wrote a ufologist in 1975, and she told her story to abduction investigator Raymond Fowler in 1977.

Raymond Fowler had studied UFO cases for several years before he met Betty Andreasson. He employed the services of a professional hypnotist to try to recover Betty Andreasson's memories. The events she described under hypnosis were even stranger than those of Betty Hill, whose story Betty Andreasson had read before her own experience. Interestingly, Betty Hill and Betty Andreasson shared a number of characteristics beyond their first names:

• Both women lived in New England during the 1960s;

• Both had disturbing dreams that they *later* attributed to strange events preceding their dreams;

• Both told their stories publicly only after a significant amount of time had passed (five years and ten years, respectively);

• Both became revered by their followers as modern-day UFO figures.

In January 1967, there was considerable stress in the Andreasson household because Betty's husband had been seriously injured in an automobile accident and was laid up in the hospital. Under hypnosis, Betty Andreasson said that while she and her daughter were at home, several strange beings floated into the house through the walls and took Betty on a very unusual journey. Betty's journey included travel to a distant planet where she saw beautiful cities. She describes being transported great distances through tubes of liquid. Her captors introduced her to a large Phoenix-like bird.

The Andreasson affair is notable for the large number of investigators interacting with the family as interviewers and hypnotists. The "controlling hypnotist," Harold Edelstein, made leading statements to Betty (Fowler 1979, 30, 40). As Fowler reports, Edelstein said, "Do you need a little refreshing? To the incidents leading up to where we left off?" (95). Besides Edelstein, five other people (including Fowler) joined in the hypnosis sessions. It is thus not surprising (and is even ironic) that Betty describes the interaction with the aliens as a "strange hypnotic-like influence" (119). Fowler makes a significant statement late in his narrative, regarding Betty's remarkable recall of strange events from ten years earlier: "We tend to forget that prior to her recall via hypnosis, Betty had remembered little of the UFO incident" (131).

Fowler and his hypnotist associates interviewed Betty over a period of years and wrote five more books about her. One serious problem with the hypnosis sessions involves the highly leading questions put at numerous points by the investigators. Interviewers consistently appear to confabulate her remarks. Debunker Philip J. Klass (1989) indicates that with encouragement her accounts became increasingly elaborate and quasi-religious in content.

Compared with contactee accounts, AANs contain a greater variety of messages. In addition, some aliens disembark from UFOs, as in the Hill case, but many arrive without UFO disks or other vehicles (for example, many of Mack's "experiencers" are whisked from their beds directly to an alien laboratory and back again). The tone of some AANs is transcendental (Strieber 1987), while others are sexual (Mack 1995; Jacobs 1999), and most involve medical molestation (Fiore 1993; Newman and Baumeister 1996, 1998). Many of the alleged experiences are remembered as frightening, and their content may be interpreted by some in religious terms as diabolical or demonic (Sagan 1997). While contactee narratives emphasize the positive intentions of alien beings, the more recent AANs, with their fear components, present the perspective of a struggle with negative forces. Taken together, these two perspectives parallel the light and dark side of religious narratives.

Seen in the context of a cultural mainstream (which also provides the context for what is considered strange), AANs are only one among many types of anomalous narratives, along with stories of miracles, apparitions, ghosts, and other spiritual experiences (Hufford 2005). For those cases that meet the criteria, David J. Hufford identifies the etiology of the experience to the objective physiologically based phenomenon of *sleep paralysis* (SP). He also takes to task modern science, medicine, *and* theology for mischaracterizing such "real" experiences as hallucination, psychopathology, and heresy, respectively. In each case, he says, there is an incorrect assumption of preexisting ignorance, delusion, or unorthodox belief. Hufford benefits from having experienced the SP phenomenon firsthand, as I have. However, his insightful analysis nonetheless implies a future materialistic solution to the problem of weird experiences, whereas my focus is on the dynamic role of such experiences as mediators (what I call *working facts*) between individual psychological structures and social institutions.

A generalized interpretive framework for anomalous narratives has not yet been developed. Such a framework would integrate the perspectives of many fields,

8.1. Thousands of people claim to have been abducted and
experimented upon by aliens called Greys. One common theme
of some alien abduction narratives is the impregnation of
humans by aliens for a hybrid breeding program.

including psychology (Spanos 1996; Clancy 2005), physiology (McNally et al. 2004; Cheyne 2003), sociology (Lewis 1995), rhetoric (Kelley 1999), religious studies (Whitmore 1995; Partridge 2003), folklore (Bullard 1982; Ellis 2001; Hufford 2005), and other disciplines. Whatever the origin of the experience (SP, trance, other altered states, suggestion, hypnosis, group worldview, or an interactive combination of several elements), we must focus on the ways the experience is interpreted. In the case of AANs, one step I have taken to control the domain for study is to separate the examination of the narratives themselves from what I call *UFO forensics,* which includes scientific assessment of the empirical facts of an alleged anomalous event. One good reason for making this distinction is that the government, the Air Force, hundreds of journalists, and dozens of UFO organizations possess far more resources than I do for tracking down crop circles, grassy burn marks, and skin scoops. Without dismissing the importance of physical evidence, I am more interested in the role that AANs play in the development of new knowledge and worldviews as the interrelated components of both scientific and religious concepts.

My research on AANs (Scribner 2003) studied the descriptions of fears in widely available AANs compiled by five prominent authors, whose popular books describe accounts from approximately two dozen primary informants. The sample included John Fuller, Raymond Fowler, Budd Hopkins, Whitley Strieber, and John Mack. Using a *narrative-phenomenological* approach, I found striking indications of very human sources for the "alien" actions and imagery. My study employed a phenomenological model proposed by archetypal psychologist Robert Sardello (1999). He asserted that humans experience fear phenomenologically as an *autonomous psychological presence* that originates from one of nine distinct sources that he called *fear worlds*. These include nature (the physical universe and all living things), the human body, emotions, threats of terror or violence, the experience of time, human passions, the economic realm, interpersonal relationships, and awareness of suffering and death. In the sense that they are experienced as autonomous psychological constructs, Sardello's fear presences are strikingly similar to the "waking terror" presences of sleep paralysis as identified by Hufford (2005).

My research hypothesis proposed that if the fear descriptions in widely available AANs reflected Sardello's fear model, it would indicate that the alien abduction experience originated within *human* conditions, albeit unusual ones that required further study. The survey of fear-related references in the data found all nine fear types, with the highest incidence occurring in the most immediately personal areas: the human body, emotions, and interpersonal relationships. Within individual accounts, fear descriptions were found to reflect specific personal and social life problems as described by those who had the experience. It is unlikely that such findings could be consistent with a phenomenon originating from a nonhuman source. However, they suggest existential conditions and real experiences that have been addressed as religious themes throughout history, which, of course, vary according to culture and historical period.

My research also uncovered suggestive parallels between AANs and traditional religious narratives, including their imagery (e.g., beings from the sky; apocalyptic themes), use of language (expressions of fear and awe; longing for "communion"), and even the explicit influence of verses from the Bible. In the course of my research, I found it helpful to distinguish between the second-hand narration used by the various authors on the subject and the first-hand testimony of those who reported having the abduction experiences. I use the term *Tellers* for the primary informants who originate alien abduction accounts. Other terms have been proposed for primary informants, such as "contactee" and "abductee," but terms such as these contain too many assumptions about the event. The late John Mack (1995) preferred the terms "experiencer" or "witness," which he considered more objective than "abductee." In a scientific sense, however, we must admit a lack of first-hand knowledge about what kind of experience has actually occurred.

Both abduction investigators and social scientists struggle with an appropriate language to label the events they study, which further complicates this area of research. Tellers may indeed be giving reliable firsthand accounts of what they experienced. Then again, preexisting belief systems and other persons may have influenced them before and after the fact. From a social psychological perspective, researchers need to know the operating social contexts from which the narrative emerged. For example, the affiliations of some Tellers—as members of a specific type of support group or clients of a particular therapist—may affect the content and direction of their narratives. I use the term *Narrators* to indicate those promoters or secondary informants (usually media-oriented professionals who may or may not be believers) who collected and redacted Teller accounts and also added their own interpretive context (as narration). Narrators bring their own layers of interpretation to the collection and selection of "original" accounts, and this is important for students of the phenomenon to take into consideration. In the following section, I extrapolate a number of parallels between alien abduction narratives and religious narratives taken from my research in this field.

Religious Parallels with AANs

If the dozens of book titles each year are any indication, a proliferation of alien abductions flows through our culture, indicating encounters with some kind of mysterious forces beyond our control. Leaping full-blown from another dimension—as *Twilight Zone* creator Rod Serling used to say, "not of sight and sound but of mind"—AANs are often creatures of the night, escalating the human predicament toward fear and awe. The phenomenon is not new. As the ancient Israelites declared: "For who is there of all flesh, that has heard the voice of the living God speaking out of the midst of fire, *as we have* [italics added], and has still lived?" (Deuteronomy 5:26). Reports of awe before wondrous experiences behave like the grain formative of the religious narrative's pearl.

Interpretations of AANs crystallize within existing belief systems, where they sometimes offer quasi-scientific explanations of the phenomena. In terms of contemporary religion, AANs already play a role in supplementing today's religious cosmologies. Various authors make explicitly religious interpretations of AANs (Downing 1968; Thompson 1993) as does Christian evangelist Billy Graham (1994), who sees UFOs and alien visitors as God's angels. Some Christian fundamentalists (Lamy 1999; Missler and Eastman 2003) view AANs and UFOs as indications of activity that anticipates the apocalyptic "last days" of our planet. One example is Charles "Chuck" Missler, who is unequivocal in his opinion that "aliens" are anti-God demons. The steady development of UFO religions clearly indicates that UFO reports and alien abduction accounts can have powerful religious implications.

New Age mystics, contactees, and religious fundamentalists may incorporate AANs as part of their own belief narratives. In such cases, AANs are not essential, but they become supporting players that supplement explanations of good and evil using UFO imagery. Although such worldviews do not form their entire group focus around alien abduction, UFO religions center on explaining its spiritual meaning. For instance, Unarius would say such an experience was a memory of a past life (Tumminia 2005), or Raëlians might venture that Elohim space travelers are introducing new genetic material into human DNA (Palmer 2004).

As viewed from the perspectives of social science and ordinary common sense, AANs share a similar narrative status with revealed religions (Hetherington 1993). When someone reports visions or other highly personal experiences that have led to a religious conversion, that testimony constitutes personal knowledge based on a perceived event that he or she interprets as real. AANs differ from traditional witnessing in that they assume a modern technological worldview, but they are similar in bypassing the normal verification requirements of scientific or social consensus. Even if an AAN does not describe a verifiable physical event, it still can inspire personal awe and transformation while remaining resistant to scientific verification.

Even if alien abduction "events" cannot be independently corroborated (as critics point out), we cannot know what "really" occurred, *and* we might not be sure even if we had been physically present. The New Testament gospels are anomalous narratives in a similar sense. Similar epistemological uncertainty applies in cases of alleged past-life regression (Jacobs and Hopkins 1992) and many other types of hypnotically obtained recollections, which are highly vulnerable to aggressive scientific critique. Skeptical or debunking interpretations (the perspective of the dominant scientific worldview) appear to be ineffective in dispelling the personally transforming effect of such experiences. In cases of religious belief, intellectual coolness or abrasive rejection may even strengthen the adherent's resolve (Festinger, Riecken, and Schachter 1956; Tumminia 1998). What really happens empirically may recede in importance once a person is already committed to an alien abduction explanation of their feelings and perceptions.

Both AANs and religious stories can lead to a dramatic reframing of a person's

Weltanschauung, or worldview. Similarly, a relatively small shift in perspective might turn a biblical account into an AAN (Williams 1991; Lieb 1998). Consider the two Bible passages below, which represent firsthand and secondhand accounts, respectively. Allow yourself to consider, "To what extent are these Biblical accounts also AANs?" To what extent might their narrative forms be interchangeable?

Example 1

On one such expedition I was going to Damascus, armed with full powers and a commission from the chief priests, and at midday as I was on my way, your Majesty [King Agrippa], I saw a *light brighter than the sun come down from heaven* [italics added]. It shone brilliantly around me and my fellow travelers. We all fell to the ground, and I heard a voice saying to me in Hebrew, "Saul, Saul, why are you persecuting me? It is hard for you [to resist]." (Acts 26:12–14, *Jerusalem Bible*)

This firsthand account is simple and direct and employs vivid descriptive language. The next account is presented as secondhand:

Example 2

I *know a man* [italics added] in Christ who, fourteen years ago, *was caught up* [italics added]—whether still in the body or out of the body, I do not know; God knows—right *into the third heaven* [which is the highest; italics added]. I do know, however, that this same person—*whether still in the body or out of the body* [italics added; it is significant that such a distinction was recognized in the First Century], I do not know; God knows—was caught up into paradise and heard things which must not and cannot be put into human language. . . . In view of the extraordinary nature of these revelations, to stop me from getting too proud *I was given a thorn in the flesh* [italics added; the reader is encouraged to consider this parallel with the alien implants reported in AANs], an angel of Satan [literally: messenger from the adversary] to beat me and stop me from getting too proud. (2 Corinthians 12:2–4, *Jerusalem Bible*)

This secondhand account is more complex and introduces a number of abstract concepts (e.g., knowledge, out-of-body travel, the limits of human language). The differences between the first and second example suggest a process of story refinement in which preexisting religious contexts play a part. Both New Testament passages presented above contain elements that are remarkably similar to those found in modern AANs.

Like religious narratives, AANs may form the basis for regular social activities, when meetings, comparisons of experiences, and agreements to agree can occur. Sociologists who study cult development have reflected on the affiliative effects that occur when groups of people share such unusual stories (Lewis 1995, 2000, 2003a; Partridge 2003). Because the dominant, skeptical culture identifies with the scientific approach to reality, AANs may serve as an alternative, antiestablishment worldview (Dean 1998). Some of this antiestablishment stance is echoed in the healing narratives that alien abduction circles use. Healing narratives often reflect spiritual worldviews and alternative views of healing (paranormal therapies, folk healing, Christian salvation from demonic forces, and so on). In such venues as psychotherapy or support group meetings, testimonials of experience serve as the proof of the efficacy of treatment. AAN support groups can be seen as budding forms of ritual healing or folk medicine (Bader 2003; Tumminia 2005) if viewed from a cross-cultural perspective. Such support groups employ talking therapies and rely on the subjective experiences of members to heal the reputed negative effects of abduction. Like religious beliefs, AANs have psychological impacts and implications.

Like religious narratives, AANs frequently emphasize the "chosen" status of their Tellers. Whitley Strieber explicitly develops this theme in *The Secret School* (1997), the fourth book in his alien abduction book series. If self-worth is enhanced through identification with superior beings (alien or otherwise), then the belief that "I've been selected" certainly implies specialness and provides a universal context for a unique, individual life. Deep psychological roots are tapped by AANs, and current psychological tools are not adequate or even intended to get at underlying spiritual motivations. Therefore, it is critical to look at the development of spiritual self-identity when seeking to understand the enduring power of AANs.

Like some religious visions, AANs can become the topic of apocalyptic anxieties. The anthology *The Gods Have Landed* (Lewis 1995) characterized the UFO myth as millenarian, that is, concerned with the end times both in its view of history and its social dynamics. A segment of the larger UFO myth involves abductions, and many groups have elaborated on that theme (Peebles 1994; Dean 1998; Lamy 1999; Barkun 2003). The spread of Christianity made linear time important, especially when measured as the clock counts toward the end times. Before the Christian era, the source of transcendent meaning tended to be "outside of time" (or perhaps in "missing time"). Tellers now, as then, become a new elect standing against the secular worldview. They await "revealed" aliens to vindicate (or even possess) them. For example, initially, under hypnosis, Betty Andreasson repeats the words of an unidentified alien voice:

Betty A.: I have faith in Jesus Christ.

[Betty repeats what she hears a voice say]: We know, child, that you do. That is why you have been chosen. I am sending you back now. Fear not. Be of comfort. Your own fear makes you feel these things. I would never harm you. It is your fear that you draw to your body that causes you to feel these things. I can release you, but you must release yourself of that fear through my son.

Fowler: Betty's face literally shone with *unrestrained joy* [italics added] as tears streamed down her beaming face. (Fowler 1979, 100)

In a later session, Betty appears to channel the speech of an alien named Andantio:

Fred [hypnotist]: Andantio, is there a more favorable time or place to communicate with you?

Betty A. [channeling the alien Andantio]: I can communicate with you when you are sitting at work, when you are driving in your car.

Fred: What is the most favorable time and place?

Betty A. Time with us is not your time. The place with you is localized. It is not with us. Cannot you see it?

Fred: I still would like to have you come directly to communicate with us telepathically now. Won't you please do that?

Betty A.: Would the vessel tell the maker what it prefers to have in it? (Fowler, 1979, 159)

This conversation taps into an explicit religious source: the Bible. The "alien" question reveals Betty's awareness of Isaiah 45:9 (*Jerusalem Bible*): "Woe to him who strives with his Maker! An earthen vessel that strives with him who made it from the earth! Does the clay say to the potter, 'What are you making?' Or 'am I not the work of your hands?' " While such Space Age religiosity (trance or possession in an anthropological perspective) is sometimes interpreted by the larger society as a trend toward irrationalism, we should take heed that this dismissive attitude was very much how the educated Roman elites viewed the early Christians before Christianity became the official religion of the Roman Empire.

Some AANs include descriptions of graphic apocalyptic images in which the aliens show the human beings the destruction of the planet and the natural world. Since the late 1970s, themes of environmental degradation and destruction have developed into a central element of AANs. Strieber came to believe that his aliens sought a spiritual union, which influenced the title of his first book about his abduction and its implications. Strieber's *Communion* (1987), in which he acts as both

Teller and Narrator, included apocalyptic elements concerning environmental fears, including degradation of the environment, destruction of the Earth by natural disasters, and destruction of the Earth by nuclear war. Strieber subsequently became interested in changes in weather patterns and wrote *The Coming Global Superstorm* (Bell and Strieber 2000) with radio talk show host Art Bell about the weather becoming highly destructive over the next several years. Strieber believes that aliens told him of the degradation of the ozone layer before its problems were publicly known.[2]

John Mack's narratives, assembled in the early 1990s, contain numerous references to apocalyptic fears, many relating to threats to the environment. Dr. Mack was an antinuclear and environmental activist before his alien abduction research, so when he selected particular stories for publication from a larger sample of unpublished alien abduction stories, they may have been selected in part based on his specific interests. Five of Mack's thirteen Tellers described fears of the loss of the natural world through environmental destruction: (Catherine), epidemic (Scott), natural disasters (Ed and Arthur), and nuclear war (Jerry).

AANs deal with issues of good and evil, and such issues can divide believers into contending factions. In addition to positive and negative fundamentalist Christian attitudes toward AANs, intense debates have arisen in the ufological community by those who differ about the intentions of the alleged sources of the phenomena, even among those who give full credence to the claims of alien contact. In my view, there are three main factions. The first, represented by Jacques Vallee, David Jacobs, and Budd Hopkins, fears alien invasion, human conspiracies, or both. Another camp, characterized by psychologists Leo Sprinkle and Richard Boylan, appears to welcome alien salvation. The third group, which includes Raymond Fowler and Whitley Strieber, reserve judgment about alien intentions. Is this the beginning of a UFO religious denominationalism?

AAN believers and debunkers also constitute de facto congregations, in the sense that their common narrative arena consists of disputes about the phenomenon's "reality." Each side accuses the other of making misstatements, while holding

---

2. In his professional life as a fiction writer, Strieber manipulates fear images for a living. Before *Communion* he suffused most of his literary work with images of natural world fears, running the gamut from animal threats to nuclear destruction. Prior to his 1985 encounter with aliens, Strieber had written fiction books about superintelligent wolves (*The Wolfen*), vampires (*The Hunger*), and nuclear war (*Warday*). Following his series of books on alien encounters, he continues writing horror novels, for example, *The Wild* about werewolves.

to the absolute truth of its own narrative. In effect, reality becomes not the evaluation of evidence, but the decision as to what *qualifies* as evidence. This difference of opinion also occurs with other controversial narratives, such as out-of-body experiences, near-death experiences (NDEs), past-life regression, and channeling. Some researchers see these other types of anomalous narratives as directly related to AANs. Stanislav and Christina Grof (1989) propose that they represent instances of what they term *spiritual emergencies.* Similarly, Kenneth Ring (1992) sees such narratives as symbolic of psychospiritual developments that may reflect a response to trauma. Many AANs indicate that the Tellers entered altered states of consciousness characteristic of known types of religious phenomena, like trance or possession, when seen in terms of typically historic and universal forms of religious expression.

Religious Contexts of Tellers

Both my own research and the preceding historical review suggest that AAN Tellers bring their own personal and social histories into the events, "experiences," and testimonies surrounding their "alien abduction." From a psychosocial perspective, they are influenced by a number of factors, including their religious backgrounds, personal spiritual styles, quasi-religious movements around abduction, leadership and integration into specific groups, narratives of conversion, and rituals of conversion.

When religious contexts are already operating within an individual's social network, they can influence the process by which a personal narrative develops. Just as seemingly ordinary events can acquire new meanings during a process of religious conversion, it is not difficult to see how a series of attentional changes and anomalous perceptions can be integrated into an AAN. In addition, AANs can influence the personal religious context by adding a new subjective component to an existing religious framework. It is not surprising that Betty Andreasson—as a professing Christian—characterized her visitors as having religious intentions and attributed to them religious-sounding speech.

Narrators like Budd Hopkins, Whitley Strieber, and John Mack are influential within their own abduction constituencies, which have different (even competing) theories on abduction. Existing social forms may carry an AAN component within their "gospels," or their members may add such a component. The scientific challenge is how to discern the ways that the new context is communicated and constructed in terms of religious elements (leadership, membership, organizational structure, and so on).

The issue of conversion raises issues of set and setting. Some AANs emerge in social settings where a kind of conversion experience can occur such as conferences, support groups, and therapy sessions. Under the tutelage of Hopkins, Strieber came to believe that his suffering could be explained by the events that were already Hopkins's specialty. Like Strieber, many Tellers struggle with the adoption of the explanation of an alien abduction explanation for their experiences or symptoms. Set and setting refer to the internal and external response contexts in the Teller's situation. Set comprises the person's subjective, experiential frames of reference, and setting refers to the environmental conditions at the time of the experience, whether an abduction "event," a support group session, or a hypnosis session that prompts a recovered memory.

If we view the interpretations surrounding AANs within a context similar to that of religious conversion, we can better understand the contents of these reports. An AAN supplies meaning according to the type of explanatory framework that has been adopted. Spanos called these frameworks *belief templates*. Religious conversion can be seen as an interpretive reframing process wherein events are not altered, but interpretation is (Tumminia 1998, 2005; Kenny 1998; Benford and Snow 2000). Conversion is perhaps the most critical issue for those concerned about the potentially destructive effects (Robbins 1988) of AANs and UFO beliefs. Often people take some time to assimilate an abduction explanation (Hufford 1982). They are not true believers at first. It is significant that many struggle with believing the alien abduction explanation of their accounts. Depending on the context and content, alien abduction narratives serve as mediums for worldview conversion, and in many cases, this worldview is religious. One can also argue that some people are preconverted. They are searching for a mystical framework, and they have a predisposition toward the worldview of the groups that they join. In turn, they learn the nuances of the particular groups that they join (Balch and Taylor 1978; Dolby 1979; Lewis 1995; Goode 2000; Partridge 2003).

Conclusion

As unusual narratives with nonetheless scientific aspirations and truth claims, alien abduction stories bring with them a number of parallels to religious themes and spiritual phenomena, including interactions with supernatural beings, struggles between good and evil, encounters with overpowering benevolent ("light") forces or malevolent ("dark") forces, conversion and reframing of interpretations (belief templates), the notion of being chosen, visions, testimonial evidence, the occasional channeling of otherworldly beings, altered states of consciousness, healing narratives, and apocalyptic pronouncements. Previous work on the literary and rhetorical forms of AANs (Matheson 1998; Kelley 1999) should be extended to consider their similarities and differences with religious narrative forms, and inquiry into other aspects of the phenomenon can also prove fruitful. Exploring alien abduction narratives could lead to a number of promising lines of research.

Closer looks at the lives of willing Tellers may unlock much more information. Thus far, clinical assessment of Tellers has proved inconclusive, except to suggest that Tellers do not differ significantly from other individuals on key psychological measures (Clancy et al. 2002). However, the psychology of religion provides research tools for tracing the religious history, development, and affiliation of AAN Tellers, such as childhood religious training, adult commitments, and denominational orientations. To evaluate these factors in psychosocial terms, the religious histories and identifications of Tellers should be surveyed in greater detail to determine whether such narratives exhibit any relationships to specific categories of religious meaning. Such research would help determine the extent to which the religious contexts in personality, family, and society affect the formation of meaning, especially as precursors to beliefs about extraterrestrials.

Because of their possible roles as *secondary believers,* as well as their varied motivations for involving themselves with the dissemination of alien abduction accounts, Narrators present a different subject for religious study. Some of them (for instance, Whitley Strieber) publicize their own personal accounts. Others (for example, Budd Hopkins and David Jacobs) present themselves as scientific researchers, although their qualifications for such a role are sometimes unclear. Psychotherapists such as John Carpenter and the late John Mack may come to be perceived—at least by their followers—in a quasi-religious role as facilitators of a spiritual journey. However, it might prove fruitful to examine the religious histories and attitudes of Narrators to explore the role that religion might play in their activities as potential modern-day prophets of the alien abduction message.

Further study of the religious contexts of AANs and the persons who originate them may provide clues to the formation of new types of religious belief. A research model that predicts the need for meaning along a religious dimension, for example, might predict whether participation in AAN support groups occurs primarily among those without personal or family religious identification—and whether such activity leads to more permanent religious forms. Research in the area of AANs must take a wait-and-see approach to discern how far the phenomenon will progress and what part it will play in the religious culture of the twenty-first century.

Close Encounters of the French Kind

The Saucerian Construction
of "Contacts" and the Controversy
over Its Reality in France

Pierre Lagrange

> "Excuse me, sir?" he said with an edge in his voice, "but I believe you also claim to
> have visited other planets by flying saucer—planets unrecognized by astronomy."
>> "That's right," . . .
>> "Just where are those planets?"
>> "Oh, they're . . . places," . . . "Real planets don't let themselves be bossed
> around by a pack of astronomers!"
>> —*The Wanderer*, Fritz Leiber

Is it possible to study and to explain science and parascience, black holes and flying saucers, scientific theories and ufological beliefs with the same methodological tools? Not so long ago, research on subjects such as sorcery were considered studies of human inanity. It took all the energy of scholars such as Jeanne Favret-Saada (1980), to show how biased this judgment was, and how, in effect, such an assessment actually revealed a researcher's prejudice. Today the academic study of flying saucers is in the same state as the analysis of peasant witchcraft was before Favret-Saada broke through. Most scientists shelved the saucer phenomenon as irrational or pathological (Bartholomew 1989). This stigma makes the subject a *sociological untouchable.* Is it possible to do a sociological study of the flying-saucer phenomenon without reducing it to a sociopsychological phenomenon? Sociologists, historians, and folklorists have made a few attempts, and their efforts have helped to realize some progress (Jacobs 1975; Dégh 1977; Westrum 1977). Let us review briefly those achievements before going further.

The majority of sociological studies on UFOs have concentrated on UFO religions, contactees, and their followers (Lewis 1995, 2003a; Partridge 2003). Newer studies take a radically different approach from the reductionist and psychiatric-oriented view common in the sixties. For instance, the psychiatric-oriented diagnosis of H. Taylor Buckner claimed, "Men in the audience tend to be either young schizophrenics or aged with advanced senility. I have never seen a male saucerian who could make a successful presentation of normalcy" (1966, 13). Such assessments have been severely criticized by sociologists like John Lofland (1966), who studied the same groups without noticing what Buckner had claimed to see. In fact, many researchers (Wallis 1974; Balch and Taylor 1978; Lewis 1995, 2003a; Tumminia 1998, 2005; Partridge 2003) showed that these people were spiritual seekers influenced by the cultic milieu and not necessarily abnormal. David Stupple and William McNeece remark, "This pathological model of cult membership is both gratuitous and inaccurate" (1979, 47). They further state that the many different reasons that may bring someone to join a group indicate, "It is faulty to assume that cult members are alike in psychological or sociological characteristics." After the 1970s, studies of contactees took a nonpsychiatric turn in sociological circles (Lewis 1995).

UFOs have ended up in the classification of scientific anomalies, and the social activity around UFO phenomena has been relegated to the realm of parascience. The analysis of parascience has also made some progress since the seventies and eighties with the emergence of academic disciplines focused on the social construction of knowledge and the sociology of science itself (Gilbert and Mulkay 1984; Latour 1995). These fields helped advance the analysis of controversies about scientific anomalies by moving the analysis from epistemology to sociology, from content to context, from the facts to the people who study them, and from scientific *thinking* to scientific *practice*—without abandoning the content for the context, or the facts for the people who study them (as sociology does when it studies "mentalities" or "beliefs"). Thus, the analysis shifted from epistemology to sociology—thanks to a new perspective within sociology itself.[1]

The sociology of science rethought sociology and produced new analyses to

---

1. Scholars like Bruno Latour (1993), showed that so-called social and cultural factors (beliefs, cultural origin, historical context, political pressure) also played a role in the production of scientific culture, just as much as they do in the construction of nonscientific culture.

show how content and context, facts and scientists, are produced at the same time in the same processes. Such studies showed that material factors (scientific instruments, laboratories, etc.), and not just scientific thinking, play an important role in the production of facts (Bloor 1976; Wallis 1979; Mulkay and Gilbert 1982; Latour and Woolgar 1990). In turn, this new analysis contributed to a new definition within sociology applicable to both science and parascience. Thus, historians and sociologists of science also have come to focus on controversies over scientific anomalies and to some small extent over alternative disciplines, such as parapsychology and ufology. In the wake of research on the social construction of science, studies of the "parasciences" created the conditions for a more symmetrical analysis, which moved from the notion of pathological science to the idea that within parascience "nothing unscientific is happening," as Harry M. Collins and Trevor J. Pinch (1979, 237) remarked. Ron Westrum (1977) showed that we could study controversies on scientific anomalies without assuming there was a priori any difference between UFO facts and scientific facts.

Paul McCarthy (1975) was the first to take into consideration the work of Thomas Kuhn and to study the career of University of Arizona professor James McDonald. McCarthy also examined the work of skeptical astrophysicist Donald H. Menzel, as well as the efforts of debunker-journalist Philip J. Klass. These thinkers attempted to show that there is no "Great Divide" between scientific and pseudoscientific minds (McCarthy 1975; Wallis 1985; Latour 1983, 1993; Lagrange 1993). By moving from psychological arguments about the pseudoscientific mind to the material conditions in which works are produced, they have shown the role that methods of interpretation play in the acceptance or rejection of anomalies and phenomena. Furthermore, they argue that this should not be a cause of concern because even in normal science specific lines of reason are necessary to the production of scientific facts. By taking into consideration the context, cultural setting, and social dynamics, they have revealed that the cultural milieu (previously only mentioned in regard to a sociology of knowledge or the history of scientific errors) plays a role in the acceptance of truth, reality, and new phenomena (Shapin 1982; Latour 1993). Thus, David Bloor's (1976) strong claim that a symmetrical analysis of scientific truth and error was feasible proved to be correct.

Although progress has been made, it should be noted that most studies are still performed as if there was a divide between science and parascience. More important for our purposes, the borderline has moved from an asymmetrical relationship between science and parascience to an asymmetry between ufology and contactees. For instance, sociologists who study contactees do not necessarily study ufology and vice versa. The two domains remain for the most part ignorant of one another, and there is no debate on the feasibility or need for symmetrical study. The problem of interpretation has never been raised, and it has never even been discussed. Instead, the community of researchers has responded as if there was no problem, or as if the solution clearly indicated that there is a great division—a fundamental difference between *minds*—between science and other systems of thought, such as ufology or contacteeism (Latour 1983, 1993).

For example, Festinger, Riecken and Schachter's (1956) superb study of Marian Keech's followers, *When Prophecy Fails,* is seen as a way to explain a psychological mechanism that elucidates religious beliefs and beliefs in general. At no time does Festinger even suggest that his theory could apply to scientists or his own research team. However, the sociologist of science Bruno Latour discovered the very same phenomenon of cognitive dissonance in the history of science. In his books *Science in Action* (1995) and *The Pasteurization of France* (1993), Latour demonstrates how Pastorians found themselves in a similar situation to that of Mrs. Keech's followers when they had to explain why their predictions about the abatement of certain diseases were refuted by the facts.[2]

An Example of Asymmetry: How David Jacobs Discusses Contactees

If we consider, for example, one of the few studies on UFO controversies, the pioneering work of David Jacobs's *UFO Controversy in America* (1975), we see how the author gives an asymmetrical treatment of UFO researchers and contactees. The bias becomes clear when he studies contactees, because his tone shifts from sympathy to criticism. Jacobs says that contactees have had prejudicial consequences for the serious study of UFOs, and he recalls how ufologists had to fight against the publicity engendered by contactees. Why a priori should we consider that the ufological approach to UFOs is sounder than that of contactees and contactee religions? Is it because we trust more in a scenario that mentions words like "evidence" and "scientific method" than in scenarios that imply following the word of a guru without discussion? Thus, the question is not, Why are the contactees less serious than ufologists? Rather we should ask, What are the criteria for being serious in ufology and in contacteeism?

2. See the French edition of Bruno Latour's *La Science en action: Introduction à la sociologie des sciences* (1995), page 452 and pages 458–59. This part is not reproduced in the American edition, *Science in Action.*

David Jacobs also stresses what he considers to be negative aspects, in particular the fact that the contactees do not submit their claims to the expertise of UFO investigators. This argument seems acceptable when viewed from the perspective of ufology, but from another perspective, that of the contactees, it may appear obtuse. In fact, the argument is close to that of historians who study religion from the point of view of anticlericalism; religion can only look faulty to them. This antithetical attitude is incorrect. If we use the same method to analyze the world of ufology from the point of view of its skeptics, like CSICOP (Committee for the Scientific Investigation of the Paranormal), then we would not describe them, but only condemn them.

David Jacobs also thinks that the followers of such contactees are gullible, and he explains their behavior only in terms of belief. However, terms, like "gullible" and "belief," are not good explanations of contactees, but the very interpretive points that need to be explained. Jacobs does to contactees what most educated people do to ufologists; he presumes they are all wrong or deluded by their own convictions. Jacobs avoids the trap of treating ufologists as believers, but he falls into the very same trap when it comes to characterizing contactees. He moves the line of asymmetry from the boundary between science and ufology to the boundary between ufology and contactees. However, if asymmetrical explanations utilizing terms such as belief and gullibility are not suitable for ufology, then they are not suitable for contactees, either. The question is not, Are contactees and their followers gullible people? Rather, we should ask, How is the boundary between being serious and being gullible constructed for ufologists and contactees alike? This question aims at understanding how these categories were constructed and applied. Therefore, if we want to understand the vocabulary used by ufologists, we have to recall the history of its invention.

David Jacobs clearly discusses the way ufologists draw on the rhetoric of UFO skeptics; in his book (1975) they appear as skeptical as the skeptics themselves. However, Jacobs has a different view when it comes to contactees; he attributes knowledge to ufologists, but only beliefs to contactees. While he avoids using the rhetoric of skeptics in his description of ufologists, he reproduces the rhetoric of the ufologists toward the contactees rather than explaining its use and characteristics. In describing a situation, one should be careful not to use the interpretive arguments employed to socially construct that situation, in this case the empiricist skeptic versus the gullible believer. This characterization of belief is an accusation, not an explanation.

Historical contexts deeply affect meaning. As historian Alain Boureau (1990) showed, there was no objective concept of belief in the Christian Middle Ages—merely a concept of truth. During that time, priests, nuns, and others concerned with the public good used cautionary stories about morality called *exempla*. These tales sometimes described the lives of saints and their miracles or sinners and their paths to damnation (e.g., Chaucer's "Pardoner's Tale"). Exempla represented normal truths. In a penetrating study, historian Jean-Claude Schmitt (1994) demonstrated that we cannot compare the medieval exempla of dead people returning among the living to the modern concept of NDE (near-death experience) because exempla did not connote any "paranormal experience." The contexts are completely different. By analyzing the context of meaning, we can understand the context of interpretation.

The Hoax Argument

Another example of the asymmetrical treatment of contactees and ufologists in David Jacobs's book is the hoax argument. For Jacobs, if the contactees are not merely naïve people, then they must be hoaxers. Indeed, investigations have revealed that many photos show fakery, not "real" interplanetary saucers. However, the hoaxes of contactees should not astonish historians, nor stop them from analyzing the phenomenon. Rather, they should be astonished by the fact that other social actors, such as skeptical ufologists or reporters, use this argument to exclude contactees from legitimate dialogue. Historians and other social scientists should not stop analyzing UFO phenomenon when notions of "proofs" or "hoaxes" enter the scene, but rather they should explain why these arguments are used and how they are constructed. The hoax is not an explanation of the contactee's attitude; it is the very issue that must be explained by a careful description of the relations between ufologists and contactees. The question is not, Why are contactees hoaxing? Instead, we should pursue the question, Why do ufologists use the hoaxing argument to stop all discussion on the validity of contacteeism as a genuine UFO experience?

The mystery is not necessarily why people follow contactees who are hoaxing. Instead we should ask, "Why do we label this or that a hoax?" For example, most textbooks print pictures of stars and galaxies in false colors that have nothing to do with films used by scientists in their daily work. We never speak of this as hoaxing, even if these pictures have no scientific value. Why not try to understand the role of hoaxing as constructed by contactees in the same way that we understand the reasons popular scientific magazines and textbooks alter pictures of stars and galaxies?

A Martian Anthropologist Facing the Hoaxing Argument

We remember E. E. Evans-Pritchard's (1937) argument that although all Zande are witches, some of them are not. Intrigued by this apparent contradiction, the anthropologist learned from the Zande that there was a difference between warm and cold witches. However, this seemed to be an ad hoc explanation, and these two contradictory beliefs troubled the Western anthropologist. How can people believe in ambiguous and contradictory things? Sociologist David Bloor (1976) imagines how a Zande would react to some of our contradictions. For example, in our society people who voluntarily kill other people are killers, but bomber pilots are not killers. They are soldiers. Thus, we are just like the Zande: we believe in contradictory things by producing differentiating labels and explaining away the contradiction.

Regarding the contactees, if a contactee falsely states that he is a professor, he is a liar and everything that he says is suspect. French sociologist Gérald Chevalier (1986) used this argument to show the pseudoscientific status of paranormal amateurs. Let us consider another argument: when Leon Festinger and his colleagues entered Marian Keech's group, they used false identities. They used deception. Is their study, *When Prophecy Fails,* suspect because of this deception? No, in fact, it is considered to be a major social-psychological work—and it is! Thus, we are just like the Zande: we believe in contradictory things. According to Jim Schnabel (1994), we believe that people who tell lies are liars, but we also believe that there are warm and cold liars. Take, for instance, the American notion of "white" acceptable lies and "black" unacceptable lies. A Martian anthropologist might be as astonished by us as we are by the Zande.

George Adamski is sometimes called the father of contacteeism, but he was also the purveyor of great hoaxes. I am not saying that "Professor" George Adamski was a great academic, like Leon Festinger, but only that we should take into consideration the context of his deceptions to understand his motive. It is not an excuse, just a method to explain apparently bizarre contradictory facts. The sociologist needs to ask Martianlike questions. He or she needs to be astonished by what is commonplace to everyone else. He or she must be as astonished by Festinger's lie as others are by Adamski's. Like the sociologist of science who "naïvely" asks how the scientific evidence and proof were constructed (a foolish question for an epistemologist, a positivist, or a rationalist), a sociologist of contactees should ask how the notion of fraud was constructed, who constructed it, and what context it served. Taking the examples of Pritchard and Festinger, we see the boundary of interpretation between the observer and the observed. The meaning and the context of words evident to members of a group should be considered by those who analyze that group.

Strangely enough in areas of ufology and contactees, no sociologist has ever tried to analyze the social construction of hoaxing.

Charges that Adamski's story was based on hoaxing do not take into account that there is anything else to explain, as if words like "hoax" and "truth" were self-explanatory. The next standard procedure is to look for psychological or psychiatric rationales to better understand the attitude of the "hoaxer," a practice that adds weight to the arguments the skeptics have already stressed. However, this method adds nothing to the social analysis of how we construct the argument, "It's a hoax and Adamski is a liar or a pathological case." Instead of describing what happens when people speak of a hoax, they assume the role of critic. As David Stupple says, "It's pointless to dismiss Adamski and his successors simply as lunatics and liars. That diverts us from an examination of the social processes and historical conditions that produced this modern variant of utopian thought" (1980, 271).

In one of the rare French anthropological works on contemporary belief in extraterrestrials, Wiktor Stoczkowski (1999) notes that Adamski's pictures are most probably faked. But like John A. Saliba (1995), to whom he makes reference, he also refuses to reduce his analysis of this and other similar cases to this "evidential" aspect: "Encounters with extraterrestrials cannot be reduced to that. To neglect their religious dimension means that we refuse the possibility of understanding the main reasons for explaining the fascination of the phenomenon with the majority of those who are the actors or the followers" (Stoczkowski 1999, 267).

A sociologist who moves from a description of ufology to a denunciation of contactees is like a scientist who studies the physics of planetary orbits and then makes moral judgments about the fact that meteors strike the earth. Thus, without an impartial scientific explanation for meteors, the researcher stands to lose credibility for all other work. Along the same lines, why would a social explanation of extraterrestrial contacts be finished merely by asserting that they are probably staged hoaxes or they are the products of alleged pathological liars? Why should we shift from the practice of using descriptions when we refer to science, only to use denunciations when we refer to extraterrestrial contacts? This makes no sense! Metaphorically speaking, the "orbital path" of the contactee should be studied and explained with the same tools used to study and explain the "orbital path" of ufologists.

Alison Lurie's Symmetrical Novel

One of the few symmetrical arguments presented on contactees and science is Alison Lurie's novel, *Imaginary Friends* (1967). In contrast to Festinger's book, which focuses only on the UFO cultists (who as a result, appear peculiar), Lurie's book discusses both the cultists and the sociologists. With this symmetry, the sociologists appear as peculiar as the cultists. However, the point is not to imbue sociologists with an aura of irrationality, but to cease crediting cultists with one. Thus, Lurie describes sociologists the same way she describes cultists. Lurie's novel does not pass for social science, although it points to the sociological idea that someone should be analyzing the scientists.

What seems evident and taken for granted when we read Festinger becomes strange and anomalous when we read Lurie. This is a perfect example of why we should maintain the obligation to examine fully all the social actors in the description: ufologists, skeptics, the contactees, and scientists (physical and social). Thus, any description of the actions of scientists and skeptics should look as interesting, as strange, and as exotic as the description of contactees.

The French Case

This chapter contributes to the sociology of the flying saucer (or more specifically, of ufologists and contactees) without reducing any aspect of it to a sociopsychological phenomenon. The obvious trap is in pushing the sociology to one side and concentrating only on the subject at hand, or inversely, of abandoning the subject by smothering it with sociological explanation. The obvious traps are often the most lethal. The methodology applied here will be to consider, above all, the accounts of the people involved and *their ability to furnish explanations.*

The case studies here discuss contactees and scientists from the French UFO scene. Reviewing the first French flying-saucer authors and investigators initially requires an assessment of how they considered contact cases. Then, a study of two contactee cases will be presented. The first case consists of a UFO group founded by a contactee named Pierre Monnet, and the second famous French contactee case is that of Jean Miguères. Additionally, the last section describes how scientists and ufologists investigated the Cergy-Pontoise abduction case of Franck Fontaine in the late seventies. No one actor is considered as a priori more significant or more valid than any other. On the contrary, every attempt will be made to show how the actors themselves reached their conclusions, and by what mechanisms they defined who was right and who was wrong or who was credible and who was not. These accounts allow the actors themselves to *create the differences.* In other words, the various protagonists will do the sociology, rather than some researcher.

If no one doubts the correspondence with reality of texts on endorphins or on interstellar gas, there is no reason to introduce such doubts for saucers. Therefore, the need arises to see how the saucers themselves go from hand to hand in the "circulation" of the stories. Verification of the reality or unreality of saucers is not a prize awarded by the observer at the end of the process, for it is the very issue at stake for all the protagonists in dispute. It is this dispute that will gradually construct and deconstruct the phenomenon. At one moment, the narrative may collapse under the weight of certain actors, while at another moment it may regain its realism. It is not for the analyst to decide in advance if the saucers are real or not. On the contrary, the researcher must follow the tribulations of ufologists and contactees alike.

What Ufologists Did: The Invention of Endless Controversies

Contacteeism did not appear in France until the 1970s, apart from a few unpublicized cases in the wake of Spiritualism about 1900 (Flournoy 1983; Evans 1986). Before the 1970s, books by American contactees were translated, but they were not widely read except by UFO researchers. The translated books of Major Donald E. Keyhoe (1950, 1951), Frank Scully (1950, 1951), and Gerald Heard (1951a, 1951b) appeared early in the fifties. Following them, British author Desmond Leslie and American contactee George Adamski published *Les soucoupes volantes ont atterri (Flying Saucers Have Landed)* in 1954. In 1965, Howard Menger's *From Outer Space to You* appeared in French, reaching a limited audience.

It is not enough to say that different categories of people were interested in flying saucers or that flying-saucer investigators were either opposed to or sympathetic toward contactees. Rather, what needs description is what these people achieved and how they created differences between themselves. We will first follow several major French figures prominent in the flying-saucer milieu of the fifties to see how they discussed contactee cases (Lagrange 1990). These French figures include the people involved with the first UFO magazine, *Ouranos,* the first UFO authors, Jimmy Guieu and Aimé Michel, who wrote two of the most famous books on flying discs. Then, the discussion will shift to other groups, like GEPA (Groupe d'Etude des Phénomène Aériens), that appeared in the early sixties.

Ouranos and the Invention of French Ufology

What we now call ufology began with thinkers nicknamed saucerians. The French called the field of inquiry by the blanket term *saucerism (soucoupisme* in French), because it covered all aspects of the UFO phenomenon without the distinctions and separatism that exist today. The first French flying-saucer magazine, *Ouranos*, unwittingly paved the way for setting up divisions within the field. The inaugural issue appeared on June 24, 1952, in both French and English. Its editors were Eric Biddle and Marc Thirouin, who practiced law and followed the "Atlantean" Paul Le Cour.

This first issue was the size of a pack of cigarettes, and it was subtitled "An International Bulletin Devoted to the Serious Study of Flying Saucers and Kindred Subjects." It is clear that the effort started from scratch and lacked an organized network of contributors. Biddle and Thirouin were not linked to any flying-saucer groups, but rather to Atlantean societies in Paris and London. They referenced books by authors such as Keyhoe, Heard, and Scully, and various news clippings.

Originally, *Ouranos* sought all perspectives. In the second issue, Eric Biddle mentions on page 25:

> Through the kindness of Mr. Egerton Sykes, Chairman of the Atlantis Research Centre, London, we have received a large batch of flying saucer material published by the Borderland Sciences Research Association of San Diego, California. This offers a different and, to my mind, highly significant, approach to the problem and in our next issue I propose to deal with it at some length.

The fourth issue of *Ouranos* (April 1953) published and discussed Borderland Sciences Research Association (BSRA) views. *Ouranos* also devoted considerable space to various topics: discussions of sightings, astronomers' views on flying saucers, conferences organized by scientific or aeronautical circles or by *Ouranos* members, and bibliographies of articles published in the press. One of the goals of *Ouranos* was to investigate sightings.

The first issue of *Ouranos-Actualités*, a supplement, appeared in May–June 1953. It was a mimeographed magazine of fourteen pages. Marc Thirouin wrote the first article, entitled "The Fantastic Revelations of Professor George Adamski, Astronomer at the Mt. Palomar Observatory." He begins by making a statement that *Ouranos* has already shown that it is objective and that it is not seeking sensationalism. Further, he writes that he has no reason to suspect Professor Adamski or Borderland Science Research Associates, the American group that provided documents on Adamski.

Thirouin then reports that Adamski revealed that he had seen a flying saucer and its occupant in a meeting organized by the BSRA and in the presence of "a dozen personalities." Thirouin mentions the status of several participants in the dialogue (a specialist on electromagnetism, an electronics expert from the U.S. Air

Force, an economist and writer, an anthropologist, and the director of the BSRA). The remaining pages of the bulletin devote discussion to sightings and investigation reports.

French veteran saucerian *(soucoupiste)* Henri Chaloupek (1997) remarks that soon after this article was written, Marc Thirouin read Adamski's book in English and concluded that the story was a crude hoax because all the elements that encouraged him to endorse Adamski's claims had proved undependable. For instance, George Adamski was not an astronomer, and although he did live on Mount Palomar, he did not work at the observatory, as implied.

In order to understand why these criteria are important for Marc Thirouin, a review of another flying-saucer case is valuable. This famous landing occurred during the 1954 UFO wave in northern France. On October 10, 1954, Marius Dewilde from Quarouble saw a flying saucer land and observed two little men marching toward him. A ray of light, which came from the saucer, paralyzed him. His story made headlines. At first, Thirouin was skeptical because of the way the story was told by the press. From one account to another, the details of Dewilde's story differed. However, when he met Marius Dewilde, he realized that the press had invented the incredible details, not Dewilde, the actual witness to the flying-saucer event (Thirouin 1959).

By comparing the situations of Adamski and Dewilde, we understand on what criteria Thirouin based his acceptance or rejection of a narrative. He initially accepted Adamski because of his social status, and then rejected him when he realized that Adamski was systematically shifting from one status to another, multiplying his identities and the versions of his story. On the other hand, although Marc Thirouin initially rejected Dewilde's testimony because of inconsistencies in the particulars, he changed his mind when he realized that journalists had introduced the disparate details, not Dewilde.

The differences between contactees and typical flying-saucer witnesses appear in these two examples. What matters to Thirouin is that the story can be checked and that the same witness tells the same version consistently. For him, the fact that Adamski's identity is never the same or that his story may not be the same represents a serious problem.

Ouranos was inventing a basic criterion of flying-saucer reality. As Thirouin says in his preface to Jimmy Guieu's first book: "In 1951, when my friend, Eric Biddle, and I founded *Ouranos* we had in view the solution of a problem whose vast importance we realized, but we had very little idea as to the practical methods of attaining this end" (Guieu 1956, 11). By the end of the fifties, some members of *Ouranos* con-

9.1. In 1954, Marius Dewilde heard a loud sound at night and went to investigate. He saw a large object on the railroad tracks. After various news reporters interviewed him, his story became distorted by the press. Courtesy of Mary Evans Picture Library.

sidered it impossible to mix the two aspects of saucerism—thereby creating two aspects. They decided to start a new scientifically oriented society, GEPA. Thus, a new division appeared between ufology and contactees. In Thirouin's mind, however, there was no divide between the two saucerian narratives.

It is noted that for a pioneer ufologist like Marc Thirouin, it was important that a story remain the same from one account to another. Nonetheless, the history of UFO discussions in France indicates that Adamski did not disappear from the spotlight the moment Thirouin declared him a hoaxer. Apparently, other ufologists found ways to maintain the discussion on his case. It seems that ufologists have a strong tendency to reopen cases that are considered closed by other investigators. An example is noted in the following interpretation of the Adamski case by another investigator and friend of Thirouin's, Jimmy Guieu.

Jimmy Guieu: From Field Investigation to Occultism

In September 1952, Marc Thirouin met a young science-fiction writer named Jimmy Guieu (Chaloupek 1997).[3] Jimmy Guieu (1926–2000) began a career as a writer at the Fleuve Noir publishing house in 1952 after briefly selling insurance. His early attraction to all things of a scientific or occult nature led him as a young schoolboy to perform experiments in alchemy. After reading the first accounts of flying saucers, he was intrigued and was soon convinced that the phenomenon was real. After meeting with Marc Thirouin, he began generating publicity for *Ouranos* during appearances on radio shows and in his science-fiction novels, which underscored saucer and paranormal themes. He became an *Ouranos* investigator, the delegate for the southeast of France, and he was quickly promoted to the rank of chief of Investigating Service of the Commission. From then on, Guieu became the most visible spokesperson for *Ouranos*. In 1954, he published *Les soucoupes volantes viennent d'un autre monde (Flying Saucers Come from Another World)*. The book's appearance was well-timed, released just before the UFO wave hit France that autumn. Two years later, Guieu authored a second book, *Black-Out sur les soucoupes volantes* (Black-out on the Flying Saucers), with a foreword by French poet Jean Cocteau.

Jimmy Guieu's *Flying Saucers Come from Another World* is of special interest, because it is the first such work published by a French UFO investigator (a second book was published by Aimé Michel later that year) and because Guieu discusses contactees. In the first chapters, he reviews historical cases. He then presents both the positive evidence and the skeptics' position. A chapter is devoted to Donald H. Menzel, the Harvard astrophysicist who published the first attempt at a systematic explanation of all UFO sightings in 1953. In chapter 11, the discussion turns to George Adamski. Jimmy Guieu had interviewed Desmond Leslie for his show on Radio Monte Carlo, and he returned convinced of the latter's authenticity. He iden-

---

3. Other sources are my interviews with Jimmy Guieu on February 16, 1987 and with Georges Hilaire Gallet on November 2, 1991. Guieu was born in 1926 in Aix-en-Provence in the southeast of France; his actual first and middle names are Henri René.

tifies George Adamski as an "amateur astronomer." Unlike Thirouin, he did not allude to any inconsistencies in Adamski's story. Instead, Guieu describes the story "as told [to] me by Desmond Leslie" (1956, 232) rather than focusing on any dissimilar, contradictory accounts. As independent confirmation, Guieu also mentions that a saucer similar to the one photographed by Adamski was photographed in England. Guieu writes, "This sighting confirms the existence of saucers like the one which Adamski examined at close quarters" (1956, 238). It is particularly intriguing to compare Guieu's rhetoric with that of another author who published a book that same year: Aimé Michel.

Aimé Michel: The Divide Between Eyewitness and Contactee

In 1954, Aimé Michel published a book on flying saucers, *Lueurs sur les soucoupes volantes* (Light on flying saucers), as did Jimmy Guieu. Its release at the beginning of the summer came a few months before one of the most important waves of French UFO sightings and supposed landings. Concurrent with the publication of Michel's book, Leslie and Adamski's *Flying Saucers Have Landed* was translated. In the first edition of *Lueurs sur les soucoupes volantes*, Michel mentions Adamski. In a footnote, he expressed strong criticism of Adamski's tales and doubts about his saucer stories, as well as misgivings about another testimony that was supposed to corroborate his sighting. Thus, Michel doubts the very same element that Guieu considers independent evidence for Adamski's claim. Michel concludes, "Does not this evidence corroborate Adamski's startling narrative? It would be more convincing if the two amateur astronomers [who took a picture of a saucer similar to Adamski's saucer] had not told us that they had previously read Adamski's book and knew it well" (1967, 99). The symmetry between Guieu and Michel is complete.

Aimé Michel initially made no distinction, but he would later contribute to the invention of a powerful division between contactees and witnesses to landings. His first book mentioned saucer crashes in the Spitzberg, Norway, area and Aztec, New Mexico, as reported by Frank Scully, and he included the first stories involving landings of little men that had gained some fame. In the second edition of *Lueurs,* printed during the autumn of 1954, Michel added a little extra material because there were many reported landings. His skepticism shows in this quote:

> Let us add one more word about the numerous cases reported in the newspapers during the summer and fall of 1954, especially those in which "little men" emerged from saucers on the ground. All the implausibility records were broken during

those months. The scientific probability that the incidents really took place is infin-
itesimal. Nevertheless we must not forget that if the saucers exist, they have been
constructed by living beings, and that life itself is simply the result of a long perse-
verance in the improbable. . . . Therefore it would be only after a long and difficult
investigation that we could decide about these cases—unless, of course, there are
sensational new developments. (Michel 1967, 99)

At that early stage, Michel drew no lines between landings and contacts, or stories told by Frank Scully and those told by George Adamski. Michel also considered
that there were no major differences between the American landings as told by
Scully and the French ones, the reports of which had multiplied in the press. Any
possible dissimilarities were less important than their tabloid origins. Thus, while
his opinion had already been formed regarding Adamski and Scully, he preferred to
wait for an investigation on the 1954 landings before reaching a conclusion. It was
not until he discussed the issue with Jean Cocteau, investigated the matter, and received additional information from his network of correspondents (which he
gained after the publication of *Lueurs*) that he started to change his views.

By 1958, when Michel published *Flying Saucers and the Straight-Line Mystery
(Mystérieux objets célestes)* first in the United States and then in France, he had
evolved in his thinking about the landings.[4] The book is dedicated to the analysis of
the 1954 UFO wave, and it also devotes some space to contactees. A clear distinction
appears now between landings reported in France and stories like Adamski's. He
even used Adamski as an argument *ad contrario* to reinforce the legitimacy and authenticity of the landings. Michel had followed the advice of Jean Cocteau: to be less
skeptical regarding cases containing incredible details and to look for some logic behind the French saucer stories. Michel discovered that when placed on a map, flying-saucer sightings had a tendency to generate straight lines for cases of three or
more sightings. To legitimate the landings and to discover this straight-line trait of
the phenomenon, Michel had to suspend disbelief, to stop "distrusting the facts, an
attitude too often developed in the course of scientific research." He had to accept
the apparently absurd landing stories that he had rejected in his first book. Michel
states, "Cocteau himself believed the witnesses who said they had seen saucers on
the ground, with their occupants" (1958a, 51).

4. Aimé Michel's evolution can be compared with that of Civilian Saucer Intelligence of New
York. For a description of the way ufologists changed their minds on landings in France and in the
United States, see Lagrange (1990).

In *Flying Saucers and the Straight-Line Mystery,* Michel pioneers his theory of *orthoteny,* a theory that said investigators could find straight-line patterns by plotting reported sightings of UFOs. However, in the same book where he suspends disbelief on saucer landings, he introduces a division between stories of landings and stories of contactees. Thus, on the one hand, Michel constructed the legitimacy of landings by suspending his disbelief, and on the other, he deconstructed the legitimacy of contacts by maintaining his disbelief. He does not ask for proof from eyewitnesses to landings, but demands proof only from the contactees. In part 6 of the book, Michel constructs an argument designed to reject contactee stories. He builds an analogy between the tales of the contactees and tales told by armchair travelers of antiquity and the Middle Ages, like Pomponius Mela and John Mandeville. Michel explains how such travelers' tales produced religious art and beliefs, and how contactee tales now produce contemporary religious beliefs. He introduces an analogy between religion and contact *and* between hoaxer and contactee claims. Michel constructs a new division between religious aspects of flying saucers and what eventually becomes ufology.

Following different strategies, instead of simply opposing contactees and ufologists, we have seen how researchers constructed their acceptance or rejection of contact stories and how ufologists differed from each other. Later on, an example of the difference in strategy between the ufologist and the scientist will be the highlighted using the Cergy-Pontoise abduction case of Franck Fontaine.

GEPA: Starting Again at Zero

In 1962, a group of dissident members from *Ouranos* headed by engineer René Hardy left Marc Thirouin's group to found GEPA (Groupe d'Etude des Phénomène Aériens). GEPA was one of the first respected ufology associations. It lasted from 1962 to 1977. René Hardy, René and Francine Fouéré, and General Lionel Chassin started the organization as an association of scientists, citizens, and military for the study of UFOs. It would go on to publish fifty-one "bulletins" before it dissolved, all of which defined further divisions between ufologists and contactees.

GEPA's founders thought that Thirouin had gone too far in the realm of occultism and pseudoscience, and they believed scientists and engineers should investigate the problem in a scientific manner.[5] However, the first issues of their bulletin

---

5. Information from my interview with Francine Fouéré in Paris on June 25, 1996, and from Chaloupek (1997, 27).

gave none of these reasons and did not even mention *Ouranos*. They created a new localized division between scientific and (what they considered) occult-oriented ufology. Thirouin and Guieu did not really construct a barrier between typical UFO cases and contactees, only between cases they accepted and cases they rejected. Michel invented a division between landings and contacts, and GEPA introduced a new partition between serious UFO researchers and occult-oriented ufologists. The tendency of *Ouranos* collaborators to take at face value extraordinary testimonies, like those of Adamski, Scully, and others, was the reason for this dissidence.

The border between contacteeism and ufology was also moving. René Fouéré wrote an article for GEPA's bulletin no. 6, which contributed to formulating this new divide, in which he said, "Among those who admit that flying saucers are piloted craft of extraterrestrial origin, a profound divide has been established for years. We find, on one side, passionate followers of Adamski and, on the other side, his firm adversaries" (1964, 3). René Fouéré discussed Adamski's evidence (photographs and testimony about the moon) and found it wanting. He also suggests that Adamski may have been fooled by his extraterrestrial friends. When Adamski died, Fouéré wrote another article (1965) in which he elucidated his reasons for rejecting Adamski's claims. It was not because Adamski was a contactee with an occult-oriented testimony, but because his worldview was nothing new to a philosophy student like Fouéré. At the same time, Fouéré recognized that Adamski's writings did not give him "an impression of a deliberate falsification." He also acknowledged that many people became interested in UFOs because of the publicity generated by Adamski's claims.

Nonetheless, René Fouéré maintained an ecumenical attitude, and even if he was a skeptic, he did not close the door. In contrast, GEPA's bulletin rarely discussed contactees, and it generally ignored contactee claims. Considering the diversity of opinions expressed so far regarding Adamski, it can be noted that the early UFO researchers did not share a common viewpoint. Indeed, René Fouéré withholds concluding anything substantial about Adamski, and this ability not to conclude will become one of the most important behavioral characteristics of ufologists. It serves to differentiate them from both scientists and contactees.

What happened to the first ufologists? Did they hesitate between serious study of ufology and the shadowy world of contactees? Did they vacillate between a scientific and a religious attitude? Perhaps the truth is somewhere else. At first, ufologists did not see any difference between UFO landings and contacts. They could not have known that the contacts belonged to another category because this knowledge required biographies and bibliographies of contactees—a difficult task in the absence of any sort of network, to say the least. It was necessary to have a library on the subject, and the first investigators had to collect, translate, and publish the available literature. Lacking such a compilation, Thirouin did not know that Adamski was not a professional astronomer and that his address at Mount Palomar, California, had nothing to do with the Mount Palomar Observatory. He did not know that Adamski served as the former guru of a Royal Order of Tibet who channeled information from eastern Ascended Masters in the 1930s, or the leader of an Advanced Thinkers Club that had published his inspired science-fiction novels in the late 1940s. Although it can be argued that taking for granted the story of a meeting with Venusians is already indicative of a questionable research methodology, the controversy over UFOs was new at that time and its ground rules unknown. Thus, little by little, France's first ufologists conceptualized the distinctions between cases they considered legitimate and those they did not.

There is also another area of differentiation between Thirouin, Guieu, Michel, and Fouéré. It is not so much their acceptance or rejection of contactees, but the fact that these divisions were more localized than globally accepted ones. From one group to another, the criteria were not the same and the border shifted elsewhere. Ufologists spent most of their time creating not only differences, but also localized differences; thus, they showed a strong capacity for reopening debates and creating a relativistic universe where every detail could be discussed again and again. What one ufologist said or wrote appeared simply as an opinion, a personal point of view. Michel was apparently one of the few who succeeded in creating a discussion that forced others to develop arguments. Among Thirouin, Guieu, and others in the field discussions appeared to multiply, but nothing like a common shared knowledge emerged before going further. Each new participant started again from zero. Michel himself was at the source of this relativistic policy in ufology. He advised UFO groups like Lumières dans la Nuit (LDLN) and UFO journals like GEPA's *Phénomènes spatiaux* to publish everything so the reader could "judge for himself." [6] Obviously, scientific journals do not publish everything, because initial selections are challenged and culled by referees and editors. Such an open-door policy defied scientific norms.

However, we should also remark that with the creation of GEPA and the evolution of groups like LDLN in the late sixties, a divide not only appeared, but it was maintained between UFO cases and contactee cases. Since the discussion on UFO cases can be endlessly reopened, the fact that ufologists put aside contactee cases

6. Information from interviews with Francine Fouéré, 1996.

shows that they considered them to belong to a different domain. The result was not rejection but silence. Contactee cases were not discussed in UFO journals. LDLN did not reply to letters of contactees (Monnet 1978) or persons suspected of being contactees. When the French UFO prophet Raël appeared in the media in 1974, LDLN published a brief note to mention the case without reaching a conclusion regarding its authenticity.

GEPA maintained a boundary between "legitimate" UFO stories and contactees. Their UFO journal, *Phénomènes spatiaux,* published narratives of abductions or close encounters with dramatic details, but they did not publish other stories, for example, of Dr. X, a physician who claimed a UFO miraculously healed wounds on his body. The reason is unclear. Often, the reason given has more to do with "feelings" than with clearly expressed arguments. "We thought the case didn't belong [in] the category of UFOs," recalled Francine Fouéré in an interview.[7] Therefore, although there seemed to be a clear borderline between UFOs and contactees, closer inspection indicated that discussions became ambiguous, and cases jumped easily from one category to another. So in due course, GEPA sustained a boundary of interpretation between UFO cases and contactees in this collection of data from their publications.

What Contactees Do: Message Versus Evidence

Having described the endeavors and discussions of the first ufologists regarding contactee cases, this study now turns to the 1970s to assess some of the first French contactees. Two cases reflect the relations that existed between contactees and ufologists. These cases will be used to elucidate how ufologists deal with contactees and how contactees construct their rhetoric (how the boundary of interpretation is constructed from their points of view). These dual interpretations show how ufologists and contactees form patterns of divergent logic. Psychological or psychiatric explanations for the contactees will be avoided. Following the methodology used in studying UFO investigators, symmetry must be maintained, and the same kind of explanations used for ufologists and scientists must also be applied to contactees.

The tenuous situation of contactees versus ufologists is best illustrated by Pierre Monnet and Jean Miguères. The case of Monnet remains salient because it provides a systematic comparison between the work of a contactee and the work of a ufologist. The Jean Miguères case shows us how a contactee evolves, how his testimony

7. Information from interviews with Francine Fouéré, 1996.

changes with time, and how a logical narrative that is consistently different from the discussion over "evidence" is constructed.

How a Contactee Group Became a Ufology Group: GREPO

In March 1975, Pierre Monnet founded GREPO, Groupe de Recherche et d'Etude du Phénomène Ovni (Group for the Research and Study of UFO Phenomenon).[8] Monnet was not a ufologist; on the contrary, he was a contactee. He made his first appearance on the UFO scene around 1972 when he sent a letter to the French UFO group Lumières dans la Nuit, to let them know about an extraterrestrial contact he claimed to have had in 1951 in the southeast of France. LDLN did not bother to investigate the case or to reply to the letter. It was only when a Belgian ufologist named Roger Lorthioir, a member of the Fédération Belge d'Ufologie (FBU), rediscovered the letter in LDLN files that the case was reopened ("Contact," 4). Investigators from the FBU met Monnet on June 7, 1974, and they accompanied him to the place of contact. Their first report then appeared in *Ouranos* in a series of articles on contactees signed by a pseudonymous Pierre Ensia (1974).

What did happen to Monnet? While on a bicycle ride one night in July 1951 in the little town of Courthezon, Monnet was suddenly teleported five kilometers to the entrance of a large, deep rock quarry. As if under hypnosis, Monnet entered the area, where he saw a light some sixty meters ahead. A metallic craft radiated light, and as Monnet drew closer, background noise disappeared. He then realized that along one side of the craft stood four humanlike beings who then initiated a telepathic discussion.

Monnet wrote to several UFO authors, such as Jimmy Guieu, Guy Tarade, and Jean-Claude Bourret, and decided to establish a UFO group known as the GREPO in March 1975.[9] What happened with GREPO is of interest. From Monnet's point of view, and as he explained later to members of the group, he started GREPO to learn about other extraterrestrial encounters because he wanted, above all, to have an-

---

8. See "Contact," a special issue of *Vaucluse Ufologie* (no. 2: 1979, 19). *Vaucluse Ufologie* is the name of an amateurish UFO magazine, which had several special issues. One of these was called "Contact." There were no authors cited for the issues. Further citations to page numbers for this issue are given in the text.

9. See "Editorial," a special issue of *Vaucluse Ufologie*, no. 8 (May 1978). Further citations for this issue are given in the text.

9.2. In 1975, Pierre Monnet founded GREPO, a French UFO research group. He later left the group. In 1978, he published *Les extra-terrestres m'ont dit* (The extra-terrestrials told me). Courtesy of the Mary Evans Picture Library.

other meeting with the aliens. He wanted to renew the contact initiated in 1951 ("Contact," 11).

A young UFO buff named Jean Manuel Cervantès and another ufologist, Christian Langlumé, joined GREPO in November 1975. Although the membership slowly grew, the situation did not last because despite the fact that the members were newcomers to the field of ufology, their motive was to investigate, not to become followers of a contactee. In 1976, Langlumé left GREPO to set up SOVEPS (Société vauclusienne d'Etude des Phénomènes spatiaux). At the end of that same year, GREPO planned to publish a journal called *Infor Ovni*, but it never did. Monnet communicated with other UFO groups with the goal of creating a French UFO Federation (Fédération française d'ufologie). However, as a contactee, other ufologists did not take him seriously, and they did not trust him as a UFO researcher ("Editorial," no. 8). In December 1976, a discouraged Monnet gave up all his projects, left ufology, and quit GREPO ("abandonna tout projet, l'ufologie, et le GREPO"; "Editorial," no. 11). He left GREPO, which then became a "normal" UFO group ("Contact," 12), and GREPO changed its status to a local delegation for LDLN, GEOS (Groupe d'Etude des Objects spatiaux), and the CUFOS-France (a later controversial French delegation of the Center for UFO Studies). In 1978, Monnet finally published a book on his contact experience under the title, *Les extra-terrestres m'ont dit* (The extraterrestrials told me).

However, what is interesting is that since the GREPO investigators had access to Monnet in 1979, they published a report on his case. This report helps to explicate the divergent logic of Monnet and of his fellow ufologists. The investigators wanted to weigh the evidence for the case and find it weak. They checked each of Monnet's claims and each time they found the evidence lacking or inconclusive. From their report, it is clear that they were not motivated by some sinister agenda. They did not draw any conclusions, only discussed their available hypotheses: fraud, pathological case, implausibility, and so on.

After detailing the story of Monnet's contact and what happened afterward, in particular his numerous claims of telepathic communications, the GREPO investigators discussed the available hypotheses. One investigator discussed the habitability of the star from which Monnet's extraterrestrials originated. The report also took note of the striking similarities between the content of Monnet's story and details from the movie *The Day the Earth Stood Still,* released the year of his contact, 1951. They did this for a good reason: Pierre Monnet had repeatedly told them that he had seen the movie in 1951 and several times since ("Contact," 43). They compared his case with that of another contactee known under the code name of Roméo-Charlie. In the report, Lilyane Troadec provided a portrait of Roméo-Charlie that took into account psychological, graphological, and astrological data. In this report, the investigators repeatedly mentioned the fact that Roméo-Charlie had come back from Indochina because of a "nervous breakdown." They wondered if there might be a psychiatric aspect to Monnet's adventure, but they do not conclude this in the end.

On several occasions, the investigators regretted that Monnet had so little interest in finding evidence to support his claims. It is, in fact, what surprised them most, particularly because they had done UFO field investigations with Monnet on other cases and found that he was "an excellent investigator." Nevertheless, Monnet soon returned to his position as a contactee, and several times his behavior surprised the members of the group. On one occasion, in particular, the members of the group had the opportunity to see a UFO and even took a picture of it. Their report remarked that each time Monnet had the opportunity to find empirical evidence, he turned away from it.

The need to maintain symmetry here requires that any discussion of lack of proof is balanced by an understanding of what proof meant for the members of GREPO and conversely for Monnet. Two enigmas emerge here: the investigation by the ufologists and the construction of Monnet's personal contact story. We do not need psychology to explain the situation, but only to understand why ufologists and contactees construct different definitions for the same things. The solution appears when we compare the report by GREPO and the book by Monnet. The GREPO report always focused on the evidence without attention to the extraterrestrial message. On the contrary, there was no discussion of the evidence in Monnet's book, and all the pages were devoted to a careful description of the contact and the messages received.

Monnet maintained that his contact was a real experience, and he said that he double-checked to make sure *it was real and not a dream*. He also offered criteria to formulate a difference between real contactees and hoaxers and said he did not want to be thought of as a cult or sect leader. Monnet and his former ufologist friends constructed their realities differently. As soon as Monnet claimed his experience was real, he moved to the discussion of the messages, while in contrast the ufologists from GREPO shifted away from the messages, preferring instead to devote their time to discussing the available hard evidence—ultimately finding it weak.

Monnet reacted strongly and bitterly to the publication of GREPO's report on his case. He sent a letter to the group stating that he was hurt by the text and by their desire to debunk his story.[10] While his former friends remained UFO investigators and participated in UFO groups, Monnet left the UFO milieu to create the Ordre de la Chevalerie de l'Etoile d'argent (Knighthood Order of the Silver Star), and he published a newsletter called *L'Etoile d'argent (The Silver Star)* in the 1980s.[11]

Jean Miguères: Relations Between a Contactee and Ufology

On Tuesday, July 28, 1992, a man was shot and killed by his stepfather on the streets of Lyon, France. This man was Jean Miguères, one of the most famous French contactees.[12] Born in 1940 in Algiers, Miguères achieved fame after the publication of his first book in 1977, *J'ai été le cobaye des extra-terrestres* (I was the guinea pig of the extraterrestrials). In it, Miguères told his readers that extraterrestrials first contacted him as he was about to crash the ambulance that he was driving. He claimed that while he was still in the wreckage a strange entity appeared near him, spoke to him, and put a small disc on his neck that regenerated his body.

After the accident, Miguères was rushed to the hospital, where he endured vari-

10. His letter is reproduced in *Vaucluse Ufologie*, no. 17 (Mar. 1980).

11. See Jean-Pierre Troadec in "Des ambassades extra-terrestres en France," *Nostra* 20 (Jan., 1983): 8–10.

12. See *Le Progrès*, July 30, 1992. See also Jean-Pierre Troadec (1992).

ous medical exams and surgical interventions. According to him, he should have died of his injuries, but instead he miraculously survived three clinical deaths. In the book, he provided medical affidavits detailing his injuries, as well as psychiatric evaluations concluding that he was quite sane. The meticulous description of these events and what transpired later fill more than a hundred pages of the book.

In the second part of the book, Jean Miguères transcribes the extraterrestrial messages he received while again in the hospital in 1970. He also describes his subsequent search for people who could help him understand what was happening to him. While hospitalized, he asked his wife to find him a book on UFOs. She brought him Guy Tarade's *Soucoupes volantes et civilisations d'outre espace* (Flying saucers and outer-space civilizations). When Miguères decided to write Tarade, he received a quick reply asking for some kind of evidence. Guy Tarade asked Jean Miguères to invite his alien friend to fly a saucer above Nice between January 15 and 31, 1971. Miguères sent a telepathic message to the extraterrestrials and waited. Then, on February 20, 1971, Miguères was surprised to receive a letter from Tarade explaining that he had seen a UFO.

In 1973, Jean Miguères became a member of Tarade's CEREIC (Centre d'Etude et de Recherches d'Elements inconnus de la Civilisation, or the Center for the Study and Research of Unknown Elements of Civilization), and he was promoted to the rank of vice president two years later. Miguères became friends with some of Tarade's colleagues, like Jimmy Guieu. He began speaking in public and met Alain Lefeuvre, a reporter from *L'Espoir Hebdo,* who wrote a paper on him and later became his publisher.

In his book, Jean Miguères (1977) explains that he went through several mutations: a physical mutation, which he claims everyone could see, a deep physiological mutation, and a psychic mutation, which was far more difficult to explain to other people, but which had a profound effect on him. He also mentioned how he discovered that he had a "strange power" to heal people.

In a brief conclusion, Jean Miguères reveals that in 1975 he had received a telepathic message from his alien friends regarding an artificial planet they had in orbit between Venus and Earth. Then, while reading the newspaper in January 1976, Miguères learned that American astronomer Charles Kowal had discovered a small planet in that orbit.

Several pages are devoted to reproductions of documents and pictures including medical documents to verify condition; affidavits from photographers and ufologists; pictures of Miguères with people he had the opportunity to meet; TV and radio shows that he appeared on; and the many articles written about him in magazines. Miguères and his publisher seemed intent to show the reader that the author was already well-known, respected, and taken seriously.

In his first book, he urges the reader to judge his story from the proof given, and it seems he was preoccupied with producing the available evidence to back up his claims. Miguères notes that his contemporaries are skeptical and need evidence, and he admits that his attitude would be similar. In his second book, *Le cobaye des extraterrestres face aux scientifiques* (The extraterrestrials' guinea pig faces the scientists), Miguères describes what happened to him after the publication of his initial book. He also devotes a discussion to his relations with French scientists. Then, in the second part of the book, he describes how he met Canadian and American scientists. He points out that in contrast to the French scientists the Canadians believed him. He then moves to revelations about his extraterrestrial contact that he refrained from publishing in his first book, in particular the transcript of an interview (remembered under hypnosis) in which he takes on the personality of an alien called Strôb. He also describes his experiences with the representatives of the Conspiracy of Silence, the so-called Men in Black, a government intelligence agency, and a private UFO group that was acting under sinister orders to suppress information. He informs his readers that he has changed since his first contact experience in 1969. From the first to the second book, Miguères moves his emphasis from one of evidence to one of skepticism, and more important, to an accusation of a government and scientific cover-up. At the same time, Miguères explains how he has changed— he no longer considers himself purely human.

Miguères published his third book, *1996: La Révélation*, in 1987. It takes a step further in the constructing of the narrative of Jean Miguères as the messenger of the aliens. Miguères is no longer one who has experienced the UFO phenomenon and who looks to the expertise of ufologists. He is finished giving proof of what happened to him. The book is entirely dedicated to the transcript of his message from the aliens.

In *1996: La Révélation*, Jean Miguères shifts to another kind of evidence. On several occasions, he insists that the reader must decide the truth of his story on a personal basis. Jean Miguères suppresses the distinction between fact and fiction. In order to attain this goal, he introduces distance between himself and his alien alter ego, Strôb, writing his book as though it were fictional. Anticipating discrepancies between the content of this book and his preceding books, and to forestall difficulties that the reader might encounter, Miguères explains that it was good that he purposely blurred the picture ("c'est bien à dessein que j'ai 'brouilé les cartes' ") (1978, 42).

What is of special interest in Miguères' case is the evolution from his first book to his third and last. Although he always speaks of evidence, he always constructs a new message in a new context, and thus, his notion of evidence is amassed in a predominantly religious way. He shifts more and more from "scientific proof" to the idea that one must look within to find the answer. Incrementally from his first to third book, he moved away from the ufologists and scientists and from their discussions of evidence. Many ufologists concluded that it was a hoax, while others continued to consider Miguères a genuine contactee. Thus, as noted in other cases, while ufologists can hold diverse points of view, debates over unseen evidence are lost in the case of Miguères, whose message is ever more elaborate, and who is not the same person/contactee from one book to the next.

We have described how ufologists discuss contactee cases, always reopening them, never concluding, and we have compared the logic of UFO investigators and contactees and have seen how a contactee can move from the position of an investigator to that of a messenger for the aliens. We have also noted how contactees presented their stories, which evolve from their first encounters with the aliens to the construction of their key messages. The discussion now turns to scientists and how they deal with contactees in a prominent case study. This discussion will emphasize the differences between scientists and ufologists. To place this discussion in perspective, it must be noted that few scientists actually study UFO phenomena because of the stigma attached to it.

What Scientists Do: The Construction of Networks

In November 1979, the French media revealed that a young man from the Paris suburbs named Franck Fontaine had been abducted at Cergy-Pontoise. Two of his friends, Jean-Pierre Prévost and Salomon N'Diaye, testified about his disappearance. The media explored that angle, while the police, suspecting some more sinister event, searched the area (dragging the river, etc.). Franck Fontaine had completely vanished. Exactly one week later, Fontaine reappeared, apparently, at the same spot from which he originally disappeared. From then on, the controversy took a new turn because of the ufological aspects of the account. Although initially Fontaine remembered few details of his abduction, everything changed when *Paris-Match,* the French equivalent of *Life* magazine, offered a significant amount of money for an exclusive story complete with details of the abduction (de Brosses 1979). Suddenly, Fontaine began to remember details. Shortly, a GEPAN team arrived at Cergy-Pontoise to investigate.

GEPAN (Le Groupe D'Etude des Phénomènes Aerospatiaux Nonidentifiés, or the Group for the Study of Unidentified Aerospace Phenomena) was founded in May 1977 thanks to the efforts of Claude Poher, an engineer with a keen sense of science policy.[13] Poher did a statistical study of eight hundred UFO cases that helped influence the National Space Center (CNES), the French equivalent of NASA, to conclude that the subject could be studied with some promise. As the military had been in charge of collecting UFO reports since the beginning of the modern UFO era, and more systematically since 1974, they decided that a copy of each report would go to Poher. For a year or two, he worked alone on the subject, and then in 1977 his work was officially recognized with the creation of GEPAN. A team of scientists from the CNES agreed to participate in this venture in their spare time. Hence, they produced a series of field investigations and statistical research projects.

However, Poher left GEPAN in 1978, and Alain Esterle, a young, highly trained engineer became the new director. Under Alain Esterle, GEPAN published a series of monographs detailing case investigations, statistical studies, psychological experiments, and research on propulsion systems as in the field of magneto-hydrodynamics. This was because several scientists, most notably, French physicist Jean-Pierre Petit, had suggested that this could explain certain enigmas attributed to UFOs (absence of sonic booms, changes of colors, and sudden right-angle adjustments in trajectory).[14] In 1983, CNES decided to put an end to the GEPAN venture and closed its office, replacing it with a new service much reduced in scope, called SEPRA (Atmospheric Reentries Phenomena Expertise Service). Candidly speaking, SEPRA is what is known in French bureaucratic slang as a *placard,* a facade. It has practically no budget, half a secretary (no secretary during several periods), and very few technicians or help from other services.

With the Franck Fontaine abduction at Cergy-Pontoise, GEPAN wanted to check the details of the case, in particular to submit the abductee to several medical tests. For instance, if Fontaine had gone into space, his blood pressure would have been altered. This "test of the cosmonaut," as journalist Robert Roussel (1994) called it, was never performed because of the reluctance of the abductee. (Of course, cos-

---

13. On the history of GEPAN, see Robert Roussel (1994). See also Perry Petrakis's 1998 interview with Claude Poher in *Phénomèna* (Poher 1998).

14. For a personal account of Jean-Pierre Petit's relations with GEPAN, see Jean-Pierre Petit (1990).

monauts, astronauts, and more precisely, *spationauts* in French, do not pass medical exams to prove they have been to space.) Several other unsuccessful attempts at verification ultimately led the investigators to conclude that the case was a crude hoax. Hence, GEPAN published in 1981 its report and conclusion in a monograph, entitled "Note technique no. 6," which was available to the public.[15]

However, the story did not end there. Apart from GEPAN, the witnesses also met with private UFO researchers, and more important, Jimmy Guieu. After writing his first two books in the fifties, Guieu kept on studying UFOs, and after Marc Thirouin's death in 1972, remained with *Ouranos* for a while. In the late seventies, he founded a new group, the IMSA (World Institute for Advanced Studies). Upon hearing about the Fontaine case, Guieu went to Cergy-Pontoise to investigate. In April 1980, he published a book coauthored by Fontaine and his two friends (Guieu et al. 1980). In this book, they say that the Cergy-Pontoise story is authentic; moreover, the real contactee was not Franck Fontaine, but his friend Jean-Pierre Prévost. Under hypnosis, Prévost had discovered how he had been contacted, and that the extraterrestrials wanted to work through him. Jimmy Guieu opened the book by attacking GEPAN and its methods. For Guieu, GEPAN was another Condon Committee. Physicist Edward U. Condon, who directed an official study in the United States, between 1966 and 1969 concluded that nothing scientific could be gained from maintaining a study of UFOs (Condon and Gillmor 1969). Many considered this action an official attempt at covering up the issue of UFOs, and the Cergy-Pontoise case looked like a similar cover-up.

After Guieu published his book, a number of French ufologists concluded the same thing that GEPAN did. In their minds, the Cergy-Pontoise alien abduction appeared to be a hoax. The case became the special interest of a private group named Control, headed by Michel Piccin, who was living in the area and did an extensive investigation from the outset. But here again, we see a difference in the work of amateur and professional scientists, although it has nothing to do with the quality of research, but rather with the duration of the debate and the ability to reopen the case. For these scientific investigators, that meant the end of the story, and no one reopened the case. Control similarly issued a document with full details of the encounter that also concluded that it was a hoax.[16] Michel Piccin even collaborated on

15. The source for this information is Esterle et al. (1981).

16. The source for this information is Marcel Piccin's *Cergy-Pontoise,* which was privately published in 1982.

several articles written by Hilary Evans that were published in the magazines, *The Unexplained* and *Fate*.[17] In 1983, Jean-Pierre Prévost, who had left the group and the influence of Guieu, explained (most ufologists say "revealed") that the entire affair was a hoax.

From then on, most UFO researchers definitively put the Cergy-Pontoise case in the hoax category, but certain other ufologists simply ignored Control and GEPAN's conclusions, touting the case as a real abduction or suggesting other scenarios to explain it. An important characteristic of ufology appears here: the impossibility to conclude or to have everyone in agreement about a particular case. Earlier, we discussed how ufologists in the fifties expressed different views on George Adamski, but with the passage of time, it seemed that this ability to keep a case open indefinitely became a characteristic of the milieu. In ufology, for each case and for each research topic there is always someone who reopens the discussion or who publishes a new book with fresh revelations. There is always someone who has another opinion or another interpretation of the same facts, and this opinion can end up in a book or article only to launch a new controversy. Adamski was no exception, and Cergy-Pontoise is no exception, either. For years after the publication of GEPAN's work and Control's articles and reports, and even after Jean-Pierre Prévost had confessed to the hoax, Jimmy Guieu continued to say that the case was authentic, and he continued to publish articles about UFO incidents occurring in the area.

In the meantime, rumors spread that the case was not a real abduction but actually a government deception. Jacques Vallee (1979) published *Masters of Deception* in which he claimed that the Cergy-Pontoise case was much more complicated than the investigators stated. While there was no UFO abduction, government agents engaged in a deceptive program had abducted Fontaine. Since there are no official spokespersons for ufology, the state of ufological interpretation varies according to who is speaking. Even today, people debate Vallee's theory on Cergy-Pontoise, which he reiterated in a later book called *Revelations* (1991). Vallee and others with additional theories about Men in Black (MIBs) helped to keep the case open.

17. See Hilary Evans (1982a, 1982b). Also see Hilary Evans and Michel Piccin (1982). Editor's note: For photos and more details on the Cergy-Pontoise case, see Richard Williams (1991). Numerous Web sites discuss Cergy-Pontoise and some have pictures. In reaction to Guieu, Jean-Pierre Prévost wrote his own book, *The Truth about the Cergy-Pontoise Affair.* He attracted followers and formed an organization. Before he ever admitted it was a hoax, a large number of his followers assembled in a field in 1980 to greet the saucers.

Case Closed?

For GEPAN, these endless discussions had no appeal. GEPAN considered the case closed and moved on to other questions. The Cergy-Pontoise case became a black hole labeled a hoax. Theoretically, a scientific case can be reopened, but a scientist needs very good reasons, and more important, he or she needs funding, an approved project, colleagues, and laboratory tools to function. If a scientist reopens a case for reasons that are not shared by colleagues, that scientist can be labeled a maverick and run into professional trouble. In comparison, it is much easier to reopen a case in ufology. However, even if ufologists use categories to differentiate "serious" from "not so serious" ufologists, the absence of a global ufological network makes it far more difficult for UFO investigators because they usually work on the margins of respected research. In contrast to established researchers, ufologists usually take their cases to the public, and there is a greater tendency on their parts to proliferate divergent points of view outside accepted academic science.

The contactee stories mentioned earlier are just a few examples. However, they are special because they show the socially constructed divisions between ufologists and scientists, and thus, help to clarify the differences between their respective methodologies. Since the seventies, there have been many other cases. Of course, Raël (Claude Vorilhon) is the most famous (Palmer 1995, 1998, 2003, 2004) with his International Raëlian Movement, although many other new groups have coalesced around messages from aliens. Despite the claim of teaching the ultimate heavenly science, Raël has been of more interest to social scientists than to physical scientists. Most of the newer contactees had no prior relationships with ufologists. Both methodologies (ufology and science) led to the publication of books and journals, but the participants did not associate with one another. Of course, they knew of each other but they did not engage in dialogue, except, for example, when contactees like Raël made headlines. Therefore, when ufologists began to investigate contact cases in the eighties, they did so from more or less a sociological perspective and sometimes from a psychiatric stance (Troadec 1983) because some had preconceived ideas about the abnormal origin of the phenomenon.

Conclusion

Good scholarship requires that we present the two versions of UFO investigation that were most generally used when describing the divisions amongst ufologists, scientists, and contactees in France, although it must be noted that both versions are biased. The first version describes the contactees as following a path fraught with ambushes from the obstinate scientific rationalists and the ufologists. The rationalists and certain ufologists are unwilling to recognize the existence of privileged close encounters with extraterrestrials. The second prejudicial version of the story proceeds as if the contactees had made mistakes and persisted in their errors. Worse, they had been just a bunch of lunatics and liars. Of these two narratives, the second version is the one most often presented, as noted in the beginning of this article with the work of David Jacobs. He and others object to the publicity sought by contactees, and their lack of submission to self-appointed ufological authorities. Nevertheless, the two versions contain similarities.

When disbelief is suspended regarding the existence or nonexistence of UFOs and alien contact, the possibility arises of describing how the actors went about reaching their conclusions. As in the case of the French contactees, all the necessary phenomenological explanations are provided by the social actors themselves. Scientists and many ufologists doubt the stories of the contactees because they "know" that psychological explanations account for their sightings. The contactees, in turn, doubt the explanations given by the scientists and ufologists, and they prefer to ally themselves with other people who seem to accept their accounts. More important, we have seen how the actors can shift from one world to another. Ufologists were not always severely critical of contactees, and contactees have spent some of their time discussing evidence.

Straddling the borderline between the two intellectual territories in ufology, Pierre Monnet could simultaneously be both a contactee and a UFO investigator. A ufologist can be a skeptic and a UFO advocate; a scientist can work in a laboratory and become a cultist upon emergence from the lab. How do people believe in contradictory things and move from one world of interpretation to another? Each day we have access to sundry social worlds. This access allows us to understand how people can live in different worlds concurrently, and be at the same time astronomers and ufologists—or ufologists and cultists. The actors must not be judged as backward or progressive, rigorous or frivolous, honest or dishonest, but as equally understandable within the context of their aims.

While there is no evidence of any kind supporting the existence of a "Great Divide" (Goody 1977) between scientific thinking and other systems of thought like ufology or contacteeism, there is considerable evidence for the existence of numerous yet small material discrepancies between the social actors and their different social worlds. It is normative for ufologists to adopt this view in their efforts to distinguish themselves from people they reject, and we have described how these perceived differences were formulated. However, it is not wise for historians or sociologists to take for granted such divisions that are socially constructed and not a priori, since they know these divisions are the actual results of historic negotiation and controversy.

However, the existence of interpretive differences is a fact. The question arises, What really happened, and what are the interpretive differences amongst scientists, ufologists, and contactees? Reviewing the particularities of each category of actors, scientists must end controversies; therefore, they reduce the number of hypotheses and actors. As Latour would say, the characteristics of scientists exist in their ability to multiply black boxes. They can do this thanks to the proliferation of instruments of measurement and empirical validation. It can be argued that scientists do not think, nor do they look at reality. Instead, scientists build instruments and fill the world with them. From their perspective, their instruments document an objective reality, as opposed to the notion that their brains and their processes of interpretation construct a situated *reality*. Resultantly, this *reality* is not seen by the scientists themselves, who instead, look at diagrams and data trails emanating from their instruments. As Latour explained, an instrument can be either a technical tool or a human being, but it has to be disciplined to perform a given task. When a scientist diverges from the accepted paradigm, this excludes him or her from acceptance and proper consideration. The divide between what is scientific and what is not was invented for that purpose.

In contrast, ufologists multiply the number of hypotheses and encourage unconventional thinkers. Ufology also provides numerous arguments and controversies against the establishment and within its own ranks, but the divisions never really work, and they are not maintained for very long. Hence, people considered by other researchers to be cranks or debunkers are much more difficult to exclude from the discussion. Thus the controversy is prolonged. The border between who is or is not a ufologist is much more difficult to define than the border between who is or is not a scientist. An important characteristic of many segments of ufology is the quasi-absence of laboratories and technical instruments. For example, the debate remains the same now as in 1947 over the objectivity of testimonies because the witnesses are simply that, witnesses, and not equipped observers. Thus, ufology now comprises a world of debates in which few nonhuman instruments are involved; hence, it lacks those very instruments that render possible the closure of scientific controversies.[18]

18. To see how scientists close controversies, win over their colleagues, and move rapidly from one subject to another, see the classic work by Bruno Latour, *The Pasteurization of French Society* (1993).

Accordingly, it is rare to reach the end of UFO controversies, and, most of the time, they appear to just start up again after a while. This leads to two questions. Why is it so difficult to "learn" something "positive" about UFOs? Why is it so difficult to add new knowledge to existent knowledge without always reopening the discussion?[19] French astronomer Pierre Guérin says that ufology is characterized by a simple law: each new fact debunks the preceding facts. Guérin's law is a sociological law that explains a characteristic of ufology: the impossibility of coming to a conclusion. Each new thinker discredits the facts submitted by previous thinkers, as each new commission debunks the assessments of earlier commissions. This could be viewed as a negative effect; however, the analyst need not be a judge of what is right or wrong regarding the behavior of the actors. Because science is considered the frame of reference for our reality, this description of the perpetual state of controversy within UFO groups appears negative to many observers.

However, this aspect of ufology could also be seen as a positive attribute. If the chief characteristic of ufologists is their ability to multiply controversies without ever concluding any of them, then ufologists can be viewed as being quite open-minded, and much more open to contradiction. In fact, they encourage the propagation of other views. With that in mind, they build few barriers between what is normal and what is not; when they do construct such cordons, they do not last. Research indicates that the diversity of beliefs of UFO adherents is widespread, eclectic, and inconsistent; they all have firm beliefs, but they never agree. Thus, the views proliferate instead of reducing in numbers.

The focal point is that those who suggest new ideas never construct them in such a way as to end the debate. It may be that this proliferation of hypotheses and controversies is owing to ufology's not being constructed *en dur* (in a hard or solid manner), and that the arguments are not structured along the same lines of strategy used in science. A good scientist is one who builds an argument in such a way that colleagues feel obliged not only to take it into account, but to abandon their own arguments in favor of it. Scientists attain this end thanks to their instruments, funding, and the like (Latour 1995). In contrast, the ideal form of a good ufologist is one who suggests a new hypothesis that exercises no constraints, whatsoever, on the

19. A perfectly clear example of a UFO discussion that is always reopened is the famous and premier Ken Arnold case. Almost every year someone comes forward with a new explanation for this case, and the Internet has helped in this regard. Even the most select Internet newsgroups, like the Project 1947 Discussion List (invitation only), carry many discussions on this classic case without any ufologist ever succeeding in putting an end to the controversy.

work of others. Therefore, a good ufological argument does not generate mere interest, but passion.

Distinctively, contactees are not building networks like scientists, and they are not focusing on controversial evidence like ufologists. What are they doing? How can we maintain a nonreductionist definition of contactees when they repeatedly change their stories and fabricate details? The temptation to assign psychological explanations should be mitigated by remembering Bloor and the Zande: what appears contradictory (asking to be believed while fabricating a story) may have a normal explanation. Remembering that the actors themselves should do the analysis, then, what are they saying and doing?

Returning to the celebrated contactee George Adamski, when speaking of his claims ufologists always focus on his photographs. For the ufologist, any doubt regarding the authenticity of the alien saucer photographed by Adamski precludes any further discussion of his experience. In spite of this, we should not ask, Why do contactees have so little evidence? Rather, we should pose the question, Why are ufologists so fascinated by evidence, when it seems that it is of so little import to contactees and their followers?

For the contactee and for those involved in contactee religions, the discussion over scientific proof is secondary and thus is not a sign of either honesty or dishonesty. Even if the photographs are forgeries, the message still has meaning. There is an example that clearly shows how a contactee can consider the message to be more important than how it is obtained. In a work that compares scientific and religious rhetoric, Bruno Latour (1990) shows that the scientific and religious modes of transmitting a message are different. In science, the source of the data must be clear, and the researchers must be able to put in a straight line all the *maillons de la chaine* (links in the chain). Conversely, what is important in religion is the meaning of the message for the listener. The message has meaning here and now for the reader, it is not simply the last representative of a long chain of mediations. The message must transform the reader rather than construct an external reality. In contrast, in science the message must remain the same all along; in religion, the message can change depending on the context, but its meaning should remain the same.

In their book on George Adamski, Swiss follower Lou Zinsstag and Timothy Good (1983) revealed how Adamski had reprocessed (in the context of his Venusian contacts) messages he had previously used decades before in another context, those of the Royal Order of Tibet. Adamski had simply changed the words "Royal Order of Tibet" to the words "Space Brothers." It is impossible for a UFO investigator (or scientist or journalist) to give credence to a fabricated narrative such as this. To better understand the contactee's position, we should refrain from asking, How can Adamski take his followers as fools and fake what he is saying? Instead, it would be more useful to inquire, Why is source of so little importance to Adamski that the same message can be attributed to both Tibetan masters and Venusian philosophers?

In *Watch the Skies! A Chronicle of the Flying Saucer Myth,* aviation historian Curtis Peebles describes how Adamski's claims were challenged and shown to be fraudulent. In lectures, George Adamski asserted that his material had been cleared by the FBI. Then, when confronted by the FBI, he denied making the claim. However, he provided a letter signed by three FBI agents in order to stop certain rumors regarding fake documents. In 1955, James Moseley revealed that most of Adamski's claims did not accurately reflect what was supposed to have happened (Peebles 1994). The witnesses he quoted had not, in fact, seen what he alleged in his book, which had been "edited, expanded, and improved" by a friend. Additionally, Adamski took pictures, which he then attributed to others.

In either a ufological or scientific context, this lack of evidence can be devastating. In a contactee context, it only illustrates that a book by a contactee should not be read like a scientific paper. Readers of scientific papers are supposed to be able to reopen every black box constructed by the author to discuss its content and mode of production; if they cannot check every detail, then there is a problem. In contrast, books by contactees are not required to pass this inspection, because they are meant to inspire. Hence, deconstructing Adamski's proofs is secondary because the logic of George Adamski's behavior and message is elsewhere.

When skeptics read Jean Miguères' book and see how the content evolves, changes, and even contradicts what the author first said, they can only offer a medical diagnosis on the case or unmask the hoax perpetrated by Miguères.[20] Nevertheless, for Miguères this evolutionary change in his basic story is not a problem. On the contrary, it is what makes the transmission of the message possible, and like Miguères, the reader must be transformed by the message. Typically, in his first book, Miguères shows a poor quality picture of the wreckage of his ambulance, and he says that he sees a face and a man with an oxygen mask. However, the picture was taken several days after he was removed from the wreckage. For the UFO investigator, this is evidence that the contactee is either insane or assuming his readers are

---

20. See the papers published by UFO researcher and longtime Miguères adversary Perry Petrakis in a UFO magazine, *Bulletin de l'AESV,* which became *Ovni-Présence* (in particular no. 10, Apr. 1979, and no. 25, Mar. 1983). OVNI or Ovni means UFO in French.

particularly gullible. But the author is only maintaining the meaning of the message; he is constructing in another context and through other means.

Following Pierre Monnet's case, we discover that his meeting incorporated details very similar to the movie *The Day the Earth Stood Still,* which he viewed in 1951. Thus, more doubts arise. Is this a similar situation to Adamski's in which the American contactee first wrote a science-fiction novel, and then incorporated details from it into his contactee story? Perhaps, but we can only begin to understand why contactees mix the different genres of fiction and reality in an effort to attain their goals if we stop looking for evidence.

When learning English, it is unimportant if the sentence—My tailor is rich—refers to any reality. The task is to learn English through examples. It seems that here we have a similar situation as evinced by the sentence—My tailor is from Venus. The task for the student is to understand. Of course, unlike the English teacher who does not claim to have met the tailor, the contactee claims to have had a meeting with the Venusian. Nevertheless, the reality is embedded within the message, rather than the evidential documentation of the experience. Had they irrefutable evidence, contactees would submit themselves to UFO investigations instead of recruiting followers. Thus, the sentence is not as real as a scientific formula, nor is it entirely fictional because the narrative is used as a learning tool. It only becomes real when people agree to be changed by the meaning of the narrative. Another comparable situation is that of medieval exempla, which were mentioned earlier. Preachers would tell the tales of ahistorical biblical sinners in order to pass the message on to believers. Thus, the desire to check the reality of the tales dulls the point because the importance lies somewhere else within the structure of religious belief.[21]

It is necessary to understand the practical differences between contactees' construction of reality and that of ufologists or scientists. It is intriguing to see how contactees use their logic when forced to answer questions on evidence. Because they are constantly obliged to shift from scientific evidence to the content of their message, the situation appears rather complicated. For instance, similar to Miguères and Monnet, the 1950s American contactee Howard Menger was another perfect example of how contactees change their stories. Initially, Menger said he met an alien woman. Then, when faced with the need for evidence, he shifted, saying that the meeting was an allegory. The circumstances appear rather difficult for the con-

---

21. See Bremond, Le Goff, and Schmitt (1982); see also pages 170–203 and in particular pages 189–90 in Berlioz (1990).

tactee. The contactee hears so much about science and evidence that he or she almost accepts the vocabulary of adversaries, thereby producing the type of evidence that cannot help but make the critics' case.[22]

The contactee, the ufologist, and the scientist—all live in parallel worlds of interpretation and meaning, alien to one another. In the collective process of the social construction of knowledge of UFOs, their worlds separated along boundaries of meaning and methodology. The French case reveals the ways that saucerism divided into different territories with few border crossings. By deconstructing the case of French saucerism, we can better understand how boundaries of interpretation cordon off and defend as real the internal logic that constructed them in the first place. This exercise will help us analyze what we call science and what we call parascience in a more balanced fashion.

Will the last person to leave the social studies of UFOs please turn on the tape recorder?

22. There is a considerable difference between the way science is described and used as rhetoric by skeptics and the way it is used in actual scientific practice. For an illustration of the use of science as rhetoric by CSICOP and its limit when skeptics are obliged to move from discussion to practice, see Pinch and Collins (1984).

PART THREE

Myth, Folklore, and Media

10

Consciousness, Culture, and UFOs

Jacques Vallee

Many years ago I had the privilege of working with J. Allen Hynek, the astronomer who served as scientific consultant to the U.S. Air Force on the topic of unidentified flying objects (UFOs). I especially remember a time when we had just finished speaking to a large audience in California. We had been stressing—as we always did—the great need for a genuine scientific investigation of the unidentified flying object phenomenon. Then it was time for questions, and none of the questions from the audience had to do with science. We should have anticipated this. What people wanted to know was, Would the occupants of the UFOs help humanity solve its problems? Did they have a God? Were they responsible for the miracles in the Bible? What kind of philosophy did they bring us? In other words, not only had the audience already jumped to the conclusion that the objects were spacecraft controlled by extraterrestrial beings, but all the questions were concerned with spiritual issues.

There is nothing wrong with this concern, so we tried our best to provide some answers. Then, as we left the stage, Dr. Hynek made a remark I have never forgotten. He told me, "Jacques, nobody will ever give you or me a dime to do serious research on UFOs. But if we were to cross the line of professional ethics, if we went back up on that stage, pretending we had the answer with a capital 'A,' and if we told these people that ufology was the cure to all their spiritual anxieties, we could raise a million dollars today!" In the last few years, that fine ethical line has been crossed again and again by many people claiming to provide both spiritual and scientific answers. As a result, the study of UFOs has turned into a complex intellectual maze where one person's certainty becomes another person's blasphemy.

With this observation in the background, I will present here my grave misgiv-

10.1. Dr. J. Allen Hynek was one of the most significant
scientists in the study of UFOs. Hynek, a professor of
astronomy, conducted many investigations for the Air Force.
He was also a cofounder of the Center for UFO Studies
(CUFOS). Courtesy of CUFOS.

ings regarding the dominant view on the nature of UFOs. The "standard scenario"
usually includes elements such as seeing lights in the sky or some highly advanced
technological spacecraft, observing short, humanoid aliens with large dark eyes,
and being abducted to a spaceship for medical examination, biological experimentation, and blood or tissue sample-taking. I am very concerned about the state of
UFO research because the focus is almost exclusively on finding data to fit this scenario. I will now offer a critique of the "standard scenario" from my own (admittedly limited) point of view. Please keep in mind that I do *not* have a solution to the
nature of the UFO problem, although I have been studying it for a long time. I cer-

tainly do not offer you any spiritual answers, and you should be very skeptical of anybody who does.

This chapter has two parts, the first one dealing with the challenge of anomalies, especially with the notion of higher intelligence, and the second one following up on a discussion I had with John E. Mack about abductions. Dr. Mack was a distinguished Harvard psychiatrist and a leading investigator of UFO abductions as anomalous manifestations. When he came to San Francisco a few years ago, he spoke to a small group of consciousness researchers at the Institute of Noetic Sciences, inviting us to think about the impacts of the UFO phenomenon if it turned out that abductions were real. I will conclude with a few words on the challenge the enigma places before us in this new millennium in the context of high technology.

Anomalies Throughout History

I would like to start by asking you to imagine, if you will, that we have been transported back in time to the year 436 A.D. An earthquake has destroyed Constantinople; famine and pestilence are spreading. The cataclysm has leveled the walls and the fifty-seven towers of the city. Now comes a new tremor, even stronger than all the previous ones. According to Brian Croke (1981), the historian Nicephorus reports that in their fright "all the inhabitants of Byzantium, abandoning their city, had gathered in the countryside."

They prayed that the city be spared total destruction. They were in no less danger themselves. The movements of the earth had nearly engulfed them, when a miracle, quite unexpected and beyond all credence, took place. It filled them with awe. In the midst of the crowd, a child was suddenly taken up by a strong force, so high into the air that they lost sight of him. Afterward, the child came down as he had gone up and told Patriarch Proclus, the emperor himself, and the assembled multitude that he had just attended a great concert of the angels hailing the Lord in their sacred canticles.[1]

The bishop of Constantinople, Acacius, states, "The population of the whole city saw it with their eyes." Baronius, commenting upon this report, adds the following words:

1. Historian Brian Croke (1981) documents the event of the Constantinople earthquake and the "miraculous" ascension of a young boy into the sky. According to the *Oxford Dictionary of Byzantium* (1991), Nicephorus was patriarch of Constantinople between A.D. 806 and 815, a historian, and a saint. Proclus was bishop of Constantinople beginning in 432, and he was also a saint.

Such a great event deserved to be transmitted to the most remote posterity and to be forever recorded in human memory through its mention every year in the ecclesiastical annals. For this reason the Greeks, after inscribing it with the greatest respect into their ancient *Menologe,* read it publicly every year in their churches. (Croke 1981)

Over the centuries, many extraordinary events have taken place and chroniclers have transmitted them to "the most remote posterity." We are that posterity (Vallee 1988). It is our responsibility to assess the data they have transmitted to us. Upon their authority and their accuracy rest our concept of history and our vision of the world. Whether we like it or not, history and culture are often determined by exceptional *incidents.* Strange beings and extraordinary events have always influenced us in an unpredictable fashion. Our vision of the world is a function of the old myths with which we have grown familiar, and of new myths we pick up along the way (Thompson 1991).

The importance and antiquity of myths were noted by anthropologist of religion Mircea Eliade in *Myths, Dreams and Mysteries: The Encounter Between Contemporary Faiths and Archaic Realities:*

What strikes us first about the mythology and folk-lore of the "magical flight" are their primitivity and their universal diffusion. [The theme] is one of the most ancient motifs in folk-lore: it is found everywhere, and in the most archaic of cultural strata. . . . Even where religious belief is not dominated by the "ouranian" gods [those of the sky], the symbolism of the ascent to heaven still exists, and always expresses the *transcendent.*[2] (1975b, 103)

Yet, the lessons from the past are often forgotten. We tend to jump to conclusions every time we hear about a UFO incident, anxious as we are to follow instructions that appear to come from above. There is a process through which the myths of humankind become implemented as social and political realities (Vallee 1992), and knowledge of that process is what I call a "forbidden science." By forbidden science, I mean that despite the large amount of historical and contemporary data regarding "unidentified flying objects" or similar celestial apparitions, mainstream science is unwilling to investigate the phenomena seriously.

2. See Eliade (1975b) in the section entitled "The Magic Flight" in chapter 5. See also "Symbolisms of Ascension and Waking Dreams" in the same book.

The Power of Mythical Reality

In the early days of flying-saucer contactees in the fifties and sixties, I remember seeing an advertisement in a UFO magazine offering *an actual hair from a Venusian dog* for the affordable sum of five dollars! Such stories make us smile. We may laugh at the simple souls who become so obsessed with a legend, or are taken in by a hoax, that they lose sight of everyday reality, and we are naturally leery of hoaxers and con artists who exploit the idealistic tendencies of an unsophisticated public. However, there is another side to the seductive nature of unexplained phenomena.

Among the notions of humankind none is more pervasive or powerful than the myth of contact with higher intelligence—with another level of reality where gods, demons, angels, and extraterrestrial and spiritual entities function. Here I am not using the word "myth" to designate a legend or a false belief, but rather any notion that is "truer than truth": a level of belief that transcends the world of factual observations. "Truer than truth" is a phrase my friend Gordon Creighton once suggested to me to indicate a mode of belief supported by experiences beyond observable, measurable data.

It is from a high level of mythical reality that some of the great movements of humanity have soared, giving us many of our religious structures, our ancient moral and legal codes, numerous paintings, sculptures, examples of great architecture, and the guiding stories of Moses, Buddha, Jesus, Mohammed, and lesser figures. In that sense, the invocation of higher intelligence is the most powerful force in history, more powerful than the atom bomb or the space rocket, or any of the other modern products of human intellect. This *is* reality, or at least social reality, whether the rational scientist likes it or not. In the new millennium, the concept of higher intelligence is playing an everyday role in visions of our own survival, giving us the collective inspiration to go on living in a world of increasing complexity and danger.

The Universe Is Not So Simple

Carl Jung (1959) spoke of something he called "the collective unconscious," a shared, transpersonal reservoir of experiences, which is the source of universal images, motifs, and symbols common to all humanity. He saw flying saucers as instances of an innate human need for profound symbols. He spoke of UFOs as an *archetype:* a preverbal, even preexperiential, primal "force" that operates at a primordial level of being, and that underlies manifestations of both psychic images and physical shapes. If he was right, as I believe he was, then the existence of an alien archetype has at least three important corollaries.

First, the UFO phenomenon, as it is seen in America today, should not be unique. We should be able to find many situations that are analogous to our own in the history of all the cultures that have preceded us. It is for that reason that I began with a mention of the Constantinople episode and the child lifted to heaven.

Second, it would be easy to trigger the archetype artificially under conditions involving hypnosis, suggestion, hallucinogenic drugs, or other altered reality states.

Third, the resulting belief system would be open to manipulation by sophisticated social engineers. A recent chilling example was the murder/suicide of fifty-three members of the Order of the Solar Temple in Switzerland and Canada, a cult involved with supposed ET contact (Leleu 1995; Hall and Schuyler 1997). Whether or not there are "real" UFOs flying around in our skies, belief in UFOs provides a back door to manipulating the unconscious.

From these observations, one could easily propose that close encounters and abductions are "simply" the result of mental processes, and the study of UFOs could then be relegated to psychology, neurophysiology, sociology, or anthropology. That is indeed the dominant view among the academic community today, but it fails to explain the facts.

If UFOs are a manifestation of archetypes, that means the phenomenon is much more anomalous (within the standard Newtonian mechanistic paradigm) than any theory of extraterrestrial aliens in spacecraft would suggest. Not only the UFO phenomenon, but the universe itself, would be much more complex and intellectually challenging than our science has heretofore indicated. It could even be that the nonphysical UFO archetype could manifest physically.

Let me remind you again that the phenomenon is indeed a real manifestation in a physical sense. Those hard scientists who did take the time to sort through the reports and to examine them closely, such as J. Allen Hynek, James McDonald, Claude Poher, and a few others, have all come to the same conclusion. We are dealing with physical objects that interact with their environment through the emission of light and other electromagnetic radiation, through mechanical and thermal effects, and through psychophysiological changes in the witnesses who are in close proximity to the phenomenon.

Researchers disagree about the secondary effects of the objects and about their probable origin, but the consensus is remarkable, from country to country and from period to period, about the underlying (archetypal) patterns. In particular, the model that Claude Poher and I developed in the seventies, starting from different

databases in France and in the United States, has held up well as new data were acquired from other regions (Poher and Vallee 1975).

Problems with the ET Hypothesis

Nowadays, theoretical physicists are developing models of reality that involve hy-
perdimensionality and such interesting cosmological concepts as wormholes and
superstrings. Given these revolutionary models of physical reality, objects that behave as UFOs are reported to behave in the earth's environment represent an opportunity to test fascinating hypotheses, and to enrich the scientific debate.
Furthermore, they also offer the opportunity to look beyond the mechanistic universe and technology itself.

William Irwin Thompson writes in his remarkable book, *Evil and World Order*:

> To see technology in proper scale, we need cosmic consciousness. . . . The human-
> istic movement that began with the Renaissance has reached its limit, and at that
> limit Western culture has broken apart as mechanism and mysticism move in op-
> posite directions along the circumference of human civilization. . . . To under-
> stand contemporary culture you have to be willing to move beyond intellectual
> definitions and academic disciplines. You have to be willing to throw your net out
> widely. (1980, 78)

In spite of all the lessons the UFO phenomenon (whether it is physically real or
not) could teach us about contemporary culture, academic researchers have not
heeded Thompson's advice to throw their net widely. Even a student of mythology
as astute and open-minded as Joseph Campbell avoided the subject. Another irony
is that the field is sinking into disrepute just as a lot of money has become available
to study it. The money comes from individuals who, it seems to me, even with the
best intentions misunderstand the nature and process of research, and who have not
surrounded themselves with open-minded experts. Starting from the idea that the
phenomenon is physically real, for which there is evidence, they have summarily
jumped to the conclusion that it can represent only an extraterrestrial intervention
on the part of intelligent creatures who look like us. This is a valid theory *but only
one among many*. From this naïve and overly simplistic view of the data, it is but a
small step to use research merely as an excuse to advocate a certain theory and to
lobby for its recognition by political authorities.

This approach to research is sterile, no matter how much money is poured into an effort to promote the "space alien" theory to the exclusion of all others. It does not matter if you spend one dollar, one million dollars, or one billion dollars to promote the theory, you will simply not get anywhere. Good research is not done that way. In science, you do not pick a conclusion before you have analyzed the data. That is how science differs from other fields, such as politics or advertising. In science, you are supposed to go out and look for facts that contradict your theory.

The problem with the extraterrestrial theory is that it does not explain the facts as we know them today. I can say this with all the more freedom because I was one of the early proponents of the theory, at a time when the data were scarce, and when it did seem that UFOs behaved like spacecraft. We need to account for the following:

The plausibility of extraterrestrial intelligence. Given the enormous number of galaxies in the visible universe, and the high probability that physical conditions similar to our own exist elsewhere, we must expect that other intelligent life-forms have achieved the ability to travel through space. They may even be traveling under conditions that would seem to violate some limitations of physics as we know it, for instance by appearing to exceed the speed of light. Indeed, works by Harold Puthoff (1996), Miguel Alcubierre, and others have shown that reduced-time interstellar travel could be envisioned within our own present concepts of physics. It is fair to assume, therefore, that we are not alone in the universe, and even that some alien civilizations may have developed very advanced technologies, including intergalactic space travel. However, beyond the technological considerations, other parameters of the reported cases contradict the extraterrestrial theory. Take, for example, the historical extension of the sightings, their high frequency, the humanoid appearance of the "operators," and the consistent absurdity of the abduction reports. (Each of these I discuss below.)

The long history of the phenomenon. If our visitors are technically savvy space travelers as some theories claim, they could obtain massive amounts of information about us in the course of a few expeditions. They would not require the millions of landings that statistical analysis indicates on the basis of even our current files alone.[3] This figure would be multiplied to absurdity if we were to extrapolate ET visits back though the centuries, for instance, to Constantinople in the fifth century.

---

3. A survey of typical Americans, conducted in the summer of 1991, was aimed at uncovering the frequency of such experiences as unusual presences in their room, seeing a ghost, or feeling paralyzed. It was interpreted as indicating the frequency of abductions by aliens. In later published reports based on this survey, UFO researchers claimed it supported a number of actual abductions ranging between 3.7 million and 9 million in the United States alone. See Hopkins, Jacobs, and Westrum (1992).

Applying statistics to the long view of history, therefore, seriously challenges the ET-visitation thesis.

Abductions for genetic engineering. This is perhaps the strongest argument against the ET-visitation hypothesis. If our "visitors" were sufficiently technologically advanced to travel between galaxies, it is highly unlikely (to put it mildly) that their level of biological engineering would be still on a par with our "seminal" biotechnology and genetic engineering. If they wanted to create a hybrid race, it would be safe to assume that they could do so unobtrusively without inducing trauma in their victims, and without resorting to crude biological scenarios: the painful taking of egg and sperm samples, or the insertion of implants described by abductees. Techniques to achieve all these objectives already exist within Earth science, or can be extrapolated from available knowledge. We would expect space visitors to do much better.

Yet one of the most common themes in contemporary abduction reports is this kind of intrusive biological experimentation. The reports are real. Hundreds, perhaps thousands, of people have experienced *something,* which they are moved to describe as alien abductions for the purpose of what appears to be biological experiments. Such reports require explanation, and it is extremely difficult to square them with the "nuts and bolts" theory of extraterrestrial encounters. Given the implausibility of "spleen and gene" ET abductors, we need to find some other explanation. We must consider the following:

Humanoid appearance of the "abductors." Considering the vast, almost unimaginable, variety of shapes and sizes of creatures that have evolved on our planet—on land, in the oceans, in the air—why should extraterrestrials appear so humanlike? Defenders of the ET thesis must resort to ad hoc speculations, such as "They take on human form for our benefit."

Consistent absurdity of the abduction reports. Taken together, the frequent accounts of "blood and sperm" experiments and the "humanoid" features of the abductors underline the consistent absurdity of the reports, especially in the context of highly advanced alien technology.

Therefore, far from fitting comfortably into an extraterrestrial scenario, or even into our more ambitious science fiction projections, the UFO phenomenon challenges much of what we know about reality and consciousness itself. That is why the phenomenon is so interesting. This makes it all the more surprising that, as far as I can see, nobody has initiated an open exchange of ideas to attract independent, critical thinkers to the field, and to bring them in contact with the people who have real data.

What Is the Meaning of Alien Abductions?

Of greater concern is the fact that some abduction researchers believe all this on faith, without making a serious effort to grasp the underlying phenomenon. This is where I part company with some researchers when they take these impressions literally, without asking deeper questions. I want to dwell on this topic because, as I have said before, I have serious doubts about both the nature of the data and the methodology used in the research. If the abduction phenomenon really is an expression of an archetype, and if archetypes may be triggered by either physical or mental stimuli, then we should expect that when subjects are placed in situations where consciousness is deliberately altered, the *situation itself* could be the trigger that releases the archetype. Hypnotic induction of memories is a clear example of such a situation.

Hypnosis is a notoriously easy setting for the reinforcement of belief. It is an ideal tool for mind control, which is why experienced psychiatrists do not use it, or do so carefully, in very well-defined cases, such as some forms of hysteria. You may recall the celebrated case of the "Jet-Propelled Couch" in Robert Lindner's classic book on psychotherapy (1954). He went out of his way to explain *why he decided not to hypnotize* a leading aerospace engineer who presented a delusion of traveling throughout the galaxy in another reality. After careful investigation the patient's condition was traced to sexual molestation in childhood. The engineer eventually recovered his sanity under Dr. Lindner's care. I shudder to think what might have happened to this patient if he had fallen prey to some of today's amateur hypnotherapists or if he had joined a "support group" of UFO believers.

In my own view, hypnotic regression of abduction victims, as commonly practiced by ufologists, is unscientific, unnecessary, and unethical. The conclusions that are drawn from this practice are unwarranted. I do believe that in most cases the witnesses have had a real, extremely unusual experience, but that experience may be very different from the scenario so heavily promoted in the literature and in the media today. In this standard scenario, interviews with abduction victims report the recall of a very structured series of events that go from seeing a light in the sky to observing some short gray aliens with big black eyes, to being transported inside a spaceship, to being medically examined on some sort of table prior to sample-taking and to eventual release.

I see another side of the experience. I get letters from abduction witnesses complaining that their stories have been taken out of context by UFO investigators. They call for help, sometimes in painfully dramatic, terrifying terms, telling me that the stories in books on abductions represent only a small part of their total experience, that the nightmare is still with them, and that in many cases it does not relate to space aliens at all! Typically, these victims tell me that what the hypnotherapists did to them was "worse than what the entities did." Then they want to be hypnotized again to be healed of the nightmare.

One of the things we must understand about hypnosis is that the experience is not reversible: You cannot rehypnotize someone who has been hypnotized sloppily by an amateur who was convinced that he or she already knew all the answers. On those occasions when I have taken these witnesses to a professional therapist trained in the *clinical* use of hypnosis I have been told that the earlier process had so badly altered the person's awareness of the experience that there was little hope of reconstructing what had really happened. These victims have to go on living with their nightmare.

Beyond the "Standard Scenario"

Over the past twenty years, I have accumulated data concerning seventy cases of abductions. In some respects, my data agree with those of other ufologists, but in many other respects they are at variance with their findings. For example, in his public lectures Dr. Mack eloquently described an interview he recorded last year with a South African shaman who experienced missing time, an encounter with various beings of the classic alien description, and a horrible sexual episode when he was raped by a woman whose flesh felt like that of a cadaver. He emerged near his village, covered with ash, and stinking of rotten fish.

The case would actually fit much more nicely into the literature of demonology than in the literature of extraterrestrial life. In an earlier work (Vallee 1994), I have quoted at length from medieval scholars who discussed how demons, *who often smelled of rotten fish,* could animate dead bodies to perform sexual intercourse with humans and steal their seed. This idea is not new, nor is it specific to the domain of ufology. Theologians have argued about just this topic for centuries. As one author puts it, "The Devil transformed himself into a sprightly maiden, who allowed herself coyly to be wooed and won. That he performed the entire act of copulation in this aspect of his enviable versatility there is no question, from the records of servants of the Holy Church too pious to lie and too learned to permit of their being misinformed"[4] (Bulliet 1956, 91). Furthermore, the implication drawn by abduc-

---

4. Bulliet goes on to say, "While Satan was father of a rather extensive progeny through virgins he had ravished during the wild orgies of the Sabbath, there is no record that he ever became a mother."

tion researchers is that we are being visited by space aliens who want to save the environment. I believe they are making deductions too hastily from biased samples. The abduction database has been censored by the promoters of a very particular interpretation to the detriment of all others. Four years ago, for example, I was approached privately by two state directors of one of the largest civilian UFO groups in the United States. They described to me how the cases they submitted were rejected when they did not fit as "classic" abductions, which were supposed to involve short beings with large black eyes performing certain actions in a certain sequence. I know of equally good cases from equally reliable witnesses that involved other scenarios that never made it into the databases.

Yet such cases exist, as shown in the following passage from a letter sent to me by a woman who lives near Los Angeles. This episode, which she first thought was a dream, happened in 1976. She writes:

> I found myself lying on a table. My clothes were gone and my legs were slung over the arms of a man, or so I thought until I looked up at his face and saw that it was not human. There stood a being that had the head of a dog with long pointed ears, a long muzzle, reddish brown fur on the face and neck, light color eyes. His body was human looking, it was pale but the sexual organ had reddish stripes as well as his lower abdomen. . . .

As she struggled with him, his eyes began to spin around like a pinwheel. She felt intense fear, thought she would lose consciousness, and woke up with a terrible start, her heart pounding very hard. Later she began seeing twinkling lights. Later she discovered that she was pregnant. She had a normal pregnancy and gave birth to a son.

Twelve years later in 1988, she was looking through a Time-Life book she had just received through the mail. It had pictures of mythical creatures and she was shocked to recognize the being in question as the Egyptian god Anubis. Her son looked at the book independently, came to this picture, and remarked, "Mom, I've seen this guy in my dreams a few times!" She goes on to write:

Noting that the Devil can "scarcely be blamed" for not wanting to be a mother, Bulliet adds, "The holy fathers must be blamed for their neglect, in the interest of science, to learn of his method of birth control" (1956, 91).

I became very upset but I didn't tell him. He said the dream was always the same, he would be walking into this pyramid and when he got inside this guy Anubis would step out from behind this wall and start talking to him. He couldn't remember what was said. I asked him to describe what he looked like, he said the thing had dark reddish brown fur on the face, and the skin was peach color and he wore a skirt-like thing that was red. Now the picture in the book had no color to it, and I never told him or anyone about the thing I saw.

What this suggests to me is that the current interpretation of abduction episodes in terms of space visitors from another planet is a terribly narrow view of a much larger and much older tapestry. In a wider view, we would simply accept the fact that human consciousness is impacted by images and experiences of other realities.

What Kind of Research Is Possible?

Eastern mystics and the songwriter Donovan have observed that "first there is a mountain, then there is no mountain, then there is." The same observation applies to the UFO kind of incident. When you first become involved, everything seems very obvious: the witnesses seem to be reporting some sort of spacecraft and their occupants, patterns are emerging, and contact seems to be just around the corner. After some years of work and lots of data, things no longer seem so simple. Contradictions emerge; cases that seemed cast in concrete turn out to be made of sand; new doubts arise about the reliability of human testimony and the complexity of consciousness. My advice is to keep going. After a few more years of hard work, the mountain reappears. But it is a different, far more majestic and inspiring mountain. The main thing you discover is that instances of apparent contact with another form of consciousness are not isolated to a particular time, place, or culture. Let me give you another example.

A book about the life of a respected leader and shaman of the Lakota (Sioux) nation, a man named Black Elk, reports an episode when he was struck by an illness that nearly paralyzed him while he traveled with his family:

When we had camped again, I was lying in our tepee and my mother and father were sitting beside me. I could see through the opening and there two men were coming from the clouds, head first like arrows slanting down. . . . Each carried a long spear, and from the points of these a jagged lightning flashed. They came down to the ground . . . and stood a little way off and looked at me and said: "Hurry! Come!" (Neihardt 1932)

The narration continues:

> They turned and left the ground like arrows slanting upward from the bow. When I got up to follow my legs did not hurt me anymore and I was very light. I went outside the tepee, and yonder where the men with flaming spears were going a little cloud was coming very fast. It came and stooped and took me and turned back to where it came from, flying fast. And when I looked down I could see my mother and father yonder, and I felt sorry to be leaving them. Then there was nothing but the air and the swiftness of the little cloud that bore me and those two men, still leading up to where white clouds were piled up like mountains on a wide blue plain, and in them thunder beings lived and leaped and flashed.

This symbolism brings us back to Jung's concept of archetypes. Why should there not be, in physical reality, certain stimuli that can activate an archetype and trigger extraordinary states of perception or unusual states of consciousness in certain human beings? In those states, why should we not become aware of other forms of consciousness? The believer's mistake is to ascribe meaning and credence to the secondary perception, the mental image created by our brain to account for the stimulus. The skeptic's mistake is to deny the reality of the stimulus altogether, simply because the secondary perception seems absurd to him or her.

What we take to be reality may, in fact, be a mere *appearance*, or projection, onto the "screen" of our four-dimensional space-time world from a much more complex, multidimensional, more fundamental reality. More than two thousand years ago, Plato described this very scenario in his allegory of "the cave," where sensory reality turned out to be mere shadows on the cave wall, projections from the higher reality of Ideal Forms beyond the cave. Real progress lies between the two equally close-minded attitudes of the believer and skeptic.

I have seen medieval engravings that claim to record something remarkable, the hand of God in the sky, holding a bloody sword ominously pointed at the earth. Such events were carefully recorded by our forefathers, like the wonderful abduction of the child in ancient Byzantium, because they were widely regarded as predicting terrible events such as wars, famines, and the death of kings.

Today we would say that the witnesses of these events were mistaken. What they were seeing in the sky was not the bloody sword of God, only a simple comet. Modern astronomy would suffer today if the event had not been recorded at the time, providing us with precious information about the comet's periodicity. We no longer believe that the comet was predicting anything, or had any religious significance. However, we do know that the stimulus was genuine. There was something in the sky. It was curved like a sword. It was pointed at the earth. Why cannot we approach UFOs in the same way?

Implications for research are clear: If there are physical stimuli that act upon the collective unconscious, as Jung had speculated, then *we should expect to find continuity* in abduction reports throughout history. That is exactly what a careful examination of old records has proven—witness the episode of Constantinople and the experience of Black Elk, and there are many more.

In every age, the witnesses came back with their own explanations or interpretations of the meaning of these incidents. The child in Constantinople thought he attended a concert of angels, and Black Elk met thunder beings. The modern theory happens to be oriented toward space aliens, who give us a message about the protection of the environment. The supposed extraterrestrials are allegedly telling us that we are harming the planet and threatening our survival, as if we did not already know it.

Then There Is a Mountain

What is the nature of this mountain, which keeps appearing and disappearing before our eyes? The mountain is a phenomenon, a real physical phenomenon that is unrecognized by current science. We have not even started to approach it seriously with the tools we do have.

Think of all the attention directed at the Roswell incident, or at claims of strange lights over Area 51.[5] Think of the abductions where the witnesses recall not

5. Area 51 is a classified test site near Nellis Air Force Base in Nevada. The mystery stems from the fact that luminous objects are often seen at night over the region. Any technically trained person who follows high-technology developments can understand the nature of the reported objects, even if the actual performance and manufacturing methodology of these platforms remain classified. Such "data" pale into insignificance compared to those of a London-based video distributor named Santilli, who revealed that he knew of an actual film of alien autopsies shot at the site of the Roswell crash in 1947. The movie (widely shown around the world and edited as part of a Fox Television documentary in the United States in August 1995) showed a humanoid cadaver being examined by a team of army doctors. They are seen sawing its skull, cutting open its body, and casually lifting out various organs, with little effort to control for possible contamination by an unknown virus. Such stories do little to help professional scientists overcome the "giggle factor" that surrounds the whole field.

just aliens but human figures among their tormentors. *We are not dealing with spir-itual transformation here, but with social trance-formation.* We are far—very far in-deed—from the simple patterns of interaction with alien visitors trying to help us clean up the earth. Therefore, it may be more important for us to break the trance and snap out of it than to surrender to it as many sincere, well-meaning people are inviting us to do.

Abductions may involve a class of beings, or a form of consciousness, that oper-ates well beyond the scope of current science. Understanding them may even be, as French UFO researcher and science writer Aimé Michel argued for a long time, be-yond the capability of the human brain. Perhaps we should be paying more atten-tion to what the beings themselves are communicating. According to the seven Sylphs who visited Facius Cardan in August 1491, the beings on the other side of re-ality feel that "we are like monsters to them." They believe that they cannot bring us anything of advantage, "except apparitions, then fear, and then knowledge."

Remaining Open

I am acutely aware that I have not offered any answers, not even a new theory of what UFOs are. Beginning as an active researcher, I have become a sorrowful by-stander in this field. My impression, as I watch this "festival of absurdities" from the sidelines, is one of unceasing amazement with a touch of sadness.

The amazement comes from the realization that even in our supposed Age of Technology, there is so little critical examination of the facts before us. Someone re-cently sent me a message over the Internet, assuring me that an American television network had paid $150,000 for the film showing the alleged alien autopsy at Roswell. I never thought I would live long enough to see the day when paying five dollars for a hair of a Venusian dog would sound to me like a pretty good deal.

The sadness comes from my observation that, in the middle of all this passion and in spite of all the money spent on ufology, what little real research was being done is grinding to a stop everywhere in the world. That is easy to understand: Why should any scientist take the trouble to go out into the field for long and tedious hours of investigation if the answer is waiting for us in the archives of some com-fortable government office, or inside Area 51, or on some old film of alien autopsies? I see no credible, ongoing effort to come to grips with the underlying UFO phe-nomenon, which I continue to believe is real and important, perhaps not for today's science, but certainly for tomorrow's science and for the future of consciousness.

I continue to hope that someday we will be able to sort out the signal from the noise and get to work on the real UFO phenomenon. If I feel one major responsibility, it is the same one the historians of Constantinople did, namely to transmit the data to posterity, hoping that future scientists will be able to make sense of what seems to us hopelessly tangled. If we can resist the temptation to jump to hasty conclusions, then we may emerge intellectually better and spiritually stronger in the twenty-first century.

In closing, I am again reminded of the words of William Irwin Thompson (1980, 81):

We are like flies crawling across the ceiling of the Sistine Chapel: We cannot see what angels and gods lie underneath the threshold of our perceptions. We do not live in reality; we live in our paradigms, our habituated perceptions, our illusions; the illusions we share through culture we call reality, but the true historical reality of our condition is invisible to us.

Aliens from the Cosmos

A Discourse of Contemporary UFO Myths

Anna E. Kubiak

> Everybody who has a computer and access to the Internet can take part in
> looking for aliens in the cosmos.
>
> —*Gazeta Wyborcza*, Warsaw, Poland

UFOs and aliens are the subjects of mystery, media, and myth. Public UFO discourse began in 1947 with the news of Kenneth Arnold, who told the press that he saw nine strange metallic objects. Rumors of an alleged flying saucer crash at Roswell followed shortly. On the heels of these rumors, Hollywood movies distributed new worlds of imagery about aliens and saucers, for example, *The Thing* (1951) and *The Day the Earth Stood Still* (1951), which helped the embryonic myth grow. Widely circulated contact reports came by 1952, when George Adamski claimed to have met a Venusian named Orthon. Adamski's books about his encounters became best sellers. Adamski and others like him organized groups devoted to contacteeism. Historically, we know that the ranks of doubters and believers grew, along with a multitude of myths and legends about UFOs, in the succeeding five decades. Today, some UFO researchers maintain that approximately ten million people have had close contact with UFOs (Skórzyński 1996), although this and similar estimates may be part of the myth of contact itself.

Identifying those interested in UFOs, John A. Saliba mentions the following social groups: "(1) natural scientists, (2) social scientists, (3) government officials and military experts, (4) adventurers, and (5) religious individuals" (1995, 17). Saliba identifies some natural constituencies for UFO data and contact narratives; however, these groups represent only part of the widespread interest in a subject that has branched out into many areas of popular culture, embedding itself in everyday language and media consumption. The ubiquitous themes of UFOs and aliens go in many directions, and they are interwoven into the fabric of the postmodern culture from religion to media and beyond.

Reputedly, UFOs come in many shapes, including saucers, cigars, and orbs. The aliens also take many forms. The Internet presents the following types of aliens, among others: Nordics, Giants, and classic Greys with big heads, big dark eyes, small noses, and strange rachitic bodies. Richard Hall (1988) proposes the following classifications: Diminutive (Humanoid form), Average (Human form), and Giant (Monster form). In comparison, Alvin Lawson (1980) goes into greater detail: Human, Humanoid, Animal, Robot, Exotic, and Apparition. Additionally, many contactees prefer to think of extraterrestrials as angels, gods, higher-dimensional creators, and ultraterrestrial beings (Lewis 2000, 2003a; Partridge 2003). Published guides to what aliens look like are available in bookstores (Huyghe 1996), and the variety of types and planets of origin seem to be increasing every year.

J. Allen Hynek developed different categories for UFO encounters: (1) close encounters of the first kind, in which a flying saucer is seen at a distance of a few hundred feet; (2) close encounters of the second kind, when a spacecraft has left some tangible sign of its presence, such as a scorched landing area; (3) close encounters of the third kind, where contact with aliens has been reported; and (4) the more recently coined, close encounters of the fourth kind, or those that involve abductions (Spencer 1991; Lewis 2000). Newly adopted by some ufologists, the close encounter of the fifth kind involves conscious human-initiated contact with extraterrestrial intelligence. These are abbreviated for everyday parlance as CE-1, CE-2, CE-3, CE-4, and CE-5.

Alien abduction narratives, or close encounters of the fourth kind, play a large part in more recent UFO mythmaking (Bullard 1989; Peebles 1994; Pope 1998; Jacobs 2000). Abduction narratives often begin with typical scenarios, for instance, people are riding in cars or they are lying in bed. Then, they see a light. Next, they meet the occupants of the UFO and lose consciousness. Afterwards, the many abductees realize that time periods are missing from their memories, and some conclude that they have abduction amnesia. Following the story line, hypnosis reveals abduction by aliens, medical tampering, sexual molestation, and a return trip to terra firma. One such abduction was depicted in the 1975 movie *The UFO Incident,* directed by Richard A. Coll. Based on *The Interrupted Journey* (1966) by John G.

Fuller, the film highlighted the ordeal of Betty and Barney Hill, who were supposedly taken by aliens in 1961 while returning home from a weekend trip. Their subsequent revelations about the event under hypnosis encouraged many others to come forward with their experiences.

Some abductees are mythmakers themselves, like the Hills. Other examples include the renowned Whitley Strieber (1987) and Adriano Forgione (Burakowska 1999), who was supposedly abducted as a child. Today, Forgione participates in international conferences where he presents research papers, such as the "History of Conspiracy Contacts Between Aliens and Governments." Many people report nightmarish experiences with UFOs and others tell of blissful journeys, leading some to speculate that there are good aliens and bad aliens, hence the need to categorize them carefully. John Whitmore (1995) commented that the accounts of abductions contain the essence of strangeness and horror. Jodie Dean (1998, 34) concludes, "Abduction can't be captured or encapsulated. A miniseries, even a good one, can't sum it up or confine it." Yet the mass-media industry still tries by producing a multitude of UFO stories (e.g., the pop-culture heroes Dana Scully and Fox Mulder from the television show *The X Files*) for a vast, almost international, audience. This vast audience has mushroomed in the era of Internet communication, where some of the most sought out information is about alien abduction (Dean 1998).

As noted by J. Gordon Melton (1995), meetings with UFOs are religious experiences par excellence. In popular culture, some movies frequently portray extraterrestrials in spiritualized ways. Although extraterrestrials are sometimes cast as monsters (e.g., the 1979 film *Alien* and its sequels), many films also depict aliens as spiritually developed, as in the movie *Contact* (1997), which featured Jodie Foster in a close encounter of the fifth kind. Scientific efforts in the area of SETI (Search for Extraterrestrial Intelligence) took on a spiritual slant in *Contact*, a film based on a Carl Sagan novel. Movies and television give us some of our strongest images of spiritual contact with aliens, as do reports from "real" contactees.

Contact with alien worlds can be a highly mystical experience. According to Rudolf Otto ([1923] 1950), *mysterium tremendum* is an important aspect of the sacred. *Mysterium tremendum* is a Latin phrase that means being awestruck, overwhelmed with humility, and filled with energy in the presence of the sacred. James R. Lewis comments on the cinematic illustration of that condition:

> According to Otto, one encounters the sacred as a powerful, alien reality that does not belong to the world of ordinary human existence. This experience contains

components of both fear and attraction: The sacred simultaneously repels and fascinates; it is "uncanny" and "awesome." The sacred is also mysterious—something we cannot grasp with our rational minds, yet which we endlessly attempt to understand.

The parallels between religious experiences and UFO experiences are straightforward enough. UFOs seem uncanny and mysterious. Because of the tremendous technological power they represent, they also evoke fear. If the reader has seen Steven Spielberg's 1977 film *Close Encounters of the Third Kind,* she or he will recall the penultimate scene in which the mothership appears: This enormous piece of alien machinery is experienced by the gathered officials and technicians as both beautiful and frightening—an incomprehensibly awesome power before which they feel like helpless children. This is precisely the kind of encounter that Otto characterizes as religious. (2003b, 96)

Following a UFO encounter or so-called contact with an alien, some individuals respond by being awestruck. Among the awestruck, contactees seem to be the most persuasive in conveying their experiences to others. Contactees often have imminent metaphysical messages for humanity, which include moral injunctions, apocalyptic pronouncements, and themes of being *chosen* by a higher power (Whitmore 1995; Saliba 1995). Such people often classify their own experiences as spiritual and transformational, and their messages become new mythological material for anyone who will listen (Lewis 2003a; Partridge 2003).

Are UFO myths useful? Carl Jung thought so. It was probably Jung, who first said that UFOs were a contemporary myth (1959). Thus, he proposed a psychological interpretation of the UFO myth, in which he speculated that the powerful shape of the archetypal circle evoked a mystical response. The evocative flying saucer was parallel to the circular *mandala* of sacred Hindu art, a symbol of spiritual fulfillment and a symbol for selfhood. However, Ken Wilber (1997) sees nothing archetypal in UFO myths. John A. Saliba (1995) notes that UFO myths contain humorous aspects and various kinds of trivia, as well as religious imagery. Valerii Sanarov (1981), on the other hand, proposes to classify narratives about meetings with UFOs as folkloric material. Diana Tumminia and R. George Kirkpatrick (1995) indicate that certain UFO groups, like Unarius, create emergent myths as the basis for meaning within their social organization and as the touchstone for their reality. Such myths become part of larger meaning systems that fuel the interpretive worlds of new religious movements (Tumminia and Kirkpatrick 2003), and they are now part of the psyche of the postmodern age.

11.1. Carl Jung suggested that the circular shape of the flying saucer evoked a psychological archetype in human consciousness and the mythic imagination. This illustration by Unarius depicts a spaceship piloted by Space Brothers. Courtesy of the Unarius Academy of Science.

An analysis of UFO symbols and myths inevitably points to the nature of postmodern fragmentation. These myths contain numerous elements from popular culture and esotericism. They combine and splice themes like these: aliens, angels, gods, astral bodies, megalithic architecture, crop circles, a hollow Earth, dolphins (from Sirius), space monsters, Edgar Cayce, the ancient culture of Sumer, alien architects of lost civilizations, and the Bible Code to name a few (Andersson 2000; Denzler 2001; Lewis 2003a). One also finds in parts of the UFO subculture an eclectic language derivative of pop psychology or alternative therapies with occasional references to the latest scientific discoveries. In this respect, one can attend a support group to heal oneself from a negative alien contact or go to another group to be healed by contact with flying-saucer energy. A person can take an astral flight to Venus, or communicate telepathically with ETs, as well as be saved from the wheel of reincarnation. A new wrinkle in the terminology of some UFO religions defines their experiences as scientific or nontheistic. The images and symbols of this genre go in many contradictory directions, crossing the boundaries of science and religion and jumping the fences between movies, television, and everyday life. This runaway cultural swapping of themes and iconography that challenges all former representations of reality is called *intertexuality* by postmodernists (Kuhn 1990).

Some regard the stories of strangers from the cosmos as a paranormal phenomenon. A Polish scientist from the University of Otago, New Zealand, wrote a monograph on how to communicate with aliens. He commented that some skillful methods of connecting with extraterrestrial visitors are telepathy, reiki, chi, orgone, meditation, and yoga. Sociologist Erich Goode (2000) places flying saucers and extraterrestrial contact beliefs squarely in the subcultures of paranormal beliefs, where participants borrow ideas from one another. Many different occult philosophies and myths cross over and become new variations on old themes in the name of UFOs.

Jodi Dean observes that UFOs have become a scattered icon of postmodern anxiety and defensive ambivalence. The main message of Dean's work is that UFO discourse reflects the essence of contemporary (late modern and postmodern) culture: the impossibility of finding the truth, while, at the same time, compulsively searching for it. The same message is imparted in the film and television series *The X Files*. Dean notes:

> Through its construction of the problem of truth as a question of credibility, UFO discourse incorporates the reflexivity and skepticism lauded as signs of the rationality and rightness of science and law. Because it adopts the very practices that excluded it, UFO discourse has always depended on the skeptic, critic, and debunker. When Carl Sagan makes the effort of writing several hundred pages to discredit reports of alien abduction, he confirms the importance of the phenomenon. Moreover, because the skeptic enters into dialogue, engaging in a discussion about the truth of flying saucers and a hybrid human-alien breeding project, the discourse itself is confirmed as open and reflexive. (1998, 55)

There are even pseudodocumentary films about UFOs, chronicling the catastrophe at Roswell, for example *UFO Crash at Roswell,* directed by Jeremy Kagan, Kevin D. Randle, and Donald R. Schmitt. The Roswell myth runs deep in contemporary folklore with charges of alien autopsies and the secret development of alien technology. Rumors of cover-ups and conspiracies are potent mythmakers especially when made into speculative films that do reach a wide audience (Tumminia

2003). In this category, there are theories of government conspiracies against aliens, and theories of conspiracies about government collusion with aliens (Dean 1998; Denzler 2001). It seems that any theory can to find an audience and "facts" to support its case in this age of mass media. Alien conspiracy theories are smaller legends that feed off bigger myths (Barkun 2003).

I conclude with a question from a friend of mine: If a UFO landed in the middle of Warsaw, Poland, would this be proof that UFOs exist? I answered, "No, there would still be many possible explanations, such as collective hypnosis, the film set of a new science-fiction movie, a paranormal phenomenon, or even NASA playing a joke on Poland." This persistent ambiguity about the meaning of the phenomenon makes UFO myths fine examples of postmodern myths.

All I Ever Want to Be, I Learned from Playing Klingon

Sex, Honor, and Cultural Critique in Star Trek *Fandom*

Jennifer E. Porter

Star Trek is, of course, a television show. When it first premiered in 1966, the studio billed the series as a futuristic Western with the starship *Enterprise* as a "wagon train to the stars." Given its ongoing popularity, it is sometimes surprising to recall that the original show lasted only three short seasons, and if not for the massive letter-writing campaign launched by fans, it would have lasted only two. *Star Trek*'s cancellation in 1969, however, simply marked the beginning of the *Star Trek* phenomenon. The enduring appeal of the series and the dedication of hundreds of thousands of fans worldwide have made the *Star Trek* phenomenon unique in television history. The commitment of fans to the ideals portrayed in *Star Trek,* their idealization of Gene Roddenberry's vision, and their determination to live their own lives in light of the meaning they found, raises the *Star Trek* fan phenomenon to mythic levels. In terms of their ideological agendas, utopian visions, sacral sense of community, moral commitments, and participation in ritual events, *Star Trek* fans can be said to construct, participate in, and embody a fictional, but mythically real, sacred universe (Jindra 1994; Porter 1999; McLaren 1999). In this universe, several species of extraterrestrials, such as Vulcans, Romulans, Ferengi, and, of course, Klingons, serve as metaphors for human cooperation and conflict. The characteristics of each species reflect parts of the human psyche and experience. For example, Vulcans are calm, spiritual, and logical, while Ferengi are avaricious and volatile. Romulans are deceitful and imperialistic. Earthlings are torn between rationality, emotionality, and spirituality.

Star Trek fandom, however, is not uniform in terms of its organizational structure or conceptual orientation. Euphemistically called Trekkies (or Trekkers), *Star Trek* fans participate in fandom to varying degrees. Some fans are simply lovers of the *Star Trek* television shows, and are unaffiliated with any organized fan club. Others participate in local, national and/or international fan clubs, attend conventions, participate in online discussion groups, read and write fan fiction, and subscribe to fan magazines (fanzines). Organized fandom circles the globe through fairly autonomous local clubs with creative names (e.g., USS Powhatan, Starbase 71, and Kronos One), often affiliated with broader national organizations such as the United Federation of Planets, United Federation of Planets Internationale, and the Klingon Assault Group. *Star Trek* broadcasts to over one hundred countries, and satellite connections, tapes, books, and DVDs make it widely available through the globalization of media.

One particular expression of *Star Trek* fandom, Klingon fans, stands as an identifiable subculture. Klingon fandom is dedicated to the appreciation, and often playful emulation, of the Klingon species. Klingons are one of the most ritualistic and spiritual, as well as most militaristic, races within the *Star Trek* universe. To "play" Klingon, therefore, is in many respects to play at religion. Fans draw upon the Klingon species to provide exemplary models of being and acting in the world, just as Klingons themselves are shown to draw upon their religious heritage for such models. In the context of Klingon fandom, playing a Klingon allows a fan to redefine and explore questions of gender and sexuality, as well as questions of what it means to be human. In challenging gender stereotypes through play, Klingon fans ultimately reenvision how human beings relate to one another.

The original *Star Trek* series portrayed Klingons as the ultimate enemy: an evil, brutal warrior race bent on conquest, and as such, they were the thinly disguised communists of American fears. Individual Klingon characters, such as Commander Kor (portrayed by John Colicos) in the classic episode "Errand of Mercy," quickly became fan favorites, but fan organizations dedicated to the Klingon species as a whole did not initially emerge.[1] In the 1980s, however, three factors contributed to the emergence of organized Klingon fandom. The first was the release of the film *Star Trek II: The Wrath of Khan* in 1982. This film featured Klingon characters prominently (albeit, as the bad guys of the plot), and it showed numerous details of

---

1. For details on all episodes and characters, see http://www.startrek.com.

Klingon physiology, culture, and dress that would become standard in future *Star Trek* movies and television shows. This film firmly established the lumpy-headed look for Klingons. (It had been only briefly portrayed in the first *Star Trek* film, and it was entirely absent from the original *Star Trek* series.)

Second, and more important, *The Final Reflection* by John M. Ford was released in 1984. This novel, one of the early Paramount Studios/Pocket Books *Star Trek* editions, explored Klingon culture, history, and physiology in depth. It presented Klingons in a positive light for the first time. Ford discreetly explored and explained inconsistencies between the "old" Klingon look and the "new" Klingon look. He elaborated on the martial virtues and warrior worldview of Klingons, and introduced a terminology for articulating rank hierarchies. Both the production and the popularity of this book represent, to some extent, the ownership of *Star Trek* that fandom has maintained since the success of the initial letter-writing campaign to save the show. Although officially sponsored and published, the book was written as a fan attempt to construct, and to some extent alter, the "official" or "canonical" portrayal of Klingons presented on the television show and the first two *Star Trek* films. It remains the basis for much of the Klingon lore accepted and developed within the context of Klingon fandom.

In 1987, *Star Trek: The Next Generation* premiered with the Klingon character of Lieutenant Worf on the bridge crew. Worf was the only Klingon in Starfleet, a Klingon raised by humans and therefore presumably a bridge between the two species. The series showed Worf to be preoccupied with honor and duty, very militaristic in attitude, and physically formidable (actor Michael Dorn is about six foot four). Although not particularly an original fan favorite, the character of Worf gradually came to attract more and more fan admiration as episodes dedicated to explaining the details of Worf's character and broader Klingon culture were produced. Instead of the brutality and sadism implied in the original series, *The Next Generation* portrayed Klingons as a warrior race with strong ties of honor, kinship, and loyalty to the Empire, as well as a complex system of mythology, ritual, and practice, which fostered a strong emphasis on individual martial prowess. The Klingons, it seemed, had been redeemed from their early "evil" personas and had now become characters worthy of respect and emulation. The first Klingon fan club emerged in the years between the publication of *The Final Reflection* and the premiere of *The Next Generation*. By far the majority of Klingon fan clubs, however, emerged following the second and third season of *The Next Generation*, once the character of Worf and Klingon culture had been sufficiently explained. This creative information attracted a larger following. Since that time, new fan clubs and new chapters of already established Klingon fan clubs continue to emerge every day.

The Culture and Religion of Klingons

Klingons are one of the most richly detailed and unique species in the *Star Trek* series. Both genders are portrayed as warriors—physically imposing, military in bearing, armed, aggressive, and very dangerous. Klingons hail from the planet Kronos (Q'onoS), where they organize their society by clans, or Houses. They rank honor as the highest value and despise weakness. Male and female Klingons display a robust egalitarianism (especially in the later *Star Trek* series and episodes). Their mating rituals involve combat as foreplay, and the females have a high sexual appetite. The Klingon language sounds harsh and guttural and is now available for study by fans at the Klingon Language Institute. Tall, aggressive, and threatening by human standards, Klingons evoke the diplomatic necessity of bypassing appearance for the sake of promoting cross-cultural understanding.[2]

Klingons possess extroverted personalities—they are blunt, honest, and radically individualistic—but they also show a strong sense of military hierarchy and loyalty to the Empire. Their code of honor is called the Code of Kahless, named after the central figure in Klingon mythology. Kahless, an Arthurian-style warrior hero, overthrew a corrupt leader, led his people righteously until they needed him no longer, and then vanished, leaving them with the promise to return should the need ever be great. Myths call him Kahless the Unforgettable, both a hero and a god. Other gods and heroes in Klingon religion include a creator god and a first-Klingon equivalent to the biblical Adam named Kortar, who slew the gods who created him. Klingon religion embraces a belief in an afterlife in which those who die with honor live in the warrior paradise of StoVoKor and serve in the Black Fleet, a ghostly armada engaged eternally in glorious battle. Those who die in dishonor are taken on the Barge of the Dead to Gre'thor, the Hall of the Damned, where they suffer eternal torments. The first Klingon, Kortar, condemned for his crime of deicide, steers the barge. He eternally ferries dishonored Klingon souls to their doom.

Klingon religion is primarily a model of and a model for exemplary action. It carries a mythic dimension in which Klingon religious stories are presented both as descriptive of Klingon prehistory and prescriptive of honorable Klingon behavior. According to religious studies scholar Wendy Doniger, human mythology encompasses both of these dimensions: myth in this regard is both a verb and a noun, a

---

2. You may ask, is it Kling (short for Klingon) or Klin? Some people pronounce the "g"—but others do not. Klin is a term (spelled as written) borrowed from John Ford's book *The Final Reflection*, which influenced Klingon fandom.

story or set of stories that can be told, but also a model and requirement for action (1988, 33). Comparative religionist Mircea Eliade also makes this point. According to Eliade, myth "supplies models for human behavior and, by that very fact, gives meaning and value to life" (1975a, 2). Given its mythic qualities, therefore, Klingon religion as depicted in the *Star Trek* series has less to do with dogma, worship, and organization than it does with providing an idiom for acting in the world. One should follow in Kahless's footsteps, avoid the hubris of Kortar, and obey the Code of Kahless not because Kahless or the gods direct one to do so, but because by doing so one acts righteously in the world. According to religious studies experts Adam Frisch and Joseph Martos, the science-fiction genre generally portrays religion in limiting terms, stressing inflexible dogma, corrupt hierarchies, and unthinking obedience to arbitrary codes of behavior that are restrictive to true freedom and limiting of social change (1985, 24). *Star Trek*'s depiction of Klingon religion transcends this critical dimension of science fiction's portrayal of religion, while maintaining the emphasis on religion as a way of acting in the world. The fictional Klingons learn how to act in the world based on their rich mythological heritage and the cultural traditions that emerge from it. Klingon fans borrow those rich cultural traditions and, through play, come to reenvision how one can and should act in the human world.

Play and Persona in Klingon Fandom

According to religious studies scholar Darcee McLaren (1999, 232), the *Star Trek* phenomenon can be considered modern myth because fans not only watch, and tell, *Star Trek* stories, but because they participate in and "live" *Star Trek* through their adoption of its ideologies and their adherence to the values and aspirations for the human race that the series portrays. It is this lived dimension of *Star Trek* in the fan context that makes the phenomenon mythic. In the context of Klingon fandom, the Klingon species becomes the model for a form of playing in which appropriate ways for acting in the world are explored. In particular, cultural norms governing gendered behavior are reenvisioned through play. Drawing on Klingon religion and culture as a model for exemplary action, new possibilities for human action emerge. Although only a small percentage of *Star Trek* fans generally engage in costumed play behavior, approximately 30 percent of organized fandom does so. Many of these fans construct "personas," or fictional characters, which they then "act out" in various ways. A persona is a character that a fan creates and plays in the context of fan interactions. A persona can be based on characters portrayed within the series—

Lieutenant Worf, for example—or more commonly it can be the original creation of the individual fan, based on characteristics established within the official *Star Trek* canon, and on other characteristics considered appropriate for the species within fandom itself. In this respect, *Star Trek* fan personas are similar to the characters created by players of fantasy role-playing games such as Dungeons and Dragons. Unlike Dungeons and Dragons personas, however, which are constrained by random rolls of dice, *Star Trek* personas are constructed purely at the discretion of the fan. They are, therefore, individual creative manifestations, and are at least somewhat reflective of individual fan values, belief systems, and priorities as articulated within the idiom.

Playing a persona in Klingon fandom can take various forms. Often, a fan's persona is simply the character that he or she assumes for online discussions about *Star Trek* and other topics with fans over the Internet. In this respect, playing a persona requires little other than a Klingon-sounding pseudonym. Other personas are built upon characters in the ongoing fictional narratives written interactively with other fans. These personas are often much more elaborate—you must know who and what your character is, in order to "write" the story in interaction with the characters of others. Interactive stories can be written within the context of an individual fan club, or online with numerous fans participating. Still other personas are even more fully delineated, and are acted out in or out of costume in the context of fan club get-togethers, charity fund-raisers, and conventions. In this context, fan personas are well-developed, with personality quirks, demeanor, family history, military record, tastes in food, clothing, sexual partners, and other sorts of information worked out in advance.

Constructing a persona is a matter of defining the history, House affiliation, economic background, political leanings, marital status, and other details of a character, then working out a chronology of events that places the fictional character somewhere in the time line of the *Star Trek* universe. Fans might choose, for example, to construct a persona who "lives" in the twenty-third century, when Kirk is captain of the starship *Enterprise*. More commonly, a persona "lives" in the time period following the one designated in the film *Star Trek VI: The Undiscovered Country* (the year 2293, when the Klingon Empire almost collapsed), or in the time frame of another film or television episode.

Constructing a persona is also a matter of defining the personality of your character. Certain personality characteristics, such as forthrightness and concern with personal honor, are generally considered integral to all Klingon personas. Other characteristics are open for individual construction. The way in which fans play their personas is therefore revealing of both general fan conceptions about "Klingonness" and of the personality traits specifically selected for expression by individual fans.

Fans construct personas for fun. *Star Trek* is fun. Fandom is fun, and playing a character makes fan participation even more fun than just watching the show or discussing the show with other fans. Scholarly literature on "fun" or "play" is fairly extensive within the fields of anthropology, sociology, psychology, folklore, gender studies, religious studies, and ritual studies (see, for example, Edwards 2000, Geertz 1973, Loy 1980, Manning 1983, Thorne 1993). Within this literature, analyses tend to focus on three main types of play behavior. First and foremost is *childhood play*, and its relationship to role socialization for children. The ways in which childhood play contributes to learned cultural behaviors has been examined in depth. The relationship between childhood play and learned gender roles is particularly emphasized within this literature. Although there are, of course, a large number of *Star Trek* fans who are children, children rarely participate fully in persona construction and organized Klingon fandom. As a result, although this body of literature lends insight into the ways in which boys (men) and girls (women) play differently, it is of only secondary importance for understanding persona construction in Klingon fandom.

More relevant to the context of Klingon fandom is the second type of play behavior frequently analyzed within the scholarly literature—*ritual play*. Anthropologists, folklorists, sociologists, and religious studies scholars have long been familiar with the prevalence of ritual play in carnival contexts. The wearing of costumes and masks, a common practice in carnival play, parallels Klingon costuming in that the individual's mundane identity is obscured, and opportunities for atypical behavior consequently emerge without the fear of identification or discovery. Dominant within scholarly analyses of masked ritual play is an emphasis on symbolic cultural inversion. Carnival masking allows cultural norms to be inverted, roles to be reversed, values to be revalued temporarily within the carnival context. Taken-for-granted cultural traits—sobriety, for example, or hierarchy, or gender divisions—are broken down in favor of parody, burlesque, inversion, and reversion of these norms. Hence, animal masks temporarily erase the distinction between man and animal. Transvestite costuming inverts gender distinctions. A cardboard crown above a ragged beggar's robe challenges social status. Excess drinking and sexuality temporarily replace the decorum of daily life.

Along with the temporary symbolic inversion of cultural norms in masked carnival play, however, goes an ultimate reinforcement of social norms. Carnival play is understood to reinforce social rules by displaying, temporarily, the absurdity of their opposite. Hence, men and women learn that it is ludicrous for men to act as women and women to act as men, for people to act as animals, for beggars to act like kings, and for civilized people to drink, drug, and carouse away their lives. Ritual play, therefore, serves a social maintenance function—a symbolic affirmation, through inversion, of the social status quo. The very outrageousness of the symbolic play behavior reinforces its fantasy (hence unrealistic) nature.

Within the context of *Star Trek* fandom generally, and Klingon fandom specifically, there is some degree of similarity to masked ritual play behavior. Klingons, as conceived within fandom and within the context of the *Star Trek* universe, are forthright, loyal, militaristic, and touchy to a fault when it comes to their personal sense (and appearance) of honor. They take their cultural and religious traditions seriously, and react with aggression to any affront to personal honor or religious faith. This is so much a given within fandom that *ludic play*—poking fun at this image without undermining or challenging it—can easily take place. All of the following examples come from my fieldwork, which has been ongoing since 1996. I conducted interviews at conventions in Pasadena, California (Grand Slam IV, VI, and VII), in Toronto, Ontario (Toronto Trek 13, 14, 16, and 18), and Las Vegas, Nevada (Star Trek Las Vegas 2003). Other interviews were with members of the St. John's, Newfoundland, Klingon fan club and with other assorted fans in 2000 and 2001. These examples represent male attempts to invert Klingon cultural norms; female fans seem less inclined to participate in symbolic inversion play.

One Klingon fan described his persona as follows: "[He's] pompous, a fraud, an iconoclast, and a lecher. He poses as a priest to avoid working, and in public appearances he mostly growls a lot and leers at women. I'm not much like him at all in real life." In constructing this persona, Karl has inverted almost every taken-for-granted Klingon personality characteristic idealized within fandom. His persona is pompous rather than proud, a fraud rather than honorable, iconoclast rather than faithful, and a lecher rather than an honorable family man. He also poses as a priest rather than as a warrior, and he is lazy and animalistic in public. As in masked carnival play, however, these inversions simply serve to highlight normative Klingon characteristics, rather than challenge or undermine them. They can also be said to invert, and hence ultimately reinforce, mainstream human norms.

This kind of Klingon normative inversion can be seen in the recollection of one participant at the 1999 WorldCon convention:

There was this one Klingon. He's HUGE. He's like 6PRIME4, and . . . the guy's like in black, and purple, with lace, and leather, and he's got itty, bitty little purple ribbon bows in his mustache, he's got this like big silk ribbon, with a huge key on it, and actually when you look up close it says key to the boys' locker room. He's got what looks like a little weapon sheath, and on stage he pulls it out, what actually it is, is this HUGE white vibrator, and he holds it up against his hand, which is huge . . . and he says, "the weapon that *hur-rrr-rts so-oo goo-oo-ood*." Just so totally anti-, you know, macho Klingon. . . . It was just so totally out there.

Here again, we have a ludic role reversal of what is perceived as normal Klingon characteristics. The beribboned and perfumed Klingon warrior, six foot four in purple, leather and lace, armed with a vibrator rather than a disruptor, is a satirical interpretation of a fictional humanoid species. The humor of the performance lies in the very taken-for-grantedness of the "macho" characteristics that he is inverting in his performance. In portraying ludic role reversal, this Klingon fan reinforces rather than challenges normative social and gender roles.

A third example of ludic play involves an inversion of Klingon religious symbols. Within the context of Klingon spirituality, Kahless the Unforgettable was the mythological hero-king who ruled his people with honor and set out the code of honor that other Klingons should follow. The Throne of Kahless is therefore a symbol of the Klingon Empire and stands for honor, loyalty, military strength, and endurance. At a 1999 TorontoTrek Convention, however, fans involved in ludic play inverted this symbol remarkably. Spray-painting a porcelain toilet with fleckstone paint, they created an archeological "artifact" that served as the perfect punch bowl at a Klingon fan-room party. This Kahless's Throne came complete with "warrior wipe"—sandpaper rolled like toilet paper—and a thick, sludgy liquor made of melted ice cream and rum that partygoers dipped from the bowl. Kahless, it seems, might be the ultimate Klingon role model, but even he cannot escape the ludic play of Klingon fans. When asked why he had chosen to turn Kahless's Throne into a punch bowl, the fan answered:

I think presentation is everything, and I got to thinking, what is the most disgusting thing I could do with it? And so the toilet . . . [but] the people in this room are all part of the Klingon club, and I think the biggest thing is, [that this is] not so much about sacrilege as [it is about] irreverence, you know? We're fans. Basically, we're all fans.

The "inverted" throne was not intended to challenge normative Klingon characteristics (or in this case, sacred mythology) so much as it was intended to celebrate
it through play. As fans, the people at the party could laugh at the toilet, knowing
that they shared with others a fundamental appreciation of the meaning behind the
original symbol.

Symbolic or role reversals certainly play a part in Klingon fandom, and they add
tremendously to the fun of fandom, role-playing, and costuming, but they are not
typical in terms of persona construction in fandom. According to the majority of
fans, the personas they construct reflect both what they feel are normative Klingon
personality traits and qualities that they feel reflect their own mundane personalities. Another type of play behavior analyzed within the scholarly literature focuses
on this dimension of role-playing as a kind of fictional portrayal of the self. Folklorist Gary Allen Fine (1980) calls this simulation of the self "role identification."
Role-identification play often has a dimension of serious social criticism. Players
can choose which characteristics to maintain, and which characteristics to change,
in relation to their own personalities. Exploring the ways in which constructed personas mirror, and the ways in which they differ from, everyday personality traits
highlights those areas of accommodation to, and resistance to, cultural norms.

Cultural Studies scholar Henry Jenkins argues that fans are "spectators who
transform the experience of watching television into a rich and complex participatory culture. . . . Fans construct their cultural and social identity through borrow-
ing and inflecting mass culture images, articulating concerns that often go unvoiced
with the dominant media" (1992, 23). Through role-identification play, Klingon
fans participate in the dominant media culture by idealizing and emulating fictional
characters and consuming mass market products, yet their emulation of chosen
Klingon characteristics also carries a serious social edge. Just as Klingon religion is
portrayed in the *Star Trek* series as providing exemplary models for Klingon living,
so the construction of Klingon identities and the idealization of Klingons by fans
provide patterns of exemplary living by and for humans in our contemporary
world. Many *Star Trek* fans are implicit participants in the contradictions inherent
within the ideologies of democracy, capitalism, and by extension, economic imperi-
alism. However, they act as social critics by idealizing the egalitarian, nonsexist,
nonracist, noncapitalist, and (officially) nonimperialist ethics portrayed on screen.
As a consequence of this social criticism in *Star Trek,* fans frequently participate in
charity work intended to help bring about, in some small way, the utopian ideal portrayed in the series. In doing so, they question the social status quo. This overt social

activism is not the only way in which social norms are challenged in fandom, however. Klingon fans also challenge rigid definitions of gender.

Gender in Klingon Fandom

It is within this latter dimension of play that clear gender differences among Klingon fan personas emerge. Women play at being Klingon in ways that allow them to challenge restrictive female gender roles. Role-playing allows women to deconstruct gender hierarchies, to erase the dichotomy between sexuality and self-assertion and authority for women, to reappropriate the body as a legitimate expression of the self, and to express sexuality without fear of male sexual aggression. As such, it represents an overt expression of the feminist critique of patriarchal cultural norms that folklorist Camille Bacon-Smith suggests is characteristic of female fandom in general. According to Bacon-Smith, however, "the mask of play protects the [female fan] group from detection as a serious alternative to masculine culture" (1992, 291). In contrast, the female Klingon fans with whom I spoke saw themselves as aggressively challenging masculine cultural norms that define femininity in restrictive stereotypical ways. Many female Klingon fans are explicit and reflexive in terms of the values that they find in portraying Klingon females. As Heather Joseph-Witham found in her 1996 study of *Star Trek* fans and costume art, female fans find empowerment in costuming as Klingons. According to Joseph-Witham, "self-empowerment is part of the Klingon philosophy" (1996, 24), and female fans express this self-empowerment through sexual self-expression.

According to Carinne, the leader and founder of an influential Klingon fan club, participation in Klingon fandom is simply a fun way to express the same desire for female equality being expressed by women in other contexts in our society. Carinne explained in this manner:

> There's a lot of aspects of Klingon society that females nowadays wish they could do. In our society, we've had a point where, [in the] 1950s view of females, you know . . . your goal was to get married and have kids and that was the be-all and end-all of life. . . . And then there was the whole liberalization of femininity [in the 1960s and 1970s], of you know, burn your bra, and the whole thing of women's equality. And now it's sort of like a ricochet backwards. Women do want their femininity, but they still want the equality . . . of being regarded as an equal being in their own right, but of not being a man. Whereas in the '80s, you know, we had this

whole thing of power dressing . . . it was like women had to be a man, to succeed. But [now] its like no, no, no, no . . . I think today a lot of women are saying yes I can do that job, but I still want to be a woman. . . . [So as a Klingon] you can be something that is strong, powerful, and still be female. There's not many places in today's society where you can do that.

In addition to challenging gender stereotypes and gender hierarchies, many female fans also find that playing Klingon allows them to erase the cultural dichotomy between sexy and authoritative in female gender roles. Women frequently find gender roles fragmenting when it comes to expressing these two aspects of their identities. Although sexuality is a legitimate expression of femininity in our society, social, political, or moral authority for women is kept independent from sexual expression. In contrast, female Klingon personas can reintegrate these fragments. One female fan said:

> The reason that I think there is an attraction, especially to women to play Klingons, is: we are not encouraged in our society to be aggressive, and to be real sexual . . . we're taught to be sort of meek . . . and in-line and quiet, and subservient, but Klingon women are the total opposite of what we're *supposed* to be.
> I don't want to get harassed because I'm being outrageous just walking around on the street, but you know [as a Klingon], I mean nobody is really going to mess with you. . . . And so, its like you've got an excuse, you know, you go to the convention and you stick your boobs out . . . its like its encouraged, you are empowered . . . so, it's a real attraction, especially for women.

Costuming as a Klingon allows women to reappropriate their bodies as legitimate expressions of their whole persons. Social condemnation of the display of the female body in public is still strong. Images of women as either whores (and hence sexual, physical beings) or saints (and hence entirely asexual in a physical sense) are still dominant images in our society. Female Klingon fans challenge these stereotypical images by using their bodies as mechanisms for empowerment. Carinne commented:

> Because they are Klingon females . . . they project themselves in such a way that nobody will mess with them . . . this way they can wear any kind of, you know, interesting costumes, very comfortable but assertive feeling . . . a little on the slinky side, a little bit sexy, a little bit aggressive, whatever. . . . You know, you wear that

out on the street and people are going to try to pick you up, or figure you're a hooker, or . . . a slut, or something, so you know there's not really that many chances to show that kind of persona, without being taken for something cheap. And this way [as a Klingon] you're not cheap, you're just taken as [someone who is] SO self-assured of your sexuality, and whatever, that you can wear it without anybody taking you the wrong way. And I think that is probably one of the best things [about costuming as a Klingon].

The freedom to be both authoritative and sexy, independent yet feminine, in the context of Klingon fandom is a criticism of the absence of those opportunities in mainstream society. Yet fans also find in this freedom a spillover to their everyday lives. Ultimately, the qualities that female fans find in their fictional personas are qualities that exist in themselves. One fan ventured this explanation:

[A person's persona is] often a reflection, or a stronger view, of what they are in real life. So sometimes people who are fairly, I wouldn't say mousy, but fairly, quiet and restrained in real life, you turn them, whether to dress them up or expose them to Klingon society, its amazing what comes out of them. They really lose a lot of inhibition. The self-confidence, the esteem, the whole feeling, you [can] almost see them glowing. [It] just really, really [gives] them a whole power feeling, that, they probably had but they just needed something . . . a catalyst, to bring it out. And oftentimes, being a Klingon [will do it].

If women find the freedom to challenge limiting gender stereotypes through the construction of Klingon personas, what is it that men find? Male fans in general are somewhat less explicit and reflexive of the values they find in playing Klingon. Nevertheless, male fans stress a number of consistent themes when they speak about the appeal of Klingons and their motivations for participation in Klingon fandom. Like female gender roles, male gender roles have been redefined over the last forty years. Unlike the redefinition of female gender roles, however, which have been self-consciously sought by women activists, male gender roles have tended to be redefined "in the breach," so to speak, in consequence of the redefinition of women's roles rather than by conscious deliberation in their own right. To some extent, this has left the majority of men in our society willing to work toward female equality without knowing how to reconstruct male gender roles and expectations in light of a changed gender environment. This "crisis of masculinity," as it has been called, gave rise to the mythopoetic men's movement in 1991. The movement rapidly gained hundreds of thousands of participants across North America and Europe and, like the women's movement, is presumably reflective of the concerns of a broad section of North American society. Like the women's movement, the mythopoetic men's movement has an agenda to redefine gender roles so as to liberate individuals from the harmful and restrictive fragmentary roles that mainstream society forces men to adopt. Just as female fandom is reflective of the broader social concerns of the women's movement, therefore, male Klingon fandom can be seen as reflective of the concerns of the broader mythopoetic men's movement.

The mythopoetic men's movement represents a loose amalgamation of issues, literary sources, and individuals that share a concern to liberate men from limiting social roles and relationships. In the words of scholar Michael Schwalbe, the movement allows participants to be "emotional, noncompetitive, and nurturing, and still get their identities as men affirmed by other men—with no feminist criticism to spoil the celebration" (1996, 25). Within the context of the mythopoetic men's movement, participants placed emphasis on these values:

• Fostering bonds to other men on the basis of camaraderie rather than competition;

• The adoption of warrior metaphors that nurture rather than dominate;

• The recognition of a spiritual rootedness of self, family, and community;

• The criticism of societal gender roles that teach men a cutthroat, me-first definition of success, which fosters distrust of other men, of themselves, their emotions, and of women.

Although Klingon fandom is certainly not identical to the mythopoetic men's movement, male Klingon fans do stress many of the same themes when it comes to articulating their reasons for participation in fandom. One of the most common themes stressed is the camaraderie with other Klingon fans. For example, one Canadian fan said:

> There are approximately 55 people from all walks of life from all parts of North America . . . [on] the [Klingon] Listserv that I subscribe to. With the exception of two or three of these people, I have never met any of them. Yet through the common bond of Klingdom we all share in each other's lives on a daily basis. . . . I consider these people to be part of an extended family. My day isn't complete, unless I've taken time to bond with these warriors.

"Bonding" with "warriors" is a central tenet of the mythopoetic men's movement. According to the men's movement, our society only allows for relationships between men based on friendly aggression and competition. Supportive friendship, close emotional bonds, and sharing is discouraged among men by the social categorization of these qualities as "feminine" or "gay." In the context of Klingon fandom, however, the physical characteristics associated with Klingons (physical size and strength, martial skills, aggressive posture) negate the socially constructed feminine or homosexual implications of close emotional bonds and allow fans to experience a sense of genuine closeness that, in the words of one fan, is hard to find in "normal" society. Male Klingon fans can be macho in terms of their physical appearance, but still form bonds that are deeply meaningful outside the "competitive" masculine mode of friendship. One fan expressed it like this:

> I think I can say, although *Star Trek* fans are usually thought of as "geeks without a life," I have met some of my best friends through Fandom/Klingdom. . . . Just next week I am going [to] visit some dear friends I met through the club. I will say it has proven to be a venue for meeting some of the most *quality* people I know. People who are down-to-earth, fun, honorable, and have their sights set on the stars.

The personas of the majority of male Klingon fans are very macho when it comes to physical appearance, personality traits, and personal histories. Like female fans, male fans tend to identify within themselves the qualities they most admire in their Klingon personas. For women this identification translates into an authoritative and slightly sexy kind of aggression. For men, it translates into a personal stress on honor and integrity, coupled with a flirtatious nature, a sense of fun, and an impatience with the "political correctness" emphasis within contemporary North American society. On the topic of personas, one fan pointed out:

> My Klin alter ego is a very strong willed, outgoing, fun loving, flirtatious warrior, who uses his strengths to provide assistance to the community. In this manner [he] doesn't differ much from me. About the only real difference between my Klin persona and my mundane persona would be that [he] can speak his mind and people won't take offense. When a human speaks their mind, certain groups in society can get upset and say that you are too blunt.

About his Klingon persona, another fan believed:

[My Klingon persona] is an extension of me in some ways and is totally different in others. [He] has no mate and is a big flirt among the females. I am married and couldn't flirt my way out of a paper bag. [He] works hard but plays hard; also he is never far from his tankard of bloodwine or warnog. . . . I draw [on his] inner strength . . . when I need it in real life, and [he] allows me to laugh at myself. Together, we make a great person.

For male fans, therefore, as for female fans, constructed Klingon personas both reflect and differ from the mundane personas of everyday life. Sexuality, or in the case of males, flirtatiousness, is also a central part of persona construction. Whereas female fans use the sexuality of their personas primarily to criticize social restrictions on women's freedoms, male fans seem to use it primarily as a secondary characteristic in their persona construction. A preoccupation with honor and integrity seems to dominate the constructed personas of male Klingon fans. This emphasis on honor, like the women's emphasis on sexuality, reflects a criticism of societal gender norms. In their emphasis on honor and integrity, male fans are primarily critical of the cutthroat, competitive ethic of success, which they feel society fosters for men. On this subject, one fan commented:

What appeals to me most about Klingons is their concept of honor and loyalty. I have a background in martial arts, so these concepts are very appealing. My persona is that of an individual who takes concepts of honor and keeping his word to heart and that is much like I am as an individual.

Consider [however] the every day practices of business in general! How often is it seen or heard about someone undermining or backstabbing to get ahead in the world? The values of "honor" are not held highly in the business world. Nor is the concept of "loyalty." An employee who is loyal to the company nowadays is overlooked or forgotten when it comes time for a promotion. Working in the banking industry, I see a lot of this type of behavior, which is why I cherish the concepts of "honor" and "loyalty" [as a Klingon fan].

Similarly, another fan clarified the attraction to honor:

[The Klingon] concept of honor is a collection of human concepts from all over the world and all times known. In everyday life, one is always confronted with a lot of law and less fairness. Money counts more than truth or honor. Klingons, as shown in *Star Trek,* do not corrupt their ideals for money—that is what I like! I guess most people who are fans of the "Klingon idea" feel that there is something missing in their everyday life. Some do not exactly know what, but [that is because] honor is not always something you think of, it's something you feel.

Yet another fan voiced similar sentiments, when he told me:

> I think that society as a whole, and by this I mean North America, not just Canada, has forgotten what honor and integrity are. Too many people are out for number one and don't care who they step on in their personal pursuits. Klingon fans, however, have a better idea of those concepts than many. With regards to the value systems [of honor and integrity], those are something you bring with you to the table, not something you find when you get there. In other words, Klingdom tends to draw people with strong values and sense of honor to it, as opposed to instilling it in its members after the fact.

By far the vast majority of male fans with whom I have spoken have stressed the honor, loyalty, and integrity of Klingons as their primary appeal and what they perceive as the absence of these qualities in everyday life. Fans conceptualize Klingons as "space-going samurai" or, as Heather Joseph-Witham found, "bikers" with a code of honor (1996, 23). Just as many people admire the Japanese samurai for their value system or bikers for their loyalty and commitment to one another, fans respect Klingons for their sense of honor, duty to community, and loyalty to family. These ties take precedence over any concern for self-aggrandizement, and, thus, are an implicit criticism of society for failing to nurture those qualities in everyday life. If to be male is to be cutthroat, individualistic, and competitive, these personas are constructed to challenge such normative models of masculinity. That may sound contradictory because male warrior cultures, like the samurai and historic biker gangs, did intimidate others with their much-deserved reputation for violence. However, Klingon fans have shaped a compensatory self-image for themselves: the warrior with a softer side, a noble person connected to the legitimating behavior of community involvement.

Within their own context, Klingon fans have constructed a warrior model of masculinity in which success is judged by individual integrity, communal (fan) validation, and community service. This model has translated into a commitment to charity work on the part of many (although not all) individual Klingon fans and the majority of Klingon fan clubs. Both male and female fans dedicate themselves to charity. For the male fans with whom I have spoken, however, this emphasis on charity work is closely tied to with their emphasis on honor and integrity as "Klingon" characteristics. Within the context of the broader mythopoetic men's movement, dedication to public service is one way in which "warrior" metaphors are used to nurture, rather than dominate, society. This "nurture-not-conquer" thread is common in the narratives of male Klingon fans. One fan stated:

> The primary "mission" for our ship—[the main purpose of our participation in Klingon fandom]—is for our members to do charity fundraisers and provide a unique twist to various public events. The majority of our fundraising efforts are directed to the Children's Wish Foundation of Canada; however, we have also provided our services to raising funds for food banks and Mental Health Awareness.

Another fan noted, "[We've done] blood drives, MDS and Children's Wish Foundation drives, [and fund-raisers for] battered women's homes. . . . All charity aspects are good publicity for the group, but also are good honorable causes for Klingons." Nonetheless, fans couched their commitment to charity work and nurture-not-conquer goals in the idiom of Klingon warriors—the idiom of battle. Recently, for example, the Atlantic region Klingon fan clubs in Canada challenged the Central Canadian fan clubs to a "duel" to see who could collect the most aluminum cans for the Children's Wish Foundation. The commander of the winning Atlantic region fan clubs agreed to show up for breakfast the next day in his Klingon underwear, as a sign of his victory, but also his humility. The commander of the losing Central Canadian fan clubs promptly presented the winner with her own Klingon underwear in tribute after the final tallies. Together, the clubs collected over a quarter ton of pop can tabs, which were sold to a recycling center and the proceeds donated to the charity. The cans were also recycled.

Although charity work might be considered an "honorable cause" for Klingons, the militaristic idiom adopted within Klingon fandom can sometimes result in misunderstanding and rejection from nonfans. One fan club based in Nova Scotia ran into rejection from a battered women's home when they tried to make a charitable donation. Having collected more than one hundred dollars in donations for this purpose, the women's shelter in question rejected the funds. Although Klingon fans have adopted a nurture-not-conquer ethic of dedication, this ethic is still foreign to mainstream society. The women's shelter did not and could not believe that any organization named the "Klingon Assault Group" could possibly have the best interests of women in mind. For male Klingon fans, however, a large part of the appeal of fandom is the chance to construct alternate models of community, alternate models of masculinity, and alternate models of morality, to challenge mainstream social mores. As in the case of female fans, male fans construct and adopt Klingon personas in such a way that restrictive gender roles are challenged and alternate possibilities in terms of gender roles explored.

Conclusion

Star Trek is just a television show, and *Star Trek* fandom is just "fun." Speak to any *Star Trek* fans long enough, and they will inform you of these facts. They will also inform you that they have, in the words of actor William Shatner, "a life." *Star Trek* fans have been negatively characterized in popular perceptions ever since the show first aired in the 1960s. In a famous (or infamous) guest appearance on *Saturday Night Live,* actor William Shatner, who portrayed Captain Kirk in the original *Star Trek* series, told fans to "Get a life!" apparently because he felt that fandom was a trivial pastime with no redeeming social features. In a skit in the same show, fans were portrayed as geeky nerds living in their parents' basement, wearing artificial Spock ears and wearing T-shirts saying, "I grok Spock." [3] Media attention on fandom has always focused on its more flamboyant aspects and has consequently fed this stereotypical and derogatory image of fans. *Star Trek* fans, however, are not the geeky nerds of *Saturday Night Live* portrayal. Within organized fandom, the majority of fans are university educated, professionally employed or trained, and socially and/or politically conscious. Many fan organizations participate in charity work, supporting Red Cross blood drives, the Children's Wish Foundation, the Heart and Stroke Foundation, local food banks, and a host of other charities. Far from living in a fantasy world, *Star Trek* fans live in the real world, and many are active in attempting to change it for the better.

The construction of fandom personas is one way in which changing the world for the better is subversively (and often unconsciously) attempted. Through "play," fans are engaged in a subtle process of accommodation and resistance to dominant cultural norms. The Klingon species as portrayed in the *Star Trek* series is immersed in a religion that serves as a source for models of exemplary behavior. The Klingon species itself then becomes the source and the idiom for models of exemplary be-

---

3. *Grok* is a term borrowed from Robert Heinlein's book *Stranger in a Strange Land.* To *grok* means to understand something deeply and intuitively. Some people define the word as "to love." It is not a Klingon or Trek term; it is just something sci-fi fans in general would recognize.

havior within which fans can criticize contemporary human social norms. Although the majority of Klingon fans do not emulate the religious behaviors of Klingons, they are, nonetheless, influenced by the portrayal of religion in the context of the Klingon species. One fan put it this way:

> The spirituality of Klingons is an inspiration to correct living—to having the right stuff, in a way. One of our favorite after-life references is to the Black Fleet, where honorable Klingons will continue to fight gloriously throughout time. Those who do not believe in a true "after-life" will still make such references, intending them to be an exhortation to correct action, in line with our belief in personal honor. As fans, we loved [the final episodes of *Star Trek: Deep Space Nine,*] where Worf challenges the corrupt Chancellor Gowron in the name of true Klingon honor. As pseudo-Klingons or perhaps proto-Klingons, we were inspired to return to an older, purer standard of honorable behavior. As fans who have been challenged, is it not the responsibility of every human being to try to make this world a better place for all? Yes, some of these artificial honor notions do cross over into real life.

Some of the aspects of "real life" that fans are trying to "make better" can be seen in the characteristics they choose to highlight in their Klingon persona construction. In particular, fans are engaged in an attempt to redefine or push the boundaries of accepted gender roles and behaviors. For women, this effort is compatible with efforts in the broader women's movement to reappropriate the body as an expression of self, and with the women's movement's efforts to expand the narrow limits of what it means to be feminine. For men, this effort is equally compatible with efforts in the broader contemporary mythopoetic men's movement to foster masculine values that nurture bonds to other men, and that nurture society in a nonpatriarchal or paternalistic ways. For both men and women, the effort is compatible with the idealized philosophy of *Star Trek*, in which poverty, racism, and intolerance vanish and humanity lives in harmony with itself and the galaxy. Although *Star Trek* fans generally, and Klingon fans particularly, are just "having fun," therefore, they are participating in and accomplishing through play what others attempt to participate in and accomplish in other social arenas.

PART FOUR

Ufological "Science" and Therapy

Observations from Archaeology and Religious Studies on First Contact and ETI Evidence

13

James F. Strange

What happens when human beings encounter remains or artifacts suggestive of extraterrestrial intelligence (ETI)? Is there any analogous situation that would enable us to gain a useful perspective on this scenario? In particular, is it possible that the science of archaeology or anthropology can give us any guidelines? Does ethology, the study of animal behavior, have anything to help us?

There are several theories and descriptions of cultural contact in anthropology, the parent discipline of archaeology. These insights are also maturing in ethnoarchaeology (Webster, Evans, and Sanders 1993; Sharer and Ashmore 1993). In general, it is surmised that the contact of Culture A with Culture B will follow some predictable paths. In general, if the two cultures compete for the same resources, then:

- One culture might kill, scatter, or enslave the members of the other culture, as in the New World at the arrival of the Europeans (Clendinnen 1987).
- One culture might absorb or manage the other, as in the Roman practice of managing its "client states" (Luttwak 1976).
- The disadvantaged culture might flee from contact.
- The two cultures might borrow from one another in not-so-predictable ways (e.g., the diffusion of African-American musical influences and slang language into dominant American culture).

In the case of a disadvantaged culture during first contact, it typically works through a scenario in several steps when receiving a foreign culture. First, the members of the disadvantaged culture literally do not know what they are seeing at first contact. Often they might stand frozen in fear or in awe of the others. Second, those who move first are often responding to a mistaken identity of the visitors (and vice versa). Members of the receiving group often think of the visitors in terms of a cultural group that they know or in terms of a cultural myth about visitors. They respond to the visitors in terms of this perceived identity. If the group is understood to be friendly, the receivers might invite friendship. If they are understood to be a threat, they meet the visitors with a hostile reception.

It is only when the culture realizes that these visitors are new and previously unknown that things get interesting. Then the receivers attempt to understand the visitors in terms of other cultures they have dealt with. This is a period of trial and error in which the two cultures get to know one another. At that point knowledge is power, and it is in everyone's self-interest to get as much knowledge of the other as possible. That is, even the visitors need to know their hosts (Richter 1993).

With increased knowledge comes a fundamental decision on the part of the host culture—the decision whether the visitors are to be regarded as threats or not. Commensurate with the identification of the visitors as threats comes fear, and with fear comes flight-or-fight responses, though denial is always a possibility. If the fear can be used or channeled in some positive way, then it may become a motive and a source of energy for the fight response. Those who come to terms with their fear are better able to understand what they see, and therefore are less able to deny their senses, so it is advantageous to come to terms with fear.

Do studies of interspecies contact help us understand a possible reaction to contact with extraterrestrials? Contact responses can be seen in observations made by ethologists of gorillas and chimpanzees, our native cousins. Montgomery (1991) reports that the great apes fled from Dian Fossey's presence at first. The gorillas had ample experience with human beings as predators, and Dian Fossey was at first simply a predator, as far as they were concerned (261). Jane Goodall noticed that the chimpanzees were naturally cautious at first, but they generally ignored humans if they observed or perceived no threat (Goodall 1990, 238). This was also the relationship of chimpanzees to baboons (124).

In terms of our hypothetical Culture A and Culture B, there is another response possible, and that is awe. It may be that Culture B, the host culture, comes to understand that the power, mobility, and resources of Culture A are simply overpowering. There seems to be nothing they cannot achieve. They are positively godlike in their attributes. In this case, awe borders on religious reverence, and in fact on occasion overflows into religious awe, reverence, and wonder (Pandian 1991). Indeed, Cortez and his men found themselves worshipped and held in religious awe by the inhabitants of Mexico. Furthermore, American soldiers in certain parts of Melanesia found themselves in a similar situation in World War II. After they withdrew from certain local islands, the locals actually founded new religions, called cargo cults, to worship the absent visitors and induce them to return with their heavenly cargos (Trompf 1990). It is possible that this parallels the awe-struck behavior of chimpanzees when faced with a thundering waterfall (Goodall 1990).[1]

I point out that awe and approbation or praise, even joy, will seem to be the appropriate responses to the visitors if the host culture has identified them as the long-promised bringers of salvation. In this instance, the host culture needs to have a time-honored myth that promises that those who visited in the past and delivered salvation, knowledge, or cargo will come again at the appropriate time and renew their relationship with the host culture. Cargo cultists have such a myth. A similar hope surrounds the idea of the *mahdi* in Islam, the rightly guided one, who will someday return to establish justice (Rahman 1966, 209). The idea of the coming of the Messiah is, of course, a cardinal element in various forms of both Judaism and Christianity. Some contemporary UFO religions carry elements of such myths, which include stories of coming of space messiahs and even cargo from millenarian spaceships (Tumminia and Kirkpatrick 1995; Lewis 1995, 2003a; Trompf 2003).

Some Theoretical Reactions to ETI Artifacts

It is possible to argue by analogy that humans will follow similar patterns when and if they encounter artifacts, or perhaps merely one artifact, that possibly stem from some extraterrestrial intelligence. (I note that the operant definition of an artifact in archaeology is an object made by humans. In this case, I suggest we extend the definition to include ETI as the agent of manufacture.) We would be dealing with an object or objects that we could possibly perceive not to be of earthly origin. We might

---

1. On an outing with the several chimps, Jane Goodall witnessed their "wild displays" as they approached a waterfall. They excitedly swung on vines, hurled rocks, and charged the water. Goodall asks, "Were the chimpanzees expressing feelings of awe such as those which, in early man, surely gave rise to primitive religions, worship of the elements?" (1990, 242).

come to that startling conclusion for a variety of reasons. After exhaustive analysis, we might recognize that the kind of technology required to manufacture this artifact is quite beyond the scope of earthly tools. We might also recognize a material that we believe humans do not know how to produce.

We can predict that we will feel fear, awe, and bafflement, or some combination of the three. If we feel awe and wonder as we turn this artifact over in our hand or in our mind, it is because we possess or think we possess a specific kind of knowing. We know, or think we know, "Earthly humans didn't make this. Some other intelligence out there made it."

We insist that this artifact is not human. I reiterate because we are looking at technology that we do not recognize or we are dealing with materials on a scale (either quite small or very large) that we cannot handle. We may be recognizing a type of material with properties we could not produce, or we may be overwhelmed by the aesthetics of this object. We may be bewildered by the purpose of the object, a purpose that eludes us in the twenty-first century. For example, we may deduce that this small object is designed to displace Jupiter from its orbit. Therefore, we conclude, those who manufactured it are far beyond us in terms of their scientific and technological knowledge.

Notice that we have not yet perceived a threat. If we perceive a threat, all these emotions of awe and wonder are whisked away by fear, and fear disables a host of mild responses and enables a host of other, more aggressive responses. In fact, fear disables both the mind and the heart. We all know stories of the odd things people do in a panic, such as saving the dirty dishes in the sink when there is a fire. Fear wonderfully focuses the mind, but usually not via our intellectual, creative, or spiritual faculties. Rather, our hormones and central nervous system simply shriek at us to get out of there or to attack. Sometimes, however, we suffer a kind of shutdown of our reasoning systems, and we enter into denial.

In fact, fear can be quite insidious if we do not come to terms with it. Unabated fear has a way of reinforcing itself so that no need gets responded to except the fundamental need for security. The need for careful thought, or thoughtful exploration, or even dialogue about the problem, is not met. Unreasonable fear thwarts new knowledge. After all, it was surely fear (and possibly other things) that kept Galileo's contemporaries from looking through his telescope, or from seeing what could not be there when they did look (Koestler 1959, 374). Nevertheless, even without fear, we may be overwhelmed, dazed, even overcome, that is, our cognitive functions reduced so that our visceral functions take over.

We could perceive two kinds of threats from those who made our hypothetical alien artifact:

• We are defenseless before their technology. This is equivalent to the sinking realization of the Bronze Age warrior, "We are defenseless before their iron spears."

• They are *not* like us, so they have no human feelings for us and will treat us as available slave labor, protein, or chemicals. In the history of the human race, we treat inhumanely those whom we define as "other." Does it not follow that they will probably treat us the same way?

On the other hand, there are a set of positive responses that could be made. These responses go with a kind of conscious not-knowing. In this case, we answer the question, "Do we know what this is?" with a strong "No." We recognize that the artifact fits none of our categories, and we most decidedly do not know what it is. In this case, we suffer bafflement and confusion. We may suspect or we may sense that this artifact is not of this world, but we are overwhelmed. We see that it is an object whose intricacy, beauty, and materials we can describe, but which we simply cannot identify, as for example, the Coke bottle in the movie *The Gods Must Be Crazy*.

However, bafflement or confusion often gives rise to intense curiosity. If this is not anything like what we know, then what is it? What does it do? What is it doing here? What is it made of? Who made it? Where are they now? Why did they leave it here?

There is only one way to reduce the dissonance that we feel when we are at the mercy of our bafflement: investigate further, that is, explore. Mount an expedition. Mount a slide, or mount a mule, but in any case take action. In this response, we simply get on with satisfying ourselves that we can find out about this thing, this artifact, this manufactured puzzle. Also, in this response we give expression to a kind of fundamental human optimism, a kind of hope that we will not remain stumped and that we need not be victims of our own lack of knowledge. There is more to learn, and we will learn it.

I would like to point out that awe and curiosity are great enablers. Perhaps they are as powerful as enablers as fear is a disabler. Awe and curiosity prompt exploration and investigation, two responses that lie at the core of science, religion, and art. Doubtless, some will be surprised to find religion in this threesome, but think for a moment. Are not the claims of religion in effect awesome, testable hypotheses? Are not priests, rabbis, imams (Islamic clergy), and bodhisattvas (future Buddhas) continually inviting us to satisfy our curiosity and enter into new realms of knowledge? Science, religion, and art all oversee their own domains of knowledge, but out of the same core motivation of a response to awe and curiosity.

ETI, Archaeology, Public Opinion, Religion, and Future Research

Presently, we are discussing our response to the possibility of finding an ETI artifact on Earth or even of finding ETI artifacts on Mars during an expedition (McDaniel 1993; Carlotto 1991; Harrison 1997). What is an appropriate response?

It is quite possible that fear would be the initial response. We may decide that the simple presence of something inexplicable in common scientific terms is a threat to the autonomy of science and scientists, or to our well-being as scientists, or to the political advantage that science and scientists have in America today. In that case, flight, attack, and denial are predictable responses. We would not flee the putative artifacts or attack them, but we could preserve our peace of mind by distancing ourselves from those who suggest that the structures on Mars (i.e., the stone face in the Cydonia region) might be artificial, or by vigorously attacking them in print. Either way we are indulging our fear rather than giving expression to awe or investing in our curiosity.

For the same reason, I should mention that some have argued that we should not investigate ETI, since that could be destructive of organized religion should the investigation prove successful. Yet as early as 1960, the Brookings Institution in a study commissioned by NASA ventured to predict that proof of an extraterrestrial presence, which at that time was hypothetically linked to UFOs, could be deleterious to religions, especially fundamentalist religions (Denzler 2001). Parenthetically, we must note the current opposition to ETI by certain Christian fundamentalists, who have gone as far as to claim that UFOs represent demonic forces (Pacheco and Blann 1993), and some even say that fallen angels pilot the spaceships. Some fundamentalists profess that alien abductions are real and dangerous. This perception exemplifies the fear factor hypothesized by the Brookings study. Nevertheless, the idea of extraterrestrials seems to be gaining acceptance with some Americans. By 1982, the Gallup Poll on religion reported that 46 percent of Americans believed in life on other planets. This compared with 41–54 percent of American natural scientists and 25 percent of American medical scientists who believed in "human life" on other planets (Gallup and Proctor 1982, 193, 208, 209; see table 13.1). (I suspect that the addition of the word "human" in the question asked of natural scientists and medical scientists significantly lowered their positive responses.)

On the other hand, the Bigelow Foundation (Alexander 1994, 2003) asked 1,000 rabbis, priests, and Protestant ministers whether positive proof of extraterrestrials would have severe negative effects on the country's moral, social, and religious foundations (see table 13.2). Fully 77 percent of the 230 religious leaders who re-

Table 13.1

**Do You Believe There Is Human Life
on Other Planets?**

	Yes	No	No opinion
United States	46%	41%	13%
Male	50	37	13
Female	43	44	13
White	45	43	12
High School	47	41	12
Nonwhite	35	43	22
College	49	39	12
Grade school	36	47	17
East	50	36	14
Midwest	45	40	15
South	37	48	15
West	54	39	7
Under 30 yrs.	55	35	10
18–24 yrs.	54	36	10
25–29 yrs.	57	31	12
30–49 yrs.	47	40	13
50+ yrs.	38	47	15
Protestant	43	43	14
Catholic	52	37	11

Source: Gallup Poll data from 1982, in Gallup and Proctor
(1982).

sponded disagreed or strongly disagreed. Some 8 percent agreed or strongly agreed that the discovery of ETI would be destructive of religious faith, and 14 percent did not know (Alexander 1994, 2003). The Bigelow Foundation survey (Alexander 1994, 2003) pressed the question with the rabbis, priests, and ministers. Even when a more contentious question was posed, namely, "If an advanced extraterrestrial civilization proclaimed responsibility for human life, it would cause a religious crisis," a full 54 percent of the clergy still disagreed or strongly disagreed.

In contrast to other clerics who have already condemned ETI contact and who associate UFOs with evil, the American evangelist Billy Graham insisted that his faith would not be undermined if extraterrestrial intelligence were encountered. In

Table 13.2
The Bigelow Foundation's UFO Religious Crisis Survey Responses

1. Official confirmation of the discovery of an advanced, technologically superior extraterrestrial civilization would have severe negative effects on the country's moral, social, and religious foundations.
    strongly agree: 8%   strongly disagree: 77%   neither agree nor disagree: 14%

2. My congregation would perceive any contact made with a technologically advanced extraterrestrial civilization, direct or indirect, as a threat.
    strongly agree: 16%   strongly disagree: 67%   neither agree nor disagree: 16%

3. The discovery of another intelligent civilization would cause my congregation to question their fundamental concepts regarding the origin of life.
    strongly agree: 12%   strongly disagree: 82%   neither agree nor disagree: 6%

4. If highly advanced intelligent civilizations exist elsewhere in the universe, the basic tenets of religion would be present.
    strongly agree: 70%   strongly disagree: 5%   neither agree nor disagree: 25%

5. Genetic similarities between mankind and an advanced extraterrestrial civilization would challenge the basic religious concepts of man's relative position in the universe.
    strongly agree: 9%   strongly disagree: 77%   neither agree nor disagree: 14%

6. If an advanced extraterrestrial civilization had religious beliefs fundamentally different from ours, it would endanger organized religions in this country.
    strongly agree: 14%   strongly disagree: 70%   neither agree nor disagree: 15%

7. Scientific confirmations of contact with advanced extraterrestrial civilizations are probable in our lifetime.
    strongly agree: 13%   strongly disagree: 47%   neither agree nor disagree: 39%

8. It is unlikely that direct contact with an advanced extraterrestrial civilization has occurred or is currently ongoing.
    strongly agree: 59%   strongly disagree: 12%   neither agree nor disagree: 29%

9. My congregation would question their beliefs if an advanced extraterrestrial civilization had no system of religion.
    strongly agree: 11%   strongly disagree: 72%   neither agree nor disagree: 17%

10. If an advanced extraterrestrial civilization proclaimed responsibility for producing human life, it would cause a religious crisis.
    strongly agree: 28%   strongly disagree: 54%   neither agree nor disagree: 17%

11. I believe my answers to the preceding questions represent the views of my congregation.
    strongly agree: 69%   strongly disagree: 3%   neither agree nor disagree: 28%

Source: Alexander 1994. The survey was conducted by Victoria Alexander.

fact, Graham has suggested that UFOs might be holy angels (Fitzgerald 1979). On a similar positive note, Michael Ashkenazi's research with twenty-one Jewish, Christian, and Muslim theologians and clerics in Israel (1992) found that the major response to possible communication with extraterrestrial intelligence (CETI) was "amusement." In fact, John Whitmore (1995) has suggested that one type of possible CETI, namely abductee reports, stem from the religious unconscious itself. In other words, abduction reports are expressions not of any scientific reality but of an innate religious tendency.

However, the CETI question as it is posed here should remain within the bounds of science, not religion. Sidestepping the complex number of religious responses that might possibly arise in the event of credible ETI evidence, some people in the twenty-first century seem remarkably open to the subject (Ziegler 2003). A Roper Poll found in 2002 that 74 percent of Americans believe they are psychologically prepared to hear about proof of extraterrestrial life. According to a Gallup Poll in 2001, over a third of Americans believe life in some form has existed on Mars. A 1997 Time/Yankelovich poll found that one-third of Americans think that intelligent beings from other worlds have visited Earth (Ziegler 2003).

If we can set aside any perception of a threat or deal realistically with our fears, we may enable our formidable faculties of careful and sustained exploration and investigation, including archaeological exploration and investigation, to kick in. Such reasoned responses in turn have the potential of moving us through awe to appropriate scientific—and yes, ultimately religious and artistic—responses.

One such response could be required from the discipline of archaeology: if we find possible ETI artifacts here or on Mars, we need to proceed in a scientific way via high-resolution satellite photography, infrared analysis, soil-penetrating radar, and perhaps other technologies that have not been invented yet. We would have to travel to Tibet, or New Jersey, or even to the Cydonia region of Mars (whenever it becomes humanly possible) to do these things. In archaeological research, we can inspect from the air or from space all we wish, engage in fly-overs and satellite photography forever, but we will not settle the question of the presence of, nature of, or significance of ETI structures without an on-site visit. In the normal state of affairs in archaeological investigation, we walk the site in a systematic grid pattern after analyzing the results of remote sensing. We perform a close inspection, sometimes dragging along behind us the sensors and cables for radar, magnetometers, and soil resistivity gear. There is no substitute for walking the site and eventually engaging in systematic and controlled surveys and excavation, should the findings warrant it. It appears to me that this approach would be the appropriate direction for further research. We cannot resort to fear and loathing that might stem from a religious perspective or even a primal need for a territorial imperative. We must utilize deep objectivity and the best science in any possible encounter with ETI evidence or any viable contact with ET visitors—if that ever happens.

A Confederacy of Fact and Faith

Science and the Sacred in UFO Research

Anne Cross

> If you graphed religion and science on a continuum, in the center, I see a UFO.
> —Joe Lewels, a participant at the UFO Experience Conference

Many of us are not quite sure what ufology means or rather what it has come to mean in its course of development. Strictly speaking, it encompasses the study of UFO-related phenomena, but to some adherents it also represents research about extraterrestrial contact. British UFO researcher John Spencer defines ufology by stating, "It is not a science, though many in the field would like to ensure scientific principles are applied, and it is unlikely ever to be a science since true understanding of the phenomenon is likely to reveal that it is several sciences rather than one thing" (1991, 303).

Conventional scientists have criticized the use of the term "ufology" as if "ufologists" are trying to make themselves seem scientific when they are not, but that has never been the purpose of the term; it has always been a simplistic usage designed merely to describe an overall study field.

Established by those dedicated to scientific investigation and systematic data-collection, ufology picked up some rather mystical fellow travelers on its trajectory through the last half of the twentieth century (Jacobs 1975, 1983; Peebles 1994; Denzler 2001). Whether intended or not, ufology has become an umbrella sheltering many essentially religious worldviews under its broader interests. Inside the scientific exteriors of its research institutes and scholarly journals, certain segments of the UFO research community do what religious clerics and mystics have done for centuries: they consult the heavens for clues about the meaning of life and human destiny. Despite its packaging as an ordinary scientific specialty, a subset of UFO research involves some themes common to traditional religions. This type of inquiry is an elaborate mix of facts and beliefs that adherents say explains most of what needs explaining about the universe, including the genesis of humankind, the meaning of the Bible, the moral order of the cosmos, and the origins of portable electronics—all in one complicated fell swoop.

Alien astronauts traveled to Earth, it is said, and they combined their genetic material with that of early primates in a high-tech breeding project that created the first human beings (Sitchin 1995). According to some ufologists, humans owe their very civilization—and science itself —to aliens. Extraterrestrials, they say, taught early humans to harness fire, seed crops, and manage the flow of rivers. Aliens have made frequent trips back to check up on humans throughout history, it is said, abducting people who subsequently have foggy (if any) recollections of their experiences. Many ufologists believe that in 1947 the U.S. government seized remnants of an alien spacecraft that crashed in Roswell, New Mexico, and then used it to develop advanced technologies and products like nonstick coating and fiber-optic communications. Under the utmost secrecy, they say, the wreckage was subjected to "reverse engineering," a process by which the extraterrestrials' sophisticated technology was unraveled by examining its machinery and materials. Elements of the craft's technology were reworked into products like lasers, state-of-the-art bulletproof vests, and integrated circuit chips (von Däniken 1971; Blumrich 1974; Corso and Birnes 1997).

A novel approach to both religion and science marks all facets of the UFO research community—its culture, its personalities, and its institutions. It considers itself a science, working through self-styled scientific institutes because it lacks acceptance by the mainstream. Its research findings are disseminated at UFO or New Age conferences and in journals that speak to its own constituency. UFO research is considered by its practitioners and followers to be a science based on empirical evidence. Yet some of the things ufology claims to reveal—that, for one, superior beings from the sky tinker in human destiny—have significant life-organizing, sacrosanct dimensions that go beyond the modern bounds of science. The blurring of the conventional boundaries between religion and science does not stop there. While certain segments of ufology scienticize religion, they also bring a religious and mystical dimension to scientific methodologies, using, for example, sacred writings, channelers, and hypnotic recollections to collect data.

Employing a self-styled scientific framework, much of ufology attempts to confirm the validity of the UFO-based worldview. This proof is to be found not only by observing UFOs, but also, according to certain authors, by combing the Bible and other sacred documents for UFO references. They use such literary evidence to establish a pedigree for UFO involvement in human affairs that goes back thousands of years. For example, UFO researchers have reinterpreted many of the phenomena described in the Bible as extraterrestrial activity, especially anything that flew, glowed, or seemed to radiate. They say that ancient observers misunderstood these phenomena to be the work of gods and angels (von Däniken 1971; Blumrich 1974; Clark 2000). Prophetic texts, mystical cave drawings, and other ancient records become primitive laboratory books and early research papers from long-lost extraterrestrial knowledge (von Däniken 1971; Temple 1999; Sitchin 2001).

Although such assertions deviate from mainstream practices and definitions, adherents to these theories accept the research as wholly scientific. In addition to challenging conventional ideas about who or what joins us in the universe, many ufologists crash through conventional boundaries around science and religion. It wreaks havoc on conventional understandings of science and religion, yet many of its adherents do not accept those categories in the first place. In interviews with conference attendees, I asked about the relationship between science and religion, and they gave scores of provocative answers.[1] One said simply, "Science *is* a religion." Just as emphatically another attendee said, "Religion is a science." Many said that the separation between science and religion is artificial and misleading, constituting a false dichotomy that serves some people's interests at the expense of truth.

A World of Scientific Research

UFO research was effectively removed from the agenda of mainstream university and laboratory-based science in the late 1960s (Condon and Gillmor 1969; Hynek 1972; Denzler 2001), but the knowledge that certain ufologists produce is nonethe-

---

1. I attended twelve UFO research conferences between 1997 and 2000. I conducted interviews with conference participants, ufologists, and event organizers at each conference I attended. I conducted participant observation research that included attending presentations by UFO researchers, going on UFO watches, and running a T-shirt stand in the exhibition area of conferences. I administered an anonymous survey to attendees of the thirtieth annual Mutual UFO Network (MUFON) International UFO Symposium, Transcending Politics and Comfort Zones in Ufology, which was held in Arlington, Virginia, July 2–4, 1999. The remarks included in this chapter are drawn from those surveys.

less inscribed in a universe of books, articles, and videotaped speeches considered wholly scientific by many. It is a self-contained literature, accepted by its adherents as a compendium of scientific fact and comprising hundreds of books and articles that take an assertively scientific approach to unraveling the mysteries behind UFOs. Carefully modeled after mainstream scientific publications, some ufological journals have publication histories spanning several decades. Although the articles do not adhere to strict standards of scientific integrity, the mission statements of UFO journals highlight their scientific intent. One journal, *The Flying Saucer Review,* published in England since 1955, claims its authority in its mission statement: "With the collaboration of a team of more than seventy experts and specialists from Britain and twenty other countries," including, it adds, "Ph.D.s, doctors of medicine, astronomers, physicists and other scientific experts."[2]

The *Journal for UFO Studies* (JUFOS) is another self-described scientific UFO journal. Established in 1970, its publishers describe it as a "refereed scientific journal dealing exclusively with the UFO phenomenon" (Center for UFO Studies 2002a). There is also the official publication of the Mutual UFO Network called *The MUFON UFO Journal.* Published since 1969, it features articles written by leading ufologists and analyses of current UFO sightings (Mutual UFO Network 2002). A broader publication that regularly features UFO research is *The International Journal for Scientific Exploration* established, according to its mission statement, "to provide a professional forum for the presentation, scrutiny, and criticism of scientific research on topics outside the established disciplines of mainstream science" (Society for Scientific Exploration 2002).

Along with UFO journals, UFO research conferences provide a forum for building and spreading many strains of ufology and, more important, perhaps, to present it as a science. Several dozen UFO research conferences occur annually wherein papers are presented and UFO researchers describe their work to audiences. While insiders do debate the validity of the many levels of research on extraterrestrial life, particular lines of inquiry enjoy a special scientific status, at least among supporters. Some ufologists publish studies based on statistical correlations of data derived from abductees' hypnotic recollections. Others compile and analyze the "scientific evidence" of extraterrestrial contact. Still others analyze the science behind alien transportation and energy systems that enable the purported interstellar travel of UFOs. For over thirty years, the Mutual UFO Network (MUFON) has organized annual symposia, which regularly draw hundreds of attendees. Many types of ufologi-

2. *The Flying Saucer Review*'s mission statement can be found at http://www.fsr.org.uk.

cal knowledge, some touting the existence of extraterrestrials, are spread at various conferences held annually in the United States and around the world by MUFON and similar organizations.

Methods are, of course, a natural question. To begin with, how does one study things that are by definition unidentified? UFO research methodologies are contained in the UFO *Field Investigator's Training Guide* of the Mutual UFO Network, subtitled *An Introduction to Methodologies, Techniques, and Scientific Disciplines for Performing UFO Investigations,* and it is required reading for those who wish to be MUFON-certified UFO investigators (Spencer 1995). While it sometimes presents itself as an ordinary line of research, ufology is not an ordinary collection of scientific disciplines. It largely deals with anomalous events and anomalous theories. In certain forms of ufology, both religion and science are mined for raw materials: mainstream science contributes methodologies and religion supplies some hard data.

The Bible and UFOs

Clusters of UFO researchers have claimed that the Bible holds evidence of ancient alien contact. UFO scholar Barry Downing mines scripture for evidence of UFO activity. In *The Bible and Flying Saucers* (1968) he notes that the Bible contains evidence that when Moses came down from Mount Sinai with two stone tablets in his hands, his face "shone" from talking with God. Therefore, Downing says, Moses was probably interfacing with a glowing UFO. Downing notes that when the Tabernacle was built the priests serving it were told to wear special clothing. He argues that they were likely told this by extraterrestrials, who were trying to protect their human followers against the radiation emitted by their nearby UFO. Downing remarks that this safety precaution may even have brought about the Jewish practice of wearing a yarmulke, the small skullcap, in a house of worship.

Similarly, Josef Blumrich writes about the mysterious "wheel" described in Ezekiel, arguing that it was probably an extraterrestrial spacecraft. He even fashioned the Bible's descriptions of the wheel into crude blueprints and built a model of the craft (Blumrich 1974). Such interpretations are a means of legitimating the UFO worldview and of explaining religion in a rationalized manner. UFO researcher Joe Lewels does the same thing in a paper entitled, "Angels or Aliens?" He draws additional links between UFOs and religious works by connecting Jesus with spaceships and by linking a reptilian race of aliens with the temptation of Eve in the Garden of Eden. In a lecture, Lewels said:

There are lots of examples in ancient times of women being impregnated by heavenly beings. Jesus' birth was heralded by a UFO . . . and the reptilians (a reptile-like race of alien beings). Let's think about this. Was the serpent a reptilian before he had to crawl on his belly for his sins in the Garden of Eden? The ancient Hebrews—they also had sentient beings who were reptilian. (1998)

Several works of Christian art have been analyzed for possible references to UFOs. One that turns up frequently in the lectures and articles by UFO researchers is Filippo Lippi's fifteenth-century *Madonna and Child*. In the painting, one can see a strange object hovering in the sky behind Jesus and Mary, a machine-like object that appears to catch the attention of other characters in the painting. A dog appears to bark at it, and a man shields his eyes to look in its direction. Among many others, a reproduction of this painting is contained in the photo archives of the Center for UFO Studies (CUFOS). The Christian tradition is an important source of data, but UFO researchers turn to a slew of other faiths and frameworks in their pursuit of UFO truths.

Other Religious, Cultural Traditions, and UFOs

Many agree that some religiomythic lore is based upon misunderstood facts rather than on supernatural happenings, and they aim to unearth and publicize these facts in their research. UFO researchers draw on Egyptian hieroglyphics, ancient Sumerian passages, Aztec sculpture, and other religious and symbolic sources for proof and factual grounding. Among the best-known researchers in this genre are Zecharia Sitchin and Erich von Däniken. Sitchin believes that an extraterrestrial race created both human beings and Sumerian culture, basing his claims on interpretations of ancient inscriptions on clay tablets buried for millennia, which he says demonstrate that the roots of humankind stretch back to 450,000 B.C. Analyzing the structure and orientation of the pyramids at Giza, he finds that the giant monuments were built as landing markers for the extraterrestrials. In these cultural and religious artifacts Sitchin finds "proof." With books like *Genesis Revisited: Is Modern Science Catching Up With Ancient Knowledge?* (1995) and *The Lost Book of Enki: Memoirs and Prophecies of an Extraterrestrial God* (2001), Sitchin refashions religious and cultural materials into empirical data.

Similarly, Erich von Däniken presents what he has called "irrefutable evidence" of UFO-based history from scripture and lore. In a lecture I attended, von Däniken argued for new ways of thinking that unite the "ancient wisdom" of sacred texts with a scientific approach to truth. He stated, "We must look with modern eyes. We must fight for a new way of thinking. Wisdom from outer space. Ezekiel. The evolution of technology. Everything completely turned upside down" (von Däniken 1998).

Like many others, Erich von Däniken claimed that myths represent a misidentification of alien astronauts as gods and angels. He claimed also that the scientific community's guiding principles are misunderstandings and, in a sense, myths. As he pointed to a slide of a giant pattern of grooves in a mountain, he explained that the ancient patterns had something to do with UFOs and extraterrestrials. He lamented that the mainstream scientific community will not admit this and instead advanced different theories that fit its "outdated" view of the universe, "I have gone through every theory from the scientific community and I have crashed them all down and I have good reason to. If someone here understands something about mathematics, this is very complicated" (von Däniken 1998).

Regarding his own motivation, von Däniken said his research was a quest for a larger understanding of the human condition and of God. When asked by an audience member how he got his start in UFO and extraterrestrial research, von Däniken explained that his interests grew out of religious curiosity and morphed into something he viewed as both more real and more inspired:

> I was educated as a Christian and a Catholic. I was a deep believer in God. God doesn't have to make an experiment and wait for the results. God is timeless. This is the idea of God I have kept in my mind even today. I found things in the Bible, during translation of it, that were not talking about God. This started the doubts about my own religion. But I never lost God. (von Däniken 1998)

Articulating the ambivalent position that some UFO researchers have toward science and religion, von Däniken spoke of a God not bound by religion, but one who is essentially a scientist and whose godlike powers rest therein. Further, he claimed to have sold over sixty million copies of books containing his brand of UFO research.

Martyrs, Pilgrimages, Conversions

The native religious significance of religious materials is often drained when certain enthusiasts take hold of them for analysis, but they do not completely shy away from meaningful religious rites and relics. For example, a 1997 UFO convention in Roswell, New Mexico, held a scientific research symposium in conjunction with a

Navajo prayer ritual at the reputed 1947 UFO crash site. Many now recognize Roswell as sacred ground. Pilgrims mark the landscape with crosses and American flags; entrepreneurs sell vials of earth. A small vial sells for ten dollars plus postage through mail order.

There are organizations (e.g., the Center for the Study of Extraterrestrial Intelligence) that conduct group meditation rituals designed to attract UFOs, drawing loosely on Eastern religious traditions as well as on alien communication principles uncovered through their brands of research. At these research rites, potential UFO "contactees" sit in a circle, meditating according to the leader's instructions. On cue, they mentally "pulse" colors into the sky, which the leader simultaneously "releases," using a giant flashlight and colored transparencies. There is a genre of music associated with the UFO community. While not exactly hymns, the songs underscore, nonetheless, the depth of UFO devotion. They include the compositions of abductees who sing about their experiences, and a wide variety of synthesizer artists who create "mood music" inspired by the reported sounds of UFOs.

Religious martyrlike figures, said to have sacrificed their lives for the cause of ufology, are celebrated and memorialized. A collection of martyrs were described in a lecture on "UFO research perils," in which researcher Ken Thomas (1999) examined "case histories of ufological researchers who have died under mysterious circumstances, or whose lives have been otherwise disrupted as a result of their work on the topic."

Some members of the UFO research community organize observational forays to established areas of research interest. They travel to the outskirts of reputed alien holding areas, including "Area 51" near Rachel, Nevada. They trek to UFO "hot spots" where sightings occur frequently, such as Gulf Breeze, Florida. UFO "relics" believed to be pieces of craft wreckage are treated as sacred material, and purported "alien implants" are displayed in glass cases at UFO research conferences. Those of the most mystical persuasion go on pilgrimages to faraway places like Machu Picchu in the Peruvian Andes.

Learned Conversions: From Darkness to Light

For many, ufology provides a broad religious philosophy, including information about life after death, a code of conduct, and a comprehensive worldview that subsumes all others. Many of its adherents have converted to subcultures of ufological mysticism from other religions, they say, through learning about UFO sightings and other anomalous phenomena. While their descriptions of their entrée into the UFO worldview often sound like more traditional born-again experiences, it is ufology's emphasis on book learning and the preponderance of empirical facts that generally leads to changes in belief.

Although some ufology addresses sacred themes and acts as a religion for many who follow it, proponents insist they are engaged not in belief but in science. They make frequent references to scientific methods and empirical grounding in the ufology community and other straight-science staples, like double-blind tests, statistical correlation, and systematic data collection. Jack "Kewaunee" Lapseritis, for example, stressed that he relied on empirical methodologies to research his book, *The Psychic Sasquatch and Their UFO Connection* (1998b), but he made it clear that his methods included things not normally considered scientific, such as telepathy, time travel, and intuition. Kewaunee defended his research techniques by stating, "When people say, 'You really believe in Bigfoot?' I say no. It's not what I believe. It's what I empirically documented using scientific methods" (Lapseritis 1998b). Kewaunee claimed that data collected telepathically or metaphysically counted as empirical observations. His empirical methods include guarding mystical portals for time traveling beings, interviewing metaphysical creatures, and communicating telepathically with Sasquatch. The search for Bigfoot does not represent the whole of ufological research, but it thrives as one line inquiry now included under the overly broad category of ufology.

These types of topics and methods are not without critics in the UFO research community. During my field research, I observed an audience member gently challenge UFO researcher Marianne Horrigan's research methods, specifically her use of telepathically channeled drawings made by an abductee: "The head of MUFON fired a guy who was into channeling. That's a part of trying to get it to the level of a recognized science. Even though it might be legitimate, it takes something away from the credibility of our undertaking." Horrigan defended the methods, claiming that channeling was sometimes the only way information could be gathered about the extraterrestrial problem: "Many channelers are illegitimate, but since we're dealing with people from other planets it transcends that. What other means for communication do we have?"

Modern-day mysteries become straightforward data for analysis in ufology. Some ufologists subject seemingly supernatural happenings to analysis within empirically styled research models and theoretical paradigms. How valid these studies are is open to question. A research initiative of the Center for UFO Studies and its partners, for example, seeks to investigate correlations between abduction experiences and the home environment. Its methodologies involve outfitting alien abductees with tracking devices. The Fund for UFO Research's (FUFOR) Web site posted this call for researchers and subjects:

> The UFO Research Coalition (composed of the Center for UFO Studies, the Fund for UFO Research, and the Mutual UFO Network) is searching for abductees with ongoing abduction experiences to participate in a research project. The project involves correlating abduction experiences and the environment in an abductee's home. As part of the project, a monitoring device is installed for a four- to six-month period in the home. An abduction investigator must work with the abductee to install the device and be the liaison with the Coalition. There are no costs involved for either the abductee or the investigator. If you are an investigator or abductee and are interested in this project, please contact the project's principal investigator. (Center for UFO Studies 2002b)

When studies like this are complete, the results are often disseminated in the manner of ordinary scientific studies.

Although claiming allegiance to scientific methods, many ufologists do not back all of the practices of modern, mainstream science. Ufologists frequently complain that conventional science has become a set of vested interests, no longer concerned with the truth, and separated from its original quest for real knowledge and human meaning. Science is, they say, caught up in outmoded, alien-free understandings of the universe—understandings that make no room for the evidence that alien-curious ufologists present.

Many ufologists argue that the mainstream scientific worldview is composed of a set of myths and outdated paradigms. They reject many of the core principles and practices of mainstream science (e.g., Hynek 1972; Pye 1998). UFO researcher Jacques Vallee (1965) would have liked to consult scientists, he writes, but "unfortunately, communication between scientists still follows medieval patterns and any attempt on my part to bring the subject into the open would have resulted in misunderstanding." This long-standing rift between established science and ufology runs deep, and it may never be repaired. When established science and government funding turned its back on the studies of UFOs and related anomalies by the 1950s, it stigmatized any further research in this area (Denzler 2001). This defensiveness on the part of ufologists has some merit in light of the historical relationship, but when taken to the extreme, their iconoclastic stance on science remains questionable.

Just as many in ufology attack scientific practices, they also eschew mainstream scientific principles and theories. Some ufological scholarship aims to overturn scientific staples, for example the big bang theory, the theory of evolution (natural selection), and the theory of relativity, in favor of highly unconventional explanations of the universe, human origins, and the space-time continuum. Admittedly, elite avant-garde physicists of our day pose criticisms of such established paradigms, but they do so without an extraterrestrial notion of causation. Researcher Lloyd Pye, author of *Everything You Know Is Wrong* (1998), claims, "Darwinism does not, as advertised, explain either how life first came to be on Earth, or how it has subsequently developed into the millions of plant and animal species that have existed since then." Darwin could have been wrong, but is Pye right? He contends that according to hard scientific evidence handed down from the Sumerians, aliens brought human DNA to planet Earth (Pye 2002).

Another area in which some ufology parts company with conventional science—almost as an official policy—is its quest for an integrated theory that explains both the physical and the spiritual dimensions of life in one unified framework. UFO researcher Robert Dean believes that explanations presented by both mainstream science and traditional religion are dead wrong. Speaking at a 1997 UFO conference, he explained his opinion that mainstream scientists and conventional religions reject and ignore what he calls "the truth" about the existence of more evolved extraterrestrial beings. Dean hints at the potential of UFO research to overturn both conventional science and religion and to take on their responsibilities:

> It's just too ego shattering for some people to accept. Just to admit that there are superior species shatters one's view of the world. You have to change everything and too many people are too comfortable. They like the comfort of the old way of thinking. They're clinging to the old reality—the religious and scientific version of reality. And that reality is just not true. (Dean 1997)

The fifth man on the moon, former NASA astronaut Edgar Mitchell, defected from science's "old way of thinking" toward a worldview sympathetic with ufology. He developed an interest in UFOs, extraterrestrials, and consciousness several years ago. A NASA mission sparked his curiosity; when returning to Earth he saw the universe as an extraterrestrial would. Lecturing at a UFO conference, he made the case that science fails to address deep questions about the nature of the universe and the meaning of human consciousness:

I have looked out the window and contemplated the universe as an ET. I saw it as personal. I knew that the molecules of my body were manufactured in an ancient generation of stars. Suddenly, . . .it became clear that those were my molecules. For ancient questions, scientific explanations are flawed. And cultural explanations are not adequate in a space faring civilization. . . . Both mystical and religious experience, and scientific dogma have been totally wrong. Our best hope is to use scientific techniques to track phenomena in a non-locality—in what mystics have called for centuries, the beyond. New scientists are looking at these phenomena. This is our best shot at it. (Mitchell 1998)

Many ufologists are critical of the conventional scientific community, sometimes charging them with spreading and perpetuating untruths or with being stuck in old paradigms. This stance is not unique to ufology, and criticisms of science abound even within the academy. Academic science ideally welcomes healthy debates, but it wrote off anthropomorphic references to extraterrestrials several decades ago, leaving all ufologists stigmatized whether they believed in ETs or not. For highly disparaged strains of ufology, this theme of scientific exclusion carries enormous weight (O'Leary 1996; von Däniken 1998).

For instance, Michael Cremo in a public lecture talked about a process of knowledge filtration whereby science ignored and hid evidence that contradicted its findings. Citing evidence of human bones being found in geological strata, where according to mainstream science "they don't belong," Cremo repeated over and over the phrase, "I'm convinced that archaeologists have buried as much evidence as they have taken out of the ground." He displayed a time line summarizing what the scientific establishment argued happened in human development, juxtaposed with his own time line. Cremo claimed:

The writing of ancients in Sanskrit tell us that in ages past there were intelligent ape-like creatures on this planet. Alongside them were humans. . . . Of course, that's quite different from the story we'd hear from Darwin and his modern day followers. . . . I look for physical evidence. Of course, I didn't find that evidence in current textbooks of archaeology. I did eight years of research. . . . Why don't we know about this evidence if there is so much of it? This is what I call a process of knowledge filtration. We live in a knowledge culture. The fixed ideas of the scientific community are the filter. Research that goes with the fixed ideas filters through easily. If they happen to go against the fixed ideas they are ignored. Set aside. Forgotten. It's against the law in all fifty states to teach anything but the standard Darwinian views of evolution of man. That's a pretty good position to be in—to have a monopoly over the control of minds. (1998)

For an outsider looking into the stranger forms of ufology, religion and science seem to be strangely mixed and matched, critiqued and fused, dissected and debunked. However, adherents interpret science and religion in ways that avoid problems that otherwise might arise. At the annual symposium of the Mutual UFO Network in July 1999, several attendees anonymously provided me with their views during interviews. While a few felt that religion and science were in direct opposition ("Oil and water"; "Different approaches"; "Match made in hell!"), many people voiced the opinion that science and religion both have an essential role in creating knowledge and uncovering truth. One remarked, "They both lead to the truth and understanding of God." Another said, "They are complementary and they are different aspects of reality." Someone else ventured, "One complements the other and furthers the search for truth." Also expressed was, "I think they each help to enhance each other and understand each other. I personally see no conflict."

Others emphasized that religion and science are "human constructs" that get in the way of the search for answers, for example, "They don't recognize each other so information is lost." Another commented, "We should work to bring the truth together." Someone else explained in more detail, "UFO research challenges personal beliefs, habits, paradigms of behavior, which cross over self-imposed boundaries of science and religion. The study requires one to re-examine oneself. Ufology is the ultimate interdisciplinary discipline!" Another said, "Both are extreme ends of the study of everything. Both have flaws that need to be smoothed out. One is the apple and the other is an orange. We need to use the whole brain to research."

Mixing its self-styled scientific methods with what might be best understood as a UFO-based theology, the world of fringe UFO research continually ruptures the conventional separation between science and religion. Joining fact and belief, ufology raises a slew of questions revolving around faith and reason, the sacred and objective, the scientific and the religious. For decades, scholars have noticed that such research provides a way to reconcile faith in "the beyond" with a rational, scientific worldview (Jung 1959; Berlitz and Moore 1980; Saler, Ziegler, and Moore 1997; Denzler 2001).

This study has sought to show that as faith becomes scienticized in elements of UFO research, some of science also becomes infused with religious principles and practices. While faith-based and sacred things are in some ways sanitized in UFO research, practical notions of science are also reconfigured and reconceived to become something more holy and meaning-laden. Although an explicit supernatural framing of religious narratives is dropped as it is spun up into certain forms of ufological research, the essential "magic" in them is not diminished. In fact, it seems heightened, as various ufologists believe they are getting closer to uncovering the hidden nature and moral meaning of the universe thorough their multipronged research approach, an approach in which any information-gathering strategy is considered fair game. These practices demonstrate the flexibility of science and religion as concepts—concepts that are defined largely in practice where they are continuously reconfigured and rewritten by a wide range of participants.

Since at least the time of Max Weber, scholars have interpreted the forces of secularization and have tracked the victory of science over traditional and religious modes of thought. Certainly, this is an indisputable and important historical trend. Yet observers have also suggested that religion can have an enormous impact on ostensibly secular pursuits. Weber did so famously, of course, relating the spirit of capitalism to the Protestant ethic. Tackling science head on, Robert Merton (1970) has suggested a causal relationship between Puritanism and the rise of modern science in the seventeenth and eighteenth centuries. Eileen Barker (1981) describes the rise of science itself as a new religion, with scientists reigning as "the new priesthood." Others focus upon the religious dimensions of what appears to be secular culture (Taylor 1999) and modern movements (most notably New Age movements) that try to reinject secular society with mysticism and spirituality (Heelas 1996; Hanegraaff 1998).

It has also been argued that science, particularly the theory of evolution, helped launch the modern religious revival, as the fundamentalist movement mobilized to defend Christian doctrine against the teachings of science (Marsden 1982). Others have suggested that as they battled against creationism, scientists used religion to define and expand their sphere of intellectual authority (Gieryn, Bevins, and Zehr 1985).

Beyond being interrelated in practice, deliberate mixing of science and religion occurs inside various religious movements. Among the most successful movements to combine religious and scientific motifs is the Church of Scientology, which mixes both spheres—even in its name. Scientology has secured tax exemptions as a religion, yet also employs science-inspired psychological profiling as religious tools (Hubbard 1950). Other groups that combine science with religious, mythical, or supernatural matter include believers in psychokinesis and psychic healing; creationists, of course; researchers of the Shroud of Turin, the reputed burial cloth of Jesus Christ; and ghost researchers, to name a few.

Definitions of religion and science and the relationships between them are somewhat fluid and influenced by time and place—very different in, for example, Leonardo da Vinci's day than in Steven Hawking's time. Furthermore, important as conventional modern science may be, its organization does not preclude the existence of unofficial, even illegitimate, scientific communities wherein deviant, life-organizing truths are made and accepted as entirely scientific by internal audiences. Adherents of certain types of fringe ufology where science and religion blur into one another have set up a parallel world of research in which information from all sources and for all purposes is considered fair game. These enclaves represent science for those who cultivate their strange lessons, however nonstandard the lessons might be.

Ancient Alien Brothers, Ancient Terrestrial Remains

Archaeology or Religion?

Pia Andersson

Ever since its birth, the discipline of archaeology has had a close relationship with religion. Both share an interest in a number of questions concerning humanity's prehistoric past and its evolution. Archaeology and religion often use each other to find answers. Initially, the goal of archaeology was to affirm the view of prehistory presented in the Bible. Today, however, the discipline of archaeology does not seek to confirm religious testimony. On the contrary, it is religious testimony that still seeks its confirmation from archaeology.

The Precarious Relationship Between Science and Religion

The preoccupation with attempting to construct a trustworthy explanation of reality is probably as old as humankind itself. Different belief systems and different ways of interpreting our surroundings have replaced one another throughout history. A thousand years ago "the anger of the gods" served as a logical explanation for thunder. It is not necessary to go back in time to find alternate explanations of reality because there are numerous contemporary cultural examples. For instance, even today in the Trobriand Islands, people treat the pain caused by a fall from a coconut tree by cutting the skin with a special magical stone. In their worldview, healing requires magic. To examine differences in explanations of reality, we need not cross the borders of the Western cultural milieu because acceptable truths and how we access them varies greatly even in our own time and place. Western culture offers many explanations for what is real.

Religion and science are two quite divergent constructors of reality that exist side by side in the present. Although some view the problem as two-sided, upon closer inspection it can be argued that both religion and science are multifaceted social constructions, made up of numerous, inconsistent systems of hypotheses, beliefs, theories, and convictions. While only a few hundred years ago explanations of "moving lights in the sky" might have exclusively been ascribed to signs of God, today's explanations include astronomical, physiological, psychological, and sociological interpretations, as well as a range of explanations about aliens from other dimensions. How did all this happen? What turned reality into this cacophony of disparate explanations? Let us go back in time a few hundred years to see where and why the highway to truth detoured into multiple lanes.

As the world grew smaller on its way to globalization, various religions, beliefs, doctrines, and values collided head-on, generating both existential chaos and creativity in the process of finding new ways of thinking. Wading through the immensity of incompatible interpretations of reality, we invented the methods of science and divided all of knowledge into distinct disciplines, each designed to define, describe, solve, and explain its own segment of reality. Apparently, here religion and science parted ways because of differences in their sources and methods of finding truth. However, in time other explanatory systems developed that aimed at finding a coherent way to synthesize religion and science again. These synthesized doctrines are primarily of two varieties, either a "spiritualized-science" type or a "scientific-spirituality" type, and both are still active today.

Within the field of spiritualized science, we find new religious movements, such as the Theosophical Society, UFO religions, and the New Age movement, which aspire to find a synthesis of all religions, as well as to bridge religion and science. These movements argued for the expansion of the scientific method to include elements belonging to the sphere of religion, hence "spiritualizing" it, and thereby creating a more "real" science, one competent to investigate *all* there is to know about reality. In contrast, there are others who seek to incorporate science into the sphere of religion, thereby adding a "scientific" aspect to religion. For example, among those who choose this method of explanation we note a tendency to comb biblical scriptures and other religious texts, like the Hindu *Vedas,* in order to discover references to electronic devices, spaceships, nuclear weapons, and ancient astronauts (Kolosimo 1982; Knight and Lomas 1999). The religion called the International Raëlian Movement is probably one of the more obvious examples of the endeavor to add the "scientific" aspect to the domain of religion, turning the eternal life of the soul into DNA transplantation, and God the Creator into aesthetic scientists from outer space (Vorilhon [Raël] 1998).

Today, more frequently than not, we have come to label the intellectual and emotional minefield between science and religion either pseudoscience or "alternative science," depending on one's perspective. Academics from many disciplines conventionally discuss what takes place at the fringes of their disciplines as fraud or pseudoscience. Defying the established boundaries of scientific practice, the fringe practitioners themselves usually relate to their field of expertise as "alternative science." Most academic disciplines have sparked fringe activities, which differentiate themselves from their conventional counterparts principally in terms of their methodologies and their logic; their divergences help them arrive at dissimilar theories for explaining the same phenomena. Ironically, conventional science accuses alternative science of, fundamentally, the same faults and frauds that fringe practitioners attribute to academics—hence, the tense relationship between the two rivals for truth.

These contested areas of knowledge construction serve as the intellectual battleground for any identification of "real" archaeology. We shall now turn our attention to the question of prehistory, a topic cherished in both science and religion. We will continue to follow the trail of "scientific" religion and the fringe areas of science, and then we will plunge headlong into the realm of "alternative archaeology," focusing on the belief in ancient astronauts and the accompanying modern myths of prehistory (Andersson 2000). On the topic of ancient astronauts, we will take a closer look at ancient archaeological remains, the theories associated with these early remains, and how these unconventional theories of prehistory function as an alternative way of looking at the past.

The Fertile Relationship Between Old and New Myths

By the beginning of the twentieth century, on the periphery of mainstream science and conventional religion, the practices of "spiritualized science" and "scientific spirituality" instigated alternative beliefs about the past derived from new religious paradigms (e.g., Theosophy, Spiritualism, occultism) that led to novel ways of looking at the mission of archaeology. Formerly belonging to conventional religion, the old doctrines of prehistory lent themselves to inventive interpretations under these influences, thereby giving birth to new myths of human origins. Additionally, Eastern religious ideas became diffused among many of these interpretations, for example, the belief in reincarnation and karma (of both living beings and planets), a cyclical view of time (rather than a linear view), and a questioning of the position of Western civilization as the apex of human evolution.

Plato's story of the sunken continent of Atlantis (Flem-Ath and Flem-Ath 1995; Wilson 1997; Wilson and Flem-Ath 2001) received renewed attention, together with other old myths of Mu and Lemuria (Harrold and Eve 1995). As esoteric writers reinterpreted other religions and myths from different parts of the world, new myths were born. They frequently referred to an ancient, highly technological global civilization (also generally described as spiritually advanced), which was destroyed by a worldwide cataclysm occurring sometime in prehistory (Kolosimo 1982; Horn 1994; Harrold and Eve 1995; Hapgood 1996). With the help of the discipline of archaeology, there was now the possibility of finding proof for these myths. In the age of science, it was no longer sufficient just to have faith and to believe. Physical evidence was coveted and archaeology was, in the case of prehistory, the obvious solution.

Paralleling the advance of these new myths of prehistory, the UFO craze of the 1950s gave rise to a set of myths all its own (Lewis 2000). Some of these myths include the following: alien conspiracies, alliances of aliens and humans in opposition to the rest of humanity, the extraterrestrial hypothesis (ETH), Men in Black (MIB), speculations about a government investigative group called Majestic 12, the significance of Area 51, the Roswell cover-up, the Condon Committee disinformation campaign, alien abductions and experimentation on human subjects, the coming of the White Brotherhood, the existence of photon belts, and the promise of a multi-dimensional physics. Charismatic prophets such as Gloria Lee, Daniel Fry, Gabriel Green, George King, and Ruth Norman heralded a belief in spaceships and contact with aliens that encouraged an alternative paradigm of history.

George Adamski (1955) and George Hunt Williamson (1975) were among the first UFO prophets to weave ideas of prehistory into their stories of alien visitors. In Adamski's book *Inside the Spaceships* (1955), two Space Brothers, Ramu and Firkon, explain how colonies from other planets have inhabited Earth at several turns during our prehistory. The Desmond Leslie and George Adamski text, *Flying Saucers Have Landed* (1953), incorporated Leslie's proposal for a new interpretation of images described in Hindu Vedic scriptures. They contended that *vimanas* (flying vehicles) were ancient accounts of UFOs. Thus, extraterrestrials, erroneously described as "gods" in the *Vedas*, piloted these vehicles. In comparison to Adamski and Leslie, Williamson was known for his special interest in archaeology, and he encouraged the development of many new myths of prehistory in his books. For example, he was among the first to suggest that the Hopi people had their origin on another planet, and that the lines of the Nazca desert in Peru indicated an ancient alien presence in South America.

Leslie and Williamson, as well as their fellow UFO enthusiasts, explicitly used old myths in the creation of new ones, as had Theosophy, which most likely inspired many of them with its themes of Atlantis and Lemuria. They reevaluated the potential historical truth of the old myths, declaring that the people of antiquity simply did not understand the advanced technology of the aliens. Therefore, early peoples made reference to supernatural forces, "sun-wagons," and "gods from the sky." Since the 1800s, this kind of assimilation of old myths has become one of the core practices of the instigators of so-called scientific spirituality. No scripture or religious text escaped reinterpretation. Researchers sought scientific knowledge in the archaic writings of Sumer, ransacked the Old and New Testaments hunting for aliens, scrutinized classical Hindu texts, and allegedly found references to both nuclear weapons and flying vehicles (Tomas 1976; Steiger and Steiger-Hansen 1992; Harold and Eve 1995; Roland 1997; Knight and Lomas 1999). Examinations of Egyptian hieroglyphs uncovered evidence of the advanced technology of ancient astronauts (Stiebing 1984; Collins 1998; Andersson 2000) and of the advanced astronomical knowledge recorded in ancient Egypt and in indigenous South American myths. In traditional religious myths all over the world, adherents to this perspective located confirmation of what they were looking for, and soon enthusiasts were ever so ready to start combing archaeological remains throughout the world to find even more evidence of ancient visitations from other worlds.

The list of people facilitating the growth and propagation of the new myths of prehistory (including the belief in ancient astronauts) has grown quite long with the years. Among the landmarks in the ancient-astronaut school, everyone notes Erich von Däniken (1968), who popularized the belief in ancient astronauts as no one had before, and Zecharia Sitchin (1976), a journalist who turned his full attention to reinterpreting old writings in accordance with the new myths of prehistoric events. Today, the belief in the existence of ancient astronauts is both a fundamental truth of prehistory among some new religious movements (Lewis 1995) as in, for example, Raëlianism and Unarius, and a very popular and seriously considered theory of antiquity in others as in, for example, the New Age movement. Additionally, theories of ancient astronauts are frequently discussed, and they are more or less critically considered within the less organized UFO subculture in which magazines like *Quest for Knowledge, UFO Universe, Atlantis Rising, Nexus,* and *Alien Encounters* publish articles discuss mythical archaeological sites and strange artifacts from an ancient-astronaut perspective.

During the last decade, a number of authors have joined Sitchin and von Däniken. Focusing their books on ancient astronauts, they regularly include pictures and explanations of archaeological remains. For examples, see the works of Alan Alford (1997, 2000), Maurice Cotterell (1996), Robert Temple (1999), and David Hatcher Childress (2000a, 2000b) to name a few. There is also an organization known as Archaeology Astronautics SETI Research Association (AASRA), previously called the Ancient Astronaut Society, that seeks to organize interest in and research on ancient astronauts. Erich von Däniken, among others, presently oversees the building of life-sized copies of the grandest archaeological monuments of the world at Swiss Mystery Park in Interlaken. This ancient-astronaut theme park promotes the notion that humans needed extraterrestrial help to establish their civilizations.

In contrast, there are also alternative archaeologists who promote all the modern myths of prehistory but very carefully choose to omit the theory of alien visitations (Bergier 1973). Occasionally, they join forces with ancient-astronaut promoters, as in Graham Hancock's collaboration with von Däniken on the *Chariots of the Gods?* documentary. Nevertheless, it is not clear until the end of the film that Hancock (1995) disagrees with von Däniken's opinion on prehistoric alien visitors. Other promoters of the ancient-astronaut school include Michael Cremo and Richard Thompson, who are supportive of the notion, even though their book, *Forbidden Archaeology* (1996), does not mention ancient alien visitors. However, Thompson has written in favor of the ancient-astronaut hypothesis in an earlier book titled, *Alien Identities* (1993). To sum up, presently there is an apparently close-knit subculture focusing its attention on modern myths of prehistory and reinterpretations of archaeological remains, presenting and promoting an alternative view of history that is eager to criticize academic science while doing so.

The Delicate Relationship Between Physical Proof and Belief

We find them all around the world, these enigmatic, impressive, and fascinating monuments of the past, enticing our imaginations, as well as confusing us. These are some of the famous places referred to in ancient astronaut theories: the Sphinx and the Great Pyramid in Egypt; the geoglyphs and lines of the Nazca desert; Stonehenge, Avebury, and Silbury Hill in England; the lines of menhirs at Carnac in France; the statues of Easter Island; the giant spheres of Costa Rica; the monoliths of

Baalbek in Lebanon; the ruins of Nan Madol at Pohnpei in Micronesia; Machu Picchu in the Andes; Angor Wat in the jungles of Cambodia; Puma Punku at Tiahua-
naco in Bolivia; and the Mayan ruins at Chitchen Itza and Palenque in Mexico.
While most of these sites have had their share of conventional archaeological attention, some of them seem to have slipped through the academic cracks and are left
wanting comprehensive scientific investigation.

Suspicions of academic negligence have, in turn, stimulated conspiracy theories, which have transformed these archaeological remains into contemporary
flashpoints of ancient mysteries. Nevertheless, sites conventionally explained and
demystified can also attract interest and theories of conspiracy, as with the monuments of the Giza in Egypt. Although academia claims to know and to understand
the when, why, and how of pyramid construction, a whole generation of maverick
Egyptologists fight to present their heterodox views of Egyptian antiquity (Wilson
1997; Dunn 1998; Coleman 1999). Above all, they question the pyramids as graves,
redate monuments and the chronologies of pharaohs, and search for the ancient library rumored to be somewhere under the Sphinx or the Great Pyramid.

However, obvious archaeological sites are not the sole focus of the ancient-
astronaut theory. Lately, a new epicenter of ancient mystery, echoing thoughts of Atlantis, Mu, and Lemuria, has been found in the underwater structures of Yonaguni
off the shore of Japan. Although academic debate cannot determine whether these
structures are natural or man-made, most promoters of the ancient-astronaut
school are convinced of the latter. There are also those who spread rumors, mainly
through the Internet, creating new myths of clandestine excavations of real "Star-
gates" and hidden caves with artifacts such as technological "time-capsules" containing full documentation of archaic civilizations (Lemesurier 1997; Picknett and
Prince 1999). An interesting example of the latter is that of the Wingmakers, who
claim to have found the site of a bygone culture near Chaco Canyon in New Mexico
that left technology, art, and philosophy in neat order for modern humans to find.
The Wingmakers' Internet homepage (2003) asserts that careful scientific examination showed that an alien race did not create the site, as previously thought, but the
site was actually constructed by a future version of humankind that practiced time
travel.

There are also artifacts popularly referred to as "oopas," or out-of-place-
artifacts. These can be either a commonplace archaeological artifact, such as an
arrow of flint unearthed in layers that predate human existence, or a very strange
and unusual object found within the layers of human history, such as the oft-
mentioned small spheres discovered in South Africa. Michael Cremo and Richard

Thompson discuss the issue of these misplaced artifacts while criticizing academic archaeology as being both conspired and nonscientific in their comprehensive text, *Forbidden Archaeology* (1996). Chris Kenworthy (1996) talks of xenotechnology (literally meaning alien technology or the study of alien technology), buttressed by the supposed finds of ancient objects from highly technical prehistoric civilizations influenced by extraterrestrials. Some people in this field anticipate finding archeological remains of spaceships, spacesuits, medical instruments, engineering tools, and so on. These finds are expected to lead to advances in other new sciences, like xenobiology (biology of alien life-forms) and xenosociology (study of alien societies). Various "mysterious objects," gadgets, and gizmos return again and again in new and different mythological contexts, as references to an ancient knowledge of flying, electricity, or nuclear power, or to a technology not yet comprehensible to human beings. The "powerful" crystal skull exhumed in a Mayan ruin (one among many other similar skulls reportedly found elsewhere), the ancient electric "batteries" of Baghdad, and small objects found in South America that resemble modern airplanes are often mentioned in this context. These inanimate objects somehow "suggest" an extraterrestrial origin, reifying the role humans play in making the interpretation.

Just as the old writings of preceding cultures are reinterpreted and are used as evidence for the ancient-astronaut hypothesis, so too has innovative deciphering of ancient cave paintings, megalithic drawings, and wall inscriptions from Australia, Asia, Europe, Africa, and the Americas been used to support theories of ancient alien visitors. Through reevaluating such depictions as flying saucers, airplanes, helicopters, space aliens with helmets and antennas, maps of stars, and unique technological devices, art makes the argument for space travel. Likewise, the famous map of Turkish admiral Piri Reis dated circa A.D. 1513 is said to indicate the possession of arcane knowledge about topography, conceivably originated by aliens, and aerial photography. In addition, interpreters of the map spawned alternative interdisciplinary theories involving continental shifts, climactic changes, and sudden flips of the earth's crust that seem to point to a hidden Atlantis under the icecap of Antarctica. These theories intellectually support many of the other new myths of prehistory.

In summation, the types of artifacts and archaeology most frequently referred to in ancient-astronaut theories and modern myths of prehistory include the world's most impressive, magnificent, and enticing sites, along with the strangest looking, seemingly misplaced objects, pictures, and inscriptions. Besides specific sites, the majority of the world's pyramids, megaliths, monoliths, and geoglyphs are integrated in the ongoing discussion of ancient alien visitations. Thus, what alterna-

15.1. Some ufologists claim the sarcophagus lid on the tomb of King K'inich Janaab Pakal at Palenque in Ciapas, Mexico, is evidence of an ancient astronaut. Mainstream archaeologists date the tomb ca. A.D. 683 in the Late Classic Mayan Period. Mayan scholars say it shows the king entering the afterlife, not piloting a spacecraft. Artwork by Diana Tumminia based on other drawings and renderings.

tive archaeology essentially does is claim that these ancient remains, monuments as well as artifacts, prove that Western culture is far from the apex of human evolution, and that there has been at least one global, highly advanced technological civilization that probably surpassed both modern technology and contemporary religion, that of a spiritual science possibly of extraterrestrial origin.

In spite of mainstream archaeological theories of how ancient peoples quarried, transported, and raised the colossal stones on Easter Island and Stonehenge, and how they built pyramids and megaliths, alternative researchers maintain there are neither realistic explanations nor sufficient proof to make such claims of knowledge. Instead, they argued that these ancient building techniques must alert us to as yet unknown laws of nature, suggesting, for example, a relationship between sound frequencies and gravity. Likewise, certain artifacts, as well as ancient texts, maps, wall inscriptions and pictures, geoglyphs, and straight lines in nature show the presence of ancient flying machines. These early remains are said to "prove" these "facts" of prehistory, thereby supporting the firm conviction of the enthusiastic researchers of alternative archaeology.

Designating Relationship Between Hypothesis and Convictions

To practice science properly according to conventional methods, it is advisable for the researcher's passion to be focused on the questions rather than on the answers. One can even suggest that the focus of this attention may be a fair indicator of the quality of research practiced. Although the kind of heavily biased science we examine here is not found exclusively outside the safe walls of universities, scientific institutions, and academic disciplines, it still is a good example of "alternative" science that has crossed the boundary of acceptance. There seems to be a recurring focus in this field on the practice of finding new answers to questions that have already been answered, and in doing so the rebel researchers in this genre constantly redraw the borders of accepted science. To understand this constant refashioning of scientific borders, we must take a closer look at the sources of inspiration for alternative researchers, which often originate within the sphere of religion.

The great existential questions about life and death, good versus evil, right or wrong, and the beginning and end of the world tap into powerful explanations about reality that mold our thoughts and preconceptions. The questions and answers involving archaeology and prehistory all touch upon these fundamental existential topics. This makes it difficult for some researchers to disconnect their views of prehistory from their personal views, which often reflect opinions of a religious or spiritual nature. Alternative researchers often employ works of occultism, mysticism, spiritualism, and Theosophy as inspiration. These philosophies already contain established myths of prehistory. The mystic Edgar Cayce wrote quite extensively on prehistoric events (Robinson 1972), as did the Theosophists Annie Besant and Charles Leadbeater (1913), who were inspired not solely by heavenly hierarchies but also by the occultists of the nineteenth century. Indeed, some of today's advocates of alternative archaeology refer directly to the writings of these nineteenth-century occultists, intending thereby to give weight to their ideas, while others choose more implicit ways of accounting for their inspiration.

I will end this exposé of alternative archaeology by referring to the beginning, the relationship between science and religion. The quest for a synthesis of both by the practices of so-called spiritualized science and scientific spirituality proposes that the choice of either method determines the degree of implicitness or explicitness used in presenting its religious inspiration. Ordinarily, religion and science do not mix. In its synthesized alternative way of doing things, scientific spirituality indicates only a certain degree of skepticism about religious sources in favor of scientific ones; this skepticism implies a tendency to discount religious inspiration in an explicit manner. We find almost the opposite situation in the practice of spiritualized science, for this practice gives an equivalent or even superior value to evidence from biblical or occult sources (compared to those of a more established scientific nature), thus proposing that any theory in question weighs more heavily if inspired and supported by spiritually inspired findings.

An intricate spectrum of relationships, both implicit and explicit, seems to exist between today's two dominant constructors of reality: the advocates of science and the advocates of religion. Therefore, following the current trend, regardless of which methodology ultimately proves its position regarding prehistory, populist theories about our beginning and our evolution still may turn out to be determined by rhetoric, marketing skills, and media exposure rather than by the solid scientific research that rigorous academics advocate. That is, of course, if the purported "gods" referred to in speculative archaeology do not return seeking alliances with conventional, institutionalized, academic science.

The Raëlian Creation Myth and the Art of Cloning

Reality or Rhetoric?

Christopher Helland

On March 28, 2001, the leader of the largest contactee religion in the world addressed the Subcommittee on Oversight and Investigations' hearing in the United States Congress.[1] The topic concerned the ethical implications of human cloning, and the leader spoke with some authority, telling legislators that it was not a matter of *if* a human would be cloned but *when*. The religion calls itself the International Raëlian Movement, and its leader asks that people address him as "His Holiness" Raël. A few months after the hearings, the Food and Drug Administration (FDA) raided the laboratory set up by the Raëlians to attempt human cloning. The FDA subpoenaed phone records, and they warned the group that it would be in violation of regulations concerning human experimentation if they attempted to clone a child, although in the end, no charges were laid and no equipment was taken. The government was forced to act because the movement kept telling the press and the general public that they would be cloning a child soon, even though they did not have the technology and the expertise to undertake successfully the nucleus transfer techniques needed to clone a human cell. Over a year later, Raëlians held press conferences in which they claimed to have successfully cloned a baby girl, dubbed Eve, who was born on December 26, 2002. In January 2003, a Florida attorney subpoenaed the Raëlian organization, Clonaid, to disclose the whereabouts of the mother

---

1. For detailed transcripts of the hearings see: http://energycommerce.house.gov/107/hearings/03282001Hearing141/hearing.htm.

and child. Clonaid's Web site (2004) now alleges that they have produced six cloned babies with more on the way. They further announced the establishment of Stemaid, a sister company specializing in therapeutic cloning. Currently, the scientific and legal communities still seek verification of these claims of successful human cloning.

This chapter explores the concept of cloning within the Raëlian belief system. Why do Raëlians promote this form of technology and scientific development? How is it that cutting-edge science has become a central component of the largest UFO religion in the world? After an introduction to the movement and its postmillennial vision, I focus upon the manner in which the group integrates science, in particular references to cloning and genetic engineering, within its belief system. I argue that appearing "scientific" has been a strategy of the Raëlians based upon their origin myth. Furthermore, cloning has become a form of validation and sensational promotionalism, a tool used to legitimate their claims to their followers and to attract potential recruits.

The Movement

The International Raëlian Movement began under the direction of Claude Vorilhon, also known as Raël, after he reported his first encounter with an extraterrestrial, one of the Elohim (creator scientists). The goals of the organization play a strong role in the social structure of the movement. In traditional terms, the movement's beliefs qualify as postmillennial. Postmillennial beliefs hold that the return of the messiah (or in this case the Elohim) will occur only after the believers, through their work, have reformed specific components of the society. The belief system sees the world in need of reform, salvation, and purification through the works of the members of the group, not through other worldly intervention. In this case, it is the responsibility of the individual and the group to begin the reformation of the planet in preparation for the return of the space Elohim.

It must be noted that there are variations in the presentation of the Raëlian belief system with the traditional postmillennial model. The most fundamental difference is that for decades the movement did not consider itself a religious institution, and it was not until 1995 that they received religious recognition in Canada. The Raëlians do promote themselves as an "atheist" form of philosophy rather than a religious theology, but possibly for tax purposes or public tolerance they accepted the religious classification (Palmer 1998, 144).

Within the original teachings presented by Raël, there were continual warnings from the Elohim to all of humanity that if the proper reforms did not occur, there would be swift and devastating repercussions. Raël states, "But if human beings remain aggressive and continue to progress in a manner which is dangerous for other worlds, then we will destroy this civilization and its repositories of scientific wealth, and there will be another Sodom and Gomorrah until such a time as humanity becomes morally worthy of its level of scientific understanding (Vorilhon [Raël] 1998, 9)."[2]

This threat of destruction runs counter to the traditional view of salvation through good works and represents a form of premillennialism, a much more radical millennial worldview. However, that radical component was removed from the belief system after Raël reported his second encounter with the Elohim. Whether as an intentional means of maintaining a consistent form of postmillennial beliefs, or as an amendment to the continuity of the message, the movement claims the passages containing these older teachings had been improperly transcribed during the first encounter.

Despite making this correction to the teachings, which places more consistency within their postmillennial worldview, elements of "divine" wrath and intervention remain. Raël makes reference to the possibility of a nuclear war and the ability of the Elohim to save the just.[3] However, the most noted form of this judgment and punishment can be seen in the movement's teachings about Israel and its refusal to allow the building of the Embassy for the Elohim near Jerusalem. According to Raël, "This is your last chance, otherwise another country will welcome the Guide of Guides and build our embassy on its territory, and that country will be close to yours; it will be protected and happiness shall prevail, and the State of Israel will be destroyed once more" (Vorilhon [Raël] 1998, 157–58).

Raël places a conditional acceptance upon the Jewish population and religious tradition. He warns those who are Jewish in origin that they should not return to Israel if the government does not allow the embassy to be constructed. Raël focuses

2. The publication used for a majority of the primary material for the Raëlian Movement is an amalgamation of the earlier material presented by the group. Where there are discrepancies in translation or omitted material, I will refer to the original publications. Because there are multiple editions, titles, and translations for the same Raëlian publications, this does create some confusion for citation purposes.

3. This theme recurs in the teachings of Raël. According to the belief system, humanity resides in the age of the apocalypse, and believers warn of the possibility of humanity destroying itself if the teachings of Raël are not heeded. However, the main focus of his teachings concern having the aliens return after the building of the Embassy for the Elohim.

the wrath of the Elohim upon the government, not necessarily the Jewish population. This position by Raël is very problematic, and members of the Jewish community have viewed it as anti-Semitic in nature. However, the movement denies this accusation by demonstrating their vocal support against any discrimination based upon race, gender, or sexual orientation (Palmer 1998, 141).

The Raëlians urge their members to remain active within society, making them a world-accommodating tradition, according to the classification system of Roy Wallis (1984). Being in the society, but not of the society because of their connection with the Elohim, the movement calls for several reforms. Civilization as it is now functioning needs to be altered if humankind is to merge with the Elohim. The transformational goal of the Raëlians focuses upon two general components of humanity. The first is concerned with instituting worldwide social, governmental, and political reforms. The second component is the development of the individual, and the movement introduced it after Raël reported his second contact with the Elohim.

The changes called for by Raël place the group in a difficult position in relation to the society in which it is functioning. Although the movement sees humanity as reformable, it has contempt for most world leaders and advocates radical changes to contemporary society. Raël teaches that certain components of our culture, particularly governments, must be changed if humanity is to evolve to the level of the Elohim. During his first contact, Raël claimed to have received specific commandments from the Elohim regarding several issues concerning governmental and societal reform. They are as follows: geniocracy, humanitarianism, world governments, nuclear weapons, and overpopulation (Vorilhon [Raël] 1998, 85–104).

Geniocracy is a term used by Raël to describe a form of political control over the population, similar to that of a meritocracy. According to his teachings, the ideal society would be ruled by the most intelligent beings upon the planet. The teachings state, "You will also participate in the creation of a worldwide political party advocating humanitarianism and geniocracy, as they are described in the first part of this message of the Elohim, and you will support its candidates. Only via geniocracy can humanity move fully into a golden age" (Vorilhon [Raël] 1998, 171). Traditional systems of democracy, including electoral and polling systems, would be abolished.[4] Raël predicts:

4. The most recent translation reads, "For this to happen, you must abolish all your electoral and polling systems because in their present form they are completely unsuited to human development" (Vorilhon [Raël] 1998, 85). However, the earlier presentation of the same material reads, "In order for

When individuals reached a responsible age, their intellectual coefficient can be measured and included on their identity or voters card. Only those with an intellectual capacity of at least fifty percent above the average should be eligible for a public post. To vote, individuals would need an intellectual coefficient of at least ten percent above average. (Vorilhon [Raël] 1998, 86)

According to this new system, individuals of average intelligence or less would be allowed no say in the running of the community or country.

Humanitarianism is linked to the geniocracy system of government presented by Raël. It represents a strict ethical paradigm against any form of inheritance. Property is owned by the state and may be rented for a period of forty-nine years. After that time the individual may live there until death, then the property returns to the state and is again rented out. Raël quotes from Leviticus to support the argument and would institute this practice to prevent people from gaining material wealth that they have not earned (Vorilhon [Raël] 1998, 87–89).

The next aspect of reform based upon Raël's contact with the Elohim concerns the implementation of a one-world government and currency. Within this framework, Raël has also decreed that conscription into the military should be forbidden. Armies should only be used for protecting public order. He views nuclear weapons as a threat to humanity. Raël warns, "If people do not want to be exposed to the dangers any longer, all they have to do is take nuclear weapons away from the military" (Vorilhon [Raël] 1998, 94). Although it is not clear how this is to be done, the teachings advocate the use of nuclear energy only as a power source that should be distributed to those countries in need.

During the first group of teachings presented by Raël, there is little mention of the liberal sexual practices that would later become a large component of the belief system. However, he does mention the importance of birth control and the need for the population of the planet to be limited. According to the Elohim, a couple should only be allowed to have two children, one to replace each parent (Vorilhon [Raël] 1998).

The second meeting between Raël and the Elohim came in 1975 in Perigord, France; it clarified the message from his first encounter and developed a number of points new to the movement. Science remains the most important aspect of the be-

---

this to happen elections must be abolished and also votes which are completely unadapted in their present form to suit the evolution of humanity" (Vorilhon [Raël] 1987a, 109).

lief system, and there is no alteration in the secularization of the Elohim. A typical example of this belief system can be seen throughout the general teachings of Raël. "As we have already explained to you in the first part of this message, there is no God, and obviously no soul. After death there is nothing unless science is used to create something," contends Raël (Vorilhon [Raël] 1998, 138).

The teachings then placed new emphasis upon the position and authority of Raël within the belief system and on the rewards promised to the membership, including the possibility of a prolonged life, benefits of sensual meditation, and the possibility of immortality through cloning of DNA. It was the second encounter that provided the framework for the new religion, removing it from consideration as just another UFO group to that of a genuine religious belief system. The new principles outlined in the teachings focus upon a number of social and religious issues. Raël even states that the Elohim told him, "The movement you have created must be the religions of religions. I insist that it is indeed a religion, although an atheistic religion, as you have already understood" (Vorilhon [Raël] 1998, 155).

The section of Raël's teachings called "the Keys" develops the belief system and establishes the parameters of conduct and worship for the followers. The Keys are reported to be the final development of the teachings revealed by the Elohim to humanity. As they are now issued from Raël, he is designated as the last of the prophets and the last representative of the teachings of the creators to the created. The teachings encompass several components, including humanity and its place in relation to the Elohim, birth and birth control (including abortion), education, sensual meditation and fulfillment, society and government, prayer and meditation, and the ability to contact the Elohim telepathically.

Participation in the movement now requires members to give 10 percent of their wages to the organization. Although the movement claims it pays no salaries, this amount is split three ways: 3 percent goes to the national organization, 6 percent flows to the international branch, and 1 percent is for Raël. By paying this percentage of wages to the movement, members can advance within the organization and participate in the functions of the group. Initially new members are not required to pay any amount to attend meetings or retreats, but for status and responsibility within the group the tithe must be paid.

Being the only guide of guides on the planet, Raël maintains complete leadership over the movement. His authority rests solely upon his reported encounter with the Elohim. His position is one of personal charisma, and the information concerning the scientific element of the movement is founded upon his narrative vision. Raël has no scientific training or background, and where specific scientific or theoretical information is used to support his claims, other experts are quoted for confirmation.

The Role of Science in Creation

The initial message presented by Raël of the teachings of the Elohim has been called a "demythologizing" of the Christian and Hebraic scriptures; it demonstrates the most visible form of the incorporation of science within the belief system. Raël highlights certain scriptures within the Old and New Testament, and he interprets all the events with a secularized scientific explanation for their occurrence. This interpretation does not remove the myth from the scriptures but rather reinterprets it with what I term *scientific dispensationalism*.

Scientific dispensationalism is a form of biblical interpretation that divides the scriptures into seven historical periods in which God deals differently and progressively with humanity. A similar structure of biblical interpretation appears in the teachings of Raël; however, the scientific language cannot be ignored in his teachings as it replaces the mysterious, unknown dimensions of the scriptures with technological imagery.

The application of scientific concepts is done in an attempt to relocate the Judeo-Christian myth within a valid and acceptable framework, presentable to a secularized community. The difficulty with the presentation is that the scientific component remains as mythic and nonprovable as the original discourse, becoming science fiction rather than science. The rhetoric used for presenting the creation of life and humanity remains religious in nature, although the descriptive terminology employed has been altered. By drawing upon the same framework (namely the Judeo-Christian scriptures), the only modification that has occurred between the former Christian narrative and this new religion is the scientific dispensationalism presented by Raël.

The presentation of the Raëlian creation myth is in a chapter titled "The Truth" in *The Final Message*. Raël reinterprets Genesis, highlighting certain sections and stories within a "scientific" framework. Raëlians present a new creation myth that recognizes the Elohim as advanced scientists from another planet who began experimenting with genetic engineering and cloning. According to Raël, the Elohim had already developed intergalactic exploration when they decided to travel to a suitable planet to seed life and create it in their image. The entire new mythic framework is juxtaposed upon the Hebraic creation story, and it is methodically presented in a manner that attempts both to demythologize the ancient myth and to add a form of secular/scientific accountability to the new one.

Here are examples of the new interpretations of the creation myth, according to Raël:

> "And the spirit of the Elohim moved across the waters." Genesis 1:2
>
> This means that the scientists made reconnaissance flights and what you might call artificial satellites were placed around the Earth to study its constitution and atmosphere.

> "The Elohim saw that the light was good." Genesis 1:4
>
> To create life on Earth it was important to know whether the sun was sending harmful rays to the Earth's surface and this question was fully researched. It turned out that the sun was heating the Earth correctly without sending out harmful rays. In other words the "light was good."

> "Let the waters under the heavens be gathered together into one place and let dry land appear." Genesis 1:9
>
> After they studied the surface of the ocean they studied the sea bed and determined that it was not very deep and fairly even everywhere. So then, by means of fairly strong explosions which acted rather like bulldozers, they raised matter from the bottom of the seas and piled it up into one place to form a continent. Originally there was on Earth only one continent and your scientists have recently acknowledged that all the continents, which have drifted apart over many years, used to fit perfectly into one another to form one land mass. (Vorilhon [Raël] 1998, 26–27)

This sample of the Raëlian biblical interpretations clearly represents the manner in which he attempted to unite scientific-sounding principles in a remythologized version of creation. His interpretation covers most of the Hebrew scriptures, including passages from Genesis, Exodus, Numbers, Deuteronomy, Joshua, the Book of Judges, Samuel, 1 Kings, 2 Kings, Isaiah, Ezekiel, Daniel, Jonah, Zechariah, Psalms, Job, Tobit, Wisdom of Solomon, Ecclesiastes, Amos, and Micah.

The teachings of Raël attempt to remove any form of mystical or spiritual explanation from the former myth. Stories such as Sodom and Gomorrah or the flood are related to a minor skirmish that occurred between the Elohim and the population on the planet that they came from. According to Raël, the majority of the extraterrestrials on the home planet viewed the creation of life and humanity on Earth as a threat and an injustice. Certain extraterrestrials with authority attempted to destroy all the earthly life that the Elohim had genetically engineered. He explains, "The government then decided from their distant planet to destroy all life on Earth by sending nuclear missiles. However when the exiled creators were informed of the project they asked Noah to build a space ship which would orbit the Earth during the cataclysm containing a pair of each species that was to be preserved" (Vorilhon [Raël] 1998, 32). To support the belief that Noah used a spaceship and not a large boat, Raël again quotes from the scriptures using Genesis 7:17: "The ark was lifted above the Earth." He says, "As you can clearly see, it is said that the ark was lifted 'above' the Earth and not 'on' the water" (33). In another mythic reference to cloning, the spaceship saved DNA samples in order to regenerate human and animal life. The scriptural references, such as Genesis 19:11 ("And they Smote them with blindness, both small and great"), are explained and interpreted with the same formula. In this case, the angels that had traveled to Sodom employed pocket atomic weapons to cause blindness, and then they dropped an atomic bomb on the city. In Exodus, manna was actually "pulverized synthetic chemical food which, when spread on the ground, swelled with the early morning dew" (37). A water-repulsion ray parted the Red Sea, and the vision of the glory of God on Mount Sinai (Exodus 24:17) came from a large spaceship taking off. There is no longer any element or component of the unexplained, mythical, or the magical in Raël's narrative. All episodes are reduced to the influence and interference of technologically advanced beings from another planet. There are no miracles, because all events can be explained and rationalized through the understanding of "what really" occurred.

Raël draws confirmation and descriptions of the Elohim as space travelers from a number of scriptures. He interprets Ezekiel's vision in a similar manner as had been done previously by Erich von Däniken in the best-selling book *Chariots of the Gods?*[5] After quoting from the Bible most of Ezekiel's encounter with God, Raël indicates:

> There you have a description which could not be more precise of the landing of the creators in their flying machines. . . . Later, four creatures appear wearing antigravity suits with small directional jet engines attached. . . . The small saucers were

5. A number of works appeared in the early 1970s that presented this interpretation of Ezekiel's vision, including Erich von Däniken's *Chariots of the Gods?* (1971) and *The Gold of the Gods* (1973), as well as Jacques Bergier's *Extraterrestrial Visitations from Prehistoric Times to the Present* (1973). The difference between presentations is that Raël claimed direct contact with the extraterrestrials, while the other works present information concerning extraterrestrial encounters that may have occurred in the past.

something like your own LEM's—lunar excursion modules—small, short range
vehicles used for exploratory missions. Above the interplanetary vessel waited.
(Vorilhon [Raël] 1998, 50)

This form of narrative is developed and continued by Raël in his interpretation
of the Christian Canon and the life and teachings of Jesus Christ. Instead of simply
dismissing the miraculous events surrounding Jesus, Raël recounts them in accordance with his scientific dispensationalism. An extraterrestrial dimension is given to
the Lord's Prayer and the meaning of "Thy will be done on earth as it is in heaven."
Parables are also juxtaposed upon the new myth presented by Raël; the passage from
Matthew 13 about the farmer who sows seeds now refers to the Elohim attempting
to start life upon other planets.

The resurrection of Jesus occurs with the help of the extraterrestrials, in that he
is taken away in a spaceship after the crucifixion. According to Raël, "The creators
took him away after this last most important phrase: 'At the time of the end . . . if
they shall take up serpents and if they drink any deadly thing, it shall not hurt them;
and they shall lay hands upon the sick and they shall get well.' Mark 16:18" (Vorilhon [Raël] 1998, 70). This interpretation refers to humanity discovering antivenom
serums and antidotes, and developing surgery and so on—as is happening now.

This form of demystification is carried through by Raël to apply to any and all
aspects of humanity. The human body and mind are presented as a machine with no
spiritual component (Vorilhon [Raël] 1987b, 35–54). There is no soul or afterlife,
and any forms of mysticism are viewed as merely developments of the human
senses. The universe is seen as an eternal, infinite place that exists on the micro and
the macro level. According to Raël, within the smallest atoms reside full galaxies and
universes; likewise our universe and cosmos is merely an atom in another cosmos—
there is no beginning or ending and no absolute creator (Vorilhon [Raël] 1987a,
38–41).

The strongest confirmations presented by the Raëlian Movement to validate the
teachings are from three distinct frameworks. The first is similar to that used by
Transcendental Meditation (TM) to confirm the benefits of practicing their form of
meditation. The second relies upon a framework often employed by those seeking
to support a fundamentalist view of creationism, the use of scientific data that challenges the paradigm of evolution or the theory of natural selection.[6] The third

6. The method of relying upon new scientific theories that challenge the scientific paradigm of
evolution to support a fundamentalist belief in creationism has become common. Through this

draws upon recent information concerning scientific advances in the area of cloning, which they believe demonstrates the exactitude of their teachings.

The Raëlian Movement does not go to the same lengths as TM to draw upon research to support their view concerning the benefits of meditation. Instead, the benefits of sensual meditation are presented as a given, and only minor references are made to the scientific confirmation of this practice. A recent publication from the movement made reference to the "Maharishi effect," but instead of mentioning the tests done on TM, the benefits were associated with the Raëlian practice of sensual meditation. Within their teachings, experts sympathetic to the movement also provided testimonials to the benefits of meditation.

The second element of support is presented by Marcel Terruse, a chemical engineer and Bishop Guide of the Raëlian Movement, and it challenges the Darwinian hypothesis of evolution. The argument is made by presenting the scientific findings of Dr. H. J. Muller about the inability of species to mutate, survive, and then reproduce. The Raëlians promote this finding and conclude that "almost all mutations including both those occurring in the wild and provoked in the laboratory result in hereditary illness, deteriorations of survival value and genetic monstrosities."[7] This view is supported by drawing upon other literature in the scientific community that challenges the Darwinian theory, including Jean Rostand's book, *Evolution*.

The argument used to support the Raëlian view of creationism does not attempt to prove that alien beings created humanity but rather develops a polemic against the theory of evolution. The rhetoric used by the group focuses upon the challenges the Darwinian theory has faced by the scientific community itself. Problems in the methodology of the work of Darwin and the apparent inability of species to evolve to other species are used as support for the Raëlians' belief that an outside force is responsible for humanity upon the earth. The argument is problematic from several perspectives. In relation to the manner in which Raël develops it, his time line concerning the creation of humanity 25,000 years ago proves the greatest challenge.

---

method, the group does not try to prove that God created the earth and humanity, but rather to disprove the theory that life developed and evolved upon the planet as outlined by Darwin. This argument has recently allowed for the teaching of creationism as an alternative theory to that of Darwin in some American schools.

7. The source is Marc Terruse's "Obscurantism and the Neo-Darwinian Myth" from the Raëlian Web site home page at http://www.rael.org.

When questioned about life on planet Earth before the Elohim arrived and created humankind, he responded:

> The Elohim have explained that they did not create our planet. When they decided to pursue their experiments of creating life scientifically in a laboratory, they set out to search the universe for a planet which would have a suitable atmosphere, allowing them to work easily. . . . Then they came down on our planet and created the life forms we know, including humans. This means that there could have been on Earth, ten or twenty thousand years ago, other life forms, another creation which could have been destroyed by a natural or an artificial catastrophe. (Vorilhon [Raël] 1987a, 19)

There is no attempt made in the presentation to validate the claims made by Raël about extraterrestrial visitations to the planet. The Raëlian Movement does not attempt to draw upon the pseudoscientific work of writers such as Erich von Däniken. The most current attempt at validation is done by presenting material on recent developments in genetic engineering as a secular confirmation of the belief system. A large majority of the group's literature makes constant reference to the breakthrough done by scientists in cloning a sheep and the potential for cloning human beings.

Raëlians see recent medical breakthroughs as a form of confirmation and new technology as a sign that humanity is developing to become on par with the Elohim. This perspective is stated on the Raëlian Web page:

> Everyday, science is confirming the authenticity of the messages that I was given by the Elohim. In 1973 for example, we created life from inert matter in our laboratories for the first time. One day, without a doubt we will be able to synthesize a human being, bringing us one step closer to what the Elohim scientists did a long time ago, i.e. the creation of a completely artificial being. That day, humanity will have reached "divine" status, the status of creator. Several other recent discoveries anticipate that this moment is not far away. Don't the blind begin to see again thanks to electronic prosthesis? Thanks to telecommunication satellites, is not our voice carried beyond the oceans? Our progress is just as stunning in the domain of the mind.[8]

8. "How Can You Believe What Only One Man Says?" by Raël is from the Raëlian home page at http://www.rael.org.

Cloning

The Raëlian Movement does not present the issue of cloning as an ethical problem even though governments and large numbers of scientists have raised some alarm at this potential scientific development. One clear ethical problem is that the initial concept was developed as a form of genetic engineering. The potential for this practice to continue to develop as a means for the wealthy to abuse this technology to develop and accumulate genetic advantages is extremely problematic. Nor do the Raëlian teachings reveal the difficulties that occurred with the experiment of Dr. Ian Wilmut when he cloned Dolly. The experiment of nucleus transfer techniques used to clone the sheep produced a number of deformities and an extremely high percentage of miscarriages. It took over three hundred attempts to get the one successful birth.[9]

Despite sanctions from governments and an ethical controversy under the guidance of Raël, the movement has founded an international company called Valiant Venture Limited. The company has supplied funding for research and offered perspective clients the opportunity to have their DNA preserved for future cloning. Although still in the development stages, the movement offers several services including Clonaid, Stemaid, Clonapet, and Insuraclone. The prices for the services range from $50,000 to $200,000. The company has a scientific director, Dr. Brigitte Boisselier, and an international public relations person, Sylvie Chabot. Clonaid supports the view presented by Raël, and it pushes past the scientific boundaries developed by current cloning technologies, claiming that the next step in the procedure will be to clone directly an adult without the growing process and to transfer memory and personality into that body—in short, immortality for the cloned.

Although claiming that they have a substantial number of people "on the waiting list" for these services, Clonaid allegedly will not collect any money until it has successfully completed their first human cloning, which according to Jan Wong will never happen. In an investigative report, Wong questioned the current media hype surrounding the Raëlians on the issue of cloning and uncovered a trend in the

---

9. Dr. Brigitte Boisselier, a bishop in the movement, addressed these ethical issues when she represented Clonaid before the congressional hearings. However, her presentation did not explore them in any relevant ethical manner; rather Boisselier dismissed ethical considerations as being nonissues. See http://energycommerce.house.gov/107/hearings/03282001Hearing141/Boisselie204.htm.

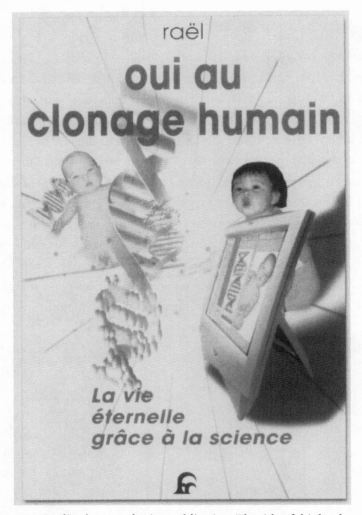

16.1. Raëlian human cloning publication. The title of this book by Raël translates as *Yes to Human Cloning: Eternal Life Thanks to Science*. Raëlians publish material in thirty-three languages. Courtesy of the International Raëlian Movement.

movement to promote themselves as a technologically advanced scientific consortium with the ability to undertake this endeavor, when in reality they are not. Wong argued, "The Raelians have a history of stunning announcements followed by zero results. In 1997, when Dolly the sheep was cloned, the Raëlians said they had more than a million customers and were building a laboratory in the Bahamas. 'It was just a P.O. box,' admits Rael. . . . 'There was nothing.' " (2001, F1)

The once-secret lab that the FDA "raided" is still open and claims to have five scientists working on the human cloning project; they are also planning to take the

FDA to court challenging their jurisdiction over the operation. Any publicity is good publicity. As Wong notes in her report that because of the cloning controversy, the Raëlians have had great press, including appearances on *60 Minutes* and *Good Morning America.*

Currently, the Raëlians are preparing to make inroads into the fertility business. A newer development associated with Clonaid called Ovulaid offered to sell fertile eggs for as low as $5,000 plus a transplantation fee. This is a market with real business potential, and it may become a very lucrative source of income for the group. New religious movements often rely upon donated labor to support their organizations (Bird and Westley 1985), and in this case female members of the group may begin to donate their eggs for free or for a minimal charge to the movement, thus gaining status for their contributions.

In turn, if the Raëlians do develop the facilities, these eggs could be fertilized and implanted for a substantial fee, giving the movement an enormous amount of profit. Their advertisement for this service reads:

THE RIGHT TO CHOOSE THE APPEARANCE OF YOUR FUTURE BABY! OVULAID® will give women and couples the possibility to choose their future babies from a catalog showing the pictures of the egg donor women, and even meet with the candidates before making their final choice so as to judge their personality and intelligence as well as their physical aspect! All will take place in our US laboratory where this is perfectly legal.[10]

The Raëlians claim they have a $500,000 investment in Clonaid made by a father wishing to clone his dead son. The movement itself may have as much as $11,000,000 in capital and property. Nonetheless, in the biotechnology world, all the movement's assets would not be enough to patent a new headache remedy in the United States, let alone get a cloning laboratory operational and staffed. Over the last three years, an anonymous billionaire has spent $3,700,000 trying to have his former dog cloned; all efforts have so far failed. Chances are any operation undertaken by the Raëlians would have the same results, although the cost (both ethical and financial) would be much higher using women to carry the cloned human embryos to term. Most people outside the movement doubt their announcements

---

10. I found the ad on the Clonaid Web site at http://www.clonaid.com/English/pages/home.html, which is no longer available.

about the births of several healthy cloned babies. So far, the group has presented no evidence to substantiate their claim.

Cloning and Creation

The International Raëlian Movement presents itself as a form of secularized religion. According to their teachings, there is no God or gods, only scientists from another planet with the ability to clone. Raël claims in his teachings that science is the "most important thing for all of humanity." He tells his followers, "You will keep in touch with the advances made by scientists, because they can solve all your problems" (Vorilhon [Raël] 1998, 181). The reason for this support of the scientific community is based upon the group's belief that science supports and validates their religious belief system. For confirmation, the movement presents recent advances in medical technology and cloning techniques as a sign of legitimation. Their secularized attempt at portraying their religious myth states that "science should be your religion." They incorporate this perspective throughout their narrative.

Their association and funding for research in cloning becomes the main scientific element recognizable within their practice, but their belief that the human consciousness will be able to be transferred to a fully developed and cloned human body is not shared by the scientific community. On February 13, 2004, South Korean scientists announced that they had achieved the first successful human embryo cloning, and scientists in the field renewed their contentious debate over ethics and the authenticity of the claim. By December 2005, their claims proved fraudulent. There is a very real possibility that human cloning will be achieved in the near future. However, the Raëlians will most likely not be the organization that accomplishes this event. For the Raëlians, cloning is a scientific development that has been used as a rhetorical tool for self-promotion and as a validation of their origin myth. They will continue to patronize this technological development and to associate their group with it to the best of their abilities, garnering free press coverage and wide-scale visibility in the hope of creating interest in their religious group and of increasing membership.

UFO Abduction Support Groups

Who Are the Members?

Christopher D. Bader

Although much has been written about abductees in ufological circles, little research has focused on the social characteristics of abductee support group members themselves. Abductees occupy the sociological intersections of folklore, religion, psychology, and experienced reality. Some band together in support groups to provide comfort to one another and to make sense out of their experiences. This study presents the results of a sociological survey that employed an availability sample of UFO abductee support group members in a specific organization. The chapter provides a brief overview of the UFO abduction movement, followed by a discussion of the method used to gather surveys. The findings of the survey will then be presented along with comparisons to the general population.

Sociologists of religion have often noted a connection between psychotherapeutic movements and the emergence of new religious groups (Bainbridge 1978; Stark and Bainbridge 1985). From a Freudian view, the relationship between religion and psychotherapy has typically been antagonistic in nature. Sigmund Freud (1930, 1961) characterized religion in many ways, none of them flattering. Yet despite the frequent negative portraits of religion painted by Freud and others, certain religious groups and quasi-spiritual therapies trace their origins to psychology, self-help, or psychoanalytic movements.

Numerous therapies today cross the line between religion and psychology. For example, Wilhelm Reich, one of Freud's earliest followers and one-time director of Freud's Psychoanalytic Polyclinic, eventually developed a quasi-religious theory re-

291

garding *orgone*—a mysterious energy given off by all organic beings (Brown 1967; Reiff 1968; Melton, Clark, and Kelly 1990). The theory of orgone energy has become popular amongst more than a few members of the holistic health and New Age movements, some of whom use Reich's "orgone accumulator," a device designed to store the energy for use in treating ailments such as cancer (Melton, Clark, and Kelly 1990). Other groups have mixed the therapeutic with the sacred to create new religious movements (NRMs), such as Scientology (Wallis 1977), the Process Church of the Final Judgment (Bainbridge 1978), Synanon (Ofshe 1980; Stark and Bainbridge 1985), and the Unarius Academy of Science (Tumminia 2005). The New Age Movement (Heelas 1996) itself contains many therapies that blend psychological ideas with various strains of supernatural beliefs such as, for instance, past-life regression therapy. Developed within the context of the Satanism scare of the 1980s (Richardson, Best, and Bromley 1991; Newman and Baumeister 1996; Newman 1997), a survivor's movement and a psychological practice surfaced based on the psychoanalytic notion of repressed memory to treat survivors of alleged satanic ritual abuse (SRA).

Along parallel lines, specific practitioners sought to heal the wounds of alien abduction (Jacobs 2000). In the 1980s, a movement emerged that exhibited a similar combination of the quasi-religious and the psychotherapeutic for so-called UFO abductee survivors. By definition, being abducted means being kidnapped and taken against your will. This movement focused upon healing members from victimization they experienced at the hands of beings with otherworldly, even supernatural, powers. By the mid-1980s, an increasing number of support groups appeared that were centered on UFO abduction (Paley 1997). Using techniques developed in psychotherapeutic circles, such as hypnosis, art therapy, and role-playing, these UFO abductee support groups attempted to help people recover repressed memories of victimization at the hands of extraterrestrials.

Many sociological studies of flying saucer, or UFO, religious groups have appeared over the years (Festinger, Riecken, and Schachter 1956; Wallis 1974; Balch 1995; Tumminia and Kirkpatrick 1995; Tumminia 1998; Bader 1999; Lewis 1995, 2003; Partridge 2003). In fact, Festinger's cognitive dissonance theory was developed upon observations of a small flying-saucer cult. Although there are various case studies of UFO cults with origins in the beliefs of the contactee movement of the 1950s and 1960s (Wallis 1974; Balch 1995; Tumminia 1998, Tumminia and Kirkpatrick 1995; Lewis 2003; Partridge 2003) much less has been written about groups centered on UFO abductions (Whitmore 1995; Bader 1999; Denzler 2001).

The UFO Abduction Movement

Soon after a series of flying-saucer sightings received national attention in the late 1940s, new religious groups appeared that made use of them in their cosmology. UFO religious groups of the 1950s and 1960s, however, differed greatly from the UFO abduction support groups that appeared in the 1980s. The first UFO religious groups were formed by contactees—people who claimed friendly interaction with alien beings (Melton 1995; Lewis 1995; Pope 1998). For example, George Adamski claimed to have met a Venusian named Orthon, who told him that Venusians were visiting to teach earthlings to become more peaceful in their ways (Adamski 1955). Other contactees, such as Orfeo Angelucci, Truman Bethurum, George Van Tassel, and Daniel Fry, soon followed, telling similar stories of contacts with benevolent, godlike extraterrestrials. Some contactees formed groups around themselves, such as George King's Aetherius Society (Wallis 1974) and Ernest Norman's Unarius Science of Life (Tumminia 2005). Others were content to speak at flying-saucer conventions and to peddle books about their experiences.

Since the late 1960s, UFO abduction stories have become one of the most popular genres within UFO subcultures (Whitmore 1995; Denzler 2001). UFO abductees claim to have been kidnapped by extraterrestrial beings and subjected to often humiliating medical procedures. In most cases, the UFO abductees claim that their tormentors have somehow erased memories of the abduction experience (Randle, Estes, and Cone 1999). The first modern abduction account to receive national attention was the experience of Betty and Barney Hill. The Hills claimed to have been kidnapped by alien beings while on the way home from a vacation. Although the couple remembered sighting a strange craft in the sky, it was not until undergoing hypnosis with Benjamin Simon that they began to recover memories that beings from a UFO had captured them and performed a series of medical experiments upon them.

A popular book recounting the couple's reported experiences, *The Interrupted Journey* by John G. Fuller, appeared in 1966. The Hills' story provided the basic template for UFO abductions, although alien abduction narratives (AANs) have evolved to include elements such as sexual encounters with aliens, ongoing abduction experiences, and philosophical discussions with the aliens. The type of beings described by the Hills, diminutive, grey-skinned creatures with large black eyes and oversized craniums, continue to be the most frequently reported. The first modern abduction was that of Antonio Villas-Boas (Spencer 1991), but his tale did not become widely circulated until after the Hills' case achieved recognition.[1] In his alleged 1957 abduction, aliens found him plowing a field on his tractor in the middle of the night. The small humanoids brought him aboard their ship, where he had intercourse with a humanlike woman who barked during the interaction (Thompson 1991).

A famous case from the 1970s had witnesses (Spencer 1991). In 1975, Travis Walton (1978) was cutting wood as part of a seven-person team removing trees in a national park in Arizona. While driving back to their base camp, they encountered a golden UFO. Walton got out of their truck to investigate, and a blue ray of light whisked him away. Walton disappeared for five days. After resurfacing, he passed a lie-detector test in which he described his abductors as large-eyed humanoids with big domed heads.

Throughout the 1970s and into the 1980s, dozens of books appeared recounting UFO abduction experiences (Barry 1978; Fowler 1979; Strieber 1987). While it is not clear when the first UFO abduction support groups appeared, their emergence and popularity were surely increased by the publication of several popular books by artist and UFO researcher Budd Hopkins (Hopkins 1981, 1987). Hopkins argued that UFO abductions were a pervasive problem and advocated the use of hypnosis to recover memories erased by the aliens. Indeed, meetings of abductees at Hopkins's apartment may have been one of the first examples of a support group on UFO abductions as a therapeutic problem.

Hopkins presented an almost entirely negative view of UFO abductions—characterizing the aliens involved as kidnappers and abusers. However, some abductees, such as Whitley Strieber and Betty Andreasson, claimed much more positive encounters with extraterrestrials. Strieber (1987) experienced his contact as frightening but ultimately a type of spiritual union. Andreasson presented a story of abduction that had much in common with the benign tales of the contactees (Fowler 1979). Such divisions about good and bad experiences are reflected in the organized support groups and gatherings that have developed around UFO abductions. Budd Hopkins's Intruder Foundation focuses upon healing the trauma

---

1. According to Denzler (2001, 51), an article about the Villas-Boas case ran in the March 1965 issue of the *Flying Saucer Review* before the celebrated book on the Hills hit the stands. However, many ufologists agree that it to took time for the story to circulate and its significance heightened as the Hill case gained notice. Some modern abductions predate the Hill case, but they were not known until after the Hill publicity. In many of these cases, abductees reconstructed the events years, sometimes decades, after they allegedly occurred.

brought by UFO abductions. Conversely, the former Program for Extraordinary Experience Research (PEER), now the John E. Mack Institute, explored the positive and spiritual aspects of UFO encounters. UFO Contact Center International, however, focuses on a variety of different experiences. Some experiences are entirely positive, from benevolent visits to other planets to meetings with wise alien teachers, while others are entirely negative, from frightening kidnappings to terrifying rapes. Still other abduction narratives represent a mixture of elements.

Given their status as support groups, rather than organized religious bodies, no reliable data exist as to the number of UFO abductees or the number of support groups operating in the United States. In fact, the research on UFO abductees and abduction support groups is very limited, focusing primarily upon historical overviews of the movement or the development of UFO abduction narratives (Bader 1995; Whitmore 1995). The Fund for UFO Research (FUFOR) sponsored psychological tests of nine abductees that, unfortunately, did not provide demographic data (Bloecher, Clamar, and Hopkins 1985).

The UFO Contact Center International

In an attempt to gather sociological data about UFO abductees, I contacted a large UFO abduction support group, the UFO Contact Center International (UFOCCI) in 1989. Aileen Bringle formed the UFOCCI in 1981 after learning of the public scorn and ridicule experienced by abductees. A certified hypnotist, she believed that abductees needed a place to gather and discuss their experiences and that she could help them recover memories erased by the aliens. As stated in a pamphlet produced by the group in 1990:

> The UFOCCI (UFO Contact Center International) was started with the purpose of helping people to examine their bizarre experiences as a result of being abducted by strange beings and taken aboard what we know of as flying discs, commonly called UFO's.

The first UFOCCI center opened in Federal Way, a suburb of Seattle, Washington, but soon expanded to sixty-five affiliate centers around the United States and into Canada. Affiliate centers were largely autonomous—they could decide when and where to hold meetings. In order to facilitate contact between centers, Bringle produced the *Missing Link,* a magazine that contained tips on recovering memories, personal accounts of UFO abductions and contacts, and news and announcements.

The Federal Way UFOCCI met on the fourth Saturday of every month. The typical UFOCCI meeting involved a combination of UFO-related discussion and the sharing of abduction and contact experiences. The group I observed held its monthly gatherings at the community center of a mobile home community. Meetings opened with an overview of recent UFO-related news provided by the group's founder. Participants would then discuss whatever notable UFO sighting, newspaper or magazine article, or television or radio show had captured their interest. When the conversation died down, members were invited to share any recent personal encounters. As one person recounted his or her latest abduction, others would join in, sharing similarities, debating differences, and arguing as to the supposed motivation of the aliens. The abduction narratives discussed at the meetings arose from therapy sessions conducted by the group's founder, Aileen. Any member who felt that he or she had experienced "missing time" (a block of time for which the abductee cannot account) could contact the founder for hypnotic-regression therapy. Through hypnotic regression, the founder believes that she is able to bring to the surface memories that have either been erased by the aliens or are simply too traumatic for the abductee's conscious mind to bear.

UFOCCI members have recovered memories of both positive and negative experiences with aliens through their therapy sessions. Thus, within the same 1996 meeting one member recalled a harrowing account of abduction and humiliating medical experiments at the hands of aliens, while another told of an invitation to board a spacecraft for a tour of the universe. A 1990 group brochure states that two alien races are "particularly frequent visitors" to Earth: the Pleiadians and the Greys. The type of alien encountered generally determined the quality of the experience. Friendly encounters were had with the Pleiadians—"Nordic types; medium builds; pleasant to encounter; by our standards attractive; and advanced in civilization by thousands of years." Negative encounters were typically the work of the Greys, described by the UFOCCI as "small and short, with large heads and large black wraparound eyes." According to the group, Greys "have, and do abduct, at will, many humans for genetic purposes and they observe and monitor us."

Despite such official group statements, the boundaries between positive and negative encounters and between the Greys and the Pleiadians were often unclear in the UFOCCI. Several members reported encounters with both types of aliens, and narratives often included other New Age elements, such as Bigfoot, ghosts, and past lives. For example, at the meeting on June 23, 1990, a UFOCCI member named Clay (pseudonym) discussed his recovered memories, which included an abduction by aliens in a past life. Clay's first memory of this sort is of flying an airplane with engine trouble. The instrument panel contained the date 1933, leading him to believe the experience occurred in a previous life. As Clay struggled to land his plane safely, a large flying saucer appeared alongside, moving close enough for him to observe several "small, gray-skinned creatures" through its windows. The shock of witnessing the craft caused Clay to lose concentration and crash the plane.

Hovering above, Clay found himself viewing his own body and the wreckage. Moments later, his "spirit" was pulled onboard the flying saucer, which then docked with "an enormous mothership." Aboard the ship, Clay noted the presence of Grey aliens and "Nordics" working in concert. His own skin had become "very white," and he was then wearing a "silvery jumpsuit." Two aliens, one humanlike and the other a Grey, led Clay into a small room and seated him in a large recliner whereupon a screen descended from the ceiling and displayed images of his life in brief flashes. From there Clay was shuttled to another flying saucer that "flew past the moon and landed on a blue-green planet." They then led him into another room filled with bodies contained in glass coffins. The aliens placed him in one. Clay's last recovered memory is that of being a baby in a crib with a Grey alien floating above him. He believes that the "Nordics" and Greys reincarnated him into his current body for some as yet unknown "higher purpose."

Administering the Survey

I first approached the UFOCCI in December 1989, asking permission to conduct a survey of group members. To provide incentive, I offered to include questions regarding the types of experiences reported by the abductees and to provide a summary of the findings to the group. Initially, the group refused the request, citing concerns that the findings might be forwarded to a "government agency" or that the government might somehow be able to identify the abductees from the survey. In attempting to survey UFO abductees, I found that many were leery of social scientists for a couple of reasons. First, abductees are frequently the targets of ridicule in the popular media, and the abductees assumed that any survey or research would be used for similar purposes. Many UFO abductees have also developed elaborate conspiracy theories regarding government cover-ups of the reality of UFOs and extraterrestrial life (Bader 1995). Some believed that members of the government would try to silence them, if their stories became public.

However, I was later invited to attend group meetings to make a case for the survey. After attending several group meetings and becoming familiar with the members, I again raised the subject of a survey. I assured members that the questionnaires would be entirely anonymous and that no reported findings would include their city or state of origin. Members were also reminded that they were free to leave blank any item that made them uncomfortable. Upon reviewing the questionnaire, several members of the group agreed to complete it. I was also given permission by the group's leader to contact the UFOCCI's affiliate centers regarding the survey. The head of each affiliate center was contacted by phone and informed about the survey. Approximately one-third of those affiliate centers declined to participate, for one or both of the reasons noted above. Those affiliate centers that agreed were sent the requested number of questionnaires with return postage. Of the 217 surveys eventually distributed, respondents ultimately returned 55.

The survey contained a series of demographic questions, including gender, age, marital status and history, occupation, income, number of children, and religious background. At the group's request, the survey also included several items regarding the abduction experience itself, such as the number of reported abductions, the abductees' feelings about the experience, dates of abductions, and methods used to recover memories.

Previous Research on the Demographics of New Age and Novel Religions

Previous research on participants in the New Age movement and membership in various NRMs suggest some hypotheses as to membership in the UFO abductee groups. Abductee groups show strong extra-institutional supernatural beliefs that coincide with the paranormal, a theme found within New Age groups and new marginal religions. Abductee support memberships are also diffuse—spread out over different support groups and focused on a variety of therapists. The problem of scattered memberships frustrates researchers who study New Age movements because there are no clearly defined boundaries or denominations from which to draw a sample (Lewis 1992).

Using New Agers and NRMs as a model for membership, one should expect the majority of abductees to be female. All types of religious groups tend to have a higher percentage of females than males (Miller and Hoffman 1995; Stark 2002). However, novel religious movements tend to be quite disproportionately female (Stark and Bainbridge 1985; Stark, Bainbridge, and Kent 1981). Participants in New Age activities like astrology also exhibit a disproportionate female-to-male ratio (Feher 1992). Rodney Stark and William Sims Bainbridge (1985) argue that NRMs especially appeal to women because such groups frequently provide a greater opportunity for positions of leadership for females than do traditional religious groups. Further, some New Age groups and movements emphasize female power or aspects of spirituality such as intuition or emotion that are associated with the feminine, thereby attracting more women than men (Mears and Ellison 2000).

Brenda Denzler's research on the UFO community in the United States shows that most writers, speakers, and visible leaders are men. By her count, men constitute 56 percent of general membership. However, she sees a shift in gender composition when it comes to abductees. According to Denzler's nonrandom surveys, 58 percent of abductees are women (2001, 164–65). The reason for this shift in gender composition may be due to the metaphysical bent of abduction beliefs. Then again, firsthand abduction narratives do not require the technical expertise that other parts of ufology utilize, the preoccupation with scientific detail that has traditionally been within the educational focus of men. Presumably, among abductees men's narratives carry no more weight than those of women.

Much of the research on age and participation in New Age movements is based on the particular historical circumstances of the baby-boom generation and increasing interest in Eastern religions in the 1960s (Brown 1992). Daniel P. Mears and Christopher G. Ellison (2002) argue that New Age consumption should be greatest among younger adults, as they will be the most attracted to novel ideas. On the other hand, Stark and Bainbridge (1985) found that subscribers to a popular magazine covering UFOs and New Age/occult topics, *Fate* magazine, skew older than the general population. Thus, the research on participation in New Age movements and consumption of New Age materials does not provide clear hypotheses as to the age distribution of UFO abductees. Research and theory of the effects of marital status on participation in New Age groups is also limited. Mears and Ellison suggest that marital status may be related to consumption of New Age materials. Marriage, they argue, is a socially approved, conventional institution. Therefore, people who reject marriage may also reject conventional ideas and be consequently more likely to express interest in unconventional topics and movements.

The most developed area of theory about the demographics of participation in the New Age and unconventional religious movements centers on socioeconomic/occupational status. For example, Stark and Bainbridge argue that cults tend to recruit disproportionately from the "more favored segments of the population. People with higher levels of education should be more attracted to new religious ideas, since higher education typically involves a greater exposure to the unconventional" (Stark and Bainbridge 1985, 395). Further, Aidan Kelly (1992) argues that NRMs tend to be created by those who express creativity in all other fields—middle-class intellectuals.

Of course, education tends to be highly correlated with occupational status and income. Therefore, we should expect members of NRMs or people expressing interest in New Age topics to come primarily from more prestigious occupations than members of sects or mainline denominations. In her research on Wicca, Margot Adler (1979) found that members of witch covens tended to come primarily from professional and white-collar occupations.

Research on the race/ethnicity of participation in the New Age suggests that participants in such movements are disproportionately white (Roof 1993). Such a finding is not particularly surprising, given the high correlations frequently reported between education, occupation, and race (Sikmus 1978; Wilson 1987). If whites in the United States have significantly higher levels of income, then they should also have higher levels of occupational prestige, greater levels of educational attainment, and hence, fit more closely the profile for cult membership. Denzler's research on the UFO community indicates that it is primarily white (90 percent) (2001, 164).

Comparing UFO Abductees to the General Population

Previous research indicates that if the UFO abduction movement operates similarly to other novel religious groups and New Age movements, their membership should be composed of a disproportionate number of highly educated, middle- to upper-middle-class white females engaged in professional occupations. The following section examines the similarities and differences between UFO abductees and the general population by comparing responses to my survey with the general population as reflected in the General Social Survey (GSS). Because it is not possible to do a random sample of all abductees, there is no way to ascertain whether the existing data are suitable for tests of significance. Therefore, the results are simply presented as raw numbers and percentages alongside data from the 1990 General Social Survey (Davis and Smith 1990). Although it is not possible to test for statistical significance, there are some striking differences between support-group members and the general population.

Gender and Age Breakdowns

The gender breakdown of the UFO abductees conforms to previous research regarding gender and cult membership. A majority of UFO abductees (63 percent) were female. Table 17.1 provides a summary of other demographic findings. The

Table 17.1

Selected Demographic Characteristics of UFO Abductees Compared to General Social Survey (GSS 1990)

	UFO abductees	General Social Survey
Marital Status		
Single	12 (22.6%)	265 (19.3%)
Married	29 (54.7%)	727 (53.0%)
Divorced/separated	10 (18.9%)	208 (15.2%)
Widowed	2 (3.8%)	171 (12.5%)
	$n = 53$	$n = 1,371$
Race		
White	48 (88.9%)	1150 (83.8%)
Black	0 (0.0%)	159 (11.6%)
Other	6 (11.1%)	63 (4.6%)
	$n = 54$	$n = 1,372$
Education		
Less than college	16 (32.0%)	738 (53.8%)
Some college +	34 (68.0%)	632 (46.1%)
	$n = 50$	$n = 1,370$
Occupation		
White-collar	29 (56.9%)	534 (41.6%)
Blue-collar/other[a]	4 (7.8%)	343 (26.7%)
Not in labor force[b]	18 (35.3%)	408 (31.8%)
	$n = 51$	$n = 1,285$

Sources: Author's data and General Social Survey (GSS), 1990.

[a]The blue-collar/other category combines the following job types: blue-collar, farm/forest, and service.

[b]The "not in labor force" category combines the following job statuses: retired, homemaker, student, and unemployed.

age distribution does not aid in the debate over whether members of NRMs will be especially young or especially old, for the differences between the two groups and the general population in age is not striking. The average age of respondents to the 1990 General Social Survey was approximately 46 (45.97). The UFO abductees were slightly younger with an average age of 44 (43.69). Neither of these findings suggests that the ranks of the movement are composed of disproportionate numbers of the young or the old.

Marital Status

The results do not provide strong support for the contention that members of novel religious movements will be primarily composed of people who reject the institution of marriage. The UFO abductees, in fact, closely resemble the general population in marital status. Approximately 23 percent (22.6 percent) of UFO abductees were single, compared to approximately 19 percent (19.3 percent) of respondents of the 1990 General Social Survey. Abductees also show similar proportions of the married, 54.7 percent versus 53 percent in the GSS, and the divorced and separated, 18.9 percent compared to 15.2 percent in the GSS.

Race and Ethnicity

My scrutiny of UFO literature led to the impression that the abduction movement in the United States and Canada was primarily composed of white members. The majority of UFO abduction accounts have been written by or about white females. Although Barney Hill, who was involved in one of the first widely reported UFO abduction cases, was an African American man, his example did not lead to black involvement in the UFO abduction movement. The survey findings confirm this impression taken from the popular literature on abduction. While approximately 12 percent (11.6 percent) of respondents to the General Social Survey were black (closely mirroring the percentage black in the U.S. population), none of the surveyed abductees reported their race as black. In my sample, a substantial majority of UFO abductees (88.9 percent) report their race as "white." This finding resonates with Denzler's results (2001, 165). The remaining 11.1 percent of abductees reported races other than black or white—specifically, the remaining abductees indicated their race as Native American. This is suspect because only 1.5 percent of respondents in the General Social Survey (1990) self-identify as Native American. One explanation is that as a contemporary trend some Americans now indicate that they are Native American when they have only a fraction of heritage. From this sample, UFO abductees appear to be primarily a movement composed of white females.

Education

As with the findings for gender and race, the educational attainment of UFO abductees appears to conform to the membership trends for NRMs. As noted above, previous research suggests as strong relationship between education and interest in novel religious movements. The survey findings suggest that the ranks of UFO abductees are, indeed, drawn from an educated segment of society. About a fourth (22 percent) of respondents to the General Social Survey have not graduated high school. By comparison only twelve percent of UFO abductees said that they do not have high school diplomas. The differences in terms of higher education (having at least attended college) are striking. Less than half (46.1 percent) of respondents to the General Social Survey have attended college. However, the majority of UFO abductees (68 percent) have attended college.

Occupation

In order to compare the occupations of UFO abductees and respondents to the 1990 General Social Survey, those occupations were coded as either white collar, blue collar, farm/forest, or service. Respondents not currently employed were classified as homemakers, students, retired persons, or unemployed.

The findings for UFO abductees suggest that the movement does indeed gather membership from favored segments of the population. Less than half of respondents to the General Social Survey (41.6 percent) reported a white-collar occupation. By comparison, approximately fifty-seven percent (56.9 percent) of abductees reported white-collar jobs. Comparatively few abductees work in blue-collar occupations (7.8 percent versus 17.3 percent in the GSS) and none reported farm/forest or service occupations. A sample of the white-collar occupations reported by UFO abductees includes "electronics technician," "professor," "therapist," and "marketing/sales rep."

Further Characteristics of UFO Abductees

Several items on the survey asked UFO abductees about specific details of their experiences. Betty and Barney Hill, whose story provided the prototype for modern UFO abduction stories, claimed only one abduction experience. With some exceptions, early abductees, such as Travis Walton, also reported singular experiences. Thus, these UFO abductions were akin to being "in the wrong place at the wrong time." More recent UFO abductees, however, report multiple abduction experiences leading to a belief amongst abductees that the extraterrestrials target and continue to follow certain people throughout their lifetimes. Respondents to the UFO abduction survey indicated that they had been abducted an average of ten separate occasions. Because the UFO literature suggests a split in the abduction subculture between those who view the experience as akin to kidnapping/rape and those who see the aliens in a positive light, the survey asked respondents to indicate their feelings about the experiences. The responses from this sample suggest that the subculture may be moving toward a more positive model of UFO abductions. The majority of the respondents (88.2 percent) find at least some positive aspects to the experience (indicating that they feel entirely positive, mostly positive, or a mixture of positive and negative about the abductions).

Conclusion

Although we know much about particular UFO religious groups from available case studies, we know very little about the organization and membership of UFO abduction support groups. If UFOCCI is a reasonable example, we can see that the group allows for a wider range of narratives that go beyond the victim scenario, for example, New Age elements like past lives, Bigfoot, and ghosts. Some narratives could be characterized as contactee narratives, accounts of visitations with supernatural beings. Given that contactees and abductees have substantially different feelings about their experiences—they have views of the aliens ranging from villainous to benevolent—it is surprising that they can belong to the same support groups.

This study attempts to increase the sociological understanding of UFO abduction and contact claims by presenting the results of a survey of abductees. The findings are in line with what researchers know about who is attracted to novel religious movements and with the limited previous research on the membership of the UFO subculture. UFO abductees in the study appear to fit the profile of people who will be attracted to NRMs. The ranks of the UFOCCI consist of mainly middle- to upper-middle-class educated white females. This finding suggests that existing sociological research on NRMs is applicable to the UFO abduction phenomenon.

However, we need further research to confirm this finding. As noted above, fear of victimization and the prevalent use of conspiracy theories make UFO abduction support groups difficult to survey. Further, the lack of a central organization from which to draw a sample of abductees raises the issue of whether any single survey of a UFO abduction support group is representative of abductees in general. If male, nonwhite, or lower-class abductees are simply less likely to join abduction support groups, then our understanding of the movement's membership, and hence our theories of abductees, would be invalid. Clearly, this phenomenon has continued to grow since I first started my study, and more investigations are needed. Thus, it is hoped that these data will spur further research on this movement that mixes the therapeutic and the spiritual—UFO abductees.

APPENDIXES

REFERENCES

INDEX

Some Known Contactee Religions

Aetherius Society: This group derives its name from Venusian Master Aetherius. George King established it during the mid-1950s in England. Aetherius conducts prayer meetings, healing services, and pilgrimages to sacred mountains. The society is headquartered in Hollywood, California, with satellite groups in Europe, Canada, Australia, New Zealand, Ghana, and Nigeria. Its philosophy draws upon the teachings of Theosophy and yogic mysticism by facilitating contact with spiritual teachers from ethereal worlds. See Saliba in James R. Lewis (2003a), which also contains other writings on and by Aetherius.

Ashtar Command: This network of believers around the world was founded on the channeled messages from Ashtar, an ascended master. The believers also communicate with Sananda, the Cosmic Christ. The group synthesizes I AM movement teachings with UFO mythology and George Van Tassel's contact with Ashtar of Venus. It also utilizes the channeled messages of Tuella (the late Thelma B. Turrell). It had about 850 members in the year 2000. Some of its different cells have Web sites. The group was renamed Guardian Action International and then Guardian Activation International. Some independent contactees also channel Ashtar, but they are not part of the Ashtar Command or Guardian Activation International.

Association of Sananda and Sanat Kumara: Sister Thedra (Dorothy Martin, Leon Festinger's Mrs. Keech of *When Prophecy Fails*) channeled messages from Sananda, a name for the New Age Christ. It is now based in Mount Shasta, California.

Cassiopaean Experiment: This "therapy" group is guided by Laura Knight Jadczyk and Arkadiusz Jadczyk. They contact "lizzies"—reptilian hyperdimensional consciousness, whom they say are "not aliens" but part of the collective unconscious. It operates the Quantum Future School, last based in France after moving from Florida.

Chen Tao (Right Way): Hon-Ming Chen, a former sociology teacher, heads Taiwanese millenarians who immigrated to the United States. It predicted that Christ would come in a spaceship in 1998 and again in 1999. The group subsequently moved to New York.

Fiat Lux: Uriella (Erika Bertschinger Eike), who serves as a trance medium for Jesus and

Mary, leads this German community of believers. The group believes the end time is near. At that juncture, extraterrestrials will evacuate the faithful on mother ships, and a new paradise called Amora will manifest on our planet. Founded in 1980, it has about 135 committed members and hundreds of sympathizers. See Partridge (2003, 2004).

Guardian Activation International: See **Ashtar Command.**

Heaven's Gate: Once known as Human Individual Metamorphosis, the small collective is now infamous for its group suicide in 1997 in Rancho Santa Fe, a suburb of San Diego, California. By dying, members planned to board a spaceship hidden in tail of the Comet Hale-Bopp. It began in 1974 with Marshall Herff Applewhite and Bonnie Nettles, who called themselves Bo and Peep, The Two. See Balch and Taylor (2003), also Lewis in Partridge (2003).

International Raëlian Movement: Also known as the Raëlian Religion, this is the largest contactee religion. Led by Raël (Claude Vorilhon), it promotes cloning and sexual freedom, even an acceptance of homosexuality. It calls itself the Raëlian Revolution, an atheist educational group that promotes scientific creationism. The members believe in the Elohim, creator scientists and space travelers. The International Raëlian Movement has church status in Canada, where it is called the Raëlian Religion. While the Raëlian Web site says the teachings are atheistic, a better description might be nontheistic (like Buddhism). See Palmer (2004) and Chryssides in Partridge (2003).

Mark-Age: Charles Boyd Gentzel (1922–1981) and Pauline Sharpe (1925–2005) established this group in 1960. In 1981, Sharpe, called Nada-Yolanda, became executive director and president of the spiritual-educational organization, which she remained until her death. Gentzel was known as Mark. After his death, he sent channeled messages as El Morya, Chohan of the First Ray of Will and Power. The group once channeled messages from Gloria Lee, El Morya, and JFK, among others. It expects the Second Coming, aided by extraterrestrial intelligence. It is now located in Pioneer, Tennessee.

New Ground Crew at Mount Shasta: This group's members channel Adama, spiritual leader of the Lemurian city Telos, which exists underneath Mount Shasta.

Nibiruan Council: The council is headed by "crystal-clear" channel Jelaila Starr (Joscelyn Kelley) in Kansas City, Missouri. The "walk-in" Jelaila contacts a ninth-dimensional cat race and guide called Devin. (A walk-in is a high extraterrestrial spirit who takes over a human body, giving it extraordinary power and knowledge.) The planet Nibiru (which is also Zecharia Sitchin's twelfth planet in the solar system) trained her as a galactic messenger and to do DNA recoding for starseed followers (descendants of positive extraterrestrials).

Pana-Wave Laboratory: This Japanese group established by the prophetess Chino Yuko in 1977 is also known as Chino Shoho (True Law of Chino Yuko). The group of about forty members wear white because of the belief that their leader is being attacked by electromagnetic waves directed by evil forces (Murguia 2005; Dorman 2005); white supposedly repels such waves. Murguia reports the group is based on pseudoscience and spiritualist channeling. In 2005, a Japanese court fined some members for a beating that resulted in the death of another member.

Planetary Activation Organization: This group was founded in 1997, having grown out of the Ground Crew Project that started in 1980s with the teachings of Sheldon Nidle and his telepathic communication with the Galactic Federation. The group prophesized the landing of 10,000 space ambassadors in 1997.

Solar Logos Foundation: This mediation group is located in Santa Barbara, California. Its philosophy is based on the teachings of Norman Paulsen and Kriya Yoga. It has a peripheral interest in UFOs.

Solar Temple: The International Chivalric Order Solar Tradition was founded in 1984 by Luc Jouret. It emerged from the Foundation Golden Way led by Joseph Di Mambro. Its beliefs say that Cosmic Masters conceive babies with humans. After death, followers will go to a planet near Sirius. It is responsible for some group suicides and murders of members in Quebec, Switzerland, and France in 1994, 1995, and 1997. About thirty members survive.

Summum: Former Mormon elder Claude Rex Nowell started the group in Salt Lake City, Utah, after contact with the Summa extraterrestrials in the mid-1970s. It advocates mummification, sexual ecstasy, and meditation.

Teaching Mission: A grassroots movement of study groups using *The Urantia Book,* which is not officially connected to the Urantia Foundation or Urantia Fellowship. Started in 1991, the breakaway group teaches contacteeism with celestial personalities. The Teaching Mission distributes transcripts of these contacts and sometimes refers to UFOs. Followers believe their celestial teachers are altering their DNA and their "deep minds."

Unarius Academy of Science: This group was founded by Ernest and Ruth Norman (Uriel) in 1954; it is located in El Cajon, California, outside San Diego. Its classes teach past-life therapy and interdimensional physics. Ernest Norman was Jesus in a past life, and Ruth Norman was Mary of Bethany, the thirteenth apostle. The group prophesized a space-fleet landing of Space Brothers in 2001. It has about sixty committed members and a few hundred less-involved correspondence students. Satellite groups study the teachings in the Toronto area and in distant Nigeria. See Tumminia (2005).

United Nuwaubian Nation of Moors: Black messiah Dwight "Malachi Z" York, supposedly from the Planet Rizq, heads this embattled group. Its fusion of black nationalism with interplanetary theology and origin myths form the content of its teachings. In 2003, York predicted a spaceship would come to pick up followers. In April 2004, a judge sentenced him to 135 years in prison on the charge of molesting thirteen children in the group. The court ordered the surrender of property in New York and Georgia, as well as considerable cash holdings. See Gabriel in Partridge (2003).

Universal Industrial Church of the New World Comforter: This church was founded in

1973–74 on the channeled messages of Allen Michael. Members believe they are trained entities of the Galactic Command Space Complex who have reincarnated into special bodies of the Andromeda Strain. Placentia is the Galactic name for planet Earth. Its One World Family Commune resides in Santa Rosa, California. It is the smallest contactee religion with about ten very committed members.

Universariun Foundation: In 1958, Zelrun and Daisy Karsleigh established this group in Portland, Oregon. The foundation publishes a magazine and has a sanctuary in Tucson, Arizona.

Urantia: This loosely structured network of study groups is associated with *The Urantia Book,* first published in 1955 (see Sarah Lewis in Partridge 2003). Urantia is the book's name for planet Earth. Fans of the book are not organized into one organization. The Urantia Foundation is based in Chicago, and the Urantia Fellowship operates out of New York. The fellowship and the foundation have more public recognition than the Teaching Mission, which is a splinter movement. Purportedly, the first contents of the book came from divinely revealed messages in 1911. In 2001, the Urantia Foundation lost its copyright on the book, which is now part of public domain. Urantia's cosmology involves multileveled celestial beings governed by the I AM. Followers once experienced a failed prophecy of atomic war. Some scholars classify it as a UFO religion, although it probably fits better into the New Age category. The group is difficult to classify because it has no specific rituals, like other religions do.

Some Types of Aliens

Accounts and descriptions vary.

Alphas: Shy; short with pointed ears and big eyes; playful demeanor.

Angels: Numerous beings from other planets described as angelic, radiating light; Ruth Norman of Unarius is revered as Uriel the Archangel.

Ascended masters or **Cosmic Masters:** Advanced minds and souls who communicate wisdom; commonly featured in contactee religions, like Aetherius, Unarius, and Ashtar Command. Terms vary in different groups. The Aetherius Society contacts Master Aetherius and Master Jesus on Venus.

Arcturians: Mentioned by Edgar Cayce. A fifth-dimensional advanced civilization that teaches love. Work with ascended masters called the Brotherhood of All; travel in spaceships powered by crystals; short and greenish with large almond eyes.

Betas: Advanced, tall Aryan-looking humanoids that look similar to Nordics, but have only benevolent feelings toward humans. Certain Betas come from Venus and are Space Brothers.

Beta-2: Humanoids with pointed chins, thick lips, and dark complexion; can have "Asian-looking eyes" (epicanthic fold on eyes); rude, rough, and secretive. Sometimes reported in Men-in-Black incidents.

Beta-F: Spiritual females who appear to be like the Virgin Mary, Hindu Kumaris, or goddesses.

Christ Beings: Several contactee religions speak with beings often described as Christ or Christlike. For example, Sananda was such a being in the Association of Sananda and Sanat Kumara. Also in Chen Tao.

Chupacabra: Means "goat sucker," a devilish creature in Puerto Rican folklore, sometimes associated with UFOs, that drains animals of blood. Cited in some alien mischief narratives.

Clarionites: Some early contactees, like Truman Bethurum and Dorothy Martin, talked with beings from the planet Clarion, a utopian world that is free from war. Bethurum met the beautiful Aura Rhanes, who captained a saucer, and he described her as "tops in shapeliness and beauty." Claronites resemble Space Brothers.

Deltas: Monsterlike creatures; for example, alien dogs.

Elohim: Advanced space travelers. Raël and Allen Michael use this term for the godlike beings who cloned humankind in their image. References to Elohim appear in the Bible, in the book of Genesis.

Gammas: Hairy bipeds, like Sasquatch, the Himalayan yeti (abominable snowman), or Big Foot.

Greys: Sometimes spelled *grays*. The most common alien reported in abduction narratives; can be one of three types, which come in different colors:

Type A: Coming from the Zeta Reticuli system, neighboring Orion. Orange Greys are best known in New Mexico and Nevada. They stand four and a half feet tall with wrap-around eyes; use human tissue for various purposes; some involved in breeding with humans.

Type B: Tall with large noses; from Orion; have advanced technology.

Type C: Shortest of the three; hostile to humans.

Humanoids: Mentioned in abduction narratives. Have fair skin and light-colored hair. Three types:

Type A: Have been abducted by Greys or are their half-breed offspring. They obey Greys.

Type B: Progenitors of humans from the Pleiades who tried to help humans but were turned away.

Type C: From Sirius; highly spiritual and want to be helpful.

Martians: Appearance depends on the eyes of their beholders. Early fantasy and science fiction depicted people and beings living on Mars. Portrayed in grotesque ways by Hollywood moviemakers, they are also described as ascended masters with advanced civilizations, depending on the contactee. Various early contactees met with them or communicated telepathically with them; some contactees took astral flights to Mars. A similar theme also applies to contacts with other planets, like Venus.

Mantis-Types: Looks like a big hungry praying mantis.

Mothmen: Creatures sighted first in 1960s and described in different ways: bat-winged, glowing red eyes, sometimes headless. They attack humans.

Nordics: Sometimes travel with Greys; mentioned in some alien abductions. Blond, fair, and tall Aryan humanoid types; their physical appearance can also fit that of Space Brothers.

Pleiadeians: Some contemporary contactees speak with them. Highly advanced, friendly, attractive, benevolent. May have seeded Earth with their genetic type.

Reptoids or **Reptilians:** Tall race of scaly creatures; highly advanced but hostile. Forced out of their home planet. Some say that they are from Planet Nibiru and that they were ancient astronauts. Possible gods of some cultures, i.e., the Dogon. Some Type-A Greys serve Reptoids. Many live underground, and they are cited as the culprits in some alien abductions.

Space Brothers: Term used in some contactee groups to refer to celestial beings whose mission is to improve humankind; for example, the Adamski Foundation and Unarius are among the groups that use this term. Many look like Betas. They communicate through clairvoyant inspiration.

Starseeds: Descendants of positive extraterrestrials, who are living as ordinary human beings and who are unaware of their parentage. Some groups help people find out if they are starseeds or reprogram DNA to starseed specifications.

Ultraterrestrials: A name given to extraterrestrials from a higher dimension. Their ships and bodies cross the dimensional void by using energy fields. Can appear halographically or telepathetically. According to John Keel, they are negative beings who want to enslave humans. Some fundamentalist Christian groups say that extraterrestrials do Satan's work and that they are really the fallen angels described in the apocryphal text *The Book of Enoch.*

Venusians: Some Venusians appear in human form and have spaceships (e.g., George Adamski's Orthon or Frank E. Stranges's Commander Valiant Thor). Some contactees say they met Venusians and have photos of them.

Venusian Masters: Guy Ballard's twelve contacts, called Lords of the Flame (a concept from Theosophy). Similar to the ascended masters. Some contactees communicate with Venusian Masters telepathically or take astral flights to Venus.

Walk-Ins: Alien beings who take over human bodies, usually to impart "higher knowledge." A term used to legitimate some contactees, for example, Jelaila Starr of the Nibiruan Council.

Zetas: Those from the Zeta Reticuli system, neighboring Orion, who are mentioned in some alien abductions, like the Betty and Barney Hill incident. Sometimes look like Greys.

References

Abrahamson, Charles, ed. 1994. *The Holy Mountains of the World: Charged in Operation Starlight.* Los Angeles, Calif.: Aetherius Society.

Adamski, George. 1955. *Inside the Space Ships.* New York: Abelard-Schuman.

Adler, Margot. 1979. *Drawing Down the Moon.* New York: Viking.

Aetherius Society. 1974. *The Twelve Blessings (The Cosmic Concept for the New Aquarian Age as Given by the Master Jesus in His Overshadowing of George King).* Los Angeles, Calif.: Aetherius Society.

————. 1996. Aetherius Society home page, http://www.aetherius.org. Accessed Dec. 28.

Aharon, Y. N. Ibn. 1957. "Diagnosis: A Case of Chronic Fright." *Saucer News* 4, no. 5:3–6.

Aho, James A. 1997. "The Apocalypse of Modernity." In *Millennium, Messiahs, and Mayhem,* edited by Thomas Robbins and Susan J. Palmer, 61–72. New York: Routledge.

Alexander, Victoria. 1994. "The Alexander UFO Religious Crisis Survey: The Impact of UFOs and Their Occupants on Religion." Las Vegas: Bigelow Foundation.

————. 2003. "Extraterrestrial Life and Religion." In *Encyclopedic Sourcebook of UFO Religions,* edited by James R. Lewis, 359–70. Amherst, N.Y.: Prometheus Books.

Alford, Alan. 1997. *Gods of the New Millennium: Scientific Proof of Flesh and Blood Gods.* London: Hodder and Stoughton.

————. 2000. *When the Gods Came Down: The Catastrophic Roots of Religion Revealed.* London: Hodder and Stoughton.

Andersson, Pia. 2000. "Ancient Astronauts." In *UFOs and Popular Culture: An Encyclopedia of Contemporary Mythology,* edited by James R. Lewis, 20–25. Santa Barbara, California: ABC-Clio.

Anonymous. 1954. "Another Flying Saucer Convention." *APRO Bulletin,* July, 13.

Anonymous Conference Attendees. 1999. Mutual UFO Network's Annual Symposia, Arlington, Va., July 4.

Arnold, Kenneth. 1950. *The Flying Saucer as I Saw It.* Boise, Ida.: Kenneth Arnold.

Ashkenazi, Michael. 1992. "Not the Sons of Adam: Religious Responses to ETI." *Space Policy* 8, no. 4:341–49.

Bacon-Smith, Camille. 1992. *Enterprising Women: Television Fandom and the Creation of Popular Myth.* Philadelphia: Univ. of Pennsylvania Press.

Bader, Christopher. 1995. "The UFO Contact Movement from the 1950s to the Present." *Studies in Popular Culture* 17, no. 2.

———. 1999. "When Prophecy Passes Unnoticed: New Perspectives on Failed Prophecy." *Journal for the Scientific Study of Religion* 38, no. 1: 119–31.

———. 2003. "Supernatural Support Groups: Who Are the UFO Abductees and Ritual-Abuse Survivors." *Journal for the Scientific Study of Religion* 42, no. 4:669–78.

Bainbridge, William Sims. 1978. *Satan's Power: Ethnography of a Deviant Psychotherapy Cult.* Berkeley: Univ. of California Press.

Balch, Robert W. 1995. "Waiting for the Ships: Disillusionment and the Revitalization of Faith in Bo and Peep's UFO Cult." In *The Gods Have Landed: New Religions from Other Worlds,* edited by James R. Lewis, 137–66. Albany: State Univ. of New York Press.

Balch, Robert W., and David Taylor. 1978. "Seekers and Saucers: The Role of the Cultic Milieu in Joining a UFO Cult." In *Conversion Careers,* edited by James T. Richardson, 43–65. Beverly Hills, Calif.: Sage Publications.

———. 2003. "Heaven's Gate: Implication for the Study of Commitment to New Religions." In *Encyclopedic Sourcebook of UFO Religions,* edited by James R. Lewis, 261–80. Amherst, N.Y.: Prometheus Books.

Banaji, Mahzarin R., and John F. Kihlstrom. 1996. "The Ordinary Nature of Alien Abduction Memories." *Psychological Inquiry* 7:132–35.

Bang, Sturla. 1996. *The Truth Is Out There: UFO som del av en religiøs verdensforst else.* Ph.D. thesis, Univ. of Bergen, Norway.

Barker, Eileen. 1981. "Science as Theology: The Theological Functioning of Western Science" In *The Sciences and Theology in the Twentieth Century,* edited by A. R. Peacocke, 262–28. London: Oriel Press.

———. 1991. "King, George." In *Who's Who in World Religions,* edited by John R. Hinnels. London: Macmillan.

———. 1993. "Charismatization: The Social Production of an Ethos Propitious to the Mobilization of Sentiments." In *Secularization, Rationalism and Sectarianism,* edited by Eileen Barker, James A. Beckford, and Karel Dobbelaere, 181–201. Oxford: Clarendon Press.

Barker, Gray. 1953. "The Monster and the Saucer." *Fate* 6, no. 1:12–17.

———. 1955. "The End of the World." *The Saucerian* 3, no. 2:55–60.

———. 1976. *Gray Barker at Giant Rock.* Clarksburg, W.V.: Saucerian Publications.

Barkun, Michael. 2003. *A Culture of Conspiracy: Apocalyptic Visions in Contemporary America.* Berkeley: Univ. of California Press.

Barry, Bill. 1978. *Ultimate Encounter.* New York: Pocket Books.

Bartholomew, Robert E. 1989. "The Romantic versus Enlightenment Debate Within the Social Sciences" Ph.D. diss., Flinders Univ. of South Australia.

Bartholomew, Robert E., Keith Basterfield, and George S. Howard. 1991. "UFO Abductees and Contactees: Psychopathology or Fantasy Proneness?" *Professional Psychology: Research and Practice* 22, no. 3:215–22.

Bartholomew, Robert E., and George S. Howard. 1998. *UFOs and Alien Contact: Two Centuries of Mystery.* Amherst, N.Y.: Prometheus Books.

Basterfield, Keith. 2002 "Waking Paralysed: Abduction or Sleep Paralysis?" http://homepage.powerup.com.au/~tkbnetw/Keith_Basterfield_3.htm.

Beckley, Timothy Green, ed. 1970. *The People of the Planet Clarion.* Clarksburg, W.V.: Saucerian Books.

Bell, Art, and Whitley Strieber. 2000. *The Coming Global Superstorm.* New York: Pocket Star.

Benford, Robert D., and David A. Snow. 2000. "Framing Processes and Social Movements: An Overview and Assessment." *Annual Review of Sociology* 26:611–39.

Berger, Peter L. 1967. *The Sacred Canopy: Elements of the Sociology of Religion.* Garden City, N.Y.: Doubleday.

Berger, Peter L., and Thomas Luckmann. 1967. *The Social Construction of Reality.* Garden City, N.Y.: Doubleday.

Bergier, Jacques. 1973. *Extraterrestrial Visitations from Prehistoric Times to the Present.* Scarborough: Meridian Books.

Berlioz, Jacques. 1990. "L'homme au crapaud: Génèse d'un *exemplum* medieval." In *Tradition et histoire dans la culture populaire,* 170–203. Grenoble: Centre alpin et rhodanien d'ethnologie.

Berlitz, Charles, and William L. Moore. 1980. *The Roswell Incident: The Classic Study of UFO Contact.* New York: Berkeley.

Besant, Annie, and Charles W. Leadbeater. 1913. *Man—Whence, How and Whither: A Record of Clairvoyant Investigations.* Los Angeles: Theosophical Publishing House.

Bethurum, Truman. 1954. *Aboard a Flying Saucer.* Los Angeles: DeVorss and Company.

Bird, Fredrick, and Frances Westley. 1985. "The Economic Strategies of New Religious Movements." *Sociological Analysis* 46, no. 2:157–70.

Bishop, Gregory, and Ken Thomas. 1999. "Calling Occupants." *Fortean Times* 118 (Jan.): 28–31.

Blackmore, Susan. 1998. "Abduction by Aliens or Sleep Paralysis?" CSICOP. http://www.csicop.org/si/9805/abduction.html.

Bloecher, Ted, Aphrodite Clamar, and Budd Hopkins. 1985. *Final Report on the Psychological Testing of UFO "Abductees."* Mt. Rainier, Md.: Fund for UFO Research.

Bloor, David. 1976. *Knowledge and Social Imagery.* London: Routledge and Kegan Paul.

Bloor, Michael J. 1988. "Notes on Member Validation." In *Contemporary Field Research: A Collection of Readings,* edited by Robert M. Emerson, 156–72. Prospect Heights, Ill.: Waveland Press.

Blumrich, Josef F. 1974. *The Spaceships of Ezekiel.* New York: Bantam Books.

Bottoms, B. L., and S. L. Davies. 1997. "The Creation of Satanic Ritual Abuse." *Journal of Social and Clinical Psychology* 16:112–32.

Boureau, Alain. 1990. "L'église médiévale comme preuve animée de la croyance chrétienne." *Terrain* 14:113–18.

Bower, Bruce. 2005. "Night of the Crusher: The Waking Nightmare of Sleep Paralysis Propels People into a Spirit World." *Science News Online* 168, no. 2:27.

Bowers, Kenneth S., and John D. Eastwood. 1996. "On the Edge of Science: Coping with UFOlogy Scientifically." *Psychological Inquiry. An International Journal of Peer Commentary and Review* 7, no. 2:136–40.

Bremond, C., J. Le Goff, and J. C. Schmitt. 1982. *L'exemplum.* Turnhout-Belgium: Brepols.

Brookesmith, Peter. 1998. *Alien Abductions.* New York: Barnes and Noble.

Brown, J. A. C. 1967. *Freud and the Post-Freudians.* Baltimore: Penguin.

Brown, Susan L. 1992. "Baby Boomers, American Character, and the New Age: A Synthesis." In *Perspectives on the New Age,* edited by James R. Lewis and J. Gordon Melton, 87–96. Albany: State Univ. of New York Press.

Bryan, Courtland D. 1995. *Close Encounters of the Fourth Kind: Alien Abduction, UFOs, and the Conference at MIT.* New York: Knopf.

Buckner, H. Taylor. 1966. "Flying Saucers Are for People." *Trans-Action* 3, no. 4:10–13.

———. 1968. "The Flying Saucerians: An Open Door Cult." In *Sociology in Everyday Life,* edited by Marcello Truzzi, 223–31. Englewood Cliffs, N.J.: Prentice Hall.

Buffalo Courier-Express. 1954. "Scoff at Saucers? You'll Be Sorry." Dec. 18.

Bullard, Thomas E. 1982. *The Airship File.* Bloomington, Ind.: Thomas E. Bullard.

———. 1987a. *Stolen Time: A Summary of a Comprehensive Study of the Abduction Mystery.* Washington, D.C.: Fund for UFO Research.

———. 1987b. *UFO Abductions: The Measure of a Mystery.* Mt. Rainier, Md.: Fund for UFO Research.

———. 1989. "UFO Abduction Reports: Supernatural Kidnap Narrative Returns in Technological Guise." *Journal of American Folklore* 102:148–70.

———. 2000a. "Forward: UFOs—Folklore of the Space Age." In *UFOs and Popular Culture: An Encyclopedia of Contemporary Myth,* edited by James R. Lewis. Santa Barbara, Calif.: ABC-CLIO.

———. 2000b. "UFOs: Lost in the Myths." In *UFOs and Abductions: Challenging the Borders of Knowledge,* edited by David M. Jacobs, 141–91. Lawrence: Univ. of Kansas Press.

Bulliet, C. J. 1956. *Venus Castina.* New York: Bonanza Books.

Burakowska, Joanna. 1999. "UFO Kongres na Sardynii." *Nieznany Świat* 10, no. 106:36–41.

Cantril, Hadley, Hazel Gaudet, and Herta Herzon. 1940. *Invasion from Mars.* Princeton: Princeton Univ. Press.

Carlotto, M. J. 1991. *The Martian Enigmas: A Closer Look.* Berkeley, Calif.: North Atlantic Books.

Center for UFO Studies. 2002a. "Center for UFO Studies." Feb. 3. http://www.cufos.org.

———. 2002b. "News Flash." Feb. 3. http://www.cufos.org/newsflash.htm.

Chaloupek, Henri. 1997. *Les Débuts de l'ufologie en France: Souvenirs d'un soucoupiste.* Le Vaudoué: Lumières dans la Nuit.

Chevalier, Gérald. 1986. "Parasciences et procédés de légitimation." *Revue française de Sociologie* 27:205–19.

Cheyne, J. A. 2003. "Sleep Paralysis and the Structure of Waking-Nightmare Hallucinations." *Dreaming* 13, no. 3:163–79.

Cheyne, J. A., I. R. Newby-Clark, and S. D. Rueffer. 1999. "Relations among Hypnagogic and Hypnopompic Experiences Associated with Sleep Paralysis." *Journal of Sleep Research* 8, no. 4:313–17.

Childress, David Hatcher. 2000a. "The Evidence for Ancient Atomic Warfare." *Nexus* 7, no. 5:49–56.

———. 2000b. *Technology of the Gods: The Incredible Sciences of the Ancients.* Stelle, Ill.: Adventures Unlimited Press.

Clancy, Susan A. 2005 *Abducted: How People Come to Believe They Were Kidnapped by Aliens.* Cambridge, Mass.: Harvard Univ. Press.

Clancy, Susan A., Richard J. McNally, Daniel L. Schacter, Mark F. Lenzenweger, and Roger K. Pitman. 2002. "Memory Distortion in People Reporting Abduction by Aliens." *Journal of Abnormal Psychology* 111, no. 3:455–61.

Clark, Jerome. 1998. *The UFO Encyclopedia.* 2d ed. Detroit: Omnigraphics.

———. 2000. *Extraordinary Encounters.* Santa Barbara, Calif.: ABC-CLIO.

Clark, S. E., and Elizabeth F. Loftus. 1996. "The Construction of Alien Abduction Memories." *Psychological Inquiry* 7, 140–43.

Clendinnen, Inga. 1987. *Ambivalent Conquests: Maya and Spaniard in Yucatan: 1517–1570.* New York: Cambridge Univ. Press.

Clinton Daily News. 1954a. "Laughs—No Alarm—After Saucer Tale." Sept. 19.

———. 1954b. "Woman Says She's Visited by Man from 'Another World.' " Sept. 17.

Clonaid Web site. 2004. http://www.clonaid.com.

Coleman, Tim. 1999. "Discoveries at the Giza Plateau: Solving the Sphinx Enigma." *UFO Magazine* 14, no. 6:32–45.

Collins, Andrew. 1998. *Gods of Eden: Egypt's Lost Legacy and the Genesis of Civilization.* London: Headline.

Collins, Harry M., and Trevor J. Pinch. 1979. "The Construction of the Paranormal: Nothing Unscientific Is Happening." In *On the Margins of Science: The Social Construction of Rejected Knowledge,* edited by Roy Wallis, 237–70. Keele, U.K.: Univ. of Keele.

Condon, Edward U., and Daniel S. Gillmor. 1969. *Final Report of the Scientific Study of Unidentified Flying Objects.* New York: Dutton.

"Contact." n.d., ca. 1979. Special issue, *Vaucluse Ufologie,* no. 2:19.

Corso, Philip J., and William J. Birnes. 1997. *The Day after Roswell.* New York: Pocket Books.

Cotterell, Maurice. 1996. *The Mayan Prophecies: Unlocking the Secrets of a Lost Civilization.* Dorset, U.K.: Element.

Cremo, Michael. 1998. Untitled lecture, New Hampshire Mutual UFO Network Presents World Famous Speakers. Portsmouth, N.H., Nov. 8.

Cremo, Michael, and Richard Thompson. 1996. *Forbidden Archaeology: The Hidden History of the Human Race.* Los Angeles: Bhaktivedanta Book Publishing.

Croke, Brian. 1981. "Two Early Byzantine Earthquakes and Their Liturgical Commemoration." *Byzantion* 51:122–47.

Damrell, Joseph. 1977. *Seeking Spiritual Meaning: The World of Vedanta.* Beverly Hills, Calif.: Sage Publications.

Davis, Isabel L. 1957. "Meet the Extraterrestrial." *Fantastic Universe,* Nov., 31–59.

Davis, James Allan, and Tom W. Smith. 1990. *General Social Survey 1990.* Storrs, Conn.: Roper Center for Public Opinion Research, Univ. of Connecticut.

Dean, Jodi. 1996. "Coming Out as an Alien: Feminists, UFOs and the Oprah Effect." In *"Bad Girls"/"Good Girls": Women, Sex and Power in the Nineties,* edited by Nan Bauer Maglin and Donna Perry, 90–105. New Brunswick, N.J.: Rutgers Univ. Press.

———. 1998. *Aliens in America: Conspiracy Cultures from Outerspace to Cyberspace.* Ithaca, N.Y.: Cornell Univ. Press.

Dean, Robert. 1997. Untitled lecture. Roswell UFO Encounter, Roswell, N.M., July 5.

de Brosses, Marie-Thérèse. 1979. "Huit jours avec les boules qui parlent." *Paris-Match* 21 (Dec.): 86–89.

Dégh, L. 1977. "UFOs and How Folklorists Should Look at Them." *Fabula* 18:242–48.

Denzler, Brenda. 2001. *The Lure of the Edge: Scientific Passions, Religious Beliefs, and the Pursuit of UFOs.* Berkeley: Univ. of California Press.

Dolby, R. G. A. 1979. "Reflections on Deviant Science." In *On the Margins of Science: The Social Construction of Rejected Knowledge,* edited by Roy Wallis, 9–47. Sociological Monograph Series 21. Keele, U.K.: Univ. of Keele.

Doniger, Wendy. 1988. *Other People Myths: The Cave of Echoes.* New York: Macmillan.

Dorman, Benjamin. 2005. "Pana-Wave: The New Aum Shinrikyo or Another Moral Panic?" *Nova Religio* 8, no. 3:83–103.

Douglas, Jack. 1976. *Investigative Research: Individual and Team Research.* Beverly Hills, Calif.: Sage Publications.

Downing, Barry. 1968. *The Bible and Flying Saucers.* New York: Lippincott.

Druffel, Ann. 1998. *How To Defend Yourself Against Alien Abduction.* London: Judy Piatcus Publishers.

Dunn, Christopher. 1998. *The Giza Power Plant: Technologies of Ancient Egypt.* Santa Fe: Bear and Company.

Eberhart, George M. 1986. *UFOs and the Extraterrestrial Contact Movement: A Bibliography.* 2 vols. Metuchen, N.J.: Scarecrow Press.

"Editorial." 1978. Special issue, *Vaucluse Ufologie,* no. 8 (May 1978).

Edwards, Carolyn Pope. 2000. "Children Play in Cross-Cultural Perspective: A New Look at the Six Cultures Study." *Cross Cultural Research* 34, no. 4:318–38.

Eliade, Mircea. 1975a. *Myth and Reality.* New York: Harper and Row.

———. 1975b. *Myths, Dreams and Mysteries: The Encounter Between Contemporary Faiths and Archaic Realities.* New York: Harper Torchbooks.

Ellis, B. 2001. *Aliens, Ghosts, and Cults: Legends We Live.* Jackson: University Press of Mississippi.

Ellwood, Robert S. 1973. *Religious and Spiritual Groups in America.* Englewood Cliffs, N.J.: Prentice Hall.

———. 1983. "The American Theosophical Synthesis." In *The Occult in America: New Historical Perspectives,* edited by Howard Kerr and Charles L. Crow, 111–34. Urbana: Univ. of Illinois Press.

Emerson, Robert M., ed. 1988. *Contemporary Field Research: A Collection of Readings.* Prospect Heights, Ill.: Waveland Press.

Emerson, Robert M., and Melvin Pollner. 1988. "On the Uses of Members' Responses to Researchers' Accounts." *Human Organization* 47, no. 3:189–98.

Ensia, Pierre. 1974. "Les contactés." *Ouranos* 13, no. 4:5–6.

Esterle, A., M. Jimenez, J. P. Rospars, P. Teyssandier, and D. Audrerie. 1981. "A propos d'une disparition." In *Enquête GEPAN* no. 79/07, Note technique no. 6, CNES-GEPAN, Mar. 31.

Evans, Hilary. 1982a. "Fact, Fraud or Fantasy?" *The Unexplained* 8, no. 93:1854–57.

———. 1982b. "Mystery of the Lost Week." *The Unexplained* 8, no. 91:1801–5.

———. 1986. "Martians of the 1890s." *International UFO Reporter* 11, no. 5:4–9.

Evans, Hilary, and Michel Piccin. 1982. "Who Took Who for a Ride?" *Fate* 35, no. 10:51–58.

Evans-Pritchard, E. E. 1937. *Witchcraft, Oracles, and Magic among the Azande.* Oxford: Clarendon Press.

Favret-Saada, Jeanne. 1980. *Deadly Words: Witchcraft in the Bocage.* Paris: Maison des Sciences de l'Homme.

Feher, Shoshanah. 1992. "Who Holds the Cards?: Women and New Age Astrology." In *Perspectives on the New Age,* edited by James R. Lewis and J. Gordon Melton, 179–88. Albany: State Univ. of New York Press.

Festinger, Leon, Henry W. Riecken, and Stanley Schachter. 1956. *When Prophecy Fails.* Minneapolis: Univ. of Minnesota Press.

Fine, Gary Alan. 1980. "Fantasy Role-Play Gaming as a Social World: Imagination and the

Social Construction of Play." In *The Paradoxes of Play*, edited by John Loy, 215–24. West Point, N.Y.: Leisure Press.

Fiore, Edith. 1993. *Encounters: A Psychologist Reveals Case Studies of Abductions by Extraterrestrials.* New York: Ballantine Books.

Fitzgerald, R. 1979. *The Complete Book of Extraterrestrial Encounters: The Ideas of Carl Sagan, Eric von Daniken, Billy Graham, Carl Jung, John C. Lilly, John G. Fuller, and Many Others.* New York: Collier Books.

Flaherty, Robert Pearson. 1990. "Flying Saucers and the New Angelology: Mythic Projection of the Cold War and the Convergence of Opposites." Ph.D. diss., Univ. of California, Los Angeles.

Flammonde, Paris. 1976. *UFO Exist!* New York: G. P. Putnam's Sons.

Flem-Ath, Rand, and Rose Flem-Ath. 1995. *When the Sky Fell: In Search of Atlantis.* New York: St. Martin's Paperbacks.

Flournoy, T. 1983. *Des Indes à la planète Mars.* Paris: Le Seuil.

Flying Saucer Review. 2002. Feb. 11. http://www.fsrnet.org.

Forrest, Burke. 1986. "Apprentice-Participation: Methodology and the Study of Subjective Reality." *Urban Life* 14, no. 4:431–53.

Fort, Charles Hoy. 1995. *The Book of the Damned.* Revised by X. London: John Brown Publishing.

Fouéré, René. 1964. "La lune ou la dernière chance d'Adamski." *Bulletin du GEPA* 6 (2d trimester): 3–6.

———. 1965. "George Adamski est mort." *Phénomènes spatiaux* 4 (May): 32–33.

Fowler, Raymond. 1979. *The Andreasson Affair.* Englewood Cliffs, N.J.: Prentice Hall.

———. 1982. *The Andreasson Affair: Phase Two.* Englewood Cliffs, N.J.: Prentice Hall.

———. 1990. *The Watchers.* New York: Bantam.

———. 1993. *The Allagash Abductions.* Tigard, Ore.: Wild Flower Press.

Frank, Emilie A. 1998. *Mt. Shasta, California's Mystic Mountain.* Hilt, Calif.: Photografix Publishing.

Freud, Sigmund. 1930. *Civilization and Its Discontents.* New York: J. Cape, H. Smith.

———. 1961. *The Future of an Illusion.* Garden City, N.Y.: Doubleday.

Frisch, Adam, and Joseph Martos. 1985. "Religious Imagination and Imagined Religion." In *The Transcendent Adventure: Studies in Science Fiction/Fantasy,* edited by Robert Reilly, 11–26. Westport, Conn.: Greenwood Press.

Fukuda, K., A. Miyasita, M. Inugami, and K. Ishihara. 1987. "High Prevalence of Isolated Sleep Paralysis: *Kanashibari* phenomenon in Japan." *Sleep* 10, no. 3:279–86.

Fuller, John G. 1966. *The Interrupted Journey: Two Lost Hours Aboard a Flying Saucer.* New York: Dial Press.

Gadamer, Hans-Georg. 1981. *Reason in the Age of Science.* Translated by Frederick G. Lawrence. Cambridge, Mass.: MIT Press.

Galactic. 2004. Universal Industrial Church of the New World Comforter and One World Family Commune. http://www.galactic.org.

Gallet, Georges Hilaire. 1991. Interview with author. Cassis, France, Nov 2.

Gallup, George, Jr., and William Proctor. 1982. *Adventures in Immortality: A Look beyond the Threshold of Death.* New York: McGraw-Hill.

Gallup Poll. 2001. http://www.gallup.com.

Gardner, Martin. 1996. "Oahspe." In *The Encyclopedia of the Paranormal,* edited by Gordon Stein, 465–71. Amherst, N.Y.: Prometheus Books.

Garfinkel, Harold. 1967. *Studies in Ethnomethodology.* Englewood Cliffs, N.J.: Prentice Hall.

Geertz, Clifford. 1973. *The Interpretation of Cultures.* New York: Basic Books.

Giere, Ronald N. 1979. *Understanding Scientific Reasoning.* New York: Holt, Rinehart and Winston.

———. 1988. *Explaining Science: A Cognitive Approach.* Chicago: Univ. of Chicago Press.

Gieryn, Thomas F. 1983. "Boundary-Work and the Demarcation of Science from Non-Science: Strains and Interests in Professional Ideologies of Scientists." *American Sociological Review* 48, no. 6:881–95.

Gieryn, Thomas F., George M. Bevins, and Stephen C. Zehr. 1985. "Professionalization of American Scientists: Public Science in the Creation/Evolution Trials." *American Sociological Review* 50, no. 3:392–409.

Gilbert, G. Nigel, and Michael Mulkay. 1984. *Opening Pandora's Box: A Sociological Analysis of Scientists' Discourse.* Cambridge: Cambridge Univ. Press.

Glock, Charles Y., and Robert N. Bellah, eds. 1976. *The New Religious Consciousness.* Berkeley: Univ. of California Press.

Goffman, Erving. 1974. *Frame Analysis: An Essay on the Organization of Experience.* New York: Harper Colophon.

Goldberg, Carl. 2000. "The General's Abduction by Aliens from a UFO: Levels of Meaning of Abduction Reports." *Journal of Contemporary Psychotherapy* 30, no. 3.

Goodall, Jane. 1990. *Through a Window: My Thirty Years with the Chimpanzees of Gombe.* Boston: Houghton Mifflin.

Goode, Erich. 2000. *Paranormal Beliefs: A Sociological Introduction.* Prospect Heights, Ill.: Waveland Press.

Goody, Jack. 1977. *The Domestication of the Savage Mind.* Cambridge: Cambridge Univ. Press.

Graham, Billy. 1994. *Angels: God's Secret Agents.* Dallas, Tex.: Word.

Grof, Stanislav, and Christina Grof, eds. 1989. *Spiritual Emergency: When Personal Transformation Becomes a Crisis.* New York: Putnam.

Guieu, Jimmy. 1954. *Les Soucoupes volantes viennent d'un autre monde.* Paris: Fleuve Noir.

———. 1956. *Flying Saucers Come from Another World.* London: Hutchinson.

———. 1987. Interview with author. Aix en Provence, Feb. 16.

Guieu, Jimmy, Franck Fontaine, Jean-Pierre Prévost, and Salomon N'Diaye. 1980. *Contacts OVNI Cergy-Pontoise.* Monaco: Editions du Rocher.

Guyard, Jacques. 1996. *Rapport: les sectes in France, Commission d'enquête parlementaire.* Rapport no. 2468. Paris: La Documentation française.

Hahn, Robert A. 1973. "Understanding Beliefs: An Essay on the Methodology of the Statement and Analysis of Belief Systems." *Current Anthropology* 14, no. 3:207–39.

Hall, John R., and Philip Schuyler. 1997. "The Mystical Apocalypse of the Solar Temple." In *Millennium, Messiahs, and Mayhem,* edited by Thomas Robbins and Susan J. Palmer, 285–311. New York: Routledge.

Hall, Michael David, and Wendy Ann Connors. 2000. *Captain Edward J. Ruppelt: Summer of the Saucers—1952.* Albuquerque: Rose Press International.

Hall, Richard. 1988. *Uninvited Guests: A Documentary History of UFO Sightings, Alien Encounters, and Coverups.* Santa Fe: Aurora Press.

Hancock, Graham. 1995. *Fingerprints of the Gods: A Quest for the Beginning and the End.* London: Mandarin.

Hanegraaff, Wouter J. 1998. *New Age Religion and Western Culture: Esotericism in the Mirror of Secular Thought.* Albany: State Univ. of New York Press.

Hapgood, Charles H. 1996. *Maps of the Ancient Sea Kings.* New York: Chilton Books.

Harrison, Albert A. 1997. *After Contact: The Human Response to Extraterrestrial Life.* New York: Plenum Publishing.

Harrold, Francis B., and Raymond A. Eve. 1995. *Cult Archaeology and Creationism: Understanding Pseudoscientific Beliefs about the Past.* Iowa City: Univ. of Iowa Press.

Heard, Gerald. 1951a. *Is Another World Watching? The Riddle of the Flying Saucers.* New York: Harper and Brothers.

———. 1951b. *Les Soucoupes volantes.* Paris: Pierre Horay-Editions de Flore.

Heelas, Paul. 1996. *The New Age Movement: The Celebration of the Self and the Sacralization of Modernity.* Oxford: Blackwell.

Heidegger, Martin. 1977. *The Question Concerning Technology and Other Essays.* Translated by William Lovitt. Cambridge: MIT Press.

Hetherington, Norris S., ed. 1993. *Cosmology: Historical, Literary, Philosophical, Religious, and Scientific Perspectives.* New York: Garland.

Hinton, Devon E., David J. Hufford, and Laurence J. Kirmayer. 2005. "Culture and Sleep Paralysis." *Transcultural Psychiatry* 42, no. 1:5–10.

Holden, Katharine J., and Christopher C. French. 2002. "Alien Abduction Experiences: Some Clues from Neuropsychology and Neuropsychiatry," *Cognitive Neuropsychiatry* 7, no. 3:163–78.

Hopkins, Budd. 1981. *Missing Time: A Documented Study of UFO Abductions.* New York: Richard Marek Publishers.

———. 1987. *Intruders: The Incredible Visitations at Copley Woods.* New York: Ballantine Books.

———. 1997. *Witnessed: The True Story of the Brooklyn Bridge UFO Abductions.* New York: Pocket Books.

Hopkins, Budd, David M. Jacobs, and Ron Westrum. 1992. *The UFO Abduction Syndrome: A Report on Unusual Experiences Associated with UFO Abduction: The Roper Organization's Survey of 5,947 Adult Americans.* Las Vegas: Bigelow Holding Co.

Hopkins, Budd, and Carol Rainey. 2003. *Sight Unseen: Science, UFO Invisibility, and Transgenic Beings.* New York: Atria Books.

Horn, Arthur David. 1994. *Humanity's Extraterrestrial Origins.* Mt. Shasta, Calif.: A. and L. Horn.

Horrigan, Marianne. 1998. "Contact of the Fifth Kind." Lecture, The UFO Experience, North Haven, Conn., Oct. 10.

Howe, Linda Moulton. 1989. *An Alien Harvest: Further Evidence Linking Animal Mutilations and Human Abductions to Alien Life Forms.* Littleton, Colo.: Linda Moulton Howe Productions.

Hubbard, L. Ron. 1950. *Dianetics: The Modern Science of Mental Health: A Handbook of Dianetic Therapy.* New York: Hermitage House.

Hufford, David J. 1982. *The Terror That Comes in the Night: An Experience-Centered Study of Supernatural Assault Traditions.* Philadelphia: Univ. of Pennsylvania Press.

———. 2005. "Sleep Paralysis as Spiritual Experience." *Transcultural Psychiatry* 42, no. 1:11–45.

Huyghe, Patrick. 1996. *The Field Guide to Extraterrestrials.* New York: Avon.

Hynek, J. Allen. 1972. *The UFO Experience: A Scientific Inquiry.* New York: Ballantine Books.

Jacobs, David M. 1975. *The UFO Controversy in America.* Bloomington: Indiana Univ. Press.

———. 1983. "UFOS and the Search for Scientific Legitimacy." In *The Occult in America: New Historical Perspectives,* edited by Howard Kerr and Charles L. Crow, 218–31. Urbana: Univ. of Illinois Press.

———. 1993. *Secret Life: Firsthand Accounts of UFO Abductions.* New York: Fireside, Simon and Schuster.

———. 1999. *The Threat: Revealing the Secret Alien Agenda.* New York: Fireside, Simon and Schuster.

———. 2000. "The UFO Abduction Controversy in the United States." In *UFOs and Abductions: Challenging the Borders of Knowledge,* edited by David M. Jacobs, 192–214. Lawrence: Univ. Press of Kansas.

Jacobs, David M., and Budd Hopkins. 1992. "Suggested Techniques for Hypnotic Regression of Abductees." 2d ed. rev. Intruders Seminar, Los Angeles, Calif.

Jenkins, Henry. 1992. *Textual Poachers: Television Fans and Participatory Culture.* New York and London: Routledge.

Jindra, Michael. 1994. "Star Trek Fandom as a Religious Phenomenon." *Sociology of Religion* 55, no. 1:27–51.

Joseph-Witham, Heather R. 1996. *Star Trek Fans and Costume Art.* Jackson: Univ. Press of Mississippi.

Jung, C. G. 1959. *Flying Saucers: A Modern Myth of Things Seen in the Skies.* London: Routledge and Kegan Paul.

———. 1978. *Flying Saucers: A Modern Myth of Things Seen in the Skies.* Translated by R. F. C. Hall. Princeton: Princeton Univ. Press.

Kelley, Stephanie. 1999. "The Myth of Communion: A Rhetorical Analysis of the Rhetoric of Alien Abductees." Ph.D. diss., Univ.of Kansas.

Kelly, Aidan A. 1992. "An Update on Neopagan Witchcraft in America." In *Perspectives on the New Age,* edited by James R. Lewis and J. Gordon Melton, 136–51. Albany: State Univ. of New York Press.

Kenny, Michael. 1998. "The Proof Is in the Passion: Emotion as an Index of Veridical Memory." In *Believed-In Imaginings: The Narrative Construction of Reality,* edited by Joseph de Rivera and Theodore R. Sarbin, 269–94. Washington, D.C.: American Psychological Association.

Kenworthy, Chris. 1996. "Xenotechnology." *Alien Encounters* 4:16–18.

Kerr, Howard, and Charles L. Crow. 1983. *The Occult in America: New Historical Perspectives.* Urbana.: Univ. of Illinois Press.

Keyhoe, Donald E. 1950. *Flying Saucers Are Real.* New York: Fawcett Publications.

———. 1951. *Les Soucoupes volantes existent.* Paris: Editions Corrêa.

King, George. [1963] 1974. *The Nine Freedoms.* Los Angeles: Aetherius Society.

King, George, and Kevin Quinn Avery. [1975] 1982. *The Age of Aetherius.* Los Angeles: Aetherius Society.

King, George, and Richard Lawrence. 1996. *Contact with the Gods from Space: Pathway to the New Millennium.* Los Angeles: Aetherius Society.

Kirkpatrick, R. George, and Diana Tumminia. 1989a. "California Space Goddess: The Mystagogue Flying Saucer Cult." Paper presented at the annual meeting of the Pacific Sociological Association, Apr., Reno, Nev.

———. 1989b. "A Case Study of a Southern Californian Flying-Saucer Cult." Presented at the American Sociological Association Meetings, San Francisco, Calif., Aug.

Klapp, Orrin E. 1972. *Currents of Unrest: An Introduction to Collective Behavior.* New York: Holt, Rinehart, Winston.

Klass, Philip J. 1989. *UFO Abductions: A Dangerous Game.* Buffalo, N.Y.: Prometheus Books.

Knight, Christopher, and Robert Lomas. 1999. *Uriel's Machine: The Prehistoric Technology That Survived the Flood.* London: Century.

Koestler, Arthur. 1959. *The Sleepwalkers: A History of Man's Changing Vision of the Universe.* London: Penguin.

Kolosimo, Peter. 1982. *Spaceships in Pre-History.* Secaucus, N.J.: Citadel Press.

Krippner, Stanley, and Susan Marie Powers. 1997. *Broken Images, Broken Selves: Dissociative Narratives in Clinical Practice.* New York: Brunner/Mazel.

Kuhn, Annette, ed. 1990. *Alien Zone: Cultural Theory and Contemporary Science Fiction Cinema.* London: Verso.

LaFleur, William, R. "Biography." 1993. In *The Encyclopedia of Religion,* Vol. 1., edited by Mircea Eliade. New York: Macmillan.

Lagrange, Pierre. 1990. "Enquêtes sur les soucoupes volantes. La construction d'un fait aux Etats-Unis (1947) et en France (1951–54)." *Terrain, Carnets du Patrimoine Ethnologique* 14 (Mar.): 92–112.

———. 1993. "Science-parascience: preuves et épreuves." *Ethnologie française* 23, no. 3:428–58.

Lamy, Philip. 1999. "UFOs, Extraterrestrials, and the Apocalypse: The Evolution of a Millennial Subculture." In *Millennial Visions,* edited by Martha Lee, 115–34. Westport, Conn.: Praeger.

Lapseritis, Jack "Kewaunee." 1998a. "Psychic Sasquatch—The Bigfoot-UFO Connection." Lecture, The UFO Experience, North Haven, Conn., Oct. 11.

———. 1998b. *The Psychic Sasquatch and Their UFO Connection.* Newberg, Ore.: Blue Water Publishing.

Latour, Bruno. 1983. "Comment redistribuer le Grand Partage?" *Revue de Synthèse* 104 (Apr.–June): 203–36.

———. 1990. "Quand les anges deviennent de biens mauvais messagers." *Terrain* 14:76–91.

———. 1993. *The Pasteurization of France.* Cambridge, Mass.: Harvard Univ. Press.

———. 1995. *La Science en action: Introduction à la sociologie des sciences.* Paris: Gallimard.

Latour, Bruno, and Steve Woolgar. 1990. *Laboratory Life: The Construction of Scientific Facts.* Princeton: Princeton Univ. Press.

Lawson, Alvin H. 1980. "Archetypes and Abductions." *Frontiers of Science* 2, no. 6:32–36.

Layne, N. Meade. 1949. "Mark Probert, Baffling San Diego Medium." *Fate* 2, no. 1:16–21.

———. 1950. *The Ether Ship and Its Solution.* Vista, Calif.: Borderland Sciences Research Associates.

Leiber, Fritz. 1964. *The Wanderer.* New York: Walker and Company.

Leleu, Christophe. 1995. *La Secte du Temple Solaire: Explications autour doun Massacre.* Paris: Claire Vigne.

Lemesurier, Peter. 1997. *Gods of the Dawn: The Message of the Pyramids and the True Stargate Mystery.* London: Thorsons.

Leslie, Desmond, and George Adamski. 1953. *Flying Saucers Have Landed.* New York: British Book Centre.

————. 1954. *Les Soucoupes volantes ont atterri.* Paris: La Colombe.

Lewels, Joe. 1998. "Angels or Aliens? The Controversy Over the God Hypothesis." Lecture, The UFO Experience, North Haven, Conn., Oct. 10.

Lewis, James R. 1992. "Approaches to the Study of the New Age Movement." In *Perspectives on the New Age,* edited by James R. Lewis and J. Gordon Melton, 1–14. Albany: State Univ. of New York Press.

————. 1995. *The Gods Have Landed: New Religions from Other Worlds.* Albany: State Univ. of New York Press.

————. 2000. *UFOs and Popular Culture: An Encyclopedia of Contemporary Myth.* Santa Barbara, Calif.: ABC-CLIO.

————. 2003a. *Encyclopedic Sourcebook of UFO Religions.* Amherst, N.Y.: Prometheus Books.

————. 2003b. *Legitimating New Religions.* New Brunswick, N.J.: Rutgers Univ. Press.

Lidsey, James E., David Wands, and Edmund J. Copeland. 2000. "Superstring Cosmology." *Physics Reports* 337, no. 4–5:343–492.

Lieb, Michael. 1998. *Children of Ezekiel: Aliens, UFOs, the Crisis of Race, and the Advent of the End Time.* Durham, N.C.: Duke Univ. Press.

Lindner, Robert. 1954. *The Fifty-Minute Hour: A Collection of True Psychoanalytic Tales.* New York: Bantam Books.

Lodge, Oliver. 1915. *The Survival of Man.* London: Methuen.

Lofland, John. 1966. "Normal Flying Saucerians?" *Trans-Action* 3, no. 5:54–55.

Loftus, Elizabeth, and Katherine Ketcham. 1994. *The Myth of Repressed Memory.* New York: St. Martin's Press.

Lore, Gordon I. R., Jr., and Harold H. Deneault, Jr. 1968. *Mysteries of the Skies: UFOs in Perspective.* Englewood Cliffs, N.J.: Prentice Hall.

Lorenzen, Carol. 1963. "The Disappearance of Rivalino Mafra da Silva: Kidnapped by a UFO?" *Fate* 16, no. 6:26–33.

————. 1970. *The Shadow of the Unknown.* New York: New American Library.

Lorenzen, Carol, and Jim Lorenzen. 1977. *Abducted.* New York: Berkeley.

Loy, John. 1980. *The Paradoxes of Play.* Proceedings of the 69th annual meeting of the Association for the Anthropological Study of Play. West Point, N.Y.: Leisure Press.

Luhrmann, Tanya. 1989. *Persuasions of the Witch's Craft.* Cambridge, Mass.: Harvard Univ. Press.

Lurie, Alison. 1967. *Imaginary Friends.* New York: Coward-McCann.

Luttwak, E. N. 1976. *The Grand Strategy of the Roman Empire: From the First Century A.D. to the Third.* Baltimore: Johns Hopkins Univ. Press.

Lynn, Steven Jay, and Irving I. Kirch. 1996. "Alleged Alien Abductions: False Memories, Hypnosis, and Fantasy Proneness." *Psychological Inquiry: An International Journal of Peer Commentary and Review* 7, no. 2:151–55.

Lynn, Steven Jay, Judith Pintar, Jane Stafford, Lisa Marmelstein, and Timothy Lock. 1998. "Rendering the Implausible Plausible: Narrative Construction, Suggestion, and Memory." In *Believed-In Imaginings: The Narrative Construction of Reality,* edited by Joseph de Rivera and Theodore R. Sarbin, 123–43. Washington D. C.: American Psychological Association.

Lyotard, Jean-François. 1987. "The Postmodern Condition." Translated by Geoff Bennington and Brian Massumi. In *Philosophy: End or Transformation?,* edited by Kenneth Baynes, James Bohman, and Thomas A. McCarthy, 67–94. Cambridge, Mass.: MIT Press.

Maccabee, Bruce. 1995a. "The Arnold Phenomenon: Part One." *International UFO Reporter* 20, no. 1:14–17.

———. 1995b. "The Arnold Phenomenon: Part Two." *International UFO Reporter* 20, no. 2:10–13

———. 1995c. "The Arnold Phenomenon: Part Three." *International UFO Reporter* 20, no. 3:6–7.

Mack, John E. 1995. *Abduction: Human Encounters with Aliens.* London: Simon and Schuster.

———. 1999. *Passport to the Cosmos: Human Transformation and Alien Encounters.* New York: Crown.

Manning, Frank E. 1983. *The World of Play.* West Point, N.Y.: Leisure Press.

Marsden, George M. 1982. *Fundamentalism and American Culture.* Oxford: Oxford Univ. Press.

Matheson, Terry. 1998. *Alien Abductions: Creating a Modern Phenomenon.* Amherst, N.Y.: Prometheus Books.

McCarthy, Paul. 1975. "Politicking and Paradigm Shifting: James E. McDonald and the UFO Case Study." Ph.D. diss., Univ. of Hawaii.

McDaniel, Stanley. 1993. *The McDaniel Report.* Berkeley, Calif.: North Atlantic Books.

McLaren, Darcee L. 1999. "On the Edge of Forever: Understanding the Star Trek Phenomenon as Myth." In *Star Trek and Sacred Ground: Explorations of* Star Trek, *Religion, and American Culture,* edited by Jennifer E. Porter and Darcee L. McLaren. 231–43. Albany: State Univ. of New York Press.

McNally, Richard J., and Susan A. Clancy. 2005. "Sleep Paralysis, Sexual Abuse, and Space Alien Abduction." *Transcultural Psychiatry* 42, no. 1:113–22.

McNally, Richard J., Natasha B. Lasko, Susan A. Clancy, Michael L. Macklin, Roger K. Pitman, and Scott P. Orr. 2004. "Psychophysiological Responding During Script-Driven Imagery in People Reporting Abduction by Space Aliens." *Psychological Science* 15, no. 7:493–97.

Mears, Daniel P., and Christopher G. Ellison. 2000. "Who Buys New Age Materials? Exploring Sociodemographic, Religious, Network, and Contextual Correlates of New Age Consumption." *Sociology of Religion* 61, no. 3:289–314.

Mehan, Hugh, and Houston Wood. 1975. *The Reality of Ethnomethodology.* New York: John Wiley and Sons.

Meisenhelder, Thomas. 1979. "A Further Investigation of the Life-World." *Human Studies* 2:21–30.

Melton, J. Gordon. 1986. *Biographical Dictionary of American Cult and Sect Leaders.* Garland Reference Library of Social Science, vol. 212. New York and London: Garland Publishing.

———, ed. 1989. *The Encyclopedia of American Religions.* 3d ed. Detroit: Gale Research.

———. 1995. "The Contactees: A Survey." In *The Gods Have Landed: New Religions from Other Worlds,* edited by James R. Lewis, 1–13. Albany: State Univ. of New York Press.

Melton, J. Gordon, Jerome Clark, and Aidan A. Kelly. 1990. *New Age Encyclopedia.* New York: Gale Research.

Menger, Howard. 1959. *From Outer Space to You.* Clarksburg, W.V.: Saucerian Books.

———. 1965. *Mes amis les hommes de l'espace.* Paris: Dervy-Livres.

Merton, Robert. 1970. *Science, Technology and Society in Seventeenth Century England.* New York: Harper and Row.

Michael, Allen. n.d. "My Encounter with Galactic Space Beings." Santa Rosa, Calif.: ETI Messenger.

———. 1982. *The Everlasting Gospel: God Ultimate Unlimited Mind Speaks.* Stockton, Calif.: Star Mast Productions.

———. 1994. *Spirit God's Seven Churches: Revelations Revealed.* Santa Rosa, Calif.: Star Mast Productions.

———. 2001. *The Everlasting Gospel: The New World Bible.* Santa Rosa, Calif.: Star Mast Productions.

Michel, Aimé. 1954. *Lueurs sur les soucoupes volantes.* Paris: Mame.

———. 1956. *The Truth about Flying Saucers.* New York: Criterion.

———. 1958a. *Flying Saucers and the Straight-Line Mystery.* New York: Criterion.

———. 1958b. *Mystérieux objets célestes.* Vichy: Arthaud.

———. 1967. *The Truth about Flying Saucers.* New York: Pyramid Books.

Miguères, Jean. 1977. *J'ai été le cobaye des extra-terrestres.* Nice: Promazur-RG.

———. 1979. *Le cobaye des extra-terrestres face aux scientifiques.* Nice: Alain Lefeuvre.

———. 1987. *1996: La Revelation.* Paris: Edité par Alliance.

Miller, Alan S., and John P. Hoffman. 1995. "Risk and Religion: An Explanation in Gender Differences in Religiosity." *Journal for the Scientific Study of Religion* 34, no. 1:63–75.

Miller, David L. 1985. *Introduction to Collective Behavior.* Belmont, Calif.: Wadsworth.

———. 2000. *Introduction to Collective Behavior and Collective Action.* Prospect Heights, Ill.: Waveland.

Miller, Max B. 1963. "The Spaceniks of Giant Rock." *Argosy,* July, 34–37.

Milligan, Linda Jean. 1988. *The UFO Debate: A Study of a Contemporary Legend*. Ph.D. diss., Ohio State Univ.

Missler, Chuck, and Mark Eastman. 2003. *Alien Encounters: The Secret Behind the UFO Phenomenon*. Coeur d'Alene, Ida.: Koinonia House.

Mitchell, Edgar. 1998. "Alien Presence—Yes or No?" Lecture, The UFO Experience, North Haven, Conn., Oct. 10.

Moffitt, John F. 2003. *Picturing Extraterrestrials: Alien Images in Modern Mass Culture*. New York: Prometheus Books.

Monnet, Pierre. 1978. *Les extra-terrestres m'ont dit*. Nice: Alain Lefeuvre.

Montgomery, Sy. 1991. *Walking with the Great Apes: Jane Goodall, Dian Fossey, Birute Galdikas*. Boston: Houghton Mifflin.

Mooney, Chris. 2005. Committee for the Scientific Investigation of Claims of the Paranormal (CSICOP). Apr. 13. http://www.csicop.org/doubtandabout/sleep.

Mulkay, Michael, and G. Nigel Gilbert. 1982. "Accounting for Error: How Scientists Construct Their Social World When They Account for Correct and Incorrect Belief." *Sociology* 16:165–83.

Mundo, Laura. n.d., ca. 1975. *Flying Saucer Up-Day!* Inkster, Mich.: Laura Mundo.

Murguia, Salvador Jimenez. 2005. "Re-Enchanting a Religio-Scientific Experience: Understanding the Extraordinary with the Pana-Laboratory." Unpublished manuscript.

Mutual UFO Network. 2002. MUFON WWW page. http://www.rutgers.edu/~mcgrew/mufon/index.html. Accessed Jan. 15.

Nelson, Buck. 1956. *My Trip to Mars, the Moon, and Venus*. Mountain View, Mo.: Buck Nelson.

Newbrough, John B. 1882. *Oahspe*. Boston, Mass.: John B. Newbrough.

Newman, Leonard S. 1997. "Intergalactic Hostages: People Who Report Abductions by UFOs." *Journal of Social and Clinical Psychology* 16, no. 2:151–57.

Newman, Leonard S., and Roy F. Baumeister. 1996. "Toward an Explanation of the UFO Abduction Phenomenon: Hypnotic Elaboration, Extraterrestrial Sadomasochism, and Spurious Memories." *Psychological Inquiry: An International Journal of Peer Commentary and Review* 7, no. 2:99–126.

———. 1998. "Abducted by Aliens: Spurious Memories of Interplanetary Masochism." In *Truth in Memory*, edited by Steven J. Lynn and Kevin M. McConkey, 284–303. New York: Guilford Press.

Norkin, Israel. 1957. *Saucer Diary*. New York: Pageant Press.

Ofshe, Richard. 1980. "The Social Development of the Synanon Cult: The Managerial Strategy of Organizational Transformation." *Sociological Analysis* 41, no. 2:109–27.

O'Leary, Brian. 1996. *Miracle in the Void: The Birth, Death, and Resurrection of Free Energy*. Kihei, Hawaii: Kampua'a Press.

Otto, Rudolf. [1923] 1950. *The Idea of the Holy.* Translated by John W. Harvey. Oxford: Oxford Univ. Press.

Pacheco, N. S. and T. R. Blann. 1993. *Unmasking the Enemy: Visions and Deceptions in the End Times.* Arlington, Va.: Bendan Press.

Paley, John. 1997. "Satanist Abuse and Alien Abduction: A Comparative Analysis Theorizing Temporal Lobe Activity as a Possible Connection Between Anomalous Memories." *British Journal of Social Work* 27, no. 1:43–70.

Palmer, Susan J. 1995. "The Raëlian Movement International." In *New Religions and the New Europe,* edited by Robert Towler, 194–210. Aahrus, Den.: Aahrus Univ. Press.

———. 1998. "The Raëlians Are Coming! The Future of a UFO Religion." In *Religion in a Changing World: Comparative Studies in Sociology,* edited by Madeleine Cousineau, 139–46. Westport, Conn.: Praeger.

———. 2003. "The Raëlian Apocalypse: Playing with Prophecy, Appeasing Aliens, or Pleasing the Public?" In *Encyclopedic Sourcebook of UFO Religions,* edited by James R. Lewis, 261–80. Amherst, N.Y.: Prometheus Books.

———. 2004. *Aliens Adored: Rael's UFO Religion.* Piscataway, N.J.: Rutgers Univ. Press.

Pandian, Jacob. 1991. *Culture, Religion, and the Sacred Self: A Critical Introduction to the Anthropological Study of Religion.* Englewood Cliffs, N.J.: Prentice Hall.

Parfrey, Adam. 1995. *Cult Rapture.* Portland, Ore.: Feral House.

Partridge, Christopher, ed. 2003. *UFO Religions.* London: Routledge.

———. 2004. *New Religions: A Guide.* New York: Oxford Univ. Press.

Peebles, Curtis. 1994. *Watch the Skies! A Chronicle of the Flying Saucer Myth.* Washington, D.C.: Smithsonian Institution Press.

Pendergrast, Mark. 1996. *Victims of Memory: Sex Abuse Accusations and Shattered Lives.* Hinesburg, Vt.: Upper Access Book Publishers.

Perina, Kaja. 2003. "Cracking the Harvard X-Files." *Psychology Today,* Mar., 66–76, 95.

Petit, Jean-Pierre. 1990. *Enquêtes sur les ovnis.* Paris: Albin Michel.

Picknett, Lynn, and Clive Prince. 1999. *The Stargate Conspiracy.* London: Warner Books.

Pinch, Trevor J., and Harry M. Collins. 1984. "Private Science and Public Knowledge: The Committee for the Scientific Investigation of the Claims of the Paranormal and Its Use of the Literature." *Social Studies of Science* 14, no. 4:521–46.

Poher, Claude. 1998. Interview by Perry Petrakis. *Phénomèna* no. 39: 5–20.

Poher, Claude, and Jacques Vallee. 1975. "Basic Patterns in UFO Observations." Paper presented at the Thirteenth Aerospace Sciences Meeting of the American Institute of Aeronautics and Astronautics, Pasadena, Calif., Jan. 20.

Pollner, Melvin. 1987. *Mundane Reason: Reality in Everyday and Sociological Discourse.* Cambridge: Cambridge Univ. Press.

Pollner, Melvin, and Robert M. Emerson. 1988. "The Dynamics of Inclusion and Distance in Fieldwork Relations." In *Contemporary Field Research: A Collection of Readings,* edited by Robert M. Emerson, 235–52. Prospect Heights, Ill.: Waveland Press.

Pollner, Melvin, and Lynn McDonald-Wikler. 1985. "The Social Construction of Unreality: A Case Study of a Family's Attribution of Competence to a Severely Retarded Child." *Family Process* 24:241–54.

Pope, Nick. 1998. *The Uninvited: An Exposé of the Alien Abduction Phenomenon.* London: Simon and Schuster.

Porter, Jennifer E. 1996. "Spiritualists, Aliens and UFOs: Extraterrestrials as Spirit Guides." *Journal of Contemporary Religion* 11, no. 3:337–54.

———. 1999. "To Boldly Go: Star Trek Convention Attendance as Pilgrimage." In *Star Trek and Sacred Ground: Explorations of* Star Trek, *Religion, and American Culture,* edited by Jennifer E. Porter and Darcee L. McLaren, 245–70. Albany: State Univ. of New York.

Porter, Jennifer E., and Darcee L. McLaren, eds. 1999. *Star Trek and Sacred Ground: Explorations of Star Trek, Religion, and American Culture.* Albany: State Univ. of New York Press.

Puthoff, Harold E. 1996. "SETI, the Velocity-of-Light Limitation, and the Alcubierre Warp Drive: An Integrating Overview." *Physics Essays* 9, no. 1:156–58.

Pye, Lloyd. 1998. *Everything You Know Is Wrong.* Maderia, Fla.: Adamu Press.

———. 2002. "Outline." Feb. 5. http://www.lloydpye.com/outline.htm.

Raëlian Church. 2004. Web page. http://www.rael.org/English/index.html.

Rahman, Fazlur. 1966. *Islam.* Garden City, N.Y.: Doubleday.

Randle, Kevin D., and Russ Estes. 1997. *Faces of the Visitors: An Illustrated Reference to Alien Contact.* New York: Fireside Books.

———. 2000. *Spaceships of the Visitors: An Illustrated Guide to Alien Spacecraft.* New York: Fireside Books.

Randle, Kevin D., Russ Estes, and William P. Cone. 1999. *The Abduction Enigma: The Truth Behind the Mass Alien Abductions of the Late Twentieth Century.* New York: Tom Doherty Associates.

Randles, Jenny. 1988. *Abduction: Over 200 Documented UFO Kidnappings Investigated.* London: Robert Hale.

———. 1999. *The Complete Book of Aliens and Abductions.* London: Judy Piatkus Publishers.

Refslund Christensen, Dorthe. 1997a. "Legenden om L. Ron Hubbard—et eksempel p en modern hagiografi. Om konstruktionen af et mytologisk livsforløb og brugen af deti Scientology." *Chaos* 28:53–76.

———. 1997b. *Scientology: En ny religion.* Copenhagen: Munksgaard.

———. 1997c. *Scientology: Fra terapi til religion.* Copenhagen: Gyldendal.

———. 2005. "Inventing L. Ron Hubbard: On the Construction and Maintenance of the Hagiographic Mythology of Scientology's Founder." In *Controversial New Religions,* edited by James R. Lewis and Jesper Aagaard Peterson, 227–58. New York: Oxford Univ. Press.

Reiff, Philip. 1968. *The Triumph of the Therapeutic.* New York: Harper and Row.

Richards, Mel. 1996. "Charles Abrahamson Interview." *Encounters* 12:64–67.

Richardson, James T., Joel Best, and David G. Bromley, eds. 1991. *The Satanism Scare.* New York: Walter de Gruyter.

Richter, Daniel K. 1993. *The Ordeal of the Longhouse: The Peoples of the Iroquois League in the Era of European Colonization.* Chapel Hill: Univ. of North Carolina Press.

Ring, Kenneth. 1992. *The Omega Project: Near-Death Experiences, UFO Encounters and Mind at Large.* New York: William Morrow.

Robbins, Thomas. 1988. *Cults, Converts and Charisma: The Sociology of New Religious Movements.* Beverly Hills, Calif.: Sage Publications.

Robinson, Lytle. 1972. *Edgar Cayce's Story of the Origin and Destiny of Man.* New York: Berkeley Books.

Rochford, E. Burke, Jr. 1985. *Hare Krishna in America.* Brunswick, N.J.: Rutgers Univ. Press.

———. 1992. "On the Politics of Member Validation: Taking Findings Back to Hare Krishna." *Social Problems* 3:99–116.

Rogo, D. Scott, ed. 1980. *UFO Abductions: True Cases of Kidnappings.* New York: Signet.

Roland, Paul. 1997. "Extraterrestrial Archaeologist: David Hatcher-Childress." *Alien Encounters* 20:54–57.

Roof, Wade C. 1993. "Toward the Year 2000: Reconstructions of Religious Space." *The Annals of the American Academy of Political and Social Science.* 527:155–70.

Roper Poll. 2002. Roper Center for Opinion Research. Univ. of Connecticut. http://www.ropercenter.uconn.edu.

Rothstein, Mikael. 1992. "Videoer og vism 3/4nd: Traditionel og moderne kanon i de nye religioner." *Chaos* 18:83–112.

———. 1993. "Helliggørelse og religiøs argumantation: The International Raelian Movement of Claude Vorilhon." *Chaos* 20: 137–47.

———. 1994. "Nogle trek ved UFO-mytens oprindelse og udvikling." *Chaos* 22:84–111.

———. 2003. "The Rise and Decline of the First Generation UFO Contactees: A Cognitive Approach." In *Encyclopedic Sourcebook of UFO Religions*, edited by James R. Lewis, 63–76. Amherst, N.Y.: Prometheus Books.

Roussel, Robert. 1994. *Ovni: les vérités cachées de l'enquête officielle.* Paris: Albin Michel.

Royal, Lyssa, and Keith Priest. 1993. *Visitors from Within.* Phoenix, Ariz.: Royal Priest Research Press.

Ruben, Marilyn, and Doug Ruben. 2003. *Healing the Hurt of Alien Abduction.* An e-book that was available at http://www.abduct.com. (Web site has changed and the book has been removed.)

Ruppelt, Edward J. 1994. "Among the Contactees." *International UFO Reporter*, July/Aug., 3–6, 23–24.

Sagan, Carl. 1997. *The Demon-Haunted World: Science as a Candle in the Dark*. New York: Ballantine Books.

Saler, Benson. 2004. "On Credulity." In *Religion as Human Capacity: A Festschrift in Honor of E. Thomas Lawson*, edited by Timothy Light and Brian C. Wilson, 315–29. Leiden: Brill.

Saler, Benson, Charles A. Ziegler, and Charles B. Moore. 1997. *UFO Crash at Roswell: The Genesis of a Modern Myth*. Washington, D.C.: Smithsonian Institution Press.

Saliba, John A. 1992. "UFO Contactee Phenomena from a Sociopsychological Perspective: A Review." *Syzygy: Journal of Alternative Religion and Culture* 1, no. 1:59–93.

———. 1995. "Religious Dimensions of UFO Phenomena." In *The Gods Have Landed: New Religions from Other Worlds*, edited by James R. Lewis, 15–57. Albany: State Univ. of New York Press.

———. 2003. "The Psychology of UFO Phenomena." In *UFO Religions*, edited by Christopher Partridge, 329–45. London: Routledge.

Sanarov, Valerii. 1981. "On the Nature and Origin of Flying Saucers and Little Green Men." *Current Anthropology* 22, no. 2:163–66.

Sanders, Jacqueline. 1954. "The Van Tassel Saucer Meeting." *The Saucerian* 2, no. 2:15–17.

Sardello, Robert. 1999. *Freeing the Soul from Fear*. New York: Riverhead.

Schmitt, Jean-Claude. 1994. *Les Revenants: Les vivants et les morts dans la société médiévale*. Paris: Gallimard.

Schnabel, Jim. 1994. "Puck in the Laboratory: The Construction and Deconstruction of Hoaxlike Deception in Science." *Science, Technology and Human Values* 19, no. 4:459–92.

Schwalbe, Michael. 1996. *Unlocking the Iron Cage: The Men's Movement, Gender Politics, and American Culture*. New York: Oxford Univ. Press.

Schwartz, Howard, and Jerry Jacobs. 1979. *Qualitative Sociology: A Method to the Madness*. New York: Free Press.

Scribner, Scott R. 2003. "Alien Fears: Toward a Psychology of UFO Abduction." Ph.D. diss., Greenwich Univ.

Scully, Frank. 1950. *Behind the Flying Saucers*. New York: Henry Holt.

———. 1951. *Le Mystère des soucoupes volantes*. Paris: Del Duca/Les Editions Mondiales.

Shapin, S. 1982. "Is a Social History of Science Possible?" *History of Science* 20:157–211.

Sharer, R. J., and W. Ashmore. 1993. *Archaeology: Discovering Our Past*. Mountain View, Calif.: Mayfield.

Sikmus, Albert A. 1978. "Residential Segregation by Occupation and Race in Ten Urbanized Areas, 1950–1970." *American Sociological Review* 43, no. 1:81–93.

Sitchin, Zecharia. 1976. *The 12th Planet: The First Book of the Earth Chronicles*. New York: Avon.

————. 1995. *Genesis Revisited: Is Modern Science Catching Up with Ancient Knowledge?* New York: Avon.

————. 2001. *The Lost Book of Enki: Memoirs and Prophecies of an Extraterrestrial God.* Rochester, Vt.: Bear and Co.

Skórzyński, Piotr. 1996. "UFO fantomy." *Nieznany Świat* 3, no. 63:31–33.

Smelser, Neil J. 1962. *Theory of Collective Behavior.* New York: Free Press.

Snow, David A., and Richard Machalek. 1982. "On the Presumed Fragility of Unconventional Beliefs." *Journal for the Scientific Study of Religion* 21, no. 1:15–26.

Society for Scientific Exploration. 2002. "Society for Scientific Exploration: *Journal for Scientific Exploration.*" Feb. 11. http://scientificexploration.org/jse.html.

Spanos, Nicholas P. 1996. *Multiple Identities and False Memories: A Sociocognitive Perspective.* Washington, D.C.: American Psychological Association.

Spanos, Nicholas P., Patricia A. Cross, Kirby Dickson, and Susan C. DuBreuil. 1993. "Close Encounters: An Examination of UFO Experiences." *Journal of Abnormal Psychology* 102, no. 4:624–32.

Spencer, David T. 1995. *UFO Investigator's Training Guide: An Introduction to Methodologies, Techniques, and Scientific Disciplines for Performing UFO Investigations in Support of the Mutual UFO Network, Inc.* Austin, Tex.: Austin MUFON.

Spencer, John. 1991. *The UFO Encyclopedia.* London: Headline Book Publishing.

Spiegel, David. 1997. "Hypnosis and Suggestion." In *Memory Distortion: How Minds, Brains, and Societies Reconstruct the Past,* edited by Daniel L. Schacter, 129–41. Cambridge, Mass.: Harvard Univ. Press.

Stark, Rodney. 2002. "Physiology and Faith: Addressing the 'Universal' Gender Difference in Religious Commitment." *Journal for the Scientific Study of Religion* 41, no. 3:495–508.

Stark, Rodney, and William Sims Bainbridge. 1985. *The Future of Religion: Secularization, Revival, and Cult Formation.* Berkeley: Univ. of California Press.

Stark, Rodney, William Sims Bainbridge, and Lori Kent. 1981. "Cult Membership in the Roaring Twenties: Assessing Local Receptivity." *Sociological Analysis* 42, no. 2:137–62.

Star Trek Web site. 2004. *Star Trek.* http://www.startrek.com.

Steiger, Brad, and Sherry Steiger-Hansen. 1992. "The Amazing Super Science of Extraterrestrial 'Giants' in Earth's Prehistory." *UFO Universe* (Fall): 44–49.

Stiebing, William H., Jr. 1984. *Ancient Astronauts, Cosmic Collisions and Other Popular Theories about Man's Past.* Buffalo, N.Y.: Prometheus Books.

Stoczkowski, Wiktor. 1999. *Des Hommes, des dieux et des extraterrestres: Ethnologie d'une croyance moderne.* Paris: Flammarion.

Strickland, Charles A. 1962. "Adamski's Hieroglyphics." *Flying Saucer Review* 8, no. 3:12–13.

Strieber, Whitley. 1987. *Communion: A True Story.* New York: Morrow.

————. 1989. *Transformation: The Breakthrough.* New York: Avon.

————. 1997. *The Secret School.* Sydney: Simon and Schuster Australia.

———. 1998. *Confirmation: The Hard Evidence of Aliens among Us.* Sydney: Simon and Schuster Australia.

Strube, J. Michael. 1996. "The Truth Is Out There." *Psychological Inquiry: An International Journal of Peer Commentary and Review* 7, no. 2:180–84.

Stupple, David. 1980. "The Man Who Talked to Venusians." In *Proceedings of the First International UFO Congress,* edited by Curtis Fuller. New York: Warner Books.

———. 1984. "Mahatmas and Space Brothers: The Ideologies of Alleged Contact with Extraterrestrials." *Journal of American Culture* 7, no. 1–2:131–39.

———. 1994. "Historical Links Between the Occult and Flying Saucers." *Journal of UFO Studies* 5:93–108.

Stupple, David, and Abdollah Dashti. 1977. "Flying Saucers and Multiple Realities: A Case Study in Phenomenological Theory." *Journal of Popular Culture* 11:479–93.

Stupple, David, and William McNeece. 1979. "Contactees, Cult, and Culture." *MUFON Symposium Proceedings* 47. MUFON.

Summers, Marshal Vian. 2001. *The Allies of Humanity: An Urgent Message about the Extraterrestrial Presence in the World Today.* Boulder, Colo.: Society for the Greater Community Way of Knowledge.

Swatos, William H. 1990. "Spiritualism as a Religion of Science." *Social Compass* 37, no. 4:471–82.

Talbot, Michael. 1991. *The Holographic Universe.* New York: HarperCollins.

Tarade, Guy. 1969. *Soucoupes volantes et civilisations d'outre espace.* L'Aventure mystérieuse. Paris: J'ai Lu.

Taylor, Mark C. 1999. *About Religion: Economies of Faith in Virtual Culture.* Chicago: Univ. of Chicago Press.

Temple, Robert. 1999. *The Sirius Mystery: New Scientific Evidence of Alien Contact 5000 Years Ago.* London: Arrow Books.

Thirouin, Marc. 1953. "Les fantastiques révélations du professeur George Adamski, astronome à l'observatoire du Mt Palomar." *Ouranos-Actualités,* no. 1 (May–June): 1–4.

———.1959. "Marius Dewilde n'a pas menti: Des Ouraniens lui ont parlé . . ." *Ouranos* 24, no. 3:11–13.

Thomas, Ken. 1999. Untitled lecture. UFO Congress Convention and Film Festival, Laughlin, Nev., Feb. 24.

Thompson, Keith. 1991. *Angels and Aliens: UFOs and the Mythic Imagination.* New York: Fawcett Columbine.

Thompson, Richard L. 1993. *Alien Identities: Ancient Insights into Modern UFO Phenomena.* Alachua, Fla.: Govardhan Hill Publishing.

Thompson, William I. 1980. *Evil and the World Order.* New York: Harper and Row.

Thorne, Barrie. 1993. *Gender Play: Girls and Boys in School.* New Brunswick, N.J.: Rutgers Univ. Press.

Tomas, Andrew. 1976. *We Are Not the First: Riddles of Ancient Science.* London: Sphere Books.

Troadec, Jean-Pierre. 1983. "L'étude des cas de contact." *Ovni-Présence* 26 (June): 14–16.

———. 1992. "Jean Miguères assassiné." *Phénomèna* 11 (Sept./Oct.): 14–15.

Trompf, Garry W., ed. 1990. *Cargo Cults and Millenarian Movements.* New York: Mouton de Gruyter.

———. 2003. "UFO Religions and Cargo Cults." In *UFO Religions,* edited by Christopher Partridge, 221–38. London: Routledge.

Tuella, ed. 1989. *Ashtar: A Tribute.* 3d ed. Salt Lake City: Guardian Action Publications.

Tumminia, Diana. 1998. "How Prophecy Never Fails: Interpretive Reason in a Flying Saucer Group." *Sociology of Religion* 59, no. 2:157–70.

———. 2003. "From Rumor to Postmodern Myth: A Sociological Study of the Transformation of Flying Saucer Rumor." In *Encyclopedic Sourcebook of UFO Religions,* edited by James R. Lewis, 103–19. Amherst, N.Y.: Prometheus Books.

———. 2005. *When Prophecy Never Fails: Myth and Reality in a Flying-Saucer Group.* New York: Oxford Univ. Press.

Tumminia, Diana, and R. George Kirkpatrick. 1995. "Unarius: Emergent Aspects of an American Flying Saucer Group." In *The Gods Have Landed: New Religions from Other Worlds,* edited by James R. Lewis, 85–104. Albany: State Univ. of New York Press.

———. 2003. "The Mythic Dimensions of New Religious Movements: Function, Reality Construction, and Process." In *The Oxford Handbook of New Religious Movements,* edited by James R. Lewis, 359–77. New York: Oxford Univ. Press.

Turner, Ralph H., and Lewis M. Killian. 1987. *Collective Behavior.* Englewood Cliffs, N.J.: Prentice Hall.

Unarius Students and Ruth Norman. 1976. *Lemuria Rising.* El Cajon, Calif.: Unarius Educational Foundation.

Uriel and Unarius Students. 1988. *The Proof of the Truth of Past Life Therapy.* El Cajon, Calif.: Unarius Publishers.

Vallee, Jacques. 1965. *Anatomy of a Phenomenon: UFOs in Space—A Scientific Appraisal.* New York: Ballantine Books.

———. 1979. *Messengers of Deception: UFO Contacts and Cults.* Berkeley, Calif.: And/Or Press.

———. 1988. *Dimensions: A Casebook of Alien Contact.* New York: Ballantine Books.

———. 1991. *Revelations: Alien Contact and Human Deception.* New York: Ballantine Books.

———. 1992. *Forbidden Science.* Berkeley, Calif.: North Atlantic Books.

———. 1994. *Passport to Magonia: From Folklore to Flying Saucers.* Chicago: Contemporary Books.

Van Tassel, George W. 1952. *I Rode a Flying Saucer!: The Mystery of the Saucers Revealed.* Los Angeles: New Age Publishing.

von Däniken, Erich. 1968. *Chariots of the Gods?: Unsolved Mysteries of the Past.* London: Corgi.

———. 1971. *Chariots of the Gods?* Toronto: Bantam Books.

———. 1973. *The Gold of the Gods.* Toronto: Bantam Books.

———. 1998. Untitled lecture, New Hampshire Mutual UFO Network Presents World Famous Speakers, Nov. 8.

Vorilhon, Claude [Raël]. 1977. *La Geniocratie.* Brantome: l'Edition du Message.

———. 1986a. *Let's Welcome Our Fathers from Space: They Created Humanity in Their Laboratories.* Tokyo: AOM Corp.

———. 1986b. *The Message Given to Me by Extra-Terrestrials: They Took Me to Their Planet.* Tokyo: AOM Corp.

———. 1986c. *Sensual Meditation.* Tokyo: AOM Corp.

———. 1987a. *Let's Welcome Our Fathers from Space.* Tokyo: AOM Corp.

———. 1987b. *Sensual Meditation: Awakening the Mind by Awakening the Body.* Japan: AOM Corp.

———. 1998. *The Final Message.* London: Tagman Press.

Wallis, Roy. 1974. "The Aetherius Society: A Case Study in the Formation of a Mystagogic Congregation." *Sociological Review* 22:27–44.

———. 1977. *The Road to Total Freedom: A Sociological Analysis of Scientology.* New York: Columbia Univ. Press.

———, ed. 1979. *On the Margins of Science: The Social Construction of Rejected Knowledge.* Sociological Review Monograph 27. Keele, U.K.: Keele Univ.

———. 1984. *The Elementary Forms of the New Religious Life.* London: Routledge and Kegan Paul.

———. 1985. "Science and Pseudo-Science." *Social Science Information* 24, no. 3:585–601.

———. 1986. "The Social Construction of Charisma." In *Sociological Theory: Religion and Collective Action,* edited by Roy Wallis and Steven Bruce, 129–54. Belfast: The Queen's University.

———. 1993. "Charisma and Explanation." In *Secularization, Rationalism and Sectarianism,* edited by Eileen Barker, James A. Beckford, and Karel Dobbelaere, 167–79. Oxford: Clarendon Press.

Walton, Travis. 1978. *The Walton Experience.* New York: Berkeley.

Weber, Max. 1963. *The Sociology of Religion.* Boston: Beacon Press.

———. 1975. *Magt og byr krati.* Oslo: Gyldendal Norsk Forlag.

Webster, David L., Susan Toby Evans, and William T. Sanders. 1993. *Out of the Past: An Introduction to Archaeology.* Mountain View, Calif.: Mayfield.

Welch, Len. 1952. "Flying Saucer 'Passenger' Declares A-Bomb Blasts Reason for Visits." *Phoenix Gazette.* Nov. 24.

Westrum, Ron. 1977. "Social Intelligence about Anomalies: The Case of UFOs." *Social Studies of Science* 7, no. 3:271–302.

Whitmore, John. 1995. "Religious Dimensions of the UFO Abductee Experience." In *The Gods Have Landed: New Religions from Other Worlds,* edited by James R. Lewis, 65–85. Albany: State Univ. of New York Press.

Wieder, D. Lawrence. 1988. "Telling the Convict Code." In *Contemporary Field Research: A Collection of Readings,* edited by Robert M. Emerson, 78–90. Prospect Heights, Ill.: Waveland Press.

Wilber, Ken. 1997. *Krótka historia wszystkiego.* (The history of everything). Warsaw: Jacek Santorski and Co.

Wilkins, Harold T. 1954. *Flying Saucers on the Attack.* New York: Citadel Press.

Williams, Richard, ed. 1991. *UFO: The Continuing Enigma.* Pleasantville, N.Y.: Reader's Digest.

Williamson, George Hunt. 1957. *Other Tongues—Other Flesh.* Amherst, Wisc.: Amherst Press.

———. 1975. *Road in the Sky.* London: Futura Publications Limited.

Williamson, George Hunt, and Alfred C. Bailey. 1954. *The Saucers Speak! A Documentary Report of Interstellar Communication by Radiotelegraphy.* Los Angeles: New Age Publishing Company.

Wilson, Colin. 1997. *From Atlantis to the Sphinx: Recovering the Lost Wisdom of the Ancient World.* London: Virgin Books.

Wilson, Colin, and Rand Flem-Ath. 2001. *The Atlantis Blueprint: Unlocking the Ancient Mysteries of a Long-Lost Civilization.* New York: Delacorte Press.

Wilson, William J. 1987. *The Truly Disadvantaged: The Inner City, the Underclass, and Public Policy.* Chicago: Univ. of Chicago Press.

Wingmakers. 2003. Wingmakers' Home page. http://www.wingmakers.com/index.html.

Wong, Jan. 2001. "Clone Artist." *Toronto Globe and Mail.* Apr. 7, F1.

Zaner, Richard. 1970. *The Way of Phenomenology.* New York: Bobbs-Merrill.

Ziegler, Charles A. 2003. "UFOs, Religion, and the Statistics of Belief." In *Encyclopedic Sourcebook of UFO Religions,* edited by James R. Lewis, 349–57. Amherst, N.Y.: Prometheus Books.

Zinsstag, Lou. 1990. *UFOs—George Adamski: Their Man on Earth.* Tucson: UFO Photo Archives.

Zinsstag, Lou, and Timothy Good. 1983. *George Adamski: The Untold Story.* Kent, U.K.: Ceti Publications.

Index

Italic page number denotes illustration.